The Ties That Bound

The Ties That Bound

Peasant Families
in Medieval England

BARBARA A. HANAWALT

New York   Oxford
Oxford University Press
1986

Oxford University Press

Oxford   New York   Toronto
Delhi   Bombay   Calcutta   Madras   Karachi
Petaling Jaya   Singapore   Hong Kong   Tokyo
Nairobi   Dar es Salaam   Cape Town
Melbourne   Auckland

and associated companies in
Beirut   Berlin   Ibadan   Nicosia

Copyright © 1986 by Oxford University Press, Inc.

Published by Oxford University Press, Inc.,
200 Madison Avenue, New York, New York 10016

Oxford is a registered trademark of Oxford University Press

Library of Congress Cataloging in Publication Data
Hanawalt, Barbara.
The ties that bound
Bibliography: p.   Includes index.
1. Family—England—History.   2. Peasantry—England—History.
3. England—Social life and customs—Medieval period, 1066–1485.   I. Title.
HQ615.H36   1986   306.8'5'0942   85–3112
ISBN 0–19–503649–2

"Childrearing Among the Lower Classes of Late Medieval England,"
by Barbara Hanawalt, reprinted in part from the
Journal of Interdisciplinary History VII (1977): 1–22,
with permission of the editors of the *Journal of Interdisciplinary History*
and the MIT Press, Cambridge, Mass.

"Peasant Women's Contribution to the Home Economy in Late Medieval
England," by Barbara Hanawalt, reprinted in part from
Women and Work in Preindustrial Europe, ed. Barbara Hanawalt
(Bloomington: Indiana University Press, 1986).

Printing (last digit): 9 8 7 6 5 4 3 2 1

Printed in the United States of America
on acid free paper

For the men of my family:
my father, Nelson; my brother, Ronald;
and my husband, Ronald Nelson

Preface

In his great study *English Villagers of the Thirteenth Century*, George Homans lamented that "in the absence of a great contemporary novel about the husbandmen, we cannot follow them into the intimate life of their homes." In his section on village families he limited his discussion to those aspects of family life that appear so prominently in manorial court rolls, bloodlines and inheritance of family land. Writing in 1941, he could not have predicted the amazing dynamism that has transformed research in social history. Medieval historians have used those same court rolls to open up the networks of intrafamilial and intravillage interactions; they have opened the doors of village homes. Archaeologists working on medieval village sites have laid bare the floor plans of these homes. Finally, the emotional interactions of the husbandman's family may be investigated, not through a contemporary novel, but through wills and, most importantly, through the cases of accidental death that appear on the coroners' rolls. Each inquest into a misadventure reads, not like a novel or even a short story, but like a very succinct verbal snapshot of life. The intimate detail of the scenes comes through in rich texture as neighbors and witnesses reconstructed what had happened.

The present study will enter the doors of the peasant's house. The first section considers the material environment of the family, starting on the ground with the archaeological work but constructing the rest of the house, furnishing it, and filling its larders and clothes chests. The second section assesses the recent scholarship on blood and land that Homans pioneered. The third investigates the heart of the peasant household, the family economy, presenting a model for the functioning of the economic unit and investigating the contributions of husband, wife, children, and servants. In the fourth part the affective bonds of family members and life stages receive detailed consideration. Finally, surrogates for family form a fifth section dealing with godparents, neighbors, social-religious gilds, and religious institutions.

This book cannot be definitive, but it is designed to pull together information about medieval peasant families that appear in a variety of secondary works and add a substantial body of new material from the accidental-death inquests from the coroners' rolls. I have attempted to present as complete a synthesis of work on the late medieval English peasant family as is currently possible. Gaps are inevitable and not all readers will agree with the thesis. Controversy, however, will be useful to the field. For too long we medievalists have discussed family as a reply to the medieval straw family that historians Philippe Ariès, Lawrence Stone, Edward Shorter, and Alan Macfarlane constructed for us. Their descriptions of medieval peasant families are designed to show how different the modern family is from the medieval one. Medievalists have declared the straw family wrong on a number of specific points, but we have lacked a comprehensive discussion of our own to which to refer.

Some historians will object that regional variations are so great that a synthesis is impossible. I am not denying the importance of regional variations; they are vitally important in a country that was settled by Celts, Romans, Angles, Saxons, Frisians, Jutes, Danes, Norwegians, and Normans. Furthermore, the geography is not homogeneous but varies with marshes, woods, hills, plains, heath, and soils that are sand, clay, and gravel. Ecological factors are bound to influence settlement patterns and cultivation practices. But to remain rooted in one village or one region handicaps comparative discussions and obscures the broader picture of common customs and practices among medieval peasant families. Many aspects of family life cut across these boundaries, for they are more rooted in biology than in inheritance practices or variations in cultivation.

Bloomington, Indiana   B.A.H.
March 1985

Acknowledgments

In writing a synthetic study of the family, I have relied heavily on excellent regional and local studies, on the publications of county record societies, and on the work of antiquarians and historians of earlier generations. These debts are recognized in specific footnote references. In the field of English social history, however, there are exemplary historians who have substantially changed the way we have conducted research on the peasantry. To G. R. Coulton I owe the debt of his own work on the manor and also the number of imaginative students whom he trained in the field. Eileen Power, with her gift of bringing medieval people alive through fine writing, has been a model for many, including myself. She has shown us all that good scholarship need not be obscure and pedantic. J. Ambrose Raftis, in his pioneering work on village reconstitution from manorial records, permanently removed any temptation to look at peasantry as an amorphous class without internal wealth and status divisions. R. H. Hilton's many studies on the English peasantry, particularly his Ford Lectures, have brought a valued level of sophistication to the field. My debts to my mentor, Sylvia Thrupp, become increasingly obvious to both of us and bring a mutual pleasure and amusement that over the years she was actually teaching me and I learned.

Without borrowing from anthropology, a study of peasant families would be incomplete. I am particularly grateful to Eric Wolf for the training I received from him as a graduate student at the University of Michigan. More than he is aware, he had a strong influence on the direction and thesis of this book.

In taking a new direction in research, I have had to learn new areas of scholarship and new methodologies. In the summer of 1974 I took a seminar with David Herlihy on the medieval family and demographic history at the Southeastern Institute for Medieval and Renaissance Studies. His initial influence on the project has carried through the whole of it. I also attended an institute on quantification and demographic history at the Newberry Library in the summer of 1978. The lectures and readings in connection with these courses initiated my reading in the modern history of the family and confirmed my desire to present a coherent picture of the medieval family.

In the course of researching a broad topic such as this one, blocks of time free from teaching and access to archives and computers are necessary. The American Philosophical Society generously provided me with the initial funds to survey the coroners' inquests, and Indiana University granted me a Summer Faculty Fellowship to return to the Public Records Office in London for further research. The university also provided funds to purchase microfilm, hire research assistants, and have access to their computing facilities. The staff of the Public Record Office were the courteous helpers that I have always found them to be. My two research assistants, Madonna Hettinger and Benjamin McRee, have gone on to become fine medieval historians in their own right. The Newberry Library, through a National Endowment for the Humanities Senior Research Fellowship, permitted me to use their excellent collection of printed primary sources that has formed a large part of this study. At the same time the Newberry was a congenial and intellectually stimulating environment in which to work. The members of their Fellows Seminar all contributed to my thinking on this project. Finally, the Institute for Advanced Study at Princeton provided a perfect environment for writing the first draft of this book. Again, the National Endowment for the Humanities, matching a sabbatical from Indiana University, made the year possible. With the year at the institute still fresh in my mind, I would like to list everyone on the staff and among the fellows who made life so pleasant and intellectually alive, but this is not the place to reproduce their telephone directory. Two of my colleagues, Norman J. G. Pounds and George Alter, were kind enough to read portions of the manuscript and share with me their expertise in archaeology and demography, respectively. My warm thanks to all who have directly or indirectly helped on this project.

Contents

Introduction   3

I. **The Material Environment**   17

    1. Field and Village Plans   19
    2. Toft and Croft   31
    3. Standards of Living   45

II. **Blood Ties and Family Wealth**   65

    4. Inheritance   67
    5. Kinship Bonds   79
    6. Household Size and Structure   90

III. **Household Economy**   105
    7. The Family as an Economic Unit   107
    8. The Husbandman's Year and Economic Ventures   124
    9. Women's Contribution to the Home Economy   141
    10. Children and Servants at Home and in the Fields   156

IV. **Stages of Life**   169
    11. Childhood   171
    12. Growing Up and Getting Married   188
    13. The Partnership Marriage   205
    14. Widowhood   220
    15. Old Age and Death   227

V. **Surrogate Family** 243

16. Surrogate Parents and Children 245
17. Neighbors and Brotherhoods 257

Epilogue 268
Appendix: Coroners' Rolls 269
Notes 275
Bibliography 320
Index 335

The Ties That Bound

Introduction

The fourteenth and fifteenth centuries were traumatic ones for the English peasantry. Each generation faced new threats to life and livelihood. In the first quarter of the fourteenth century famine brought starvation to poor peasants and belt tightening to rich. Disease was ever present following the first wave of the Black Death in 1348 through the late fifteenth century. In addition to natural disasters, royal tax collectors and recruiters came to collect money, carry off goods, and impress peasant lads into service. Even if some of the peasants thrived despite adverse conditions or because reduced population presented new economic opportunities, the possibility of death was very close, taking life before the rewards of hard work could be enjoyed or killing heirs who would have profited from the fruits of their parents' labors. Radical changes threatened the institutions of English society, eventually resulting in the demise of serfdom in the fifteenth century. But what happened to that basic institution of peasant society, the family?

In this book I explore that question and propose a thesis: that the peasant family remained much the same throughout these two centuries of cataclysmic changes and, moreover, that the family was able to maintain its basic structure because it was a remarkably flexible institution, permitting the pursuit of a variety of options while retaining the integrity of the unit. The family was the basic economic unit for working the land, producing and socializing the younger generation, and finally passing on wealth from one generation to another. Even a sweep of plague through a community did not destroy these familial capacities. People remarried if they lost a spouse, and relatives came to claim a family holding left vacant. Constant regroupings of families

3

occurred to compensate for losses. Using a range of economic strategies, the peasant family continued to function effectively and often expanded its wealth and options as new economic opportunities opened up in the fifteenth century.

Economic necessity alone, however, did not hold families together or keep people continually regrouping into conjugal units. Traditional role structures for men, women, and children made people more comfortable within a family structure. Folklore and long custom ascribed various functions to youths, to married couples, and to children. Thus village fertility festivals were the province of single youths, but married men held village offices and married women officiated at births. Cultural roles for family members reinforced those that biology had imposed on humans. Children must be nurtured, the sexual drives are strongest in youth, and the need for food and shelter forces mature men and women into economic activities to provide for themselves and their offspring.

While family remained a stable institution during the fifteenth century, the community changed, as did the relation of family to it. In the fourteenth century the peasant community was a fairly close-knit social and political group. Their mutual reliance and emphasis on self-regulation did not mean that the community members always got along with one another, but rather that they used institutions such as village bylaws, manorial courts, and even royal courts to regulate disputes, punish offenders, and enforce contracts and debts. By the fifteenth century the traumas of the previous century began to erode these institutions of village regulation, and neighbor became estranged from neighbor.

My assertion that family was the basic unit of peasant society, and that peasant communities, not family structures, changed, requires elaboration. A few rudimentary definitions and some background description of late medieval social and economic conditions are in order.

As other historians of medieval families have noted, contemporary language was deficient in describing the institution on which we have lavished so much study.[1] *Familia* was a Latin word used in the Middle Ages, as it had been earlier, to describe the households of lords or ecclesiastical establishments and included the master, his immediate kin, servants, and other household residents. In the fourteenth century it would not have applied to a peasant with his wife and children. Nor was the aristocratic concept of "house" as a lineage used among peasantry. Instead, from Anglo-Saxon times the more specific terms for the roles in the family were used. The husband was the holder of a house, the wife (his woman) and his children completed his immediate circle at the hearth. In late medieval records intrafamilial relations continued to be specified as in "Matilda wife of William" or "John son of Richard." Manorial court records speak of "William and his wife Matilda surrendering land to the lord and taking it back for themselves and the heirs of their body." Such references to family served the peasants' linguistic needs as effectively as the more abstract category of "family" does for us today.

The household units we will encounter in this book tended to be nuclear or conjugal families. Peasants showed a strong preference for having only a conjugal family in a household. As we shall see in the first section on the material environment, one reason that this preference was so feasible in practice was that the peasants' wattle and daub housing was cheap to construct. Old people could often have a dower cottage rather than living in the family residence, and even the propertyless and children inheriting only minimal wealth could at least have a hovel of their own.

Another term demanding definition is that of *peasant*, partly because Alan Macfarlane's *The Origins of English Individualism* has so muddied the waters by defining peasants in terms of an economic and familial organization resembling that of twentieth-century Polish rural dwellers.[2] As he conclusively proved, medieval English peasants did not resemble these—not a surprising fact and already well known. But if they were not twentieth-century Polish peasants, were they peasants nonetheless? A more general definition will take us farther, and R. H. Hilton, a medieval historian, has provided one of the most thoughtful. Peasants are rural dwellers who possess (if they do not own) the means of agricultural production. The basic unit for working their holding is the family, but the families are integrated into larger units (villages or hamlets) that have some degree of collective and community interests and regulations. Not all peasants are continually involved in agricultural pursuits, and they may supplement these with wage labor, participating in the market, or providing their skilled services, such as carpentry, tailoring, or brewing, to other peasants. Crucial to the definition of peasantry is that they support, through their agricultural production, not only themselves but superimposed classes and institutions, such as landlords, churches, and towns, that dominate them politically and skim off surplus profits. In medieval England the lords raked off their share of peasant wealth through the institution of manorialism, churches through the tithe, and the state by introducing taxation. Although there has been some learned grumbling that we should not use the term *peasant* at all, I concur with Hilton, who argues that it is not the word that matters but the social stratum that the term designates.[3]

The peasantry cannot be considered a "lumpen" class, however, but can be broken down into three basic status groups within the class. As George Orwell observed at the conclusion of *1984*, societies always group into high, low, and middle. While it had been commonplace to observe that some peasants had thirty acres compared to another group who had fifteen and still another group who may have had only one or two, it was the historian J. Ambrose Raftis and his students who discovered and explored in depth what the implications of the different status groups were. Through painstaking village and family reconstitutions they, and now several other scholars, have investigated the variations in wealth, the domination of village power, the reliance on fellow villagers, marriage alliances, and a range of behavior that relates directly to the social status of the village family. It is now apparent that these status distinctions were much more significant than the differences between free and unfree (villein) peasants. Modern scholars have found that marriages between villein and free peasants and an active land market tended to obscure these old legal distinctions until the demise of serfdom in the fifteenth century made them irrelevant.[4]

The wealthy peasants, who have sometimes been called primary villagers and even oligarchs, were wealthy in land and chattels, dominated village offices, ate well, and produced relatively large families. The secondary villagers were a numerous group who also had roots in the village, but they had less land and fewer chattels. In good times they could prosper, but to make ends meet they relied on a network of other villagers to aid them. They were respected in the village, but only occasionally held the coveted offices of village governance. Below this group were the cottars, or tertiary villagers. They had only a cottage and a few acres, and consequently they had to rely heavily on wage labor or some supplementary activity, such as thatching, in order to get by. Their standard of living was low, and few of their children survived.

The demographic catastrophes of the fourteenth and fifteenth centuries brought changes to these established village ranks. In the first quarter of the fourteenth century, overpopulation created a land shortage and wages were very low. Primary villagers, with their greater landholdings, were able to pursue such strategies as educating a son or marrying one to a widow with land, but a family had to have wealth to negotiate such moves. Secondary villagers might well find themselves struggling for survival during the famine years and were certainly not in a position to hope to settle all children well if they had more than one or two. For the cottars, hunger and high infant mortality precluded more than hoping for work, stealing, and begging. But it is an ill wind indeed that blows no one good, and the diminished population that survived the famines found higher wages and more available land.

With further population loss of about a third to a half in the first wave of plague, and the continued low population levels, a new era of opportunity opened for peasants of all status groups. Cottars and others who chose to sell their labor found that they could command a high price. The laboring population became more mobile, leaving old tenements and seeking better opportunities elsewhere. Those who chose to remain in the villages could rent land from vacant tenements and add to their holdings. The landlords tried to force the villeins back to the manor, but their efforts failed, and by the first decades of the fifteenth century the demesne lands that had previously been cultivated to produce grain crops for the lord's profit were leased. Peasants who could afford further rents took up these lands, as did other entrepreneurs. The labor shortage also led to a shift from cultivation to grazing of sheep and cattle, a less labor-intensive agrarian land use. With the increased mobility of the rural population and the breakup of some of the old tenements because of the active land market, the manorial system was challenged. Peasants were willing to pay rents for their land, but they omitted to pay the other dues and services that would have indicated their servile status. Lords' officials made futile efforts to track down offenders and get them to pay. Serfdom simply withered away during the course of the fifteenth century. In sum, it would appear that the fifteenth century was a golden age of opportunity for the peasantry.

One must be careful not to present too rosy a picture of life in the fifteenth century, however, for the plague revisited about every generation and there were a number of other diseases that were new and deadly. Furthermore, a new social structure was developing in the countryside that eventually eroded some of the good features of the old communities. The social stratification within the rural population became much greater than it was in the early fourteenth century.[5] The problems that this situation created are discussed in the fifth section, on surrogate family.

In defining peasant families and discussing their fortunes during this brief review of economic and social conditions in the countryside, it is apparent that peasants had a range of economic options open to them. The flexibility of the peasant household economy permitted it to adapt to the radically different conditions of the two centuries under study. One of the major goals of this study has been to create a flexible model of peasant household economy that takes into consideration the sex roles in the household, age of members, social status, and economic options.

The model I propose is based on that suggested by the Russian economist A. V. Chayanov and on Eric Wolf's anthropological discussion in *Peasants*, but I have adapted these to the medieval English system and have added more dynamism to the model to accommodate sex, age, and socioeconomic status as factors influencing the range of peasant options. The dilemma for the peasant family was to balance the demands of their economy against their assets. The essential outlays were for their daily living, rent, ceremonial and religious expenses, and ultimately a division of property among adult children. Their assets included land, livestock and other moveable goods, and family labor. How well a family could maximize their assets depended on how large these were, the number and health of family members, the sorts of reciprocity they could call upon from neighbors, and simple good luck and cunning.

The model is a verbal rather than a mathematical one, for the functioning of the peasant economy is not sufficiently precise to sustain a mathematical model. Nonquantitative exchanges and social relations always must play a fairly large part in peasant family planning. While the third section of the book deals most specifically with the household economy, the idea that the peasants work with a range of flexible options within the constraints of their economy appears throughout the book. In the first section, on the material environment, the model explains the options for sustenance and housing. The common use of a variety of options in inheritance planning, considered in the second section of the book, indicates that the peasants were not bound by custom or law but worked out disposal of their goods to their own perceived advantage. The model also helps to explain the role of surrogate family, particularly the role of social-religious gilds, for the gilds were a way of providing extrafamilial fellowship and of defraying some ceremonial expenses that would otherwise come out of the family budget.

In its bare outline, to be fleshed out with the examples in subsequent chapters, the economic model emphasizes scheming peasants. They were scheming and deserved that reputation in the Middle Ages. They had to be. But there was also time for play, for enjoyment of a few luxuries, for drinks with neighbors in taverns, and for dinner parties with friends at home. Babies were fussed over and bounced on the knees of proud parents. Youths flirted and married couples loved as well as argued. The affective relations between family members dominate the fourth section of the book.

With relish have the early modern and modern historians painted the medieval peasants as boorish, unsentimental, unsociable, gossipy creatures without enough sense to keep the doors to their lineage and family closed. To Edward Shorter, the traditional family of "The Bad Old Days" was like a ship moored in a harbor and tied down by cables representing kin and community ties. This ship never goes anywhere, but since it has gaping holes in its sides, outsiders are forever going in and out of its open structure. A parking garage might have been a more apt analogy, for it is a recognizable, if skeletal, structure that never travels itself, but its occupants (cars) keep going in and out and provide its only dynamic. Lawrence Stone has also described the peasants ("rural proletariat," in his words) as open-lineage families. But here the metaphor is more subtle, for these families have a "porosity" about them that permits others to slip in and observe and destroy the precious privacy that a modern, affective family needs. Open-lineage families are more like sieves in which irritants come in and family goes out, to be irritants to other families. With less colorful imagery Philippe Ariès has argued that for the medieval peasant family, community rather than family played a large role in the emotional life of individuals. In all of these works, traditional families are perceived as extended rather than as simple conjugal families, and the households teem with grannies and bachelor aunts and uncles, all of whom interfere with the family.[6]

On the other hand, we have Alan Macfarlane's equally inaccurate perception that the medieval family members behaved just like modern-day Englishmen. To argue that medieval rural families were not true peasants because they lived in conjugal units, participated in local and regional markets, devised strategies for passing on land outside customary inheritance patterns, and otherwise behaved like individuals in a capitalist society is to overlook the many ways that they were peasants by Hilton's definition. Land was family land, as was the wealth produced by the household. The individual was not the basic unit of the economy, but rather the family was. Only the very poorest in the society could function as individuals, and people did not envy these wanderers but regarded them with great suspicion. While one must appreciate Macfarlane's desire to redress the balance in regards to the medieval English rural population and sympathize with his wish to point out that the English peasant was different from those on the continent,[7] this goal may be accomplished without historical distortion.

My objections to the early modern historians' descriptions of the medieval family are twofold. First, they are inadequately researched statements and often factually incorrect. The specific points of disagreement are discussed more fully later in the book, but one may say from the outset that medieval English peasant families were not exactly like our own, but they were also not extended, full of holes, porous, or solely centered on the community. The inheritance practices virtually precluded an outsider from entering into family land without some "adoption" into it. Furthermore, the family economy as outlined above was designed to benefit family members, not community. Neighbors might help out, but it was a reciprocal arrangement in which a good turn would be done in repayment. The sort of spying on neighbors that one finds in early modern court records is rare in medieval records.

My second objection is the emotive quality of these condemnations of medieval peasant families; it is completely unnecessary for the sake of the authors' arguments and leads to suspicions of a theory of progress or the ethnocentrism of modernism. The anthropologist Jack Goody has pointed out the ethnocentric biases that enter these works because historians of the modern family have tried to do history backwards, projecting the modern institution onto an imagined past. Granted, the three authors mentioned do not go as far as Macfarlane, who argues that if only we can understand the experiences of ordinary Englishmen in the Middle Ages we will be able to help the underdeveloped nations to move toward industrialism as England did.[8] I feel no need to shoulder the "white man's burden" and use history to bring the Third World into the dubious glories of the modern age. Nor do I have either a nostalgic or an antinostalgic view of our past. The Middle Ages were neither a lamented world we have lost nor "The Bad Old Days." I believe it is safe to assume that the majority of my readers will share my view and have neither a longing nor a loathing for medieval peasant life. Rather, I assume that the readers want to know how the medieval peasant families lived and what continuities and discontinuities may be found between their familial behavior and our own.

Having stated my objections to the "straw families" that historians of the modern and early modern family have erected, I must add that I am not attacking the premise that medieval peasant families and modern families have major differences. Medieval literature does not contain the same intensity of sentimentalization of family that modern literature does. Even without letters from medieval peasants, one can imagine that if they wrote to each other it would not be romantic or sexual, but more like Margaret Paston's letters to her husband. Affection certainly existed among family members—that shows up clearly in wills—but not sentimentalization. Domesticity was not an ideal, and if the medieval peasant had described the establishment of a new household, it would probably be in the terms my grandmother used: "going to housekeeping." Paterfamilias did not hold the sway over his family that he did in nineteenth-century England. In short, there are major differences between the medieval English peasant family and the modern family.

Similarities also exist, however, and I will argue that much of human and familial behavior is dictated by biological needs that cannot be culturally denied or even culturally distorted. Children must be fed, cleaned, talked to, and played with simply for their survival. This may be done with or without sentimentalizing the concept of childhood, which has little influence in the first years of child development. Furthermore, cultural change is gradual, particularly in such a profoundly basic institution as the family. One can have revolutions in government, but families are resistant to sudden change. Some of our perceptions about family are folk theories dating from the Middle Ages, and so continuities and similarities will appear. The people in this book are not unrecognizable to us.

Studies of the medieval family have progressed so far that we are able to see profound differences in family organization, household economy, and intrafamilial relations depending on the country, the demographic structure of the society, and the wealth and social class of the family. The fine studies of Mediterranean society, particularly Italy, present a picture of more complex households, more emphasis on the role of the paterfamilias, and different ages of marriage.[9] In parts of France and in Germany partible inheritance was an honored custom, where it was ignored in England. Among the aristocracy, marriage, childrearing, relations between spouses, and, needless to say, the economic base were radically different from that of the peasantry. The same may be said of urban households.[10] Thus these fine studies have been used for comparisons rather than to draw analogies or fill in information where English rural data are missing.

When Homans and Bennett did their studies of medieval peasants and their families, they both relied heavily on their travels in early twentieth-century Europe to evoke a picture of peasant households and the daily life of the peasant. Such images from one's past are inspiring and influential in forming perceptions, as are modern oral histories of fading English country life. Although both scholars wished for more contemporary evidence, they felt that more intimate views of family life would elude medievalists.[11] Medieval English records, however, are voluminous and full of information as yet untapped. The new methodologies and questions that social historians have now probed have opened up many of these records to fresh inquiry. For this study, the coroners' inquests have provided the intimate view, the vignette, of peasants at their daily routine. Because of the richness of these accounts, I have been able to reconstruct life in peasant households without relying on either modern or comparative sources.

Medieval coroners, like modern ones, investigated all sudden or unnatural deaths, whether they were homicides, suicides, or misadventures (accidents). By royal order, each county elected four coroners from among its knights so that this official could arrive at the scene of a suspicious death within a day or two of the discovery of the body. When villagers saw someone die or found a body that showed evidence of unnatural death, they notified one of the coroners. The coroner ordered the hundred bailiff to summon a jury of the vill and several neighboring vills for an inquest into the cause of death. The coroner then viewed the body, turning it over to observe all wounds or other signs that would indicate the cause of death. He inquired of the neighbors and witnesses the cause of death and what they knew about the circumstance of it, the activities of the victim before the death occurred, and the person or persons who first discovered the body.

The richness of detail in the records depended on the coroner and his clerk. Some recorded numerous details, translating into Latin the jurors' very words concerning the activities of the victim and those around him or her, the physical environment, the extent of the wounds, the value of the death instrument, the length of time the person lingered before he or she died, whether or not extreme unction was administered, the date and time of day of death, who was the first finder, and sometimes even the reactions of the first finder. Some coroners even recorded the age of adult victims, and all recorded the ages of children through age twelve. Although the wealth of detail will be amply apparent as the cases are cited in the text, it is helpful to see at least one example in full to have an appreciation for these inquests:

> It happened in the vill of Eaton in a hamlet called Staplehoe in the brewhouse of Lady Juliana de Beauchamp about the hour of none on Thursday next after Michaelmas in the fifty-fourth year that Amice Belamy, Robert Belamy's daughter and [Sibyl] Bonchevaler were carrying between them a tub full of grout, intending to empty the grout into a boiling leaden vessel; and Amice Belamy's feet slipped, and she fell into the said vessel, and the tub fell upon her. Sibyl Bonchevaler at once sprang to her and lifted her from the vessel and shouted [for help]; the servants of the household came and found her almost scalded to death. Amice had the rites of the church, and died on the following Friday about hour of prime. Sibyl, who was with her, found pledges: Gervase of Shelton and Robert Monk of Stablehoe.
>
> Inquest was made before Ralph of Goldington, the coroner, by four neighboring townships, Eaton, Wyboston, Chawston, and Colmworth; they say on their oath that they know nothing except as is aforesaid. The vessel is appraised at twelve pence, the tub at two pence, the cowl-staff at a halfpenny; and they are delivered to the township of Eaton.[12]

Sometimes the inquests were accompanied by editorial comments on the part of the coroner's clerk or the jurors themselves. One clerk added to his description of a young man's fall from a wagonload of grain that it resulted from his vanity, and jurors said that a young woman who put a dead illegitimate child at the father's doorstep had acted shamefully.

In an earlier work on crime in fourteenth-century England, I used the inquests into the homicide cases to study the patterns of homicide and suicide. While reading through the records I realized the value of accidental-death cases for studying ordinary life. The current study is based on 3118 accidental-death inquests drawn from the counties of Norfolk, Cambridgeshire, Lincolnshire, Northamptonshire, Bedfordshire, and Wiltshire. The cases cover the whole of the fourteenth century, with a scattering from the late thirteenth and early fifteenth centuries. The only county with anything approaching continuous records is Northamptonshire. The others are sporadic, with Bedfordshire having only early ones and the others spread through the middle to late fourteenth-century. The records were all very detailed and all legible cases were used. The data are too scattered to indicate trends, but they are useful for such matters as seasonality, day of week, time of day, cause of death, and sex, age, and activity of victims. The rolls provide a rather wide geographical spread. East Anglia is perhaps overrepresented, but these coroners were the best record keepers. Parts of Lincolnshire are excellent for understanding coastal life, and other parts of the county illustrate the more northern patterns. The Midlands and the west country are well represented, but the southeast does not have good records. More technical information on the accidental-death inquests may be found in the Appendix.

I am frequently asked why the king was interested in accidental deaths as well as homicides. In Anglo-Saxon times the neighbors had assessed the value of the item that killed the person and sold it for prayers for the soul of the victim who had died without extreme unction. The value of the item was called the *deodand*, or gift to God. Norman kings found this practice lucrative and, instead of arranging for prayers for the person who died of misadventure, collected the deodand for their treasury. The coroner was responsible for the collection.

I have also been asked if I am depressed by reading stories that continually end tragically. A few cases are so vivid that they haunt me—in particular the case of the trained bear who escaped from his room in the cellar of an inn and made his way to the top rooms, where he mauled a sleeping girl. But in other cases one only sees ordinary human folly end in an accident. Typical is a case in which a cart carrying three men became stuck in the mud. One man got out to urge the horses on, another went behind to push the cart, and the third, also wanting to be helpful, got in front of the stuck wheel and gave it a pull. The cart dislodged and rolled over him, crushing him. Mostly one feels awed at the overwhelming sense of being at the scene, a feeling that both Homans and Bennett had strived for.

More traditional sources have also played a major role in this study. The manorial court rolls are rich in information on the family. I am indebted to those who published the rolls and to those historians who have done village-reconstitution studies based on them. But, again, I have approached the manorial court records from a somewhat different perspective than Homans did. Rather than trying to establish the exact rules of inheritance, for instance, I looked at the occasions when these rules were applied and found that the villagers appealed to them primarily when other arrangements had not been made or there was a dispute among the heirs. The more individually tailored inheritances were also routinely recorded and superseded the inheritance rules. I also looked at nontraditional economic relationships such as retirement contracts, reciprocity, and hunting and gathering. Perhaps more than Homans and Bennett, I was less interested in establishing the rules and regularity that were supposed to govern life and more concerned with the way peasant households actually functioned.

Wills, which are not common for the peasantry until rather late in the fifteenth century, provided a quantity of information on inheritance as well as on attitudes toward godchildren, parents, and spouses, and on material comfort. A variety of other primary sources yielded surprising information. A proof of English ancestry, which York required for tradesmen suspected of being Scots, supplied valuable evidence on godparents and naming patterns. Homilies and popular advice books for parish priests gave not only spiritual advice on family but practical counseling as well. The church court records contained valuable information on divorce and marital and sexual difficulties.

Literary sources also contributed to the study, particularly the admirable modern collections of medieval folk carols and lyrics. I also referred to ballads, but with caution, for these were not recorded until the eighteenth century and some scholars would argue that they should not be used for medieval evidence. I have chosen not to rely heavily on Chaucer's *Canterbury Tales* or Langland's *Piers Plowman* because they have already been drawn on heavily for social evidence and because, being a "higher" type of literary output, they may suffer from the authors' prejudices and literary distortions. I preferred to build my case from peasant sources as much as possible.

In looking over the various types of information that I have collected on the English peasant family of the late Middle Ages, I seem to have shining nuggets and illuminating bits of data—not the sorts of materials that permit one to weave a tapestry of history, but rather to create a mosaic. It will be a richly colored one, however, and I hope it will please the eye of the reader.

I

The Material
Environment

1

Field and Village Plans

A commonplace in describing peasants is that they are bound to the ground or chained to the soil, so that it is appropriate to begin a discussion of peasant families by looking at their material environment: their fields, villages, and houses. The fields were of primary importance in providing the peasants grain and fodder for their animals. Another common phrase, "Man does not live by bread alone," is a useful reminder that social interactions, as well as economic necessity, influenced field use and residential plans. Village landscapes, through constant usage, became the social setting for the peasantry. Indeed, their marks on the land are their most enduring memorials, for the ridges and furrows of their fields and the remains of roads, ditches, and house sites are still prominent on the English landscape centuries after medieval peasant cultivation ceased. Tied to the soil, they made it their own.

At one time it seemed that most of what we would know about the material environment would come from aerial photography, careful observation of the landscape, manorial records, and some literary and artistic evidence. In the last twenty years, however, archaeology has added significantly to our understanding of village sites and the layout of village houses. Archaeology, however, provides a two-dimensional picture. The coroners' inquests and manorial court rolls permit us to see the upper parts of those houses and something of the village and home dynamics. These records people the landscape and archaeological remains.

Village and field origins have long been a subject of learned discussion, but for the current study we need only describe them briefly in order to set the stage for our investigation of peasant families.

England has been broadly divided into two types of field systems, woodland and champion. The woodland had small clusters of houses (hamlets) or individual homesteads surrounded by square and rectangular fields marked out by ditches, walls, and hedgerows. Such fields and settlement arrangements resembled our modern conception of farms, although the actual divisions of labor and land usage might be among the residents rather than falling to individual families. Champion country was characterized by nucleated villages surrounded by large, open, unhedged fields. The size of the villages and the surrounding fields varied considerably with the type of soil available and the historic foundation of the village, so that the average number of houses or acres is a meaningless figure. There were small villages of under a thousand acres, but some were closer to five thousand. The distinction between village and hamlet is likewise flexible, and hamlets and farmsteads were mixed among the villages. Sometimes the presence or absence of a parish church or the size of the population has been used to differentiate the two, but the two terms blended into one another and were not as significant as the differences in field structures.

In champion, or open-field, agriculture the village lands were divided into two, three, or more large fields in which a villager held strips scattered throughout the different fields and intermingled among those of his neighbors. In a sense, therefore, the village was a cluster of individual holdings. It was the cultivation of individual strips in fields that give them their characteristic washboard appearance on the landscape. The strips were cultivated on a system of crop rotation agreed upon by the village. Part of the land lay fallow while the rest was cultivated. In addition to the village fields there were often permanent meadow, wooded lands, and perhaps a stream or fish ponds. The open fields with their thousand or so acres of arable land provided sweeping vistas unhindered by the hedges that gave the woodland country its choppy appearance.[1]

The areas of predominantly champion, as opposed to woodland, have been reconstructed both from medieval evidence and from the later Acts of Enclosure.[2] To sketch the distribution one should imagine a broad band running diagonally across England from the North Sea coast through the Midlands to the channel on the south. Left out of this central band are the west country counties of Cornwall and Devon; the northwestern counties of Cheshire, Lancastershire, Westmorland, and Cumberland; and the southeast counties of Essex, Middlesex, and Kent. Other counties such as Surrey, Suffolk, and Hertfordshire had a mixture of the two field types. To say that the diagonal, central band contained mostly open-field agriculture is not to exclude hamlets and farmsteads from these regions as well.

The field systems began to change in the period covered by this study and, indeed, that is one of the reasons for looking at family during the late Middle Ages. In response to the contraction of population after the Black Death, the process of enclosure of open fields became more frequent. Agriculture shifted from primarily grain production to a greater emphasis on livestock rearing. Open fields required herders for livestock, but by dividing and hedging the fields herders could be dispensed with. The new hedges altered the character of champion country. The process of enclosure had started early in places such as Norfolk, but was not completed until the nineteenth century. Enclosures were not necessarily accompanied by the evictions and suffering we associate with the Tudor period, but were a result of a necessary adjustment in land use in response to a decrease in laborers and consumers of grain. Land that had been difficult and marginal to farm was abandoned first and turned into grazing lands. The villages that were deserted during this process of diminishing arable have provided the archaeological sites for village studies.

Village locations depended on terrain and the availability of land, but probably the most important consideration was ready access to drinking water. The great landscape historian W. G. Hoskins has recommended to local historians that they look for the village well to find evidence of the original village site,[3] but streams and shallow cisterns were also used as water sources. Beyond the availability of water, terrain was important. In the Fenland the "islands" were favored because they were drier. Although defensive positions on hills were not characteristic of English village sites, there was a preference for places that provided good drainage and flat areas for building.[4] In the thirteenth century, when the land was rapidly populated, daughter villages and hamlets sometimes had to locate in less desirable places to be near new fields.

The village lands were divided into three distinct regions. At the center were the cluster of enclosures that contained peasants' houses, outbuildings, and gardens. The agricultural area, both fields and meadow, surrounded the village and at its perimeter was a rough area of woods.[5] By the thirteenth century population had grown so that village boundaries were pushed to their limits against the fields of other villages, and in some areas the village boundaries were demarcated by strips of greensward.[6] The peasantry were by no means isolated in their village and the protecting rough. To prohibit encroachment of neighboring peasants, they held an annual perambulation of the boundaries, beating of the bounds, to establish their turf. They also had contacts with neighboring villages and market towns. A daily round of interaction was within a radius of five miles from the village.[7]

Because the manor was an administrative unit, not an agricultural one, the village and manor did not necessarily coincide. The manors were often imposed later than the establishment of the village. A village might be all in one manor or it might be divided between two or three different manors. If the village was divided between several manors, there were not separate fields, but rather the strips of one manor were interspersed with those of another. In villages that were divided between administrative units, the villagers themselves took a greater role in regulating agrarian practices and village bylaws were developed to establish land usage.[8] The division of villages among two or more lords or the transfer of a village from one lordship to another had little effect on the peasantry unless one lordship was harsher than another.[9]

The methods and reasons for the distribution of strips to villagers in open fields need not detain us, but the units and amount of land villagers held is important. The large fields were divided by fiscal units: virgates (yardlands) or bovates (oxgangs). The virgate reflects measurement with a rod while the bovate indicates that the land unit was assessed by the plowing capacity of oxen. The units varied somewhat from place to place, but a virgate averaged thirty acres and a bovate, fifteen acres. Kent and East Anglia had a local variation of assessment, the *sulung*. Glebe land, that belonging to the parish church, was mixed in with the villagers' strips and so might be the demesne land (that which the lord held for his own exploitation). Demesne could, however, be held in blocks of strips, and even among the peasants there was some tendency to try to accumulate holdings in a contiguous grouping.

An individual's holding in the arable varied considerably by the fourteenth century. The traditional holding was one virgate or two bovates, but it is entirely possible that in the original land distributions there were inequalities, with some people having only a few acres and others only half-virgates. Certainly, by the thirteenth century, as a result of land shortage, an active land market, and other factors, small units of an acre or less might comprise a family's sole holding. Other families had been able to accumulate more than the thirty acres, so that decided inequalities in landholding appeared among the villagers by the four-teenth century. In general, however, those with half a virgate predom-inated in the villages. As the fifteenth century progressed, the inequali-ties in land distribution became even more pronounced. Some peasants abandoned land while others accumulated larger holdings from the vacated lands. Those holding more than a virgate became more numerous.[10]

In addition to having a share of the arable land, peasants had usage of meadowland, wastes, woodlands, and pastures. Since artificial grasses were not grown as crops in the Middle Ages, meadows provided the only source of hay to tide animals over the winter. Village bylaws regulated pasturage carefully, allowing villagers to keep only a fixed number of animals on the open fields and setting the times of pasturing. Wastes were also used for pasture and for the various extra food sources that grew there: berries, nuts, greens, mushrooms, and fruit. The woodland provided fuel, building materials for houses, acorns and beechnuts for feeding hogs, and were a source of illicit protein in the form of deer, fowl, and other wild animals. In some areas the woods were still wild and bear wandered out, occasionally mauling a village child.[11]

Moving in from the fields to the village perimeter, ditches, hedges, or lanes marked the end of the arable and the beginning of the village. Bylaws governed the keeping of these barriers so that animals could not stray into crops or be allowed in the newly harvested fields until the villagers agreed.[12]

In the competition for food and a livelihood from the land, boundaries were important to medieval peasants. In the champion country the greensward demarcated one village's fields from its neighbor's. Within the fields themselves boundaries between strips were also necessary, because one of the most common petty thefts was to plow or reap into a neighbor's furrows. The jurors of Hemmingford Abbots complained about Thomas Jordan, saying that by plowing he had appropriated a whole furlong to himself and that, when he and his servants mowed, they encroached on his neighbor's land.[13] Complaints concerning violation of strips were common in manor courts, but strip boundaries were marked only by stones and stakes, so that it was easy to plow an extra furrow to the damage of a neighbor.

Maintenance of boundaries elicited strong emotional responses. Fights with neighboring villages occurred at the beating of the bounds, and people who lived outside the village were called strangers and foreigners and were treated with suspicion. Jurors from the Ramsey Abbey villages convicted 37.5 percent of the outsiders who committed felonies (larceny, burglary, robbery, homicide, rape, arson, and receiving stolen goods or known felons) within their boundaries but only 18 percent of fellow villagers. Violations of field and hedge boundaries could lead to fights to the death. The majority of homicides occurred in village fields (59 percent), particularly during plowing or harvest, when competition for crops was at its keenest in peasant communities.[14]

Within the village peasant families had a croft, messuage, or close, as the bit of land surrounding the house was called. It was enclosed by ditches, walls, or hedges and was used for garden, house, barn, and perhaps other outbuildings belonging to the family. The word *toft* is sometimes used to describe the house site in the croft. Croft sizes varied, as did a family's landholding. Some were large enough for substantial gardens and several outbuildings, while others were only large enough to contain a cottage and limited garden.

Even a simple description of land distribution and house sites indicates that the villages were not occupied by peasant families of equal wealth and status. The village population included virgaters with sufficient land to easily support a family and produce for the market; half-virgaters, who could assume to support a family; and cottages, who would have only a small croft and a few acres in the open fields. Those with little land supplemented their livelihood by hiring out their labor or practicing a craft. For instance, a smith in Stotfold, Bedfordshire, in 1276 was described as having one cow, a crop of a half acre of drege, and three rods of oats. His total worth in movable goods was only 8s.[15]

Village layouts showed a considerable variations. Geographers have tried to classify different plans from existing villages and from later maps, but because there was such an extensive rebuilding of houses and villages from 1570 to 1640, this information is unreliable.[16] The best evidence on village plans comes from aerial photographs of over two thousand late medieval deserted villages. These photographs show deep roadways running through villages, ditches and mounds of crumbled walls that marked the sites of crofts and houses, and lanes into the fields. Such evidence indicates that in some villages crofts were strung along the main road, either on one side or on both, in a linear pattern. Others had a radial pattern where several roads met. Some villages had greens in their center or next to the church while others had market areas.[17] No standard or even regional village plan prevailed, and there is increasing evidence that their layouts changed.

Medieval villages appear to have been in continual flux, changing location, distribution of plots, size, and boundaries. In the period of expanding population in the thirteenth century, some villages seem to have responded to the need for new housing by completely redoing their village plans. In Norfolk villages may have moved from arable land to waste sites in order to accommodate more rational land use.[18] In Bardolfeston (Dorset) and Wharram Percy (Yorkshire) similar replanning was done, but, rather than moving the site, the location of crofts and houses was made more regular.[19] The usual accommodation, however, was to extend the village area along the roadway running through it or to add lanes and streets as new housing sites were needed. The growth was largely haphazard.

As population declined following the Black Death, villages shrank in size, with some crofts being consolidated while others were abandoned.[20] Archaeological evidence suggests that the late-fourteenth-century response to decreased population was to replan villages by replacing the ad hoc arrangements of the thirteenth century with coherent, planned layouts. At Wawne in Yorkshire such change is well illustrated. In the Midlands extreme changes in village plans were, perhaps, more difficult because in the fourteenth century the crofts were raised on platforms of earth piled up from the ditches surrounding them and from the roadway. Their general plan shows more or less rectangular crofts with sunken streets winding between them. As yet, archaeological evidence is too limited for us to know how often villages changed plans or locations.[21]

Excavations of manors, castles, and churches have shown that these were often built on the site of peasant houses and that entire villages or substantial portions of them were moved to make way for new structures. Nor did the new locations remain permanent even for manor houses and churches. At Wharram Percy a manor house built at the end of the twelfth century was soon abandoned and a new one built on the other side of the village. By the end of the thirteenth century yet another manor house was built and a village green added to separate it from the village. Thus the village was redesigned twice in the century. The village of Northolt shows similar changes to accommodate a lord.[22]

Among the other controls that lords exercised over their peasants was the right to raze their houses and relocate them. It was not a trivial imposition, for over the generations of family occupation much loving care and manure would have been expended on making the croft garden highly productive. The loss of such investment might have been more significant than that of the insubstantial houses. No comprehensive explanation has been given for village relocation. The lords had clear title to the peasants' crofts, so that it was within their power to move them. But why would a lord enter into village planning? Contact with some of the newly planned towns may have influenced country elites' taste and aroused a desire to have a more aesthetic surrounding for their new dwelling.[23] Considering the extent of village self-governance that is present in bylaws regulating field use as well as interpersonal relations, however, it is possible that the villagers were consulted or even relocated at their own instigation. At Wawne, for instance, villagers may have wished to make a new start in a new location following the devastation of the plague.[24]

Village greens were often a feature of newly laid-out villages, but their prevalence before the fifteenth century is not known. Villages such as Hinton-on-the-Green were named for their open area, but may have received such an appellation because of the rarity of greens. Atte Green, however, was a common surname, deriving from the proximity of the family's residence to a green.

Village greens evoke such a nostalgic picture of peasant life that it is disappointing to learn that they were not routine features. When they were present, coroners' inquests show that they played a large role in village life. Women came to the well to get water in pitchers and buckets, and children of all ages played there. A little boy of three went out on a Sunday afternoon in June to play with the ducks grazing on the green and fell into a pit.[25] On a Sunday in June 1356 John Waryn went to watch an archery contest at Brune in Lincolnshire, that was being held on the church green and was killed by a stray arrow.[26] Greens were the sites of dances, drinking, and the inevitable drunken brawls.

Although even a brawl is more picturesque imagined on the green, social interactions of all sorts could equally well take place on dusty or muddy village streets. The streets could be very wide, quite a different picture than we experience in medieval cities. In the clay areas of the Midlands some sunken roadways were over forty feet wide and five feet deep. Road surfaces themselves were twenty feet wide and were drained by ditches on either side. Ditches could be as much as eight feet wide and three feet deep. Complaints about the condition of the highways and streets were frequent in all court records. The potholes were so large that a cart hitting one could overturn and spill out both driver and load.[27]

The broad streets provided ample room for social interactions. Among rural homicides 30 percent occurred in streets or highways. In accidental deaths greens are rarely mentioned, but streets and highways were the location of 6 percent of the cases. For twenty-year-old Christine and her friend Nick the street was a place for courtship as they walked along, joking together and throwing Nick's knife in its sheath back and forth.[28] Children such as Agnes, the two-year-old daughter of William Wrythe of Fordam, played with other children, jumping over ditches along the streets. Other children's street games included throwing balls back and forth, throwing stones into the water, and shooting with bows and arrows. One seven-year-old girl even found the street a place to sleep on a June day, but she was run over by a cart.[29] For their parents the streets were places to work and meet each other and exchange news. Adults, too, had games in the street. Joan, wife of William Shayle,* and Thomas Prat, Jr., were "playing at wrestling" in

---

* The medieval form of listing names often uses appositives in lieu of surnames (see chapter 5) and does not use commas to separate the appositives (e.g., Joan wife of William Shayle). To avoid confusion for the modern reader, especially when two or more persons are listed in series, commas have been added in accordance with current rules of punctuation.

June 1353 when his knife came out of the sheaf and stabbed her in the stomach.[30]

Bodies of water were as important a feature of villages as were the streets, and equally dangerous. Drowning accounted for 34 percent of all accidental deaths (1091 cases). Rivers were the most common place of these drownings, but ponds, ditches, and wells also reckoned among the sites. The communal well and the ponds on the green have already been mentioned as village features, but closes had wells, ponds, and ditches as well. Pits dug for marl, peat, latrines, water collection, and so on were common. Ditches draining highways and streets in the Midlands and draining fields in fenland were deep enough for people to drown in. The fens also had marshland with considerable standing water. Rivers and streams crisscrossed the countryside. In Lincolnshire the daring boys and young men crossed by pole-vaulting, but boating was more common. Punting was every bit as dangerous in the Middle Ages as it is for the unwary tourist on the Cam today. People got the poles caught in the muck on the bottom and made the wrong choice, clinging to the pole instead of letting go and staying with the boat. On the larger rivers, such as the Humber in Lincolnshire, seaworthy boats had to be used, and in Bedfordshire and elsewhere smaller boats provided transportation. Robert, son of Robert Dolle of Milton Ernest, was at William Passelewe's house at Bromham and after lunch (shortly before midday) he got into a small boat, intending to cross the Ouse and return home, but he fell out and drowned. On the coastal areas the sea was an important and routine feature of life, providing food and salt. One Lincolnshire boy, aged one and a half, was by a salt pan eating a boiled egg. He wanted to dip the egg into the salt pan, but it slipped out of his hand. He drowned trying to retrieve it.[31]

Each village had a church that was also an institution of village contact. We cannot know how routine church attendance was for peasants, but the coroners' inquests give some glimpses of everyday worship. At vesper services on a stormy Sunday in January 1362 John Syger, eighteen and Katherine Bony, sixty, were at church praying when a large tree was blown over in the wind. It fell on the church and dislodged stones that fell on the worshipers, killing the two mentioned.[32] Attendance at Sunday church services might be assumed, but religious observance appeared to be more regular. For instance, Alice, mother of Agnes, daughter of Nicholas Wellester of Stanford, had been heating water in her home on Thursday after Epiphany in 1385 when she heard the church bells ring for the Eucharist. She put down a container of boiling water and ran to church. A dog followed her, running, and knocked the bowl over on her one-and-a-half-year-old daughter.[33] The church bells were a symbol for villages. They marked the time of day, announced services, and signaled events of joy and sadness for parishioners.

Churchyards contained the graves of departed parishioners, but they were often an alternative to a green or the green was in front of the church. It was not uncommon for a tavern to be located next to the church. At Croscombe in Somerset the churchwardens' accounts indicate that the tavern was a fund raiser for the parish and that private celebrations and church ales were held there to the profit of the church.[34] Other villages also had taverns near the church, for Hawisa, wife of Alan Hardy of Tost in Lincolnshire, took an earthen bowl to the tavern by the church to get her husband ale for supper.[35]

Most taverns, however, were in private homes. As we shall see, village women took an active role in brewing, but the taverners named were most often men, such as John of Belling, who kept a tavern in Cambridgeshire, or William Proudfoot, a taverner in Wakefield.[36] But Simon le Prestisman and his wife, Agnes, took their ale at night at Christiane le Hunestere's house in Edworth.[37] Whoever had a quantity of ale could put up a sign—a staff with a garland or some such symbol—and sell ale. Both men and women drank at taverns after the day's work was done and brought home ale to drink with meals.

The villagers were convivial people frequently spending time in each other's homes and sharing a drink or a meal. For instance, on January 5, 1270, Adam of Banbury had a number of his friends for dinner at his house, but one guest did not reach home safely. In March of the same year Simon and Richard, the sons of Hugh Fisher, went to dinner at their sister's house and returned late at night, discovering a scandal in a haystack on the way home.[38] On feast days, such as Christmas villagers met in each other's houses, leaving their children together while they went off to church and then returned for a feast.[39]

We are used to planned towns where the alignment of houses either provides for maximum privacy and isolation from neighbors or encourages greater communication and interaction. Although peasants sought out social contacts with each other in streets, homes, churches, taverns, and village greens, they apparently did not feel the need to locate their houses in such a way as to encourage communication. Archaeological evidence indicates that until the end of the thirteenth century house sites were frequently moved around the crofts. Most of the earlier houses were located in the center of the crofts; later ones were built at the sides of the road and even facing it.[40]

No examples of medieval villages survive, and so their physical environment must be recreated from archaeological and record evidence. It is doubtful that if one did survive, we would describe it as picturesque. The wide streets could not be called broad avenues, but rather large trenches below the level of the houses. The climate was damp, and became colder and wetter in the fourteenth century, so that mud was a continual problem. Only in the late fourteenth and fifteenth centuries were cobbled stones used for streets. Houses were low, impermanent, and scattered on their lots among various outbuildings. The only substantial structure would have been the church and a manor house, if there was one in the village. It is little wonder that the church was a focal point for the community; it was often the only structure that lasted from one generation to the next.

Although the villages and hamlets were not picturesque, they were filled with lively activity during the daylight hours. The houses, as we shall see in the next chapter, were uninviting, so that as much as possible people did their play and daily routine out of doors. Villagers knew everything about their neighbors and for good or ill became involved with them in borrowing, looking after their children, and helping them with housework or fieldwork. The usual frictions of living so closely with others involved them in slanders, trespasses, assaults, and even homicides with their neighbors.

Reading the coroners' inquests, one can easily imagine this world of neighbors as a noisy one with a bustle of activity. Children ran among the crofts at play, although by the age of ten they might be herding geese or animals. Babies cried in cradles by the hearth. The usual barnyard noises of pigs, sheep, poultry, horses, and oxen filled the air. Carts rumbled through the village when the streets were dry and occasionally got stuck in the mud when it rained. A village smith might be clanging away. During the daytime women dominated the village streets, fetching water, washing clothes, calling to children, and working about their closes. The men contended that their wives spent their time drinking at the tavern and gossiping while they were away at fieldwork, but, as we shall see, women's work was no less strenuous for being largely confined to the village. The peasant communities were not sleepy villages by any means.

The distinction *as different as day and night* was very apt for these communities. Without the ambient light to which we have grown accustomed, nightfall brought impenetrable darkness. The moon and stars provided the only light, but with frequently cloudy weather, this source could also be obscured. Nights could be very dark, and even for people who were not returning drunk from a tavern or dinner party, crossing ditches and rivers was treacherous. It is not uncommon to read in the coroners' inquests of people groping in the dark for a log or plank over a ditch and falling in. When the sun went down, the nights could be horribly cold in winter, and poor vagabonds froze to death in ditches. In the inclement summer of 1351 a girl of seven died of exposure in a June tempest, and in August a pigherd died of the cold. In June 1388 a drunk man was coming home from a tavern on a Friday night when he fell into a furrow and was found dead from cold.[41]

Night brought other terrors as well. One man went out to his sheepfold at twilight and did not return. His son found him slain the next day.[42] Burglars also worked under cover of darkness, breaking into houses and killing the inhabitants. Villagers resented those who stole at night more than those who carried off goods by daylight, and although there was not an aggravated punishment for night crime, the jurors always mentioned the fact in their reports to the sheriff. It is no wonder that Thomas, son of John Rayward of Crippelowe, was suspicious when he heard a long, low whistle shortly before midnight on the Saturday before the feast of St. Gregory in 1337. He was just across from the door of Eleanor, daughter of William, and saw a certain man whom he suspected of having evil intentions. He stopped him to interrogate him, but the man would not answer and fled. Because Thomas wished to keep the king's peace, he explained, he pursued him and hit him with a staff. It was so dark that he did not recognize his neighbor, Robert Lorkyn, until he knocked him to the ground.[43] But if the outside was dark and dangerous during the night, there might be some cheer and coziness in the village houses. We must therefore move from the fields and streets into the houses themselves.

2

Toft and Croft

The family's life centered on the croft and toft, or homestead, in both champion and woodland areas. On this small property families kept their worldly goods, cared for their animals, raised their children, and entertained their friends. They called their living structure by a variety of names. *House* was the old Teutonic word for the dwelling place, and *home* evolved from the Old English and early Middle English term which included the whole village with its cluster of cottages. The initial meaning of the word *home* underscored the importance of the community as well as the family in people's lives. By the fourteenth century *home* came to have the meaning that it does today: a family residence. Contemporary records used a variety of terms: *domus* was the most common, but *domus capitalis* (dwelling house), *aula*, (hall), *mansum*, and the English word *insetenhous* all appeared.

Such terms indicated the physical structure, but symbolic identification with a house was equally strong. In English we preserve this sense in that the word *house* means both a structure and the people living in it, the "household." In medieval England the *husbond* was the bondsman who held the house, and the word *husbandry* also derived from this root.[1] The house (not simply the physical structure) had similar emotional ties as *haus* in Germany and *ostel* in southern France.[2] It was the center of the family's economic and dwelling unit.

The physical appearance of peasant houses emerges from a combination of archaeological evidence from the more than a score of excavated houses and from the detailed descriptions in record sources. Surviving vernacular houses are as misleading as surviving villages, because most of them date from the great rebuilding of the sixteenth

31

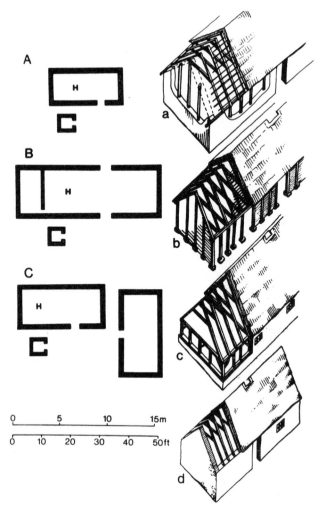

The one-bay house (A) with the hearth marked with an H was the simplest of peasant houses. The walls were of wattle and daub and the roof thatched. The two-bay house (B) was more common. The space might be shared on one end with animals. By the late Middle Ages some of the more prosperous peasants were showing a preference for the type of housing that separated the family dwelling from the animals (C). A separate barn is at right angle to the house. [Reprinted from J. G. Hurst, "The Changing Medieval Villages in England," in *Pathways to Medieval Peasants*, ed. J. A. Raftis, Papers in Medieval Studies, 2 (Toronto: Pontifical Institute of Mediaeval Studies, 1981), p. 42, by permission of the publishers. © 1981 by Pontifical Institute of Mediaeval Studies, Toronto.]

century. Excavations indicate a few basic house types. At the lower end of the social scale was the hut of the cottar, the cottage. These were either one-room houses of about sixteen by twelve feet or possibly larger two-room houses of thirty-three by thirteen feet. The typical half-virgater or virgater had a long-house. At one end was a byre that was usually separated from the living part by a cross-passage. The byre housed farm animals or other agricultural goods such as grain or farming, brewing, or dairying equipment. An internal passageway between the two parts of a long-house permitted access to either side, so that it had the appearance from the outside of being a long, low, continuous structure. Long-houses varied in size from buildings little larger than cottages to the more normal forty-nine feet in length; some were as long as eighty-two to ninety-eight feet. In addition to the basic structure, both cottages and long-houses could have outshoots that increased the floor space and functions.[3]

Long-houses have been found in excavations and in manorial records all over England, thus making them the typical peasant housing. The exceptions are in the central Midlands, East Anglia, and Kent. Their absence from these regions, at least in the thirteenth century may have resulted from a different solution to sheltering animals. These areas produced grain and so had enough straw for bedding down animals in crew yards rather than keeping them in byres attached to houses.[4]

Apparently, peasants did not live so intimately with their animals out of preference, but because of the economy of building the long-house. The more prosperous peasants planned their housing in a type called the farm. Here the house was separated from the animal shelter and a barn was set at right angles to the house, thus emphasizing the distinction between the living quarters and farming operation. The buildings might be clustered around a courtyard, suggesting that they were built in imitation of the manor houses. This type of house and barn arrangement has been found as early as the thirteenth century, but it became increasingly popular with yeoman farmers in the late fourteenth and fifteenth centuries.[5]

House sites were even more mobile than village locations. Until the end of the thirteenth century most houses were built to last only one generation (about twenty years). When the old house began to disintegrate a new one was erected, usually on a completely different alignment, sometimes turned by 90 degrees, and in a completely different location on the croft. The old structure became an outbuilding for animals or farm equipment. Even in such places as Wharram Percy, where houses were built of stone, old houses were abandoned and new ones constructed.[6] As mentioned in the last chapter, the houses were not necessarily aligned with the village street nor placed in such a way as either to minimize or maximize contact with other villagers.

Archaeological evidence provides a useful warning not to oversentimentalize village life. Peasant sons apparently did not have strong attachments to an ancestral house, not even to the home of their father, but readily allowed the old structure to decay and built a new one. Even in the fourteenth century, when houses might be built to last forty or fifty years, changes in house location were frequent. Familial feelings of identity were with family members and family property and land, not with a particular domicile.

One reason that sons were so willing to dispense with the old house was that it was often so insubstantially constructed that it had fallen apart or needed major repairs by the time they inherited it. Manorial court rolls highlight the problems of decay. In 1439 in Worcestershire the lord directed an inheritor to build a new house within two years because the old house was decayed. In another case, an old woman who had lived in a house had let it deteriorate and the new tenant was to build a new one in two years.[7] The cases explain why the house location changed. Obviously John Tailor, who took the old woman's tenement, would live in the dilapidated dwelling until his new one was ready for habitation. The old one might then be torn down or patched up for use as an outbuilding.

Decaying buildings were present in all villages and posed a threat to inhabitants. For instance, Richard Wygod came from Blomhurst church to his courtyard and stood under the wall of an old, weak building which collapsed on him. And in Lincolnshire in 1352 a whole gable fell over on three women.[8]

Peasants used a variety of materials for house construction. As long as it was readily available, wood was the preferred building material. But it was so scarce by the fourteenth century that it was only used as a frame and the walls were filled in with turf in Devon and similar areas, cob in clayland, and wattle and daub through most of England. Cob was a combination of mud and straw mixed with chalk. It would dry almost as hard as concrete but, since it was unbaked, had to be protected from water or it would gradually dissolve. Cob walls had the advantage of being very thick and thus keeping out drafts. In East Anglia clay lumps sometimes substituted for cob.

Wattle and daub was very popular for filling in the spaces in the timber skeleton and also for internal partitions. It consisted of a screen woven of twigs and small branches covered with mud and finished off with a lime wash that left the house sparkling white. The timber frame showed through, as is characteristic of the later Tudor vernacular houses with which we are so familiar.[9] Wattle and daub was a cheap, quick solution for walls but had the disadvantage of being very insubstantial. For instance, "on the night of 17 November 1269 felons and thieves came to a house in Roxton . . . broke a wall, entered, and robbed and carried away all the goods of the house." They went to the next house and broke its west wall and entered, and then on to the next house, whose windows and doors they also broke.[10]

The house frames were of two types. The cruck type was perhaps the older of the two. The cruck was a marvelous structure requiring considerable skill to make. A venerable tree, usually an oak, was cut and the trunk and the lowest branch split in half and shaped; or, possibly, two smaller trees were used. The two pieces were put together to form an arch, the branch portion providing the roof frame and the trunk providing the wall frame. The tie beam between roof and wall portions and the other wooden parts all were constructed on the ground and then the whole cruck was raised into place. As the crucks were assembled they were raised in order, starting at one end. Because trees for such a purpose were scarce, it is possible that some trees were groomed for crucks by constraining the growth of the lower branches to form the correct curve. By the fourteenth century trees large enough to serve as crucks were rare, so an alternative, the truss, was also used. In this construction posts made up the frame for walls and supported rafters for the roof. Tie beams held the structure together. Less mature timber could be used in this type of structure.

The cruck or truss made up the gable ends, the space between being called a bay. Cottages had only one bay, but the long-house might have two or more bays. Thus a house of two bays would have two gable ends and also an intermediate cruck in the center for support. Houses with more bays added another cruck.[11] By the fifteenth century on the Worcestershire estates two- and three-bay houses were the most common, and even four-bay houses are mentioned.[12] While houses could be extended by adding more crucks or trusses, the width depended on the cruck or on the length of timber available for the tie beam. Both types of frames tended to produce rather narrow houses. Outshoots, however, provided extra living space.

The roofs of the cruck and truss houses were usually thatched with straw and sometimes with rushes. Both types of frames left a natural hip that made thatching easy. Because there were no chimneys in peasant houses, the smoke exited directly through a hole in the thatch. To prevent the thatch from catching fire, tiles were placed around the opening.[13] In some of the higher-quality houses, where appropriate materials were available, stone or slate roofs, were used in the fourteenth century.[14] The wood supports for the thatch were probably quite flimsy, being made of roughly cut branches and not carpentered. A case from Wakefield manor court graphically demonstrates their insubstantiality.

Two women complained that John del Bondroke knocked off the roof of Henry's grange and Nicholas, a tenant of Henry, "carried the roof away."[15] It was the poor quality of roofs that made peasant housing so short-lived, for once water got into the mud walls they began to disintegrate.[16]

Where stone was not readily available, timber-frame houses continued to be built. The ends of the posts or crucks rested directly on the ground in the twelfth century, but as the climate became wetter and timber was in shorter supply, stone pads were used as studs to protect timber ends from the damp. Where building stone was readily available—and for the most part that meant on the site, for carting stone was expensive—houses began to be made of rough-cut stone in the thirteenth century, and increasingly so in the fourteenth century. Thus, the stone houses at Wharram Percy were built of natural chalk that could be quarried in the village itself. Lacking mortar, which is found only in manor houses, the peasants filled the cracks with clay to keep out wind and water. Like timber houses, houses built of stone were erected directly on the ground without foundation trenches. Yet another variation was the erection of a low wall of stone that kept out rising dampness; a timber structure was then placed on it with wattle-and-daub fillers. Carpenters and masons made little attempt to align squarely either stone walls or timber-frame houses, so that they seldom had square corners, straight walls, or doors opposite each other.[17]

Manorial accounts give some indication of expenses involved in building these houses. In Bishops Clyst, Devon, the lord undertook responsibility for repairing and building cottages. They were built on stone foundations with cob walls. The account rolls showed that the lord's expenses included pulling down the old walls, buying stones, and hiring a mason to lay the floor and foundation. To erect the wall he paid for straw, water carrying, and workers' wages. A thatcher was hired for the roofs, but on the higher-quality houses stone tiles replaced straw. The frames were cruck style and partitions within the houses were wattle and daub. The expenses came to £3 4s. for single-bay cottage and £5 18s. for a long-house in 1406. This compares to 10s. to 30s. in 1295–1306 in Northamptonshire for constructing cottages of unknown size and £4 19s. in 1559–1560 in Leicestershire for a one-bay cottage.[18]

Not all lords provided cottages and long-houses for tenants. On the Worcestershire estates there was a mix of solutions for bearing costs. The lord almost always granted a period of two to four years for the construction of a new house, so that the costs could be spread out, but he retained considerable control over the type of house to be built on a newly leased toft. A cottager and his wife had to agree to build a one-bay house on their new property while a half-virgater or virgater would have to build a two- or three-bay house. Two men who reached an agreement on the descent of property on the older man's death split the cost. The inheritor was to build, at his own expense, a hall with one room twenty feet long; the owner was to be responsible for the cost of the walls. Sometimes the lord helped by providing from his forest the timber for the frame.[19] But theft cases in manorial courts indicate that the peasants tried to help themselves to building materials. The tithingmen of Chalgrave claimed that three men cut down ash trees to repair their houses without paying a fine to the lord. One of the three had permission, but he sold the tree rather than repairing his house.[20]

The floors were usually of clay, although some stone, cobbles, and stone flags have been found. Wooden floors were very rare. On some house sites floors showed considerable wear. In clayland areas often the only visible remains of a house is a U-shaped depression formed by the sweeping of tidy housewives. In other sites wear from heavy traffic, such as in doorways, forced owners to repair them with cobbles and stones. In general, house sites are very clean, indicating that peasants did not live in filthy hovels but regularly swept them out and threw the rubbish in the close. Thus no well-stratified layers of deposits on the floors remain to help date houses or locate house sites. The peasants also took measures to keep the floors dry. Doorsills were often built up and were favorite places to sit, particularly for children, who could watch their parents at work and look at the chickens and ducks in the yard.[21] The line of drip under the eaves was trenched to prevent seepage; cobbled pathways led up to some houses; and within the houses themselves a drainage ditch was added if it had proved necessary.[22] Peasants apparently tried to control the mud and filth about their dwellings.

Coroners' roll cases indicate that floors were covered with straw. For instance, when Alice Saddler left the house on an errand, in closing the door she created a draft that spread the fire from the hearth to the straw on the floor and burnt down the house. Or consider the case of the fifty-year-old chaplain, John of Norfolk, who went to bed on a Friday night and placed his candle on the partition above his head. He fell asleep without blowing out his candle and it fell on the straw on the floor and burnt down the rectory.[23] Straw on the floor must have absorbed dirt brought in on shoes and droppings of chickens and pigs who were allowed to wander freely in houses, as well as giving the house a general air of coziness. When the straw was dirty, the housewife swept it out and put down new straw. Even a fastidious medieval housewife would not clean frequently enough for our sensitive noses, and floors would have seemed rank by our standards. Barn odors from the adjoining byre would have added to the smell.

Houses had substantial doors and windows that were closed with shutters. A cottage usually had only one door, but long-houses had two or more, one for each bay or one on either side of the passage between the byre and the living quarters. The doors were not simple screens of wattle or canvas, but rather substantial wooden ones. A boy of ten was killed when the wind blew one of these solid doors shut on him.[24] Excavation sites indicate a number of hinges, latches, keys and locks. Smaller latches may have been for window shutters.

The presence of locks indicates that villagers were fearful of intruders. These were not safe rural communities where people left their doors unlocked at night, although they did leave them open during the day. Doors locked from the inside with a bar of wood to close them securely. Even so, William Brien, son of John Aylmar of Salford, experienced a burglary and the very crossbar on the door was used to bash in his head.[25]

Since no pieces of glass provide physical evidence that windows in peasant houses were glazed, archaeologists have assumed that windows were small and covered with shutters. Criminal records, however, indicate that windows must have varied in size. Sometimes felons are described as entering through windows, so that some must have been large enough to permit an armed man to enter. For instance, two neighbors who had murdered their chaplain came back in the morning to check on him and were described as having "opened the windows [and] entered." But in another case a would-be burglar climbed a ladder to the top window of a house, and when he got there he discovered that the window was too small for him to enter and too small for him to remove the goods he wanted.[26]

This last case and other criminal cases suggest that houses had second stories. Archaeologists have argued that second stories were rare, but they cannot be completely sure with only physical remains with which to work. The limitations of the building materials in a cruck-style house would lead one to conclude that second stories were not feasible, but the truss style could easily accommodate them. Documentary evidence mentions second stories, but only sporadically. In the Worcestershire court rolls only one of the houses described specified that an upper room be built, and this was on a larger tenement in the fifteenth century.[27] Second stories are occasionally mentioned in the coroners' inquests. A curious case from the market town of Salisbury indicates the entire layout of an inn:

> In the middle of the night of Thursday after the feast of St. John at Latin Gate 42 Edward III a bear of Robert Cotiller broke its chain and broke through the wall of the chamber in which it was kept in

the cellar of Thomas Stoke's inn. It left the chamber and climbed
the stairs to a high room where Emma daughter of Edward Putton,
7 years old, lay sleeping in her bed. It entered her room and mauled
her.[28]

In another case a servant girl slipped out of her second-floor room by
dangling a rope from her window into the garden.[29]

While full second stories were rare, coroners' roll cases and manorial court records indicate the presence of solars, small rooms or lofts in
the rafters of houses. The solar was used for storing grain and other
agricultural products, but it might also be used as a bedroom. Retirement contracts, which are discussed in Chapter 15 on old age, sometimes
specified that a solar be built for the retiring peasant. Agnes Watrot of
Abyton, more than fifty years old, had spent a day in August 1356
gleaning and returned to her home with grain. She took her grain and a
candle up the solar, where her bed was, and fell asleep without putting
out her candle. It fell on the straw, and she burned to death. Access to
the solar and to the beams of the house, which were also used for storage,
was by ladder.[30] But all told, less than a dozen accidental deaths mention
a solar.

The general layout of house interiors on the ground floor is most
clearly seen in the case of a Devonshire farmstead, Dinna Clerks, which
burned, burying its contents. This excavation showed a central granite
hearth in the main room and a wattle-and-daub hood over it that
channeled smoke through the roof. Four small cooking pots were found,
a green glazed jug, and a cooking pot buried to its rim in the floor. The
purpose of this latter pot is not known, but it may have been used for
water. In the inner room of the house, which served as a storage or
sleeping room, there was a cistern.[31]

The use of various rooms and outshoots of the houses is not always
clear in archaeological excavations. The main room with the hearth was
the center of activity and might also have been used for sleeping, as it
certainly was in one-room cottages. Other rooms, referred to as
chambers in the coroners' inquests, served a variety of purposes including storage of grain and sleeping. One woman who was staying with a
kinsman had a separate chamber with a separate hearth. She caused a
fire when she fetched coals from the main hearth to start her own fire.
Another case described the relationship of the chamber to the main
room. John Clarice was lying in bed near his wife, Joan, in a chamber in
his house. His son was in the main room and troubled because his father
had not gotten up. He entered the separate chamber and found him
dead.[32]

Digs all over England have shown the persistence of the central hearth and a fairly common use of clay canopies, which should not be confused with chimneys, a sixteenth-century addition to peasant homes. If stone was not readily available, a clay platform was built up or the fire was built on the floor. Various postholes have been found near hearths and were perhaps used to hold spits. We know of one man who was sitting and turning a spit when he had an epileptic attack and fell on the fire.[33] Most of the cooking, however, was done in pots and pans held over the hearth on trivets. Many of the children who appear in accidental-death cases were scalded when the trivet broke or when they knocked over the unstable pots. A pair of twins, John and Joann, were sitting by the fire when a tripod holding a caldron of hot water broke, scalding the two children.[34] The open hearth was a potential cause of house fires as well, so the fires were covered at night with a ceramic lid that was shaped like a large inverted bowl and had a strap handle across the top and a series of perforations. It kept the coals glowing but prevented sparks from setting the straw on the floor ablaze.[35] The housewife removed the cover in the morning and lit her fire with straw and twigs.

In addition to the hearth, some of the houses showed signs of fire pits for baking and ovens against the side of the wall. Internal ovens were not common in England, although they have been routinely found in central Europe.[36]

Partitions divided rooms within houses. Unless an oven was built against the partition, it was probably made of wattle and daub or a thin wall of stone, although an eary-fourteenth-century Wakefield case speaks of the theft of a partition of boards from an empty house.[37] These partitions were unstable even compared to outside walls and sometimes came tumbling down on the occupants. On Christmas Day 1362 a two-month-old baby was sleeping in bed with its mother when the house partition fell and killed him.[38]

People moved in and out of houses freely; in fact, the close was as much a part of the family living quarters as the house was. By the late fourteenth century the close was often cobbled and thus a more agreeable place to work. Rather than the oven being in the house, it was often located outside in the courtyard. Brewing might also be done outside, where there was more room to maneuver the large vats. At some manor houses ovens were very large. For instance, a twelve-year-old swineherd got so cold at his task in December that he went to the manor bakery, where he stirred up a fire in the oven, put on some more charcoal and crawled inside to get warm.[39] The result, sadly, was roast swineherd.

The close might also contain a well or a pit to collect runoff water. There were, of course, pubic wells, and 2 percent of all recorded accidents happened in them. But many closes had private wells, as both archaeological and record evidence indicate. Three percent of all accidents occurred in the family's well, while 1 percent occurred in a neighbor's well. People without wells probably used a neighbor's well as frequently as they went to the village well, which might have been a longer walk. Wells were treacherous, for often they were simply pits in the ground without a superstructure over them. It was easy for a child to fall in and easy also for the weight of a filled pitcher or bucket to pull in an adult, since the ground around the well would be muddy and slippery. The wells were deep and narrow, making them difficult to get out of; they were deep enough that repairs were done by someone lowering a ladder into the well.[40]

Pits, or open cisterns, were also a common feature of closes. Like wells they served as a source of water for cooking and drinking; but they were also used for bathing, washing clothes, and watering animals. Pits, like wells, could be quite deep; one at Barton Blount was described as nine feet deep.[41]

Latrines and rubbish pits have been neglected in archaeological sites because of the emphasis on houses rather than on the whole close. Castles, manor houses, and ecclesiastical establishments left good evidence of elaborate garderobe facilities, and record sources confirm these. But of the many pits and ditches that one could fall into, latrines are seldom mentioned. In one case, a man employed by the prior of Spalding was working in the priory's latrine when he was overcome by fumes. In another case, a man fell into a latrine at Grimsby that was called Budyk. It was described as a public latrine when a three-year-old boy fell into it.[42] In two excavated sites the latrines in peasant closes have been only about three feet square and two feet deep, so that falling into one would be disagreeable but difficult for an adult to drown in. One of these had two postholes, indicating that a bench had been placed over it at one time.[43]

In general, the excavated toft sites have been remarkably clean, and archaeological evidence does not indicate what was done with rubbish. The houses were swept out, probably into the immediate area, but there is very little broken pottery on the sites nor is it obvious that it was spread over the fields. Not even the old quarries at Wharram Percy appear to have been used for rubbish.[44] Complaints in manorial courts about dung heaps obstructing village streets suggest that each house had one by its door.[45] Coroners' inquests provide further corroboration. One case mentions a dunghill in the street outside a residence, and several cases involved people carting dung into fields.[46] One ·brutal homicide also featured a dung heap. A husband and his children murdered their stepmother, cut her up, and buried her in a dung heap outside their door.[47]

Clustered around the courtyard were barns, byres, and other outbuildings. The byres in long-houses are recognizable by built-in mangers, doorways that were large enough to accommodate cows and oxen, and the wear on the floor from manure removal and the tread of animals. But byres might be used for other purposes as well, such as dairying, brewing, storing grain, or perhaps even some other cottage industry such as cloth making. In parts of England where long-houses were not typical, barns were constructed in a similar fashion to the houses. Set at a right angle to the house, the combination formed part of a courtyard for keeping in animals. The other sides were built up with clay walls as at Glotho. Crew yards or cattle yards such as this were large enough to keep fourteen adult cows or twelve draft oxen. The surfaces have been scoured away by animals' hooves.[48]

In the coroners' inquests 1.5 percent (45 cases) of the accidental deaths occurred in barns. To the extent that accidental deaths can indicate the prevalance of various structures, Northamptonshire, Bedfordshire, and Cambridgeshire appeared to have a higher frequency of barns (2 per cent of all accidents in those counties), whilst Wiltshire had the fewest (.003 percent). Barns may indicate a greater prevalance of animal husbandry, but cannot be taken as conclusive evidence.

The close might also include a separate, smaller residence, such as a dower cottage, for a retired peasant and his wife or a rental unit. In 1374 a man and his wife were staying in a cottage in the close of their landlord when it caught fire because they had not properly covered the hearth.[49]

Other features that could be found on closes were pigsties, dovecotes, cowsheds, stables, drying ovens, kilns, and haystacks. Stables mentioned in the coroners' rolls appear to belong only to manorial establishments or to very successful peasants.[50] Dovecotes may also have been more common on larger holdings.[51] Most bylaws required that pigs be confined to sties or sheds at night.[52] Drying ovens or kilns have been found throughout the highland zone in the southwest, where it was difficult to dry crops naturally. In addition to corn, they also dried beans, flax, malt, and hay.[53] Haystacks were for feeding animals, but stacks of straw served a variety of purposes. Straw from oats made fairly good fodder, but on the whole animals could not digest straw. Instead, it was used for thatching, floor covering, bedding for humans and animals, and starting fires. Isabella, wife of John, the son of Margery of Bodekesham, went early in the morning to her straw stack to get straw to start a fire. She put a ladder against the stack but fell from the ladder.[54]

Some of the tofts contained more specialized buildings and other signs of supplemental economic activites, such as a smithy and a sawyer's pit.[55] In one coroner's inquest a potter's kiln had been built close to his house and caused it to burn down when it got too hot.[56]

The croft, or garden area, was so intimately related to the toft in the claylands of the Midlands and East Anglia that no clear division was made between them, other than perhaps a drainage ditch. In the north, as at Wharram Percy, sizable ditches or walls separated crofts from tofts and prevented animals from straying into the living area.[57]

Archaeological evidence suggests that the major earthworks surrounding crofts and tofts appeared first in the fourteenth century. The ditches were predominant in the clayland areas, where it is possible that they became necessary for drainage as the weather turned wetter.[58] In coroners' inquests ditches were more prominent in Bedfordshire and Cambridgeshire, but since they figure in 7 percent (175 cases) of the accidental deaths in all counties, they must have been a common feature. While ditches may have been created chiefly for drainage, they served a variety of functions, aside from indirectly reducing population. Women washed cloth and clothes in ditches; children played in them, chasing ducks that fed there; both men and women bathed in them; farm animals watered there; the herbs on their banks were gathered for salads and seasonings; and they were an additional source of water. The ditches kept animals from straying out of the close, but planks were put across them so that the inhabitants were not isolated on quasi-islands. In Lincolnshire, as we noted, boys dispensed with planks and bridges and pole-vaulted across ditches and streams.[59]

In addition to the garden, the croft often had pear, apple, and cherry trees to supplement the family diet. The croft might also have a pit or pond on it for a water supply, a pig wallow, or keeping geese.

The toft and croft were areas for both activity and repose. During the day doors were opened and children and animals wandered in and out freely. While the baby of the family slept in its cradle by the open hearth, chickens, pigs, and the family cat rooted in the straw around the cradle. We know about this peaceful scene in detail, for the inquests often recount it when a chicken dropped a burning straw or ember into the cradle or pigs came in and mauled the baby. Toddlers sat by the hearth, keeping warm and investigating the contents of pots on the trivets. The young children also followed their parents as they did chores around the courtyard or in the croft. They set off on their own errands as well, chasing ducks and picking flowers. Older children were sent to collect the fruit from the croft or to herd geese and ducks at the ponds. The adults had a variety of activities that centered in the close: mending farm equipment and fishing nets or pursuing a craft. In August tall wagonloads of grain would be brought in from the fields in sheaves to be winnowed and a straw stack erected. In June the haystack would be made with grass from the meadow. The plough oxen or horses were kept in the byre or barn, and the wagon, plough, and other implements were stored there. For the housewife the house and close were places for washing clothes, churning, peeling vegetables, baking and brewing, and cooking the family supper. In good weather the trestle table was set out for family meals.[60]

We have a description of a family supper. William Foleweye and his wife, Albreda, were sitting at supper. Their infant son, John, was sitting on Albreda's lap. When Albreda got up to serve her husband a second helping of food and drink, the baby slipped off her lap into a pan of hot milk on the hearth. The record implies that Albreda was drunk.[61]

Was the peasant's home his castle or at least his private bastion and retreat? The phrase "A man's home is his castle" goes back at least to the sixteenth century, but we know that a villein's house was not safe from a lord, who could tear it down at will. And we also know that the homes were not substantial enough to withstand strong armed burglars. Beyond these powerful social predators, however, the houses did provide medieval peasant families with more privacy than early modern historians have assumed.[62] A three-room house with outshoots provided considerable privacy, and many so-called late developments, such as staggered entrances, can be found in thirteenth-century peasant houses.[63] The major change that took place in housing in the fourteenth and fifteenth centuries was not an increase in privacy, but rather that more substantial houses replaced badly built, short-lived ones.

The concern for privacy of housing was almost an obsession among the peasantry. Articles of frankpledge made gossiping and spying on neighbors a finable offense and a matter for the tithingmen to correct. They took their charge seriously, as is indicated by the fining of a woman who had hidden under a wall and listened to her neighbor's secrets.[64]

Human intrusions on domestic peace were not the only ones with which peasants coped. One villein complained that he could not sleep and could not have peace in his home because of noisy crows in some fine old trees by his house. The lord gave him permission to remove the trees.[65] There was also the problem of the ubiquitous rodents. Other than keeping a cat, little could be done to keep mice and rats away from granary and house. There was an incantation against them, but its effectiveness is unproven:

> I command all ye rattens that be here about,
> That non dwell in this place, nor within, nor without,
> By virtue of Jesus Christ that Mary bore about,
> To whom all creatures ought to lout . . .[66]

3

Standards of Living

One of the few extant English poems about peasant life is "The Man in the Moon" of the late thirteenth or early fourteenth century. In three vignettes the poet describes the peasant in winter; wearing torn and inadequate clothing, carrying a bundle on a forked stick, he will freeze to death. Next he is shown working very slowly, moved neither by exertion of labor nor by what he sees. And, finally, he is collecting wood illegally and the hedgekeeper catches and fines him. The peasant hopes to get his pledge back, "but the man in the moon does not hear."[1] In contrast to these pictures of misery in the material environment is Chaucer's Reeve, the wealthy peasant who grew rich as a manorial official. To indicate his wealth and status, Chaucer situates him in a tree-shaded house and tells us that he has become so wealthy through his shrewd bargains that he lent money to the lord for whom he worked.[2] These contemporary literary pictures of peasants are not contradictory, for both the very poor and the wealthy were present in all peasant communities and the contrast was starkly observable. These inequalities among villagers, which appear in the Domesday Book, became increasingly pronounced by the end of the fifteenth century. Thus we cannot make a generalized statement about the living standards for all peasants, just as we cannot for landholding or for house size.

A number of sources indicate the contents of peasant households. Perhaps the best place to begin is with the *principalia*, the household items and field equipment that the lord lent villeins when they took over a tenement. We know about these goods because they were listed in the court rolls when a villein died or fled the estate, often absconding with them. The lists are rudimentary but resemble the list a landlord would

45

give for a furnished apartment today with the expectation that the items would be returned when the tenant vacated the apartment. A cottager, such as Agnes atte Mulle, received in 1391 a gallon brass pot, a brass pan worth 6d., two chests without locks but with tops, one chest without a bottom or a top, and one trestle table with feet. Another cottager, Thomas atte Frythe, received somewhat more goods, including a brass pot and a brass pan, a mashing vat, a barrel for ale and a barrel for verjuice, a broadcloth, a chair, a spinning wheel, a chest, a brendart (cooking implement), a shovel, an ax, a harrow, and a carder and comb for flax.[3]

Half-virgaters and virgaters received the same basic issue of table and tablecloth, chests, pots and pans, and vats, but in addition they might receive more elaborate furniture and certainly more farm equipment. Thomas Mody, a half-virgater who died in 1363, had a stand and a cupboard to add comfort to his home along with the usual household items, and for fieldwork he had a cart horse with a saddle and collar, a plow with a coulter, share, and yoke, a hoe, a shovel, an ax, a sieve, a sack, and a flail. John atte Wall, a virgater and a wealthy man by peasant standards, had the usual table and pots and pans, but also had a towel, a silver spoon, a four-gallon and a twelve-gallon brass pot, a stool, a goblet, a blanket and two pairs of sheets, a mattress, a chest, a coffer, various serving utensils, a lamp, and a kiln or oven. For farming he had two iron-bound wagons, one for dung, a cord, a plow, a horse harrow, a dung fork, a sheaf fork, a mattox, a flail, an ax, a sieve, a sack, and a seed lip.[4] Neither cottagers nor virgaters were often given chairs or even stools.

The *principalia*, like the contents of a furnished apartment, did not represent the whole of a family's possessions. Other items appear in record sources and in archaeological evidence, particularly at house sites. Various types of pottery are the most common find on an archaeological site. Everyday pottery was coarse, unglazed ware for cooking pots, bowls, and jugs. These were very functional because they were cheap and could be put on a trivet over a low fire for heating liquids. In addition, all sites show some glazed pottery that was imported from regional potteries. Finally, digs turn up some very fine and highly glazed jugs that must have been prized items in peasant households. They could come from as much as a hundred miles away. One may assume that most of the better-quality pottery came from market towns where peasants sold their surpluses and bought a variety of ready-made goods.[5]

Metal objects such as locks, hinges, spurs, knives, and parts of spits, trivets, and cooking pots were also found on the archaeological sites. But perhaps the most interesting items among private possessions were querns of stone that had come from the Rhineland in Germany or from the Mediterranean. The quern stones could be twenty-four inches across and must have presented real problems to transport by pack animals over the bad roads leading to these isolated villages. Similarly heavy objects such as Purbeck marble and whetstones from France and Scotland also appear.[6] The presence of these objects for food preparation, along with imported and decorated spindle whorls, suggest that families invested rather heavily in the housewife's work and even spent some money on decorative items to make her work more enjoyable.[7]

Ephemeral items were not preserved and valuable ones were not idly lost in a house or village ditch. The former included baskets, wooden bowls and buckets, towels and other articles of cloth, rope, and so on. The latter included silver spoons, coins, and jewelry. Bits of jewelry and coin turn up on village sites, but these fragments indicate that peasants were very prudent about letting them out of their possession. Only recently a fourteenth-century silver-spoon was found in a thatched roof. The high price it fetched at auction attests to its rarity. For the peasantry silver spoons meant more than an indication of wealth and status; they were also a form of saving and accumulating profits. They played a role similar to that of women's gold and silver jewelry in other peasant societies: for both display and savings. Since the houses were so easy to break into, peasants kept silver spoons and other such valued items in locked chests.

We know about ephemeral and valuable possessions from court records. Valuable goods stolen from houses included mazers (drinking bowls usually made of maple), tablecloths and sheets, brass pans and pots, silver spoons, pieces of jewelry, and money. In all, 2 percent of the thefts appearing in jail delivery rolls included household goods; 5 percent, clothing; and 17 percent, valuables. Cloth, often stored in houses, accounted for 15 percent of thefts.[8]

Manorial court records describe people with appallingly little, particularly in the late thirteenth and early fourteenth centuries. On Chalgrave manor in 1279 a bondsman and vagrant, who had no tenement or dwelling place, could no longer hold body and soul together. In dying he directed that his surcoat be given to the Church and a cow, his only other possession, be given to his sister, who was a leper. The lord countermanded this last act of familial charity and took the cow as heriot.[9] At Wakefield manor a widow who fled the manor left some oats and mixed grain, a small hutch, an empty jar, and other small utensils worth only 4s. 2d.[10] Recognizing the poverty of many peasants, the subsidy taxes were limited to those whose assessed worth in movable chattel was at least 10s. 4d. Such poverty was much less common after the Black Death, when the standard of living for all peasants greatly increased.

Combining information from archaeology, *principalia*, court cases, and coroners' inquests, we can construct the interior of a rudimentary cottage. With additions to this picture, we can also imagine the inside of a wealthier peasant's house. In a one-bay cottage the hearth would be in the center of the floor, raised up so that the straw on the floor would not easily catch fire. There would be a trivet and an earthen pot on it and perhaps a brass pot with feet. The coroners' inquests indicate that a fire was kept going all the time and that liquids were always warming there: milk, water, wort, porridge, and so on. The cooking qualities of the fire were never wasted, there was always a *pot-au-feu*. The hearth might also have a spit and a clay canopy to channel the smoke. Various bowls, jugs, buckets, and wooden spoons and forks were by the fire or in cupboards and hutches. A trestle table would certainly be part of the furnishings. These were convenient, for they could be taken down at night to make room for people to sleep on the floor and could be carried outside to work or eat on in good weather.[11] The tables were unstable. A man was at his neighbor's and, in emphasizing a point, he banged his fist on the table, which jumped up and hit him on the head.[12] Benches served when stools and chairs were not available.

Sleeping arrangements included straw pallets for mattresses; it would have been an exceedingly poor house that could not put at least blankets on these rudimentary beds. Husband and wife shared one bed, sometimes with the infant child, while siblings slept together in another bed. The houses also had cradles that were set by the fire to keep the baby warm.[13]

Better houses had feather beds and bolsters that are mentioned in wills. But even in 1557 Harrison wrote about the laxity of the modern generation and described the beds of his youth:

> Our fathers and we ourselves have lyen full ofte upon straw pallettes covered only with a sheet, under coverlets made of dogswain or hopharlot and a good round logge under their heads insteade of a boulster. If it were so that our fathers or the good man of the house had . . . a matres or flock bed and thereto a sacke of chafe to rest hys head upon, he thought himself to be as well loged as the lorde of the towne, so well were they contented.

Servants, he goes on to say, did well have to a sheet above them because they had to sleep on pallets with the straws pricking their "hardened hides."[14]

Chests, rafters, and sometimes a separate room or outshoot provided storage for family goods. Hams and other preserved meats hung from the rafters, and rope, clothing, and cloth might also hang from rods suspended there.

Wills of prosperous peasants indicate greater comforts and more room. An animal breeder in York left a description of his house and its contents in 1451. He had a cellar that contained cloth, salt, silver spoons, and other treasures. In his chamber there were beds, blankets, sheets, chests, a coffer, and his clothing. The kitchen was separate and contained pewter dishes, ladles, trivets, and other such equipment. He also specified a variety of rings, silver objects, and broaches.[15] By 1505 a man who was comfortably well off, and had already set up his son, left his grandson seven acres of land and most of his household effects (the rest being reserved for the boy's grandmother). The will gave him "a coffer that stands in the over chamber, another coffer standing in the guest chamber, another coffer standing 'at his beds hede,'" two pair of flaxen sheets, one pair of hempe sheets, 3 pair of harden sheets, two pair of new blankets and two coverlets, two underclothes with bolsters and a tick, "the greatest brass pot," another pot, six pewter plates, six saucers, two latten candlesticks, a salt cellar, ten ewes, a plow, a share, coulter, an ox team and yoke, a painted cloth of the crucifix, and another painted cloth. When this fortunate young man married he was to receive a quarter of wheat, four quarters of barley and four of peas as well as eight marks, "an hawlyng of the story of Joobe," a pot hanger and spit, several saws and brewing equipment, two four-year-old oxen, three able horses, a broadcloth, a towel, a cart, and the best pan "save one."[16] The testator obviously had a house of several rooms, including the guest room (perhaps that vacated by the grown son), an upper story, and such comforts of life as a bed. He decorated his walls with religious art.

Recent research has suggested that comfort in housing was a sixteenth-century development coinciding with the great rebuilding and confirmed by probate inventories. Historians of the sixteenth century have been misled by the conservative Harrison, who said that the improvements in living standards were a recent corruption. But wills indicate the contrary.[17] For some of the peasantry, life had become quite comfortable by the fifteenth century.

The contents of homes were highly valued, and occasionally people lost their lives trying to save their possessions. One woman went to get water to put out a fire in her house, but whe she realized that she could not save it, she rushed back in to get her cloth.[18]

Houses were heated with wood, peat, and coal. One of the tenants' privileges, often paid for by fines, as in the "Man in the Moon," was to collect firewood in the lord's woods and waste. They were allowed to collect deadwood from the ground (the windfall) and from the trees and hedges (wood that could be pulled down using a hook or a crook; hence the phrase "by hook or by crook"). The wood was made into fagots and either carted or carried away in bundles. Women frequently carried the fagots on their backs with a strap across the forehead. The men of the family climbed into trees to get branches.[19] A good wood supply would be that appearing in a listing of a peasant's possessions in 1414: three cartloads of wood.[20] Women and children gathered straw and kindling to start the morning fire. For instance, one woman went out early one morning to get kindling from a tree in the usual way and fell from it.[21]

Coal and peat were procured by the cartload and also by individuals digging a small supply for personal use. In Lincolnshire sea coal was carted from the docks for use inland. The cart trip was tedious. Thomas Quege of Toterton, who was riding on a cart full of sea coal belonging to Robert Trubbe of Sotterton, fell asleep and tumbled from the cart, only to be run over by another cart of sea coal bound for the same destination.[22] Coal has been found on many of the deserted village sites, even those far away from sources. At Wharram Percy, for instance, the nearest supply of coal was sixty-two miles away.[23] In regions where coal outcropped, people simply dug it out of the ground, often in places that inconvenienced the community; for example, Adam Isabel dug a pit in the high road and was fined for it.[24] The exploitation of peat was similar to that of coal. Cartloads were brought in by those who could afford it, but women and children went to the turbaries (holes from which peat is cut) to get small amounts for their family's use.[25] Charcoal was also used for ovens and industrial purposes.

In discussing available fuel it is easy to assume that a cozy fire was readily available to all peasants. But one must not ignore the literary descriptions of "The Man in the Moon" or overlook the lengths to which people went to get their firewood. Getting wood by hook and by crook was not easy work, and one could fall from a tree or pull heavy limbs down on oneself. Two percent of all accidents occurred collecting wood. (See Appendix, Table 8.) The walls of turbaries were unstable because they were not systematically worked; rather, people dug out what they could get, so that walls occasionally collapsed on the diggers. Wood was not always dry, as we learn in *Piers Plowman*, for the peasants were hoarse and bleary-eyed with the smoldering fire and called a curse on those who were supposed to build fires with dry wood or blow them into a blaze.[26] In winter, when doors and windows were closed to keep out drafts, houses became "ful sooty," as was the widow's house in the story of Chanticlear.[27] Clothing, bedding, and people would have smelled of smoke the year around. Perhaps the smell was a welcome disguise for those originating from sweat and close contact with domestic animals.

Other than the glow of the fire, the chief source of light in the peasant homes were candles. In a dark environment candles were much-prized objects. The peasants carried them about for light while walking and kept them in candleholders for use in the house. Upon retiring the housewife fixed the candle to a hook or shelf on the wall by the bed and hopefully remembered to blow it out or it could burn down during the night and fall on the straw.[28] A book on urban household managment instructed the servants to put candles some distance from the bed.[29] Candles, however, were expensive items and highly valued. A pound of hard fat for candles was four times as dear as meat, and beeswax, the only alternative, was a prized possession.[30]

Equipment for farming and large vats for brewing and laundry were among the items mentioned in wills, *principalia*, and evictions. Farm equipment for agriculture would include oxen or horses, a plow, a wagon for carrying grain from the fields, a harrow, shovels, various forks, a seed lip, a flail, and a winnowing fan. There might be a dung cart and other farm tools and, very likely, cows, hogs, sheep, and poultry. John Mashon of Ombersley is a good example. He had nineteen and a half acres under crop, fourteen acres sown, and five and a half acres spring sown, so that it was estimated that he had 50s. in crops. In addition he had two oxen, a cow and calf, four hogs, twenty geese, one cock, and four hens. He had a wagon, winnowing fan, riddle, plow with iron attachments, three cartloads of firewood, 3 vats, and five bushels of malt.[31] John Mashon was well equipped to cultivate, but we have seen from the *principalia* that a cottar would probably have to borrow a team and plow to do his few acres. Court rolls and bylaws contain cases and rules covering the borrowing of plow animals. While large animals were possible only for peasants with land in the open fields, even a cottar or servant might own one to a half-dozen sheep.[32]

Regional differences were pronounced in the possession of animals. The examples we have given so far are largely from the grain-raising Midlands, but in the north sheep would have had a far more important place in the peasants' chattel.

Animals pastured on the rough and waste areas and the fallow fields. Although temporary hurdles might be erected to restrict pasturing, herders usually tended swine, sheep, and cattle. Many families designated one of their boys (six years of age or older) to do this work. Herding was a good use of the boy's time because he could not do the heavy work in the fields and the member of the family who herded was exempt from harvest work for the lord.[33] Animals had to be kept in check or they would run over crops and root in gardens. Pigs were particularly objectionable because they damaged crops and were vicious. Occasionally they even mauled a child. As one court entry commented, "Pigs, as the most perverse of animals, require the firmest and most vigorous handling." For these reasons bylaws required that they have rings in their noses.[34]

Some animals were not checked in their wanderings. The free bull, the free boar, and the free ram were owned by the lord or someone who bought the right. They wandered unhindered through crops and villages, taking their food where they pleased and their mates from the village livestock. They were such a prevalent part of village life that Chaucer compared them to lecherous parish priests.[35] These animals were a nuisance in the crops and a threat to villagers' lives. One woman met up with the lord's bull on a village street and was gored to death, while another woman, trying to avoid the free ram, drowned in a ditch.[36]

One would not expect to find peasant shopping lists or menu books, but a variety of sources help to reconstruct their diet. Remains of animal bones at archaeological sites provide some insights into the animal protein in their diet. Such digs appear to contradict the common assumption that pork was the usual protein source since it could be preserved with salt and kept for the winter. On five different sites only 4 to 13 percent of the bones came from pigs, while oxen provided 18 to 46 percent and sheep were the most common at 41 to 78 percent. The age of the animals, as determined from bones and teeth, indicate that they were kept over the winter, contrary to previous assumptions that the peasants had insufficient hay to keep the animals alive. Sheep at Wharram were slaughtered after two years, but at Upton they were kept even longer, apparently because they were grown primarily for wool. Cattle were killed at two years, but some were much older and, presumably, used as plow beasts. Other bones included domestic fowl, geese, and rabbit.[37] At least in Upton in Gloucestershire meat appears to have been very readily available, for old animals were thrown on the rubbish heap and heads and lower joints were not eaten. The slaughter of 60 percent of the cattle before they were three years old suggests a preference for tender meat. Horse meat did not form a large part of the diet at Upton.[38]

Reports on animal bones from excavations are not entirely helpful in determining the availability of meat. They do not, for instance, indicate the length of time that the bone finds accumulated on the site. Such information woud be useful, but difficult to obtain without datable layers on the digs. We know from other sources that animals were scarce in the late thirteenth and early fourteenth centuries, because almost all available land was used to cultivate grains in order to sustain the overpopulated nation. With the drastic decline in population after the plague, land reverted to pasture and more animals were grown, both sheep for wool and cattle for the market.[39] Animal protein, therefore, played an increasingly larger role in the diet by the late fourteenth and fifteenth centuries.

Likewise, on the basis of so few archaeological sites, one cannot dismiss the pig from a major dietary role. Although pigs will not eat indiscriminately, they are a hearty animal and bylaws indicate that they were a common nuisance in streets, gardens, and fields. Manorial court rolls indicate that panage, a fee for allowing pigs to eat acorns in the forests and woods, was routinely charged. Furthermore, we are confronted with the evidence of later times when the pig was fed at the expense of the household in the summer and at harvest so that the family could feed off it during the winter and spring.[40] Pork bones are soft, and the brining and boiling of this useful beast caused the bones to disintegrate. Dogs and even pigs probably consumed the remains, thus depriving the rubbish heap of its fair share of pig bones.

Archaeologists have also found few wild-animal bones. Such evidence could indicate that the prohibitions against peasants hunting the king's deer and the lord's rabbits and birds were successful, but digs also indicate a number of hunting arrowheads.[41] The absence of wild-animal bones is less puzzling when one reads poaching cases. The meat was often butchered in the forest, and the hide and some of the bones were left there so that the theft would not be detected and the meat could be brought into the village in concealable pieces.[42] Excuses for poaching were ingenious. One man, who had been caught taking a perch from a pond, told the judge that he had not really tried to take it but had only lain down by the pond with his hand in the water and the perch had swam into his hands. He would have thrown it back, he claimed, but his wife was ill and could not eat or drink, although she had a great desire for perch.[43]

Fish, both fresh- and saltwater, were important protein sources as well as being part of the Lenten celebration. The saltwater fishing industry was a major one in England and bones from saltwater fish have been found at archaeological sites located far from the sea. Some freshwater fishing was also done commercially, but boys were often sent out to fish in local streams. In seashore settlements women and children collected shellfish from the beaches.[44]

Most houses had a few chickens and perhaps geese as well. The Christmas payment to the lord was often made in poultry or eggs and the peasants might be invited to share the feast. Pigeons and doves were either raised in dovecotes or were collected from the church steeples where they roosted. Pigeon was prized at three months old (squab); these bones would have disintegrated rapidly and would not appear in archaeological sites, but there is artistic and record evidence of people collecting pigeons.[45]

Cheeses were an important part of the diet, since they could be made from sheep's, goats', and cows' milk and would withstand long storage. There were cheeses in medieval England that have left the reputation of being delectable but are no longer available.[46] Cheese, like eggs and fish, were also important in the Lenten season.

Grains of various sorts were more basic to the diet than protein. By preference, peasants would have eaten good-quality, white wheat bread. It is not accidental that white bread is a fantasy found in such disparate literature as the lives of the saints' and the ballads of Robin Hood. For preindustrial society soft white bread was a luxury sometimes only fantasized about and sometimes eaten only at holidays. We learn that just before Christmas a man went to the mill especially to grind the grain for the holiday baking.[47] Such fine flour required good-quality wheat, fine grinding, and sifting (bolting) of flour. Our modern supermarket bread could be seen as the ultimate fulfillment of the peasant's dream of white bread. Although some historians have maintained that the English ate mostly wheat bread,[48] other grains were also made into breads. Even most wheat bread would not have been a fine, soft white bread but a coarser, whole wheat bread.

If wheat bread was the most desirable, it was not necessarily the most common in the peasant diet.[49] Wheat and rye were planted together in the fields and produced a mixed grain called "maslin." In criminal records maslin was often mentioned among items stolen or goods confiscated from felons and outlaws. Although a vast amount of data is available on demesne land crops, these were chiefly the lord's cash crops from the manor and do not indicate what peasants ate. A more complete study would be desirable because the type of grain consumed would have implications for the occurrence of the nervous disorder ergotism among the population. Since rye was not grown everywhere in England, the eating of rye bread or a bread made of maslin might have been a regional phenomenon.

A hierarchy of bread consumption existed and was generally recognized. It permitted nobles, monks, scholars, and urban and country elites the pleasure of good white bread, while their servants were to eat brown bread and the peasants had to make do with bread of peas and beans, if they did not have other grains.[50] When peasant prosperity in the late fourteenth century threatened the accepted bread hierarchy, John Gower complained:

> Laborers of old were not wont to eat of wheaten bread; their meat was of beans and coarser corn, and their drink water alone. Cheese and milk were a feast to them and rarely ate they of other dainties; their dress was of hodden-gray.[51]

Langland also spoke of peasants refusing to eat bread with beans and preferring wheaten bread.[52]

In addtion to rye and beans, oats were eaten in the colder and wetter parts of England that could not produce wheat. Most barley was reserved for malt to be used in brewing, but an inferior barley, often combined with oats, was called "drege" and made into a heavy bread. Peas and beans were a nourishing supplement to the diet, either made into bread or served as a porridge. Bean shelling was done as needed; one case in the coroners' rolls describes the interior of a house in December in which the floor was covered with the husks of shelled beans.[53]

Peas and beans were so essential to the diet that elaborate bylaws governed their harvest. For a short period they could be eaten raw and were a much appreciated delicacy, but in the main they were dried. Peas and beans were partly a charity crop in villages. Bylaws from the thirteenth through the sixteenth centuries regulated when and how village paupers and cottars could pick from their neighbors' crops. They had to line up outside the pea field and could only pick for limited hours and on certain days of the week.[54] To the village poor the routine pea-picking privilege meant a week's worth of suppers in season.

The very young, the old, and the impotent had gleaning rights after harvest, but this right was not generally extended to the poor. At harvest all able-bodied men and women worked in the fields at reaping, binding, and carting. Even students and townspeople turned out for harvest, for the pay was good and the timing was crucial because of the weather. But the method of cutting grain (halfway up the stalk) and stacking it for the binders to make sheaves meant that grain dropped from the heads and some heads were missed. The gleaning of a field was profitable and, as we will see, women of the best village families often gleaned illegally alongside the impotent.[55]

Barley was made into that other staple of the English diet, ale. While Gower may have thought that the peasants drank only water in the days when they knew their proper place, the evidence is against him. Brewing was common in peasant households, with women predominating in both home and commercial brewing. The quality of ale varied greatly. Some was so thick that it was rather like fermented bread, while

the better-quality ale was more potent and clearer. Small ale was a very
light ale that went through the wort a second time. Ale was not simply a
nourishing and intoxicating drink but had a special social significance.
If one did not leave a lamb to a grandchild or godchild, one left some
malt. In joining a parish gild it was common to pay the entry fine in
quarters of malt.

Wine was rare on peasant tables, even in the better households, but
there were vats of wine in the abbot's garden large enough to fall into
and drown.[56] Cider was a regional drink in the southwest.

The basics of the diet were rounded out with fruits, greens, and
vegetables. As we have seen, the close might contain cherry, apple, or
pear trees. The garden would have cabbages, leeks, onions, garlic, peas
and beans, and a variety of herbs to flavor foods and cure ills. We tend
to underestimate the amount of gathering that was done in peasant
societies. Women, children, and maid servants contributed to the
household economy by picking greens by waterways, and nuts, wild
fruits, and berries in the woods. In famines acorns were gathered and
made into bread.

Condiments included garden herbs, vinegar (verjuice), salt, honey,
and, for those who could afford them or on special occasions, spices such
as pepper, cumin, and cinnamon. Honey, the chief sweetener, came
from private beehives. The hives were valued items left in wills and
sometimes stolen.[57] Salt was procured by salt panning. We have already
observed the case of the toddler who took his boiled egg directly to the
salt pan to dip it.[58]

A survey of the diet suggests that it was a healthy one and might
even appeal to a modern health columnist with its whole grains, a
balance of fresh fruit and vegetables, and, though probably not in great
quantities, some meat, cheese and fish. The evidence from skeletal
remains indicates that the peasants were fairly robust. At Wharram
Percy the mean stature was 5 feet 5 inches, larger than previously
thought. Of the teeth examined, dental caries afflicted 8.1 percent, less
than modern Britain but more than Anglo-Saxon Britain. Various
rheumatic diseases (osteoarthritis) were common in vertebral columns
and joints, and gall and bladder stones were found.[59] In a leper
graveyard the teeth found were in good condition and not worn as much
as the teeth in other burials, indicating that the lepers had eaten softer
foods because of abscesses and sores in their mouths. Two of the
skeletons were of people who had worked hard through adult life and
had died rather quickly of the disease.[60] Various rhymes recommending
temperate diets have come down to us and indicate that people gave
thought to healthy eating.[61]

Although healthful, it is very difficult to know how plentiful food was for different economic groups in villages. At the top of the scale is the wealthy peasant in "How the Ploughman Learned his Paternoster":

> His hall rofe was full of bakon flytches,
> The chambre charged was with wyches
> Full of egges, butter, and chese,
> Men that were hungry for to ese;
> To make good ale, malte had he plentye;
> And Martylmas fefe to him was not deyntye;
> Onyons and garlyke had he inowe;
> And good creme, and mylke of the cow.[62]

At the other end of the scale is the pathetic picture of poor peasants in late winter, when food was scarce. Langland speaks of the poor having only milk and a little meal to make porridge for their children:

> Also in winter they suffer much hunger and woe
> It would be a charity to help them
> Bread and penny-ale are a luxury
> Cold flesh and cold fish is to them like baked venison
> On Fridays and fasting-days, a farthing's worth of mussels
> Or so many cockles were a feast for such folk.[63]

Poor peasants were found throughout the Middle Ages and in later centuries, but the only period of widespread hunger was in the early fourteenth century when population had outstripped food production and the weather became cold and wet. The worst period of famine in England was 1315–1321. People died in the streets during the first two years of severe famine. Conditions improved with the decreased population at the end of the fourteenth century and into the fifteenth; higher wages meant that most people lived well, but a fringe of decrepit individuals and families always relied on charity.

Determining the peasants' caloric minimum and their actual intake is difficult. Fernand Braudel tried to make some calculations of caloric intake and what percentage of the diet consisted of grain, protein, and drink, but these are at best vague and based on no hard evidence.[64] Two English economic historians have calculated that a fully grown male ate up to five pounds of bread a day in a largely carbohydrate diet, or about five thousand calories a day.[65]

The accounts from a modest perpetual chantry in Bridport give some idea of meals in an establishment where food was neither wanting nor lavish. The priests usually drank second-quality ale and had wine only when important guests arrived. They had both bread and oatmeal. At Lent they had fresh and salted fish and dairy products, but did not eat much fish outside of Lent. During the rest of the year they ate beef, mutton, veal, pork, and poultry. Figs and spices enlivened the fare during Lent, and for their Christmas pudding they bought almonds, raisins, and dates. In addition to these items, which they purchased, they had a garden with vegetables, fruit trees, and a dovecote. Their expenses per person averaged about £2 15s. a year. Using their accounts, two historians have calculated their outlays. They spent 20 percent of their budget on farinaceous foods, 35 percent on meat and fish, 2 percent on butter and cheese, and 23 percent on drink. Food accounted for 80 percent of their budget. An additional 7.5 percent went toward fuel and light, but other expenses such as clothing were not included.[66] The priests of Bridport probably ate about the same things peasants would have, although the peasant household would have produced more of their own food rather than buying it.

Other sources provide clues to the amount of food considered necessary for sustenance. Contemporaries assumed that one person could live with a cottage garden and an acre or two of arable. Cottar families lived—not well, one imagines—on three to five acres. Hospital records also preserve the amounts of food distributed to the poor, who stopped for a meal, and served to permanent pensioners. At one of the most luxurious establishments, Sherburn hospital, each person received a loaf of bread and a gallon of beer daily, meat three times a week, and eggs, cheese and herrings on the other days. These were in addition to butter, vegetables, and salt.[67] Another clue comes from the meals that the lord agreed to provide as part of the payment for boon work, labor required during intensive agricultural seasons such as plowing or harvest. Medieval wages, even for more professional positions such as college masters and members of barons' councils, were paid partly in money and partly in food. The guaranteed meal was highly valued until the period of high wages and cheap food at the end of the fourteenth century, when employers complained to the enforcers of the Statute of Labourers that workers wanted only money and not food.

Food accompanying boons varied only a little from manor to manor and from season to season. Some were more elaborate than others, and Ramsey Abbey peasants aptly and humorously named them: *alebedrep*, *waterbedrep*, and *hungerbedrep*. In the first the lord provided ale with the meal, in the second only water with the meal, and in the third they had to provide their own food. The amount furnished was often written in the custumals or customs of the manor. An example from Bishopstone, Sussex, is illustrative. At the two plowing boons the lord agreed to give meat on the first day and fish on the second, both washed down with ale. Those who had brought teams of oxen to the plowing were allowed to come to the lord's house for supper. At the wheat harvest the boon-work dinner consisted of soup, wheaten bread, beef, and cheese; and for supper they had bread and cheese accompanied by as much ale as they wished. On the second day of labor they were given soup, wheaten bread, fish, cheese, and ale to their fill. Supper consisted of a loaf of bread apiece.[68]

Harvest meals were certainly more elaborate and varied than the ordinary fare would have been, because the labor was hard and because it was payment to villeins, who had to put off their own fieldwork to work for the lord. If the food were withheld, the peasants struck. The number of meals eaten in a day depends on which are counted. Harrison claimed that the old habit of eating included four meals a day: breakfast, dinner, beverages or nuntions, and a late supper before bed. In the *Handlyng Synne* the moralist Robert Mannyng recommended only two meals a day for adults, including working men, and three meals for children. His admonitions indicate that people ate more frequently. The heaviest meal seems to have been at noon, as Harrison observed.[69]

Peasants appreciated good food and shared with neighbors. We have already observed that the villagers enjoyed having neighbors and kin over for meals and ale, but more elaborate feasts were also part of village life. Parish gilds always held a banquet to celebrate their saint's day. The account book of a fifteenth-century village gild shows how elaborate these communal meals could be:

> . . . beef, a calf with the purtenances thereof without the skin, three other calves, two half sheep, a breast of mutton, a breast of veal, five lambs, six pigs, seven rabbits; eggs, butter, milk, and cream; pepper, vinegar, cloves, mace, conniseed, sugar, dates, and English honey.

The cook who was to prepare this quantity of meat and spices into a banquet for about one hundred people was to have 16d. in wages. The banquet was served on the gild plates and the silver salt cellars and servers were proudly displayed for the occasion.[70]

Gluttony and drunkenness were a feature of village life, and the disapprobation of such behavior even appeared in coroners' inquests. "At midnight, 17 May, Osbert le Wuayle son of William Christemasse of Elston, who was drunk and disgustingly overfed, came from Bedford door to door towards his house." He fell on a stone in front of his house and hit his head. His servant boy found him the next morning. Drunkenness also led to fights. One night in February the vicar of Bromham set out to visit a parishioner when he was accosted by four men who asked him who he was. His flippant answer, "A man, who are you?" earned him a blow on the head with an ax from one of the drunks.[71]

Drunkenness seems to have been common among adults not only after an evening of drinking at the tavern, but also while working. For instance, John Baronn, aged thirty rode his horse to a tavern and fell off on the way home. Another man, aged thirty-two, was drunk and sitting on a bench near a well in the marketplace when he fell in and drowned. One drunk man fell into the water while fishing; another went to relieve himself in a pond and fell in; and a third was walking down the village street with a pot of ale in his hand when a dog bit him, and he tripped and hit his head on a wall trying to pick up a stone to throw at the dog. Women likewise went to taverns and got drunk. One popular carol spoke of women going to the tavern during the day and bringing along meat and fish. When they went home they told their husbands that they had been at church, but they fell asleep immediately.[72]

Women were somewhat more prone to have accidents in connection with drink than were men: 2 percent of women's accidents were specifically described as related to drink while only 1 percent of men's were. It is impossible to determine whether women were more likely to be drunk or whether such behavior on their part was socially unacceptable, as it is today, and therefore considered an important fact for the record. Drink certainly played a larger part in accidental deaths than is recorded. Many of the carting accidents in which a man fell off the load during harvest are probably attributable to ale consumed while harvesting.

Were the people who went to taverns, or sat down to a humble meal of bread, cheese, and ale, or attended gild banquets uncouth louts, as we commonly assume? It is perhaps surprising to find any evidence of refinement in living and fastidiousness about table manners. The *principalia* included tablecloths and goods stolen from peasant houses often included napkins, towels, and tablecloths. People ate with their fingers for the most part and used knives, which they always carried with them, to cut cheese, meat, and bread. Spoons were used for soups and porridge. In the better households, as we have seen, the spoons would have been silver, but wooden spoons served as well. Among the upper classes we know that hands were elaborately washed before meals. Rules for polite society included not petting cats and dogs at table, not picking teeth or cleaning them with a table cloth, and keeping nails clean so as not to offend a neighbor at table. Gild regulations also included directives for polite behavior at banquets.[73]

By our standards the peasants would undoubtedly have been offensively malodorous, but it is all too easy to be overrefined in this matter. The ordinary smells associated with living in a smoky house, working around animals, and sweating from hard labor might offend our sensibilities, but they are common to farm work. It is only the accumulation of these odors on unwashed clothes and bodies that could lead to a certain ripeness of smell. Even so, toleration of odor is a matter for the people who lived with it and not a question of judgment for a historian, who does not have to sleep with a peasant man or woman. But because we are curious about the material environment, bathing is a relevant area of inquiry. Needless to say, such intimate detail is difficult to find even for the English kings, although we know that King John, whatever his other deficiences, had more entries in household accounts for hot baths than other kings.[74] Romances and illustrations accompanying the texts indicate that baths were part of erotic encounters and tubs were kept in bedchambers. Indeed, prostitution took place in the bathhouses in medieval Europe.[75] But all of this does not tell us about peasants and their baths.

The coroners' inquests report on thirty-five people whose baths ended tragically by drowning. The case contents rather than the number of cases will, of course, be more informative. First, most of the cases occurred when the weather was warm, and most involved bathing in streams, pits, and rivers. For instance, after a twenty-six-year-old harvest worker bathed himself in a stream on a Tuesday in August 1362, he was dancing around to dry himself and fell in and drowned. Boys watching sheep on hot days took off their clothes to bathe and cool off. Other cases specifically mention people washing their hands before or after eating. A ten-year-old boy was sitting and eating on a market stall. When he finished, he went to wash his bowl and hands and fell into a trough. Another man went to bathe at vespers and drowned in the river because he did not know how deep it was. In winter, basins or tubs of hot water served for bathing. In February 1349 a woman was sitting in her house by the fire heating water for a bath. Her fifteen-day-old baby was near her in a cradle. The tripod broke and the boiling water scalded the baby.[76] As these examples show, people enjoyed a bath and casually washed their dirty hands or bathed away the sweat of hot labor. What they do not show is how frequently they bathed.

Peasants laundered their clothing, and in almshouses and hospitals the warden's wife washed sheets and clothing for the inmates. Although there are only twelve cases involving laundering, they suggest how it was done and who did it. Ponds, pits, and rivers were common places to wash clothing or cloth. While women usually did the laundry, anyone might wash out their personal effects. A nineteen-year-old man finished his work on a Friday and washed his socks in a pit, into which he fell. Some laundry operations were more elaborate, with large vats of boiling water to wash dirty clothing.[77]

The style of peasants' clothing remained largely unchanged during the whole period. Sumptuary legislation in the Lancastrian period described the garb well. Men wore loose tunics and cote-hardie, hoods and wide-brimmed straw hats. Women wore loose gowns, hoods, and cloaks. Both wore stockings or socks and leather shoes.[78] The fact that the sumptuary legislation insisted that the peasants wear this homely garb is a sure indicator they were branching out in their wardrobes. From the thirteenth century on, thefts from peasant houses did not produce many furred garments, but brightly colored tunics and gowns of fine wools and silks, along with rings, bracelets, and fancy girdles, were all stolen. Wealthier peasants had always spent a part of their income on sartorial splendor, but better-quality clothing became more common with the new prosperity.

For the poorer peasants and wanderers the clothing was often inadequate, and it is instructive that the authors of "The Man in the Moon" and the "Song of the Husbandman" chose to comment on the inadequate clothing of the peasants they depicted. Almost 1 percent of the cases (excluding homicide) in the coroners' rolls are deaths by exposure. Most of these occurred in the winter, and most of the people were poor and elderly.

Having bathed and dressed themselves for, let us say, the gild feast, did they have any idea what they looked like? They would have relied on each other for comments and probably aid with arranging hair and hoods, but they were unlikely to have mirrors, athough they might have had a chance to look into one in the market town. Wells, however, gave very good reflections. An inquest over the body of a boy, four and a half years old, explained that he looked into a well and saw his face reflected there. When he tried to get at the reflection, he fell into the well.[79] One can easily imagine that adults routinely checked their appearance in such reflections, but without tragic consequences to reward their curiosity.

The period following the Black Death and the new opportunities that the decreased population afforded the peasants encouraged greater interest in material comforts.[80] Gower was not an uninformed observer in his complaints that the peasants no longer kept their station. The new opportunities meant more investment in housing, food, and clothing. It also ultimately created greater divisions in the peasant community, for some of the peasants did very well and became yeomen while some of the less successful peasants slipped in their standard of living. The fifteenth century may be seen as one of greater consumerism, but not all benefited equally.

The material environment was not a benign one, but rather one that required aggressive pursuit of a living. Success depended partly on a person's inheritance, on the other competitors, on the family economic strategies, and on luck. The wheel of fortune was a common motif for church wall paintings. In the pursuit of a living both cooperation and competition were inevitable. The community ideal encouraged sharing of labor and wealth. Alms maintained the village poor, and the man without plow animals could have his land plowed by a wealthier neighbor in return for other labor. The worst of the deadly sins for the peasantry was avarice, and yet throughout the Middle Ages peasants were labeled as "grasping."

While neighborliness was essential, the tensions of securing a living could easily lead to serious fights and criminal acts. Almost 30 percent of cases coming into jail delivery courts were felonies between people living in the same village.[81] Village bylaws attempted to regulate the inevitable tension, and court rolls show that they were enforced. But the most trivial arguments over the material environment indicate how easily tempers flared. Toward vespers in July, Alice Timpon of Harrowen came into the highway opposite Isabel Bernard's house and claimed as hers a basket that was lying in the street. William Bernard came out of the house and in the ensuing quarrel over the basket he hit and finally strangled her.[82] Competition with neighbors for food and goods reinforced the family as a unit of economic activity and as allies in an aggressive world.

II

Blood Ties
and Family Wealth

4

Inheritance

After reading through three chapters of mud, ditches, and cramped quarters, it should come as a relief to readers to know that in this section we shall be demolishing the myth that in the Middle Ages families lived in complex households. The sooty households were generally shared only by a conjugal couple and their children. The brown bread, peas porridge, and small ale of the everyday meal were ordinarily divided among the immediate family. Households with several brothers and their wives fighting for room and debilitated older generations insisting on their place by the hearth were rare. The myth of the extended family may seem an appealing one in a large nineteenth-century farmhouse, but not in a peasant's wattle-and-daub house.

In discussing the peasants' material environment I did not consider how many people actually lived in the houses. The time has come to address the problem. Likewise, in discussing the attachment of peasants to fields and hearth, I did not discuss how the land and dwelling would be passed on from one generation to the next. In this section, therefore, we must look at the demography of the peasantry, household structures, inheritance patterns, and the importance of kinship. Such matters are essential for understanding the peasant family economy, the relative rigidity of customary rules of inheritance, and the affective relationships within the family that could offset custom. Leaving aside until a subsequent chapter the problems of household size and demography, I will turn first to inheritance patterns, for in part they helped to determine household size.

Medieval peasant parents were caught in a dilemma as they arranged the devolution of family land and the accrued wealth of

67

family enterprise from their generation to the next. English custom was in agreement with that of other European peasant societies, that wealth produced from family labor on their holding belonged to all members, and those children reaching adulthood could claim either a part of these benefits as their own or continued maintenance on the family land. English peasants also shared with those on the continent the idea that the generation controlling family land was more a steward than owner, and, preferably, the land passed on as a unit.[1] Ideally, daughters were given a dowry of chattels and money, sons were provided with pieces of land or skills of a trade, and one son inherited the family tenement. While rules governing the lines of descent of the tenement were part of the customary law of every manor and prominent in common law, I will argue in this chapter that peasants put aside such rules and explored a range of options for inheritance that permitted them to resolve their dilemma and make arrangements compatible with their own needs.

The tradition has been, since the great jurist Bracton first looked at the welter of peasant inheritance customs and practices in the thirteenth century, to try to impose some rational ordering, to pin peasants down to a system of inheritance. When Homans applied a new theoretical framework to the data, an anthropologically based classificatory system for inheritance, he too tried to force peasant inheritance into neat categories. But the researcher must let the records speak for themselves and not be overanxious to impose legalistic or social-science structures on a system of make do. Peasants appealed to customary rules of inheritance only when a father died without making arrangements or when the family squabbled about the inheritance. In these cases the jurors cited the rules and decided the case. But in practice peasants exercised a range of options depending on their age and that of their children, their confidence in various children, and alternative arrangements for older offspring.

Peasants' instruments for breaking with custom were either a settlement during the parents' lifetime or a will. The Church encouraged all laymen to make wills for the good of their souls, but it was also to the lord's advantage through most of the period under investigation to encourage the smooth succession of the land from father to next of kin. Legally, the ownership of all villein land was in the lord's hands and he could in theory take it back at any time. But in practice the family claimed the right to keep the land from generation to generation, to cultivate it, and to pay such rents as the lord demanded. The lord, however, did not need to hold peasants to strict inheritance rules in order to preserve his rights in the land, but only to have the devolution of his land recorded with its present holder in the manorial court rolls.[2]

The formal inheritance rules that Homans and others have reconstructed are readily observable in manorial court rolls and custumals, and a review of them will serve as a contrast with the cases of peasants bending the rules to suit their own circumstances. Free peasants, of course, could follow the common law of primogeniture, but rules for inheritance among villeins fell to custom and thus varied from region to region and manor to manor. Consistent throughout all the various customs was the demand that the inheritor be of the family's blood, the only exception being the widow, and her claim, as we shall see, was a different one.

Two basic inheritance types emerged from early studies, which made the whole matter appear more regular than it was in practice. Impartible inheritance, that favoring one son and keeping the land intact, could be either through primogeniture or Borough English (usually ultimogeniture) and was common in champion country. Partible inheritance (gavelkind in Kent) called for the division of land among all surviving sons and was found in woodland.[3] The results of the different inheritance customs appeared obvious to these early investigators. Borough English and primogeniture kept the land intact and sent noninheriting sons scurrying for other land or labor, whilst impartible inheritance either led to joint exploitation of the land or breaking it up into smaller units.[4]

Borough English would appear in the abstract to be preferable from the peasant parent's viewpoint. Older children could be provided with their portion of the family wealth in dowry, an apprenticeship or education, or a parcel of land. When the parents were ready to retire, the young son would be grown and ready to take on the family tenement and care of his parents. The peasants, however, had other thoughts on the matter, and by the fourteenth century primogeniture replaced ultimogeniture. The change at Bookham in East Surrey in 1339 was well documented. Two of the leading villeins, Gilbert Luwyne and Thomas atte Hache, came with the whole homage and asked the lord's seneschal if the abbot might change the rule from the youngest son inheriting to the oldest because, although it had been the custom of their ancestors, it was "to the grave damage and detriment of the whole homage and tenants." The abbot agreed to the change and within a year the other villages also asked to switch to primogeniture and were allowed to do so at a cost of 40s.[5] Perhaps peasants wanted to bring their customs in line with that of the nobility, who practiced primogeniture.

Unigeniture, whether the eldest or youngest, had the obvious advantage of keeping the family tenement intact and, from the lord's viewpoint, guaranteed that it would continue as a unit of cultivation. If the family economic unit had accumulated other goods and wealth, noninheriting children would have some share of it. For daughters, dowries of animals, cash, household goods, and occasionally a bit of land would be their portion. Sons might receive some similar items or, if the fathers were wealthy, they would buy up other tenements or bits of land to establish their sons. The son inheriting the family land ended up with a higher status that his siblings, who might sink to the cottager group in the village.[6] In modern European peasant society such distinctions in social status estranged the inheriting brother from his other siblings.[7] But apparently less animosity arose from unigeniture, for fewer sibling murders occurred in impartible compared to partible inheritance areas.[8]

When the family unit had not been productive or had few resources, noninheriting children were considerably disadvantaged. In the French village of Sologne, where parents had few possessions to pass on, the children had few ties to their parents and tended to make their own way in the world. Old parents were turned out into the streets to beg.[9] Such was the case for cottars and wage laborers in rural England, as we shall see in the chapters on marriage and old age.

Manorial court records and wills give ample evidence about the provisions for noninheriting siblings in areas practicing unigeniture. A father might set up the eldest son or sons and instruct them to provide their younger brothers with land or money when they reach the age of majority. The dowry of unmarried sisters might also be specified.[10] But if the family had little wealth to go around, the siblings had the right to maintenance on the family tenement for life. The Syward family went to court to settle how much the noninheriting sisters could expect. The court judged that the two sisters should have lodging and a ring of corn (one-half a ring of wheat and one-half of peas).[11]

Partible inheritance, one would assume, would impose on the siblings the demand that either they cultivate the land together or that the patrimony be broken up into smaller fields. In East Anglia the field sizes did tend to be smaller than in open-field husbandry, but Homans may have overemphasized the amount and importance of fragmentation.[12] Partible inheritance seems to be characteristic of areas in which opportunities for supplemental economic activities were abundant. Thus in the fenlands and wooded areas where hunting and fishing provided additional sources of food less land was needed to support a family. Fenlands in East Anglia and woodlands in Kent could afford partible inheritance. But partible inheritenace in pratice did not necessarily imply fragmentation. In thirteenth-century Lincolnshire usually only two sons lived to inherit and, with the exception of one village, the landholdings tended to be large.[13] In Kent an active land market helped to counteract the effects of gavelkind inheritance.[14] Elsewhere siblings sold their interest in the land to one brother or the legal ownership would be in all siblings' names but only one worked the land. Thus family land tended to remain intact or be regrouped into units. The tendency to splinter was particularly noticeable in the land hunger of the late thirteenth and early fourteenth centuries; but other than that period of crisis, land units tended to coalesce.[15] Joint cultivation of the land seems to have been fairly rare.

Succession of sons could be delayed because the widow, at least for her lifetime, had a claim on the land. In common law the widow was allowed a third of the property for life through a dower, but customary law was far more generous. On a number of manors in the West Midlands the widow could have the whole tenement or less for life, with the most common arrangement being half of it. The widow's right was as the continuator of her husband's tenure, and consequently she did not pay an entry fine.[16] Other studies indicate a range of dower settlements. In one community widows were given interest in the land only until the age of majority of the heirs, and this could be as low as fourteen. In Orwell the widow was left with the land until the son or heir was twenty-one, and then she could claim houseroom. But the widow could be a bar to her son's succession to his patrimony, particularly if she remarried and started a new family.[17]

A more complete discussion of widows appears in a later chapter, but a few examples will clarify how the widow's right worked in practice. On Chalgrave manor (Bedfordshire) Richard, son of Thomas Ballard, claimed that he was the eldest son and that he should inherit his father's lands. The jury said that he had an elder brother who was now dead, but that he had heirs. If this older brother had held the land, his heirs would have a prior claim. Since he did not, Richard's claim was the rightful one, except that his mother was alive: "the use of the manor is that no customary tenant can enter such land after the death of his father while his mother is alive, unless the mother shall agree and that his mother will hold the land all of her life if she shall wish."[18] In one will a man gave his wife her choice of living arrangements, declaring that if she was not satisfied, she could have her third of the estate according to the law.[19]

Succession to land in the absence of a widow or surviving sons also involved customary rules. In the case of surviving daughters the land was usually divided equally among them unless some extenuating circumstances, such as an older daughter already having received her share of the family inheritance at marriage, obviated the rules.[20] In a case a Chertsey Abbey the younger daughter was declared impotent and her claim was overlooked in favor of the older daughter.[21]

Inheritance rights became more complicated when half brothers and half sisters had claims. Although the manor courts always resorted to customary rules in disputed cases, these arrangements had an ad hoc appearance, indicating that efficient cultivation of the land may have been the most important criterion. Cecily and her husband sued her half brother for ten acres in Holme, arguing that her brother had inherited it from her father and that when he died it should have gone to her rather than her half brother by her father's second marriage. The court upheld her claim probably because she had a husband who could farm the land.[22] At Chertsey Abbey practicalities argued against the daughter of the first wife. Peter Bernard died, leaving a messuage and a half virgate to his son by his second wife. When this boy, William, died while still a minor, his half sister by Peter's first marriage claimed it. Instead, the court argued that she was not William's sister but the daughter of a first wife. "None of half-blood can inherit of right." The land eventually went to the man who married Peter's widow.[23]

Bastardy posed complications because it could be a bar to direct succession of the land. Thus when John de Tothale of Chobham claimed some meadow that had belonged to Ralph de Forde and his wife, Alice, on the grounds that he was their son but born before they were married, the court disallowed it. The jurors claimed that John was "by the laws of England, a bastard, to whom no villein-land can descend, so that he has no right to the aforesaid land, either by way of purchase or inheritance." Such harshness, however, was not as uniform throughout the realm as the jurors claimed. In Wakefield a child conceived between trothplight and marriage was legitimate:

> Robert son of Richard de Risseworth of Wakefield and John his brother come and crave the land of Thomas son of Nigel de Wakefued as his heirs. John says Robert ought not to be heir because he was born before the marriage was solemnized at the church porch, but after the plighting of troth privately between them. Robert, the elder brother, says it is the custom on the lord's land in these parts for the elder brother, born after trothplight, to be heir, and he therefore prays to be admitted as heir.

The jurors agreed with Robert and he was given the land.[24]

Practical considerations led both lay and ecclesiastical authorities to take a lenient view of bastardy in order to preserve amicable arrangements and smooth succession to property. On many manors the bastard's rights might only be recognized if he were the sole heir, but he could be given land for his lifetime. If the family and the lord were satisfied with the arrangement for a bastard to inherit, there was no dispute. Common law and church law differed from customary law but were also generous in recognizing the legitimacy of children. If a marriage ended on the grounds of affinity or consanguinity, the children were considered legitimate. Even a child produced from an adulterous union in the fifteenth century was deemed legitimate, for, as one jurist put it, "Whoso bulleth my cow, the calf is mine."[25]

Although customs varied from manor to manor, the strong sentiment that property should descend to the person with the closest blood tie remained firm. In 1331, when William Totti died without heirs of his blood, his land was granted to another person "until the right heirs of the said William shall appear and satisfy the lord in court for what is due from the same."[26] The force of inherited rights appears to have played an important role in the land market. On the manor of Kibworth (Leicestershire) between 1359 and 1419 preference for family land was so strong that young people were willing to rent land with an elderly tenant on it so that they could be considered the "adopted" heir. They could thereby avoid the risk of having an heir suddenly appear and dispossess them. Fears that a distant relative would appear with a claim to the land were not irrational, for the mortality of the post-1348 plague encouraged more distant kin such as nieces and nephews to claim family land. Lords encouraged kin to take up vacant holdings by charging anyone with a blood tie to the land a lower entry fee than a person simply purchasing the right to it.[27]

While the peasantry had strong attachments to inheritance rights and knew the laws and customs that presumably governed devolution of property, a close look at the actual disbursement of land and goods shows enormous diversity. Peasants resorted to rules and customs only when a father failed to make his personal arrangements before death or when family feuds forced the issue into court. For the most part, peasants manipulated rules through settlements during their lifetime or arrangements made at their death, increasingly through wills.

Factors encouraging flexible land and wealth settlements included population decline and the consequent availability of land, opportunities for other employment, such as the tin industry in Cornwall, the amount of land a family possessed, the wealth the family unit had accumulated, the point in a member's life cycle, the number of children, the parents' personal preferences, and other opportunities such as education or wage labor. Macfarlane's suggestion that medieval Englishmen were not peasants because inheritance rules were often laid aside and because family land might be sold to non kin may not be taken as a serious explanation of the diversity of inheritance patterns one sees in the records.[28]

Let us begin with the demographic and economic changes, for they provided the constraints within which peasant families had to work. A study of the vicissitudes of real estate ownership over the course of two centuries for one Leicestershire village provides a convenient framework for discussing other village studies. Between 1280 and 1340 one finds complete continuity of surnames in ownership and five new names added to the rental lists. In most cases the descent was from father to son.[29] While few studies show such remarkable consistency as Kibworth Harcourt, all indicate a tendency for the old families to stay on their lands through the 1340s. These same studies show that the Black Death in 1348 was the beginning of dislocations of old families and selling of whole tenements, both of which were features of the late fourteenth and fifteenth centuries. Plague and other diseases killed off families, and the new opportunities for wage labor and alternative landholdings led some survivors to seek additional or better land.[30] Both the dearth of the early fourteenth century and the subsequent easing of demands for land brought adaptations to inheritance strategies but did not alter the importance of providing for family members.

The noted economic historian M. M. Postan argued that the land hunger in the early fourteenth century led to fragmentation of land-holdings as individuals and families in the inexorably growing popula-tion purchased small parcels of land in their pursuit of survival.[31] More detailed studies of landholding in the years of scarcity have demon-strated that what appeared at first as an active land market was often rentals. Some of the land transfers were really leases or exchanges, not sales, and would eventually revert back to the original holding. Such transactions permitted flexible adjustments to the family developmental cycle without involving permanent alienation of family land. Retired parents could lease a few acres until they died, or mature sons could be married and settled on rented land until the parents were ready to retire. Widows could lease land, rather than trying to cultivate it themselves, and take it back when their sons grew up. Most land that appeared on the market was in small units of a half acre to a few acres. These lands may have been pieces of assart that never belonged to a holding, or abandoned cotland, or simply temporary leases from a tenement. Even in periods of land scarcity, then, odd acres and leases of parts of tenements relieved the pressure to fragment family land permanently.[32]

With a reduced population after 1350, land became readily avail-able. As a consequence, parents had a wide range of options in providing for themselves and inheritances for their children. Wealthy peasant parents could acquire vacant tenements to set up older children when they reached the age of marriage. Even younger children in the family could look forward to receiving a full settlement rather making do with what remained of family wealth. Young people whose parents were too poor to provide them with anything could spend a few years working as servants in order to acquire some land with their savings or could take on a retirement contract with an elderly neighbor. With these new opportunities, the dictates of customary rules for division of property became even weaker in the fifteenth century than they had been in the fourteenth. In Kibworth Harcourt, for instance, the average family size declined from 5 to 3.96, while family holdings increased from an average of twelve acres to twenty-four.[33] Leighton Buzzard saw a flurry of land transfers to people outside the family from 1464 to 1508, and in the estates of the bishop of Worcester an active land market led to an increase in the size of landholdings.[34] In Kibworth Harcourt customary settlements remained strong in the early fifteenth century, but in King's Ripton the trend away from custom accelerated in the second half of the fourteenth century. By the fifteenth century, in most places the force of customary rules of inheritance weakened as land continued to be available.[35]

The demographic and economic variables over the course of two centuries did not alter the rules of inheritance; they simply provided fewer or greater options in dividing family wealth. In addition to these all-encompassing parameters on inheritance, individual solutions for passing on wealth depended on the family's circumstance.

To safeguard provisions that did not fall strictly within the inheritance rules or to ensure that land and goods woud be divided as planned, the peasants had several legal instruments. The widow's rights, for instance, were assured when the couple married. The husband went to the manor court and surrendered his tenement into the lord's hands and took it back again in the name of both. Thus when the husband died, the wife could continue on the land without special permission and without paying entrance fines. Similar arrangements might be made with a son or daughter to pass on land during the lifetime of the father. In 1313 John Perus, Parnel, his wife, and John, his son, entered one acre of land. Inter vivos settlements for children were particularly important after the plague years when peasants took up new tenements, for it was one way to guarantee that the tenement would pass to the heir rather than being rented to another party.[36] Retirement contracts with children or provisions for the devolution of land to an heiress were also done inter vivos in manorial court. Special arrangements could be made in a will, which was permissible for villeins and freemen alike. The villein could also call the bailiff or the whole manor court to dictate his final directions for the disposal of his lands and goods. In both manorial courts and common law, wills became increasingly popular in the fourteenth century to tailor property divisions to family needs and elude custom.[37]

Both the stage in the life cycle and the relative wealth of the family dictated property divisions and special arrangements. If the father had grown sons and extra land, he would try to establish them on land during his lifetime, with or without a retirement contract. Thus Robert, son of William of Denton, got a license to take seven acres and a barn from his father, but he would only have a half acre of that until his father died.[38] Half an acre was not enough to feed a family, so Robert probably was unable to marry at that time. Gerbot de Alvirthorp, however, gave a bovate of land to two grown sons, Richard and John, while he still had a younger son at home. When he retired, he took the bovate back for his lifetime and paid each of the boys 3d. a year. Presumably they then got the home tenement.[39] With a bovate between them they might have married. The extra bit of land to establish a grown son might come from land that the wife brought to the marriage. Thus Robert, son and heir of Emma, took up nine acres of land that she had received from her father.[40] These examples from the late thirteenth century illustrate clearly the tight maneuvering necessary to establish mature sons. The contrast to the late fifteenth century is striking. Before Bartholomew Atkyn died in 1500, he had bought properties with which to endow his heirs. His son John was to become a priest. If he did not, he woud have the principal house but would have to care for two younger brothers. For his wife he had a tenement "lately bought from one called Bustard with the mill and all appurtenances." To his son Hugh he gave a tenement and two closes "lately bought from Henry Serle," and to his son Richard "the tenement bought from Malpasse."[41]

In poorer families sons would have to wait until their father died in order to marry, or they pursued an entirely different strategy. They might try to marry a widow with land who needed a husband to work it, but they would then find themselves in competition with second sons of the wealthier peasants. They could also try to establish themselves through wage labor. In the early fourteenth century, when population was high, this strategy was difficult; however, during the population stagnation such an approach could be very successful for both young men and women.

Wills provide the most readily accessible overview of the variety of inheritance arrangements. Out of 193 wills from Kibworth, thirty-three men died leaving chidren who were all minors. A small majority (42 percent) preferred to give the wife the tenement and residue to raise the family, although 39 percent jointly endowed the wife and a son and 18 percent bequeathed it all to the son even though the wife was still alive. When at least some of the children had reached the age of majority, the inheritance strategy changed. Men favored mature sons in 41 percent of their wills, while they left to the wife alone or the wife with a son the estate in 29 percent of the cases. In the eighteen cases in which the testator died childless he left his estate to his wife (81 percent) or to the wife and another kinsman (17 percent).[42]

What could children reasonably expect to receive as a settlement? The 376 lay testators in Bedfordshire gave their sons (405 in the sample) animals (17 percent), money (16 percent), land other than the home tenement (15 percent), household goods (12 percent), and the home tenement (8 percent). Other bequests included a house other than the home tenement, grain, trade tools or an education, other goods such as clothing, and the residue of the estate.[43] Some testators specified that they had already provided for their sons (3 percent of the sons in the sample) and probably more had been provided for inter vivos than are mentioned.

Daughters (274 in the sample) could also expect to receive animals as their share of the family wealth (26 percent). In addition, 21 percent received money; 14 percent, household goods; 11 percent, grain; 9 percent, land other than the home tenement; and 4 percent, other goods. Other provisions included a house other than the home tenement, trade or education, and the residue.[44] Seven percent of the daughters were the sole heirs and received the home tenement.

The bare numerical breakdown of bequests in wills does not adequately capture the wide range of strategies that peasants used to endow children. A few examples better indicate the pains a father took to make equitable divisions of the wealth accumulated during his stewardship of family lands. Edward Colyn of Stapulford died in 1509. He gave each of his children sixteen sheep. The eldest son and his heirs were given a house called Hogeyard with a garden and four acres of land, and the younger son was given the testator's house and land after the death of his mother, with the provison that £10 be taken from the estate and divided equally among the testator's five children.[45] Bartholomew Atkyn was considerably wealthier, having silver spoons and other luxuries to disperse. He was very desirous that his eldest son, John, become a priest; but if he did not, he would get the home tenement and would have to pay the other legacies out of it. The other children got various pieces of land along with money and some household goods. But, to be sure that fair division continued, he provided that "if any child die, his portion to go to him who shall then have the greatest need."[46]

One can detect some agonizing scrupulousness in being fair even when the testator knew that a bequest was going to a child who was a spendthrift.[47]

The Russell family wills permit us to observe the careful planning for one large family. Hugh Russell had six sons and three daughters to provide for in the late fifteenth century. He gave four sons tenements, arable land, and meadows. Two brothers, William and Thomas, Sr., were to live side by side. Thomas was settled in a cottage with a forge. William and Thomas Russell, Jr., were to take over two tenements that were being held by their brothers-in-law when they reached the age of majority. Apparently the three daughters had as part of their dowries the right to use the land until their brothers matured. The wife was to remain on the home tenement with two younger boys who each got 40s., but she was to make a will and provide for them. The arrangement was sealed with the sons-in-law witnessing and acting as executors.[48]

Evidence from manorial courts and wills shows peasant parents juggling resources to meet the constraints of keeping family land intact and providing all members of the immediate family with some share of the goods and chattels. In this delicate balancing of claims the peasants might try to honor local inheritance rules, but they certainly did not feel bound by them. Economic opportunities, age of children and parents, children's talents, and favoritism might be more important in determining inheritances. Thus a father might decide to educate a bright son or set up an older one during his lifetime then bequeath the family land to a younger son. Or, rather than a completely equal division, a father might favor the elder son with the family land and the elder daughter with a good dowry. The younger children would receive some lesser payment from their favored brother, or perhaps nothing if the family was poor. Beyond the immediate family, kin claims on land and goods were weak. A young testator might revert his lands and goods back to his family. Old testators who had already distributed the family wealth had the freedom to give their remaining personal effects to extended family and friends. A testator dying without immediate family usually did not leave his land to brothers or cousins, but ordered that it be sold for the benefit of his soul.[49] After the parents had made their settlements with their children, the children apparently felt no further sense of material obligation to brothers or sisters, even if they died childless themselves. The parents' division was binding for that generation. Such strong identity with the nuclear family and its fortunes raises questions about the attitudes toward extended family that we will investigate in the next chapter.

5

Kinship Bonds

Claims to family land and chattels seldom moved beyond the immediate hearth or out of the bloodline, but in matters other than the dispersal of material goods, what bonds did kinship imply? English peasant kinship was bilateral—that is, individuals traced their descent from both father and mother. Marriage brought them into the kinship network of their spouse's family as well. Thus each individual had a unique set of kinship relations. These relations could be extended through fictive kinship by the selection of godparents. In a society with high mortality, remarriage regularly created stepparents and stepchildren. Thus the English peasant was hardly kin-poor, but how much did this extended kinship mean in terms of living arrangements, marriages, loyalties, and affections?

Several approaches have proved useful for providing insights into family cohesion. Kinship terminology has long been popular, naming patterns have been exploited more recently, and a knowledge of family history can be indicative of familial identity.

Kinship terminology in English is not very diversified. Anthropologists expect to find rather elaborate kinship terminology in socieites where kinship plays an important part in an individual's life, but even Anglo-Saxon had few words to describe any ties but those to the nuclear family. They did not even have a word for *cousin* until the introduction of French. This paucity of kinship terms is in startling contrast to the continent, which had extensions to fourth cousins. The minimal kinship terms already common in the seventh and eighth centuries in England did not appear on the continent until after the Black Death.[1]

Anglo-Saxon kin terminology had an easy flexibility, with the same word used for *grandson* and *nephew*, *granddaughter*, and *niece*. The interchangeability of terms suggest that the modes of behavior toward these family relationships were similar. Nuclear-family terms were virtually the only ones that were important, and compounds based on them formed lineal ascent and descent. The only extended family member meriting a unique appellation was the father's brother, indicating a special relationship with the spear-side uncle.[2]

Middle and modern English adopted from the Normans the French root words for kinship terms such as *uncle* and *aunt*, but no more complicated term than *cousin* was used for more distant kin. Although the special term for a relationship to father's brother was dropped, the kinship terminology perpetuated Anglo-Saxon practices. Thus we continued to form clumsy compounds such as grandmother or fourth cousin once removed. The lack of words for extended kin indicates that they were not a part of daily parlance because they were not needed.

Anglo-Saxon social custom, like the modern English one, was not patrilineal and did not emphasize obligations to extended kin. Modern historians have argued that inherited surnames are an indication of a patrilineal system, but they are mistaken. Instead, both then and now, society was organized into ego-centered, bilateral kinship. Only a slight preference, arising perhaps out of the warlike nature of Anglo-Saxon society, made the "spear side" more important than the "spindle side." Residence tended to be virilocal, unless a man married a woman inheriting a house and land. But even inheritance customs in Anglo-Saxon England showed the same ad hoc quality that we found in late medieval England.[3] Surnames, as we shall see, were not even necesarily patronymics.

Although the Church introduced the elaborate canonical prohibitions on marriage by degree of kinship, peasants did not adopt a more elaborate system for kin recognition. Marriage was prohibited between men and women related to the fourth degree of kinship, so that people who had descended from the same great-great-grandfather were considered consanguineous. Affinity was also a ban to marriage, so that a man could not marry the sister of a former wife and vice versa. Even sexual relations outside marriage established affinity; if one had sexual relations with a fiancee's kinswoman, the marriage could not take place. The spiritual kinship from the baptismal ceremony meant that, for instance, a man could not marry a woman who had stood as godmother to a child by his first wife. The Church must have presumed that people would know their family trees and would avoid marriage to those with either consanguineous or affinal ties. But did they?

Cases in ecclesiastical courts indicated that the populace had considerable anxiety about kinship connections in marriages and, as a consequence, people did avoid at least the obvious kin marriages.

Furthermore, few divorce cases among the general population were based on consanguinity. One would assume, given the many degrees of kinship involved, that divorce would be relatively simple because of the potential for consanguinity. But cases appearing in the ecclesiastical courts demonstrate that people did not know their kinship ties and could not find witnesses or prove to the court's satisfaction that they were related to their spouse. Apparently, parishioners did not have a good sense of their more distant kinship ties.[4]

In spite of Church strictures on intermarriage with kin, marriages within the forbidden degrees occurred. To form a rough estimate on intermarriage, one scholar looked at the marriages in various ecclesiastical act books and found that roughly 50 percent of the couples were from the same parish, and therefore potentially related. Since no routine parish register was kept, the extent of intermarriage among kin cannot be established, but a statistical model based on an individual and starting at the Norman Conquest (1066) shows considerable overlap:

> Around the discovery of America, our individual has more than 60,000 distinct ancestors. Some 95 percent of the slots in the family tree at this level are still filled by different people. But back as far as the time of Wycliffe and the Peasant's Revolt, at the twentieth generation the number of distinct ancestors has grown beyond 600,000 and nearly a third of the slots in the tree are filled by duplicate people. Just before the Black Death nearly 30 percent of the 3,650,000 inhabitants of England turned up as ancestors. [By the time of King John] 80 percent of the population are ancestors of our single individual.[5]

On an island such as England the more distant kinship relations had to be forgotten or nearly all marriages would have been within the prohibited degrees.

Two other legal situations encouraged peasants to call upon their family history. In the thirteenth century men and women went to the king's court to try to prove that they were free peasants as opposed to villeins. They supported their testimony with their genealogies showing freeborn relatives while the lord countered with his reconstruction of their family trees indicating telltale unfree ancestors. These genealogies went no farther back than to a grandfather, but they did extend laterally to include aunts, uncles, and cousins. All cases showed a mix of free and unfree relatives. In very few of the cases did the inquest jury, drawn from the community, support the peasant's claim. The evidence leads one to conclude that not only family, but community members and the lord's officials as well, knew the relationship and the status of all individuals involved.[6]

Knowledge of one's family tree could also be important in claiming land that had become vacant because of death or desertion of direct heirs. Following the Black Death, collateral branches came from other villages to claim inheritances in Halesowen, and their claims were recognized. Again, the ties were mostly limited to nieces and nephews of both the male and female lines.[7]

Lineage did not have the great importance to peasants that it did to nobility. One use of the word *house* that did not appear in the peasants' vocabulary was its association with an aristocratic lineage system, as in "the House of Lancaster." If peasants had family traditions that traced descent from some notable ancestor, such as John the Bullthrower, they have escaped record readers to date.

English peasants were ahead of those on the continent in one aspect of family identity, and that was the early establishment of relatively stable family surnames.[8] By the late thirteenth century, and certainly by the time of the Black Death, surnames had reached considerable stability. The need for surnames arose partly because English government was beginning to reach out to individuals in the countryside, particularly in such matters as justice and taxation, which required stable names, but also because peasants were using written records and found that surnames were useful to themselves as well. Thus land transactions could be traced and debts collected from the next generation.

English peasants did not necessarily use patronymics. A child might be identified by either the father's or the mother's surname, so that matronymics were not uncommon. The mother's name was not reserved for illegitimate children but, rather, was used when the mother was the inheritor of the family land. Thus one finds in manorial court cases, such as that of Henry Chyld, who married Joan, the daughter and heir of Walter Chyld, that the husband has taken the wife's name. In another case the couple changed their name to the wife's father's surname when they inherited the land.[9]

The surnames themselves suggest that the community bestowed them. Occupational surnames such as Smith and Carter described the family's work; geographical names such as de (of) Broughton or atte Townsend described the village or place of residence; and physical descriptions such as Long or White depicted a person's physical characteristics. Sometimes the names were not entirely complimentary, but they stuck as surnames because the community recognized them. Occasionally a name suggests an ancestral root in a Danish settler such as Wigeston's Herricks, who perhaps descended from an Erik. Surnames became commonplace only gradually, and the old system of identification with a father's or mother's first name continued, either as the only identification or along with a surname as in William, son of Maud Squint. At least initially it is hard to imagine a positive identity with surnames given in such a way, unless it indicated flattering personal characteristics. Pride in a family name appears not to have been a preoccupation of medieval peasants, for they had no formal adoption procedure for a child to take an adoptive parent's surname.

Another way to look at the importance of kinship for an individual or family is to investigate the rights and obligations that a peasant might expect from kin. We have already seen that the right to inheritance was tightly held to the blood relations centered at the family hearth. But did peasants rely for various services and emotional bonds on a limited family network of parents, children, and siblings? on an extended family including uncles and cousins? or, as Ariès suggested, on community contacts?

The myth of extended kinship in the Middle Ages does not die easily; and even when social scientists considered the uses of kinship, they adopted a sentimentalized argument for extended kinship being better, theoretically at least, for a peasant society. Extended families, they argue, are more efficient for agriculture in that they provide for a cooperative work force, greater security for members and less disruption from death and divorce, and ample entertainment and fellowship.[10] While it might make more short-run economic sense to invest in the wage labor of fellow villagers to help with farm work, the long-term investment in extended kin is worth more because they can be relied upon for aid in adversity.[11]

Medieval peasants did not behave in a manner modern social scientists think of as optimal for their circumstances. They did not routinely live in extended families and seem not to have relied extensively on kin. From the Anglo-Saxon period and into the Middle Ages, the only right that extended kin could ask of an individual was part of the inheritance, should that individual's direct line fail. Their duties to him/her were also few. They might be asked to stand surety and care for him/her in the event of illness, but as we shall see, immediate family and nonkin might be preferable for such roles. In Anglo-Saxon law they received compensation in the event that he/she was killed, but only a remnant of this right remained in the late Middle Ages. The wife or mother could prosecute the murderer of a dead brother, father, husband, or son.[12] Record sources do not mention exchanging work with kin or obligations to aid in hard times. Instead, reliance on the labor of nuclear family, supplemented with hired servants, and some reciprocity with neighbors dominate the records.

One vexing question that eludes researchers in medieval records is the extent to which members of village communities were related to each other. If inbreeding was common in villages, we might expect that the networks of mutual aid and pledging (surety) we see in manorial courts are, in fact, the workings of extended kinship. Even if families did not live together, they could have cooperated to further their mutual interests. Studies of networks are just beginning to be done, and those that are published indicate that an individual family was likely to have at least one other kin in the community. In early modern Terling, 50 to 60 percent of the households had kin in the village, but the link was usually with only one other household containing closely related kin— parents or siblings; more extended family was rare. Thus kinship networks tended to be loose and played only a small role in the village's social structure.[13]

What sort of mutual reciprocity, if any, did peasants expect from their kin? To answer that question we must turn to manorial court rolls. Here, again, we meet with some frustration in analyzing kinship obligations, for only the close relationships of the nuclear family are specifically mentioned and kin ties through the female line are difficult to detect. A study of Redgrave, Suffolk, shows that of the 13,592 interactions in the manor court from 1259 to 1293 only 10.7 percent were between members of the same familes, and this figure included such uncooperative actions as assault and tresspasses. The most common form of interaction (96 percent) was when families were jointly amerced (fined). Since family members are cited as defaulting on debt, they apparently borrowed from each other. In Writtle (Essex), however, only 2 percent of debt litigations were between family members. While family members did pledge for each other, they were more likely to select someone who was not in their family. Pledging, or standing surety that the other person will meet their obligations, is the area where one would expect the most family cooperation, for the arrangement required a high degree of trust since the pledger was fined or held responsible if the pledgee reneged. That studies of pledging have not found family ties predominating argues for friends being more important.[14] One reason for selecting nonkin as a pledge, however, was that recruiting a higher-status villager for the role was more prestigious.

The extent to which an individual relied on neighbors or kin depended on their community status. Both upper- and lower-status individuals in Redgrave had few interactions. The lower economic group had small nuclear families in which the children, by necessity, left home early to seek work as servants and laborers. Because they had little property to distribute, as we saw in the last chapter, they made few claims on family. At the upper end of village wealth, money and power could, in a sense, substitute for kin and neighbors. It was the middling group who relied on kith and kin. Sons and daughters might marry during the father's lifetime and even live on the same messuage, thus encouraging mutual help, but for this group as well neighbors were more important than kin in pledging and cooperating in agriculture.[15] The relationship of an individual and his family to neighbors will be considered more fully in the section on surrogate family.

While it is difficult to move beyond bonds within the nuclear family in manorial court rolls, the picture they present may not be totally unrealistic. It is possible, however, to trace the fortunes of some individuals and their extended kin through sources ranging from reconstructed manorial court "biographies" to wills and chronicles. Amassing example upon example cannot, to be sure, provide a final guide to the debts of kinship and the depth of family feeling, but they do indicate how kin could be exploited if conditions were right and the parties amenable.

In the late fourteenth century three cousins, John, Richard, and Thomas Cellarer, made such an impression on the abbey of Meaux with their joint strategy to get their villein status transferred out of abbey and onto royal demesne, that their case was recorded in the abbey chronicle thirty years later. The Cellarers, as their name implied, had risen to prominence because their grandfather Adam had been an abbey official. After Richard had tried to raise an unsuccessful revolt in 1356, John and Thomas along with two other kinsmen made a clever legal maneuver. They claimed that, in violation of the Statute of Labourers of 1351, the abbot had taken by force a plowman whom they had hired. The abbot intended to discuss the case with the royal auditors at Westminster, but since the charges had been brought, the auditors distrained the abbot's horses and he had to rent some to return to Meaux. The plea was quashed when the cousins, examined singly, admitted they were villeins of the abbot. They could not, therefore, bring charges against him. Richard then appealed to the king on behalf of the family, saying they were really his villeins and not those of the abbot, but the king delayed the case because of a fresh campaign in France. Yet another infraction of manorial rules landed John and some family members in the abbey's prison, but John crawled out at night through a shaft in the latrine system. He and William, another cousin, then tried to get their freedom declared. Throughout these legal maneuvers members always acted in the interest of the whole family and often worked together, assuming legal costs and punishments jointly.[16]

In one of the reconstructed biographies from court roll evidence, the importance of marriage in changing a person's kinship encounters is well illustrated. When Henry Kroyl, Jr., married Agnes, daughter of Robert Penifader, their union brought together the kin of the two prominent village families for the first time. While for all parties most associations continued to be with nonkin, Henry's relationship with his brother, as opposed to his father, became more important and his affinal relationships with his wife's kin were a new feature of his life. Henry's brothers-in-law, however, tended to use their new association with the Kroyl family more extensively, perhaps reflecting the greater political prominence of the Kroyl family. The women in the Penifader family also reflect their marital status in their networks. Agnes relied on her husband's network, but her unmarried sister, Christine, continued to rely largely on her natal family. The relationships between the two families remained amicable during this generation, but conflicts arose over inheritances among their children and between aunts and uncles and nieces and nephews.[17]

Wills and manorial court land transactions sometimes show the role that kin played in an overall strategy for setting up family units. For instance, John Andrew died in 1303 without heirs. His brother Roger took his land and endowed his son Andrew with it. His other son, John, took an acre of land with his uncle's widow. Eventually John and Andrew took over Uncle John's messuage together. Andrew apparently died without issue and the land went to John, son of John, the son of Roger, or the grandnephew of the original holder. Uncles and aunts on both the father's and the mother's side could be a source of inheritance. Since they received part of the family inheritance, they might return it to the children of siblings if they died childless, and in a stable population 20 percent of married adults were likely to be childless.[18]

Even if we must assume that the connections with extended family are obscured because of name changes at marriage or failure to mention the ties of blood, our few examples cannot prove extensive networks of kin.[19] If the reliance on kin related by blood is difficult to trace through the records, the importance of fictive kin and stepparents is even more difficult. We will leave these two relationsips for a separate chapter on surrogate parents.

The most difficult aspect of kinship to illuminate with medieval records is the affection felt and displayed toward relatives. Here one can only appeal to the sources for inferences about feelings. What, for instance, does it tell us when we read in a coroner's inquest that the wife of Hugh the Cobbler of Blundham expected her husband to come back from Sandy on December 11 but he did not? She searched for him the next day "because she was troubled by his delay and every day until

December 29," when she found him drowned in the river.[20] Was it the kin's duty to search for a family member who was delayed on the road or was this an act of individual concern and affection?

Of the 1704 cases in which the first finder in an accidental-death case is mentioned, only 26 percent were found by a family member. The mother was the first finder in 36 percent and the father in 31 percent. The wife was the first finder in 9 percent of the cases and the husband in 2 percent. Siblings account for 8 percent of the first finders. The rest were an insignificant scattering of other relatives and kin whose relationship is not known but whose surname was the same as the victim's. The preponderance of parents in the first-finder category disappears when one controls for children as victims, and the number of first finders who are related to adult victims drops to 15 percent. When the first finder is a relative, most likely she will be a woman, either a mother, wife, or sister. This is not a coincidence but rather underscores both the nurturing role of peasant women and the greater likelihood of adult men, as opposed to women, to die from accidental death.

A county-by-county breakdown shows large variations in kin as first finders. When one reads the coroners' rolls for Bedfordshire, it appears that a strong emphasis was placed on the family being the first finder; and occasionally the person who actually found the victim notified the next of kin so that the latter appears officially as first finder. In Bedfordshire 60 percent of the cases in which the first finder was identified he or she was related to the victim. But in Cambridgeshire only 25 percent were kin; and in Norfolk 30 percent, in Wiltshire 28 percent, and in Lincolnshire only 15 percent were kin. The lower percentages do not necessarily reflect a lack of emotional concern in these counties, but rather a difference in local legal attitudes. Since most of the first finders who were kin were females, counties that reserved legal roles largely for men, such as Wiltshire and Lincolnshire, have a lower percentage of kin as "official" first finders.

The first finder, therefore, is not a reliable indicator of concern about kin except that, once again, only the immediate family were the first finders, not extended family.

Wills, likewise, underscore the close attachment of an individual to immediate family rather than to more distant kin. Members of the nuclear family were given the bulk of the estates, and only the aged were likely to make token gifts to kin.[21] Of the 376 testators in Bedfordshire only 12 percent remembered grandchildren in their wills and they often referred to them as an undifferentiated group—e.g., "to each grandchild I leave 4d." The gifts were the token, ceremonial types that were reserved for those outside the immediate family circle. Animals (usually a sheep) were the most common (48 percent) bequests, followed by money (20 percent), and grain (11 percent). Other provisions included a bit of land or a house other than the home tenement, trade or an education, clothing, valuables, and a dowry for a granddaughter (3 percent). Some of the wills stated that the grandchild had been provided for already and some indicated that if the son inheriting the home tenement died, the grandchild should succeed him. Godchildren, as we shall see, were even less likely to be remembered, and when they are, they are given animals, money and grain.

A scattering of other kin are mentioned. The largest of this group are nieces, nephews, and unspecified kin with the same surname. This group received the usual animals, money, grain, and miscellaneous household goods, clothing, silver spoons, and so on. Only two were given the home tenement and two were given the right to buy it. Brothers were the next most frequently mentioned (21 percent), followed by sisters (11 percent), sons-in-law (10 percent), mothers, fathers, and daughters-in-law. All receive the usual ceremonial token gifts, although a few are provided with a house or land other than the home tenement. For the most part, as we mentioned in the last chapter, if a testator did not have a wife or a son or daughter, he directed that the estate be sold for masses for his soul.

Another insight into concern for kin, or lack thereof, comes from the provision for prayers for the testator's soul and others he cared to remember. In this largely spiritual matter one might expect that bonds of affection rather than economic ties would predominate. The provision for prayers would, of course, only go to people who had predeceased the testator, and this must be borne in mind in interpreting the data. Almost half of the testators left special bequests of goods and money for masses for only their own souls, while 30 percent generously included all Christian souls. Of those who did include kin in the masses, a father (10 percent) was the most common, followed by a wife (9 percent). Husbands were mentioned in 3 percent of all wills, but a high proportion of the widows leaving wills mentioned their husband. Most of the men still had a wife alive, so that the failure to include a wife is not surprising. Only two men mentioned two wives. Mothers were not specifically mentioned but included as parents (4 percent). Brothers were rarely mentioned (1 percent), and sisters never were. Priests were most likely to reserve prayers for parents or brothers in their wills. The enlightening omissions are children who predeceased the testator (only one example) and kin other than the immediate family.

The nuclear family, seen in the light of inheritance customs and practices and kinship relations, was a compact unit, not a porous one.

Inheritance customs kept the nuclear family tightly bound until the children set up their own households. The role of relatives outside the nuclear family varied with family preferences, individual bonds of affection, and the value of family assets. Kin outside the nuclear family could either play no part or a large part in family life and economic strategy. No strong cultural norms dictated that extended kin be asked to sit at the hearth or be serviceable in case of need. Even with the introduction of surnames and Church prohibitions on consanguineous marriages, knowledge of family relationshps beyond grandfathers and aunts and uncles remained shaky. Thus, contrary to the assertions of Shorter and Stone, the nuclear family was not permeable to the entrance of other kin to its hearth unless it so chose. Friends and neighbors were important for an individual and a family unit to succeed, particularly among the large group of middling peasants, but they too did not enter into the family.

The Black Death and the major economic and demographic changes of the fourteenth and fifteenth centuries had little effect on peasants' assumptions about the rights and obligations of nuclear family members; they remained as firmly binding as ever. The greater opportunities meant simply that second sons were likely to be able to do much more with their inheritances than had previously been possible, assuming they survived disease. Because of the high mortality, members of the extended kin network appeared more frequently in court records, chiefly to claim vacant family lands. Neither the dearth of the early fourteenth century nor the prosperity of the later period seems to have altered peasants' indifferance toward extended kin.

6

Household Size and
Structure

Two of the most elusive aspects of the medieval family are its size and structure, and yet both have received considerable study. The record sources are all deficient in one way or another. The two large surveys, the Domesday Book of 1086 and the poll taxes of the late fourteenth century, do not list all household members, so that the demographer must derive a multiplier from other sources in order to arrive at the number of people in the household. Other sources, however, also have their defects. Manorial court rolls do not refer to women and children with any consistency. The surveys and serf lists that survive are for short time periods and small areas. Wills are not numerous until the fifteenth century and do not necessarily indicate all of a testator's children. Coroners' inquests provide fleeting glimpses of the whole family around the hearth, but are not systematic sources for household size or structure. Thus to those vital questions of age of marriage, fertility, family limitation, and relationship of people in a household, the answers will necessarily remain somewhat tentative.

Although sources are sparse, speculation has been rife on all of these matters. Scholars of the early modern and modern family have found it necessary to fill medieval households with a number of kin in order to argue that the modern family is very different from the medieval one. Historians and social scientists have equated the nuclear, or conjugal, families with modern economic and social life, and have equated extended families, by contrast, with preindustrial and peasant societies.[1] Two sociologists, for instance, have argued that in societies with a high degree of social stratification the extended family will predominate.[2] Certainly, medieval Europe qualified as a society with a

90

high degree of social stratification, but we have already shown that in matters of inheritance the nuclear, or conjugal, family predominated and that in the recognition of kinship bonds only close relationships were noted. However, we must still investigate who lived under one roof and who controlled entrance to and exit from the hearth.

Because of source material deficiencies and because scholars have been so active in creating hypothetical structures for the medieval family, it is useful to start with some basic definitions of subjects investigated in this chapter. Two demographic historians, Hammel and Laslett, have provided some basic categories for analyzing domestic units that can serve as a guide. Their basic definition is that the domestic group "consists and consisted of those who share the same physical space for the purposes of eating, sleeping, and taking rest and leisure, growing up, childrearing and procreation." The domestic group is coresidential and functions as a household unit. In establishing this basic definition, they draw a distinction between the household and the houseful. The household is a functioning domestic unit in which the members contribute to the general well-being of the group and share in the reciprocal obligations to its members. This close relationship of the members is opposed to the houseful, which may include visitors, guests, lodgers, boarders, and even aged parents and other kin who do not directly contribute to the domestic unit.

The domestic group could be very varied in its content, but the variations fall into six basic types. Solitaries included the widowed and widows as well as single people. Groups with no familial relationship include coresident persons who were either siblings or not related. Simple families or households are based on the conjugal couple and include married couples alone, married couples with children (nuclear family), and widows or widowers with children. The extended family or household could be extended either vertically or laterally or even a combination of the two. The most usual would be parents and a married son with children. The multiple family or household included secondary units and could thus encompass two brothers and their families living under one roof. Finally, there is a catchall group of incompletely classifiable households.[3]

Most of the debate over the structure of medieval families has been whether they were simple or more complex either extended or multiple. Our discussion of inheritance would lead us to expect to find multiple families in areas such as Kent or East Anglia, where partible inheritance was practiced. If two brothers inherited the land, it could be economically advantageous for them to work it jointly. But even though they might work the land jointly, they did not necessarily live in the same

house. Thus thirteenth-century serf lists in an area that practiced
partible inheritance showed that nuclear or simple households predominated.[4]

The traditional assumption about households in peasant society has
been that they contain extended families, with the married son and his
children living in the same house with his retired parents. Thus one has a
three-generational household or stem family.[5]

One argument that historians have used for extended peasant
households is a type of architectural determinism. Housing space was
limited because a peasant house was a substantial capital investment
that prohibited expansion of housing, thus forcing married sons to
continue living with parents. As we have seen in the chapters on the
material environment, a one-bay house was fairly inexpensive and could
easily be erected to house a retired peasant or a single adult brother or
sister. Archaeological evidence suggests that father and son built a new
house on the croft as a "dower" cottage or retirement home.[6] Thus
alternative solutions to housing the older generation were both common
and preferred. Furthermore, we have seen that the houses were neither
large nor, until the fifteenth century, very substantial. Houses lasted
about one generation, so that the son would have to rebuild. While there
was attachment to the family land, it did not extend to an identity with
the physical structure of the home. Home was, literally, where the
hearth was. The late medieval English peasant houses were not the
substantial, large stone houses found in parts of France and Italy.

The two main documents that enumerate household occupants, the
Domesday Book and the late-fourteenth-century poll taxes, indicate
that simple families were the rule. Manorial records of various sorts that
have been used in the numerous village reconstitution studies also show
households containing only the immediate family. All these records have
flaws in accurate reporting, but they suggest that if stem families did
occur, they were rare or short-lived. In the coroners' inquests the
families who are described around the hearth or in the house are almost
always simple families. But one occasionally finds an ambiguous case
such as the burning of the house of John, son of Henry of Baumburgh.
In the house was John's four-week-old son and his older son's sixteen-
week-old daughter.[7] Was the latter child simply left there or did John
and his older son live under the same roof?

One might argue that the stem family was of short duration in the
family cycle but nonetheless important.[8] A reply to this argument and
an attempt to overcome the source deficiencies has been a demographic
simulation model. It shows that demographic variables provided only
very loose constraints on household structure and that in the English

case, at least after 1500, the existence of stem families would have been rare. If demographic variables were not decisive, then one would not expect to find stem families earlier, except possibly during the period of land hunger and famine in the early fourteenth century.[9] Another source of evidence is the demographic studies from the continent, where records are more complete. In fifteenth-century Tuscany over half the families were simple ones. In northern France simple families predominated, but starting in 1350 stem and joint families appeared to be more common in Languedoc and southern France.[10] All evidence, such as it is, points to simple families predominating as the most common household type.

Evidence on solitaries is also difficult to find. Thirteenth-century serf lists show that 9 percent of the households were widows living alone.[11] The coroners' inquests also mention the occasional widow living alone or coresident with a sibling. Peasants were also familiar with local clergy as a solitary living alone or with some servants.

Widows heading households, however, were rather common. Of the 252 serf households in the study mentioned above, widows headed 5 percent. A survey of a dozen hamlets on Ombersley manor showed that one tenant out of seven was a widow, and the records of ten estates in the west midlands from 1350 to 1450 show that of the holdings remaining within families, 60 percent went to female heiresses and all but 5 percent of these were widows. In 1260 in Holderness about one-sixth of the villein holdings were in the hands of women, but about one-third of the cottars were women. These women were sometimes described as widows and sometimes as daughters of tenants. Among the Bedfordshire laymen leaving wills in the late fifteenth century, 72 percent had wives living at the time they wrote their wills (usually shortly before death).[12]

The presence of extra kin and nonkin in the households is a matter of separate interest. Orphans, as we shall see in a later chapter, were absorbed into family, as has been shown for later centuries. Servants, however, seemed not to have been as prominent a part of peasant households as they were later. Families relied on servants if they could afford them, and the poll tax lists their presence, but it is not clear that they always lived with the master or that peasants routinely put their children out in a semi-fostering arrangement as was common later in England.[13] Wealthy peasant families became temporarily larger during harvest season when they sheltered extra workers and sometimes their families, but these fall into the category of houseful rather than household.

The brief summary presented here indicates how little concrete information can be amassed on medieval English peasant household structure. Such evidence as exists points to a predominance of simple, conjugal families rather than either multiple or extended families. Housing was cheap throughout the period, so that the option of a separate roof over one's head was feasible and seemed to be preferred. No evidence may be found in literary or legal sources suggesting that the extended or multiple families were an integral part of the culture. In balance, the scant information available lends itself more readily to an argument for the predominance of simple families over stem families among the English peasantry during the late Middle Ages. Those who would argue for extended and multiple families must produce evidence rather than assertions and hypothetical preferences for the behavior of medieval English peasants.

Peasant household sizes have been the subject of as much disagreement as have their structure. Again scholars have produced hypothetical arguments. It is conventional wisdom, for instance, that peasants will reproduce at near biological maximums and hence have very large families with births every year or two during the woman's reproductive life. Other scholars, however, have observed that household size tends to be small in all societies and that one finds larger domestic groups only in pastoral societies and among rich peasants whose plentiful resources make it possible to support larger households.[14]

Historians who have studied preindustrial peasant society have also observed that economic opportunities were closely related to household size. Wealthier households had more children that poorer, and wealthier regions had larger families than did poorer ones. In rural Pistoia peasants living on the hillside terrain were kept poor by the avarice of landlords who charged too much rent and did not encourage capital investment in either the land or technology. The gouging landlords prior to the Black Death so depressed the standards of living of these people that married couples failed to replace themselves. Peasants on better land, however, had substantially larger families.[15] In Halesowen land in the preplague period was so scarce that sons inheriting small holdings or cottages were unable to increase either their income or their holdings. Consequently, they had small families while the wealthier peasants with more land had larger families.

Various household sizes have been suggested for the pre- and postplague periods. In Halesowen before the Black Death the average was 5.8, a higher figure than the 4.7 and 4.9 for Redgrave and Rickinghall, respectively, in Suffolk in the late thirteenth century. The average household size in Kibworth Harcourt was 5 before the plague and it dropped to 3.96 during the course of the fifteenth century. By the sixteenth century England again had a mean household size of 4.8. The improved economic conditions following the plague may not have increased household size, but they did ease the differences between the rich, middling, and poor families in numbers of children.[16]

Most of these estimates are based on family reconstitutions derived from manorial court rolls. These rolls were never intended as census documents and demographic calculations based on them must be reconstructed from court appearances. The rolls are biased against females, children under twelve, and against poorer elements who made fewer court appearances. Even extreme care in using them will never make them a reliable demographic source. Wills are another source for family size, but they too are very inadequate, for not all living children are mentioned because they may have received a previous settlement. But some trends may be derived from them, such as that the testators had few children during the fifteenth century, with the picture improving in its closing decades.[17]

Although none of the sources leaves one satisfied, it appears that the average number of persons per household was about five before the plague, with the rich having more and the poor less. In the late fourteenth and first part of the fifteenth century the average family size may have dipped below four, while the late fifteenth century saw a return to larger household size.

If we are to talk about small households including only a conjugal couple and one to three children, then questions arise about fertility and mortality. One wants to know why population was not reproducing close to the biological maximum, as the early historical demographer Frederick Le Play predicted.[18] Various suggestions and hypotheses have been put forward to explain the small family size, including birth control, infanticide, high infant mortality, late marriages, infertility due to poor diet, high female mortality, and economic limitations on nuptiality. If one assesses the limited data available to answer these questions, once again it is apparent that firm answers will not be forthcoming. Without parish registers, censuses, and even a routine notation of age in medieval records, one can only suggest possible parameters.

The age of marriage and percentage of the population marrying is obviously important in determining fertility, for early marriages and most people marrying should foster maximum reproductive capabilities. In his classic article on the European marriage pattern, Hajnal identified the medieval English population as non-European both because people married earlier than the northwestern Europeans did in later centuries and because a larger percentage married. Basing his argument on studies of the 1377 poll tax and of the British peerage, he concluded that the medieval English population resembled that of Bulgaria or Romania. These studies have proved to be unreliable.[19] A more rigorous, recent study of the poll tax evidence suggests that the percentage of males marrying was low and those who married did so late in life. This pattern was also confirmed in a reexamination of the thirteenth-century Lincolnshire serf lists. If this study is correct, then the marriage pattern of medieval England would fall within Hajnal's classification for the northwestern European pattern. The stagnation of population in the late fourteenth and fifteenth centuries, therefore, could have arisen not only from the pervasive mortality but also from the relatively late age of marriage of the population.[20]

The conclusions a researcher draws from poll tax lists, however, may depend on the ones she or he analyzes. Suffolk poll taxes show a high percentage of the population marrying and suggest a young age of marriage.[21] Of the knightly class, 86 percent were reported as married, as were 94 percent of the peasant farmers, 77 percent of the artificers, 84 percent of the laborers, and 54 percent of the servants. The Suffolk poll tax returns demonstrate that servants were establishing their own households while still young and in service. They appear to be taking advantage of the higher wages to set up independent households. The Suffolk returns also show that in the upper-status groups marriage was very common, and those not married were either widows, widowers, or teenagers living at home.

The family reconstitution study of Halesowen showed a variable age of marriage depending on economic circumstances. In the early fourteenth century, when land was hard to come by and wages were depressed, couples married in their early twenties. With the new economic opportunities opening up following the Black Death, the marriage age for women and men dipped into the late teens.[22] Both the Suffolk poll tax returns and the Halesowen materials suggest that Hajnal's depiction of the medieval English population as non-European is correct.

One reason for the relatively early age of marriage and the high percentage of the population marrying was that medieval peasant youth appear not to have been bound by the custom of "no land, no marriage." Both historians and demographers have held this up as an inalterable principle of peasant marriages. These scholars have presumed that a peasant son waited for his father to die or retire before he secured a tenement and married, and that younger siblings without prospects remained at home, unmarried. The effects of this long wait, historians argue, is that men marry older and spend part of their youth on fantasies of parricide.[23]

Evidence from fifteenth-century wills and fourteenth-century manorial court records dispel the myth that sons waited for their fathers to retire before marrying. We saw in Chapter 4 that fathers with grown sons had already given them other tenements or pieces of land or may have given them the home tenement and themselves retired to a cottage. Even the land shortages of the late thirteenth and early fourteenth centuries did not deter marriages. In Halesowen even a small holder could establish two sons on pieces of land and in separate cottages during his lifetime. The sons then married and supported small families on their land. Larger holders likewise set up their more numerous children during their lifetime. In the preplague years about 38 percent of the sons who formed households did so before their fathers died or retired. The land shortages may have delayed marriages for the poorer and middling groups, but not for the well-to-do. With the diminished population and ready availability of land, 54 percent of all sons established households while their fathers were alive.[24]

Land need not have come from the fathers, for enterprising youth, both male and female, purchased small plots of land in order to marry, and some inherited land from childless relatives. In manorial court rolls, as we have pointed out, numerous small pieces of land changed hands. These were often purchased by an individual anticipating marriage or by the parents of a child. Young couples were willing to risk establishing a household with as little as a cottage and an acre or two of land. They would have a meager life, poor survival rates for their children, and have to find wage labor and perhaps charity to supplement their income, but they were not deterred from marriage.[25]

Other resourceful young people took up retirement contracts, as will be discussed in the chapter on aging, so that they could guarantee that they would eventually have land when their elderly charges died.[26] In the early fourteenth century, when land was so much in demand, young men married widows for their land even if it meant that they would have to compete with children from the first marriage for the land after her death[27] On the Ramsey Abbey estates, 141 out of the 426 brides paying marriage fines had earned enough money to pay their own fines and select their own partners.[28] Even vagabonds, with only stolen goods to their name, married.[29]

Another reason that the lack of an inheritance or land did not deter marriage was that it was so simple to marry. A verbal agreement to marry was all that was necessary for a canonically valid marriage.

We have been suggesting that medieval peasant youth married young, but none of our sources so far have given ages. The absence of concrete evidence places greater value on the more subtle indicators of cultural attitudes toward the age at which marriage and sexual relations were considered appropriate. We must, therefore, look at unorthodox sources to determine what the society thought was the normal age of first marriage. All evidence points to the mid-teenage years as being too young for adult responsibilities, including marriage. The poll tax itself did not tax youth of fourteen because they were not fully adult. In the prosecution of rape cases, jurors singled out as especially reprehensible those men whose victims were teenagers and were much more likely to convict such offenders. One father lost his life trying to save his teenage daughter from a rapist. She had gone to the woods to gather sticks when the rapist approached her carrying a bow and arrow. She called for help from her father, who came to her rescue but was shot.[30] The rape and attempted-rape cases indicate a feeling on the part of society that girls in their teenage years should be sheltered from sexual encounter and that violent sexual attacks on them were repugnant. Another legal indication that adult marriages were preferred was the continued custom of keeping the age of majority for inheritance at twenty-one and higher. Such a high inheritance age was a signal, if not always an impediment, to youth to delay marriage. While these bits of evidence from legal records are far from conclusive, they do indicate that early and middle teenage marriages, and perhaps even sexual contacts, were not the norm.

Moralists such as Robert Mannyng counted marriage of children an outrageous sin. His objections had practical overtones; he observed that if people marry too young, they will come to dislike each other as they grow older and the marriage partners will tend to wander. But the canon law, applicable to all Europe and not England alone, permitted a very young age for marriage contracts. Children under seven could not enter into marriage contracts, and those over that age could repudiate the agreement at the age of puberty. For boys puberty was canonically established at age fourteen and for girls it was twelve. Few cases appeared in ecclesiastical courts arguing for dissolution of marriage or contract on the grounds of the parties being too young. The situation may seldom have arisen because children so young contracted few marriages or their repudiation was accepted without a court case.[31] Although Chaucer had the Wife of Bath married first at the canonically permitted age of twelve, we may not take that as a normal age of first marriage; such an early age of marriage could have been a literary devise to shock the public and enhance the sexuality of his character.

In ballads special and tragic circumstances surround the taking of a young bride. The classic story is that of Earl Brand. A young maid, who is described as just fifteen, came to his bedside and they conspired to elope. But as they went away together an old man on the moor recognized her and went to the castle to tell her father. The father set out with her brothers, but Earl Brand killed them all. However, he did not get to enjoy his too-young bride, because he too had received a mortal wound.[32]

Popular lyrics also warned about marrying women too young or too old, for either can turn shrewish:

> Young men I warn you every one
> Old wives take ye none
> For I myself have one at home:
> I dare not say, she says peace.
>
> When I come from the plow at noon
> In a broken dish my meat is come
> I dare not ask our dame for a spoon;
> I dare not say. . . .

The speaker goes on to complain that when he asks for cheese, she calls him "boy" and tells him he is not worth half a pea.[33]

Individual cases from scattered sources occasionally provide a glimpse into the age of first marriage. For instance, on a Sunday evening in 1367 a twenty-year-old man put a ladder against a beam in his house to get a cord, but the beam broke and he fell. His wife was the first finder. But we have no idea how long they were married before his accident. Margery Kempe, daughter of the mayor of Lynn, said in her autobiography that she was twenty when she married.[34] Such pathetic shreds of evidence underscore the difficulty of establishing any firm conclusions about age of marriage.

Cultural evidence suggests that marriage of teenagers was not normal and that a young Romeo and Juliet marrying in England would have created scandal. Furthermore, the great age disparities between husband and wife found in Italy were not the norm in England. In evaluating the evidence of age at first marriage and percentage marrying, it would appear that Hajnal was correct in suggesting that in medieval England the age of marriage was lower than in the modern period and a greater proportion of the population married. But his thesis requires some modification to take into account the fact that age of marriage could vary with economic and social conditions and that it was never common to marry in the early or middle teens. Hajnal is probably also correct in concluding that most people married. After all, men and women had so few economic options outside of establishing a family unit. Some men might have entered the clergy, but few of them were peasants; and some men and women may have entered service and remained single. Marriage, however, seemed to be a robust institution in the society and one can easily believe that the estimate that only 8 percent of the women remained unmarried in the mid-sixteenth century is not far off the mark for the fourteenth and fifteenth centuries.[35] Although land scarcity and lack of access to the home tenement may not have been as effective a brake on marriage as a rational demographer or economist might assume, marriages among the poor and landless were not very fertile. Under such circumstances a high proportion of the population marrying relatively young need not have produced offspring at a biological maximum. Delayed marriage and a large portion of the population remaining celibate is not the only possible explanation for low fertility.

The most apparent explanation for small family size has been high infant and child mortality, estimated at 30 to 50 percent of the children born in the preindustrial period. In the preplague years poor mothers could very well have had such insufficient diets that their fertility was reduced, miscarriages increased, or their weak infants were susceptible to disease.

Following the Black Death, however, almost all mothers should have had adequate diets since both land and wages were profitable. Nonetheless, mean family size decreased during this period. Contemporary chronicle and literary sources suggest that some visitations of the plague attacked children and young people more than the old. And some of the current research into plague has suggested these age groups as special targets as well. As Sylvia Thrupp noted, the fifteenth century, if it was a golden age for anything, was a golden age for bacteria. Not only plague, but other types of diseases became endemic in Europe at this time. The age groups most vulnerable were young adults, those who would produce the next generation.[36]

Some scholars have argued for a conscious limitation of family size in medieval England, including the practice of birth control. Medical treatises suggested a variety of herbs, and some, applied to the vagina, may have acted effectively as a block to sperm. A plausible argument based on ecclesiastical sources has been made for a knowledge of coitus interruptus. The pastoral guides, of course, forbade their parishioners to engage in such an act, ranking incest with a daughter as a lesser sin than performing unnatural sex with one's wife. Many of the writers of these manuals had acted as confessors and probably knew quite a bit about the abuse they were cautioning against. The West, unlike many other cultures, was fortunate in having a folklore and intellectual traditions dating back to Aristotle that encouraged laity to think of contraception in terms of blocking the sperm.[37]

Abortion was also a concern of ecclesiastical and medical writers. Medical texts list a variety of herbal suppositories and potions that a woman might take to induce abortion. Bracton, in *The Laws and Customs of England,* and later the author of *Fleta* were the first English legal writers to connect abortion with manslaughter, and the methods they named included potions and hitting or pressing a pregnant woman so as to kill the fetus. Only one such case appeared in the coroners' inquests.

> On 12 Dec. 1503 Joan Wynspere of Basford, "singilwoman," being pregnant, at Basford drank divers poisoned and dangerous draughts to destroy the child in her womb, of which she immediately died. Thus she feloniously slew and poisoned herself as a suicide and also the child in her womb. . . .

Moralists warned that it was a great sin to take anything "with meat or drink" against pregnancy, but in folklore herbs were used to "scathe the babe away."[38]

Psycho-historians have delighted in making medieval peasants great practitioners of infanticide. A précis to one psycho-history article claimed that "the latrines of Europe were screaming with the cries of murdered infants" and that there was a "widespread infanticide component ... present in the medieval personality."[39] As we have seen, it is by no means clear how much latrines were used in peasant society, and archaeological evidence could neither confirm nor deny the assertion in any case, because the bones of a newborn baby would disintegrate very rapidly.

In pre-Christian Europe a child could be exposed if it had not been named, but Christianity forbade exposure and infanticide. Even after Scandinavia became Christian it continued to be permissible for the poor who could not feed the infant or for the father of a deformed child to expose it. The procedure was to put a piece of pork fat in its mouth, wrap it up, and put it out. The decision was always the father's and the execution was usually left to servants.[40]

If infanticide was widely practiced, one would expect to find a positive rationalization for it in European folklore. Instead, one finds in folk traditions that dead infants returned to haunt their mothers. In "The Cruel Mother," a woman who has murdered her illegitimate twins in the wilderness is haunted by them when she gives birth to a legitimate child. And in another popular balled, "The Maid and the Palmer," a woman washing by the well is told by an old palmer who begs a cup of water that she is no maiden but had nine children, three buried at her bed's head, three under her lead brewing vat, and three out on the green.[41]

Finding concrete evidence that infanticide was widespread in medieval England has proven impossible. Of the more than four thousand cases of homicide that I have read in the coroners' and jail delivery rolls, I have only found three cases of infanticide. Indeed, the law did not clearly state (until the sixteenth century) that a mother was culpable of murder when she killed her infant. Jurors were thus unsure about whether indictments could be brought or not and, if they were, what was to be done with the woman who proved to be guilty of killing her newborn child. The Church took an interest in the newborn child and prescribed penances for mothers who killed them. But a study of the church court records revealed that here, too, cases of infanticide were rare.[42] Finally, evidence of skeletal remains in medieval graveyards shows a disproportionately high number of adult males to females.[43] Some people have been tempted to take this as evidence of female infanticide, but it is possible that female bones rather than those of males were unearthed and scattered as graveyards were cleared for new occupants.

Theoretical arguments for infanticide suggest that when food is scarce in other cultures, babies are killed or exposed. Such an argument would be applicable to medieval England only during the subsistence crisis in the first quarter of the fourteenth century, and, indeed, one of the contemporary chroniclers mentions that mothers killed their babes and ate their flesh.[44] One never knows in chronicles of this sort whether the author knew of such instances or was simply using a standard literary device to describe how horrible the Great Famine was.

Many scholars have argued that infanticide was common but did not show up in records because mothers or midwives successfully concealed the deaths by calling them stillbirths or accidents. An analysis of the accidental deaths of infants under one year old, however, does not indicate a pattern of willful destruction. None of the seventy-eight babies were described as dying from drowning or exposure, and the majority of them died in fires in their cradle or in their house, thus indicating that they were being cared for. A mother would not risk burning down a house by starting a cradle fire to kill an infant. Furthermore, one would expect that a higher proportion of female infants would be killed compared to male infants if the parents were practicing infanticide, but the sex ratios are quite close.[45] Medieval English sources do not even contain the usual peasant complaints over the liabilities of excess female children.

A number of questions remain about attitudes toward children that would favor infanticide. Parents might have neglected children who were mentally and physically handicapped and these would then have a high infant mortality. But one occasionally finds the village idiot who has even inherited land. When Henry Swerd inherited two and a half acres, the lord had to take the land from him because of his idiocy. Illegitimacy appears not to have been heavily stigmatized, indicating either that it was rare or that all children were valued. Sixteenth-century records suggest that only about 3 percent of the births were illegitimate.[46]

In the absence of baptismal records, it is very difficult to determine if peasants were performing some sort of birth control, including infanticide. The drop in the number of people per household in the late thirteenth century has been taken as a sign of some artificial control over reproduction.[47] Scattered cases in the coroners' inquests, when, for instance, all of the children of one family died at once, tell us something about spacing of children. Robert Penlyn of Hemingby and his wife, Alice, went to market on a Saturday in December 1355, leaving at home their three children, John, aged four, Agnes, two, and Edmund, one.[48] Even with such information it is difficult to tell if the two-year gap between John and Agnes was the product of family planning or if the conception in between, assuming there was one, was terminated naturally

We have discussed much in this chapter about the structure and size of medieval peasant families. Medieval materials for appraising these two problems are weak and projections back from other English sources or across from continental ones are always suspect. One would normally console the reader at the end of a chapter with such tentative conclusions by suggesting that additional work will illuminate the matter more, but, because of the record deficiencies in this case, I believe that further research will be fruitless. What may be said with some degree of certainty is that medieval families were for the most part simple, conjugal families. Even areas that practiced partible inheritance did not necessarily establish joint households. Parents and children exhibited a strong preference for separate residences once the children were grown, and fathers tried to establish their sons and daughters with land and marriages during their lifetime. The wealthier peasants were, of course, more successful in fulfilling this ideal. Stem families were not common and, as we shall see, parents were very resourceful at forming retirement contracts that did not leave them dependent on the goodwill of sons. Most people married, so that households generally did not contain a number of unmarried siblings.

The household size was small, possibly dipping very low (2.5) for poorer peasants in the land hunger of the early fourteenth century and never averaging more than 5. Even in the century following the Black

Death, when land and wages were abundant, household size remained small and population stagnated at a very low level in spite of the new economic opportunities. Age of marriage was not excessively low but was probably not as high as the modern western European marriage pattern. In any case, the age of marriage did not determine family size. Although artificial control over conception and births may have kept family size small, high infant mortality probably played a more significant role. The usual peasant family that gathered around the hearth contained a father and mother and two or three children of varying ages. A grandmother might be sitting at the hearth as well, but not if she or her children could make separate provisions for her.

III

Household Economy

7

The Family as
an Economic Unit

"The first fundamental characteristic of the farm economy of the peasant is that it is a family economy."[1] Thus did the Russian economist A. V. Chayanov, whose work itself has become fundamental for studying peasant economy, begin his study. His discussion of peasant economy and that of the anthropologist Eric Wolf[2] have helped to shape the model that I present here for medieval English peasant families. In adapting these models to medieval English peasant society, I have tried to make them more flexible and more dynamic in order to reflect the range of options that a peasant family had open to it depending on the general economic conditions prevailing at a given time, the social and economic status of the family, and the point in its life cycle. Throughout the book we have looked at the importance of availability of land and labor for determining inheritance and family size. In addition, we noted a tendency for the peasant communities to split into three status groups of primary, secondary, and tertiary villagers depending on both wealth and social clout in the village. These factors had an enormous importance in determining what options the peasants were able to exercise in economic planning. Some of the strategies were open to all peasants, while other families had to have a sufficient level of wealth even to enter the economic game. The model presented is not a mathematical one, for much of the peasant economy had to be one of makeshift in which families followed the main chance in availing themselves of opportunities or entered into short-term reciprocity arrangements with neighbors. Such one-time ventures and mutual assistance are difficult to quantify and are best illustrated through particular cases.

The peasants' assets of land, livestock, and family labor would have to provide for the basic demands made on peasant resources. Wolf has outlined minimum expenses that the peasant family unit must meet. Foremost in their concerns was to provide a caloric minimum to feed the family. But rations could often be short, because they also had to pay rent to the landlord. Most of the lord's officials were inflexible about rent and only forgave them and waived fines when a family was destitute. Ceremonial expenses for religious services and village festivals also came out of the profits from family land and labor. And, finally, the family had to keep an eye to the future in providing for the children as they became adults and securing a portion of the family assets for them so that they could establish their own families.

Our concern in this section must be with the strategies and options available to peasant families in trying to meet the demands on their production. The matter is a complex one, for several factors must be taken into consideration. The period we are studying represents major economic shifts that changed the peasants' options considerably. In the years before the Black Death population was high and land scarce. Wage labor brought little profit because of the surplus of laborers. Peasant family strategies in these lean years would be very different from those in the period of low population in the late fourteenth and fifteenth centuries, when land was readily available and wages rose, in spite of official efforts to keep them at preplague levels. But in the period of low population persistent mortality threatened the existence of families and carried off children whose labor was needed for the prosperity of the household economy. Coupled with the major shifts in opportunities were the persistent problems of cultivators—bad weather, disease of animals, fires, debts, and loss of family members. A further complication in understanding the functioning of the household economy is that the family's initial resources largely determined the options it could pursue. A primary villager with ample land, plow teams, and able sons and daughters would have advantages and options at his disposal that would never be available to the cottager. A family in the middle years of the life cycle was more likely to farm efficiently than old couples or young ones with toddlers at home.

Our problem is twofold. One aspect concerns the strategies peasants used to maximize profits in their household economy, and the second relates to the division of labor within the household. The latter issue is treated in subsequent chapters in this section; the former lends itself well to a model that permits us to consider various economic options available to the peasants.

A model for peasant family economy is a useful tool in three ways. First, it helps to make coherent the limited sources available. Unlike the sources used for the analysis of more modern peasant economies, the medieval English records are not systematic enough to suggest their own models of household economy.[3] The manorial court cases, our major source, were recorded because some dispute arose over an economic decision within the family or in its relationships to the lord or a neighbor. The references are scattered and much is not explicitly mentioned. Other sources such as wills, manorial accounts, poll tax lists, and the coroners' inquests help to supplement manorial court roll evidence. Second, since the various options available to peasant families depended on their economic and social status in the community, a general model permits us to compare how these different groups coped and which options they could choose given their resources. Third, a model of peasant family economy aids in comparing the impact of economic change on the family's options and strategies. Using a model, it is possible to compare the household economic strategies during the overcrowded conditions of preplague England with the more open economic circumstances prevailing after successive visitations of plague.

The model has four basic parts: demands on the family economy, assets of the family to meet the demands, supplemental economic activities, and strategies to improve the family's economic standing.

Demands on the Family Economy

In part simple need and in part legal and social customs determined the outlays required of the family economy. First and foremost, the family economy had to provide a livelihood, or, in Wolf's terms, a caloric minimum, for its members. The family lands, even if they were only a few acres, would have produced most of the food. For the poor in the community wage labor, begging, and gleaning supplemented a meager diet. In addition to food, families had to allot a portion of their proceeds to replacing seed corn, farm animals, equipment, clothing, and household goods. Finally, the unit would try to find the resources to endow children with their share of the profits when they became adults. Supplying the basic livelihood for the family from landholdings was a major part of the peasants' efforts, and those with more land and labor at their disposal would do considerably better than those with only two or three acres.

Modern historians have tended to place undue emphasis on the pursuit of the caloric minimum and have called the medieval peasant economy a subsistence one. As we shall see, the appellation is inaccurate both because peasants actively engaged in a local and regional market economy and because their resources had to cover other expenses than those necessary for survival.

Wolf has emphasized that the requirement of rent and services by a lord or the state is the fundamental feature of peasant economy that distinguished it from a primitive economy—and, he might have added, from a farm economy.[4] The demands of these two social institutions were also a fundamental part of Hilton's definition of peasantry with which we began the book. The state, particularly during the fourteenth century, developed taxation systems based sometimes on assessment of movable property and sometimes on poll taxes in order to tax peasants and others in the population. In addition, they made a number of levies of animals and goods to support various war efforts. The burdens of such taxation could be heavy, and anger over them contributed to the Peasant Revolt of 1381.

The lords' collection of rents, services, fines, and other levies on the peasant economy was of long-established right and has been given the name *manorialism* by modern historians to aid in understanding what some historians would call a complicated contractual arrangement between lord and peasant and what others would call the lord's oppression of his tenants. Briefly, the lord owned the land that the peasants relied on for their house site and for their strips in the open fields. He also controlled the meadow and the woods. Even though, as we have seen, the peasants became attached to their landholdings and regarded them as "family land," both they and the lord agreed that, in the final analysis, title belonged with the lord. In order to have the right to use the land, the villeins owed the lord a money rent. They and their plow animals gave labor service on demesne land or paid monetary sums as a substitute; they also presented gifts in kind, such as poultry, eggs, and ale; they paid fines for taking up holdings, merchet for marriage of their women, and a number of other routine fines and fees. In addition, they paid fines for a variety of economic activities, such as brewing and cutting wood, and for failure to meet the terms of their lease to the lord. When the head of household died, the lord took his best beast as heriot, again underscoring his ownership of all the peasant had. Even such private matters as the deflowering of a peasant girl (legerwite) elicited a fine from the lord. All fines, land transfers, trespasses, infringements of the lord's rights, and failure to perform the required work were recorded in the manorial court, and the lord's bailiff duly collected money accruing from these sources. If peasants wanted to take their private cases to their lord's court, they paid a fee for the privilege. The profits from manorial court alone provided the lords with considerable revenue. Even free peasants were not exempt from rents and some services.

The cost of maintaining the noble class was a great and inescapable drain on peasant family resources and was ameliorated only slightly by the feasts that the lord owed his villeins for boon work and his generosity (often stingy) in forgiving fines of those too poor to pay.

Ceremonial expenses were the final demand on the household economy, and in medieval England these were substantial. The Church collected annual tithes from each household and a mortuary beast on the death of the householder. Furthermore, in the absence of state welfare systems, the villagers expected to give charity to the local poor and might even contribute to a local hospital or almshouse for the good of their souls.[5] They also participated in community and religious ceremonies—celebrations of saints' days with feasts, processions, candles, banners, and ale, repair of the parish church, village games, and so on. Finally, family ceremonies incurred occasional major expenses. Baptisms required gifts to the godparents. Marriages were a statement of a new village alliance and a new family and were marked with as much feasting as was affordable. Funerals became increasingly important in the fourteenth and fifteenth centuries, requiring that the corpse be escorted to the grave with candles and processions and that the soul be aided through purgatory with alms and masses. A wake comforted the survivors.

Failure to participate in ceremonies would lead fellow villagers to punish the culprit with loss of status, ridicule, and perhaps even physical violence. The punishment for not contributing the plow penny, for instance, was having the ground in front of the offender's house plowed up. On one occasion the bride's family failed to bring the usual gifts and the ensuing brawl left one of the wedding party dead.[6] For the primary and secondary villagers, displays at baptisms, marriages, and funerals were essential for maintaining village status, but the cottagers might have to dispense with them.

Ceremonial outlays were so highly valued that families could go into debt or even ruin themselves with heavy investment. One man, dying while he still had a young family, explained in his will that his father's commitment of money for prayer for his soul so encumbered the estate that it could not maintain his family. The expenses for prayers were 20s. annually for ten years. He importuned his brother, Richard Bune of London, to be "good and specyall friends to my wyf and to my chyldrern in the way of Charyte and to be favorable for all and syche detts as I do oowe unto him." He hoped that his children would eventually inherit the family land.[7]

The problem that the peasant family economy continually confronted was balancing the external demands of rent and ceremony against its need to provide a livelihood for members. Peasants had only two ways to introduce any elasticity into the system: either increase production or decrease consumption. In years of dearth the second was the only strategy possible. Curtailing consumption, if limited to reducing goods bought from the market, could help the peasant family through a temporary setback, but deprivations that forced them to eat seed corn and plow animals could be devastating.[8] Opportunities for increasing production, as we shall see, included acquiring more land or a manorial office, working for wages, or pursuing supplemental economic activities.

The other possibility for increasing profits was to decrease expenditure on taxes, rents, and ceremony. As we have just noted, ceremonial expenses, particularly for funerals, became increasingly important in the fourteenth and fifteenth centuries, so that few cuts could be made in that area. In the dues paid to the lord and state, however, some cuts were made in the late fourteenth and fifteenth centuries. Taxes to the state to support the Hundred Years' War had been crushing during the fourteenth century and were one of the chief contributors to the outbreak of the Peasant Revolt of 1381.[9] Following the revolt and throughout the fifteenth century taxes and purveyances of goods from the peasants decreased. Furthermore, the peasants increasingly refused either to perform or pay for the old servile-labor requirements. While they were willing to pay rents to lords for land, they would not pay the old dues of serfdom. Thus in the fifteenth century, along with more land and better wages for labor, peasants enjoyed a decrease in the drains of money to state and lords.[10]

Assets of the Peasant Family

To meet the demands on their resources, peasant households had three basic assets: their land, family labor, and capital (livestock, household goods, silver spoons and coins, and tools). As we have seen, the size of the landholdings varied considerably in the village from those having thirty acres or more to those having five acres or less. The amount of land a family held could also depend on the regional economy. In the rich fenland area large families could be supported on five to ten acres by exploiting the fens for game, fish, rushes, and grazing.[11] If the family had sufficient capital assets, they could also add to their land by renting parcels, buying them, acquiring them as dowry, or clearing them and claiming them through assarts. As we have seen, there was an active land market for odd acres of land. For the most part, it was the primary villagers who expanded their production by acquiring more land or purchasing more acres in order to establish their sons in separate households.[12] With land readily available in the fifteenth century, we have seen that wealthy fathers could easily establish all sons with separate tenements during their lifetime.

The family provided most of the labor in house and fields, but not exclusively. A variety of factors determined the labor patterns. Life cycle would certainly have played a significant role. Families with young children would hire help for their intensive periods of cultivation, if they could afford it. But the family always had to balance the number of mouths it could feed with the amount of productive labor in the household. A poor family could not afford to hire help even during this crucial period, as the "Song of the Husbandman" shows so movingly. The husband plows while his wife goads the ox. Her bleeding feet are wrapped in rags and at the end of the land their infant child lies in a bowl, and twins, two years old, cry from cold and hunger.[13] Widows with young children and families at the end of the life cycle, in old age or disability, might hire labor or rent out land if there was insufficient family labor.[14] Wealthy villagers, whatever family help was available, routinely hired laborers for harvest and employed servants from the village youth to help cultivate their extensive lands and aid their wives with brewing and other supplemental economic activities. These primary villagers were the most likely to be indicted for receiving people out of tithing because they were the chief village employers.[15] The optimal situation for a peasant family to work their land was for the husband and wife to be in their prime and have a few teenage children who could help with fieldwork and housework.

Both custom and efficiency tended to divide family labor into separate spheres according to sex and age. As we shall see in subsequent chapters in this section, the husbandman's work was chiefly in field and forest while women worked mostly about the home. Children did herding, errands, and other tasks both in the home and field.

Labor need not be solely fieldwork. Modern historians mistakenly assume that peasants were like pioneers and that households made their own cloth, clothing, tools, beer, bread, and buildings. But as common surnames such as Carpenter, Smith, Brewster, Fuller, and Tailor indicate, the society was actually one that relied heavily on specialized services. Rather than trying to put together the complicated crucks for their houses, peasants engaged a carpenter. Many peasant women did not bake their own bread but bought it from a neighbor who specialized in baking and had invested in a large oven. For the most part, clothing was made by tailors and only rough cloth was produced at home. The village craftsmen who practiced trades such as smithing, milling, and tinkering usually also held some land in the village and practiced their crafts only part-time, as a supplement to their agricultural endeavors. They received their pay in money or in the equivalent amount of goods or services. In the latter form of payment, they might enter into a reciprocity relationship with a fellow villager for whom they worked, as is common in peasant societies.

The poll taxes provide a profile of different villages, illustrating the variety of occupations. In the 1379 poll tax, Skipton, which had a large number of craftsmen and tradesmen (twenty-four) was still predominantly agrarian. And Kettlewell, a largely agrarian village, had thirty-four agricultural laborers, one cattle buyer, eleven servants, but only three craftsmen. Craftsmen that appeared in the poll tax lists included tailors, dyers, drapers, carpenters, smiths, brewers, millers, tinkers, and so on. The variety of artisans in a village depended on the regional specialties—that is, cattle-producing regions were more likely to have cattle buyers while wool-producing regions had more people in cloth production. As in the Skipton and Kettlewell examples, not all villages would have the same mix of agricultural compared to artisanal residents.[16]

In addition to the fields and family labor to make them productive, peasants' capital investments were of major importance. Livestock was so significant that dowries were often composed of animals, and the routine bequest to brothers, sisters, servants, and godchildren were animals. Livestock became even more important during the fifteenth century as more arable was converted to grazing lands. Ideally, the peasant establishment contained at least two plow oxen or horses, and most of the yardlanders and half-yardlanders had these or more. But poorer families might have to rent or borrow plow teams in exchange for money or their labor. The large domestic animals were expensive both to buy and to feed, so that owning them was necessarily limited to those of means. Even for these families the heriot of the best beast to the lord and the second best for mortuary to the Church, when the peasant father died, could leave the son who inherited the home tenement strapped during his first years. As we have seen, almost all families could keep a sheep or two, pigs, chickens, and so on, but only those with access to generous pastures could have large herds of sheep and profit from the sale of their wool. By the fifteenth century herding became more common and the yeomen often had herds of over a hundred sheep.

Metal was dear throughout the Middle Ages, so that possession of a plow and iron field implements was a major capital investment. So, too, were the brewing and cooking pots of the peasant women. Thus access to good equipment and supplemental economic pursuits such as brewing for public consumption tended to be open only to the more prosperous peasants.

Supplemental Economic Activities

While land, labor, and capital were the basic assets of the family economy, villagers engaged in a number of other economic activities to supplement these resources. All status groups in the village sought supplemental sources of food and income, but the options available to them depended on their capital resources and the time they had to devote to them.

Seeking wages as a supplement to an income from agriculture was common. For cottars some wages or a cottage industry was essential. Produce from their few acres of land could only provide the sparsest living, so that both the husband and wife would have to seek outside income. In the lean years preceding the Black Death, wages were low and competition for employment intense in the overcrowded island. But wages rose immediately following the first wave of the Black Death and remained high until the end of the fifteenth century. Thus wage labor became a more attractive option during the late fourteenth and fifteenth centuries, and many people with marginal holdings simply abandoned their land and sought the highest wages that they could get by migrating.

Cottars were not the only ones competing for wage-earning positions. Wealthy villagers with plows, carts, and other equipment often hired themselves and their equipment to make extra money. Furthermore, if primary or secondary villagers had more than enough labor for their own fields, they sent some of their adolescent children to work for wages elsewhere. Some of these younger siblings in a family would remain wage workers, because the family could not afford to purchase extra land for them to establish themselves in the same social status in which they were raised. For others, the period of wage work or servitude was a temporary one and they returned to the family lands when their parents retired. When adolescents did leave the home economy and work for wages or as servants elsewhere, it is not clear whether they were expected to revert part of their wages to the parental household. Indirect evidence suggests that they kept their wages and purchased parcels of land and arranged their own marriages.[17]

Cottage industries of various sorts also supplemented family income. Women's contribution to the home economy, in addition to

routine work in house, field, and garden, included a variety of additional activities that brought in extra income. Spinning was the most
apparent of women's work and the distaff was a medieval peasant
woman's symbol. But brewing was a lucrative side occupation for
peasant women, particularly, as we shall see, among those of the
primary village families who could afford caldrons and capital outlays
for malt necessary to brew on a large scale. Weaving was not a common
cottage industry until the latter half of the fifteenth century, when it
became a major supplemental activity. In herding districts the makers of
butter and cheese also brought in a bit of extra cash. Because family
labor was relatively cheap and the profits from utilizing it were high for
the unit as a whole, various labor-intensive supplemental activities were
common. Thus beating flax and making linen thread, while arduous and
time-consuming work, were profitable for the peasants.[18]

All peasants, unless they lived in rough and hilly territory or in
borderland regions, had ready access to a market town in which they
sold their surplus agricultural goods or the fruits of their labor. The
more fortunate peasants sold livestock and excess grain along with the
housewife's eggs, butter, and thread. Others sold items that they had
gathered or grown in their gardens. Isabella and her husband, Paganus
Horn of Saham, for instance, had gathered rushes and took them by
boat to sell at market in Cambridge. Some of the cottars bought stalls in
local market towns and took neighbors' surpluses for sale, thus acting as
middlemen for villagers at the market.[19] Proceeds from the sales were
spent on household goods such as pottery, on agricultural equipment,
and on such small luxuries as dates or raisins for a holiday pudding.

Taking in lodgers was as important a supplement to medieval
peasant families as it was to twentiety-century urban families. Since inns
were not a routine feature of the countryside, travelers sought shelter for
the night in private homes. People in search of work or those who had
found employment in a village also rented room in village houses. Thus
lodgers sometimes appear in peasant houses in reports of accidental
deaths and of some of the homicides. Maude of London, for instance,
was described as a lodger at Emma Harlewyne's house, where she killed
Emma's daughters and stole the goods of the house. People taking in
lodgers knew surprisingly little about their guests, often not even
inquiring their names. Thus a seventeen-year-old youth, whose name
was not known, died when his bed caught fire; and William le Engleys,
who had an extra house that he rented, did not know the name of the
group that lived in it. Money was sufficient contract for renting.[20]

Hunting and gathering were among the routine supplements of
peasant households for all status groups. We tend to associate these

activities with an earlier, more primitive economy, but they played an important role in the well-being of the peasantry. Many of the items hunted and gathered were controlled by the lord, and peasants caught with them were fined—a sure sign that they played a significant role in the rural economy. Collecting nuts and fruit or taking brush from the lord's hedgerows or forest were offenses punishable by fine. Fines were often so low that, even if caught, it was still profitable to gather. For instance, stealing a whole cartload of brush and firewood brought a fine of only 6d. in Wakefield. Fines were also imposed on hunting and keeping hunting dogs, and peasants caught with venison, rabbits, and squirrels paid heavily for their illicit protein. A Wakefield woman spent three weeks in prison for a dead hare found in her yard, as did a man for taking a rabbit from the field. Killing a deer cost 20s. Even access to some fishing remained in the lord's preserve. Much of the gathering was done by children, servants, and housewives. Men did the hunting, but boys were sent out to fish.[21]

Another routine source of food and petty economic advantage came from trespasses. In folklore the image of the scheming, avaricious, tightfisted peasant is common, and examples from the manorial courts confirm it. In trespass cases, for instance, people were accused of deliberately breaking down hedges so that their animals could eat the lord's crops; or they allowed the animals on the fields before all the gleaning was done; or they gleaned illegally. Trespasses could be very petty; for example one person was accused of bleeding another's animal in order to make blood sausage. Such trespasses, however, could be profitable. One was not always caught and it was often possible to make a settlement lower than the value of the trespass. If one trespassed against the lord, the low fines meant that the trespass, as in the case of illegal gleaning,was profitable even if one was caught.[22]

Theft could also augment the regular agricultural income. The most commonly stolen items were livestock, particularly the valuable horses, sheep, and cattle. Cloth, grain, and valuables were also prized objects of theft. Neighbor stole from neighbor in the same village in a third of both the larceny and burglary cases. In 15 percent of the larceny cases and in 21 percent of the burglary cases the victim and accused lived only one to five miles from each other. In all felonies, about half of the victims and accused knew each other well and stole, received, or murdered within a fifteen-mile radius of their residence. Thefts from larceny rarely exceeded £1 and a third of them were under 12d., petty larcenies that would not lead to a sentence of capital punishment. Burglary was considerably more profitable than larceny, although it required more skill and planning to execute. Robbery was not a routine crime for the ordinary peasant, but was generally committed by strong-armed robbers who were strangers to the community. Profits from illegal acquisitions were fairly good considering other supplemental economic activities, and punishment, although severe, was not likely to be imposed. Of those who were caught and tried for their crimes only 23 percent were found guilty.[23]

Because trespass and petty theft were so profitable, they attracted participants from all status groups in the villages. A linking of criminal cases with village reconstitution studies from the Ramsey Abbey villages indicated that the bulk of those indicted for felonies (80 percent) were primary and secondary villagers rather than cottars and laborers. These people had more to gain through their thefts and tended to steal items of relatively high value, while the poorer elements of the community tended to steal poultry and grain, which were often of insufficient value to be counted as felonies. Since primary villagers dominated the judicial system, they could be fairly sure of receiving acquittals for their criminal activities. Cottars, on the other hand, could be punished in the community. In general, the criminal and trespass interactions among community members indicate that illegal advantages were not shunned by the villagers and that all status groups practiced them. The wives of primary villagers were just as likely, if not more so, to glean illegally as the village poor. And the well-established village reeve or juror could use his position to protect himself from being hanged for stealing a neighbor's horse.[24]

One must strive for balance, however, in looking at village dynamics. The shrewd peasant is but one side of our perceptions of peasants. The obverse is that cooperation and neighborliness were needed to make the community function smoothly. Reciprocity arrangements included exchange of labor, equipment, and food. As we have commented, the peasants were a sociable lot who exchanged meals and expected distributions of food at weddings and funerals. Formal ties of village ceremonies and festivals became increasingly important in the late fourteenth and fifteenth centuries, and social-religious gilds, which we will discuss in the final section of the book, attempted to institutionalize village cooperation.

Individual networks of cooperation and reciprocity among villagers helped them to meet the everyday problems of plowing and building and to cushion crises when they occurrred. The arrangements for mutual assistance were often informal ones between neighbors, but when the undertakings were not honored, the cases appear in manorial court and give us a glimpse into the workings of these reciprocal agreements. A study of debt litigation in Writtle (Essex) shows that 17 percent of all debts that came into court were reciprocal. For instance, two men joined together in 1393 to buy a saw with the agreement that they would act together as sawyers for six months out of every year. Similar arrangements were made for the purchase of carts, and even the borrowing of plow animals, cattle, and other such items were arranged by contracts that could be appealed in court. Such cases indicated how widows arranged to have farmwork done and how neighbors worked as a team in investments and in marketing items. A young man with a family, for instance, might agree to provide labor for a widow in exchange for aid in purchasing a tenement.[25]

The networks of peasants on Redgrave manor indicates that, for the most part many-stranded relationships with other villagers were more common among the middling peasants, peaking with those holding three to ten acres, than either the upper- or lower-status groups. They relied on one another for loans of equipment and money as well as for assistance in labor. For them, cooperation was essential in order to profit economically. Their social interactions were not always ones of mutual assistance and pledging, but even the trespasses and assaults among members of this status group show that their interactions were more frequent than those of the other two groups. Wealthier peasants did not have to rely on such complex ties of reciprocity, but instead owned the equipment that they needed and could afford to hire wage laborers when they wanted extra help. Only in hamlets did the wealthier peasants rely on more complex economic and social ties. While wealthy peasants had no need for mutual aid arrangements, the village poor could not enter into them because they had very little to offer by way of reciprocity with anyone else. When they entered into a relationship with another person, such as over debt or pledging, it tended to be dyadic and involve specific transactions. Thus a man who worked as a laborer contracted with his master, and a person with one acre, who supplemented his income with a market stall, had contacts with others in the market.[26]

The fifteenth century brought changed conditions that somewhat modified this earlier pattern of reciprocity. The wealthy peasants, moving toward the social class of yeomen, tended to have even fewer ties of mutual dependency with other peasants. They continued as employers, but their political and social ties turned more toward the county than the village. The laborers were more mobile than they had been, and so, too, were members of the middling group. The new economic opportunities of the fifteenth century may have loosened the traditional bonds of networks to some extent, but debt litigation continued and many families had to rely on neighbors for aid, so that the breaking away from an economy based partly on reciprocity was probably only at the upper and lower margins of wealth.

Strategies for Economic Improvement

The inflexibility of demands on the peasant and the resources that the family had to meet those demands meant that either the peasant had to be wealthy initially to begin a strategy of economic improvements or the conditions had to change substantially. During the lean years of the early fourteenth century most of the population was doing well just to survive. Since rents could not be reduced and cutting out ceremonial expenses meant loss of status, only the caloric minimum and the amount of goods distributed to family members were flexible. These conditions meant that some of the poorer members of society did not survive and even some of the younger children of wealthy and middling families were subject to downward mobility. But even during this bleak period, villagers with more resources than others were able to improve their economic circumstances. Following the population loss, new opportunities opened for selling labor at a competitive price and for purchasing or renting vacant lands. The possibilities of maneuvering for economic improvement became more open.

Those who could afford the extra capital to invest in strategies for economic improvements or who had the good luck to prosper unexpectedly could look to several basic areas that might give them the edge: acquisition of more land or a change in agricultural techniques; advantageous marriages; education and officeholding; lawsuits and credit transactions.

Acquisition of additional land was the most common route to greater prosperity and community prominence. Land in small parcels was available to anyone who could raise the entry fines and, as we have seen, young single men and women often purchased such pieces, or their parents did for them, in order to permit them to marry. Other reasons for entering the land market were either that the family had the labor to work additional land or that they were releasing or selling land to meet other expenses. All levels of wealth participated in these small land transfers.[27] Acquiring half-virgates or virgates before the depopulation, however, was reserved for the wealthy villagers; and even after land became readily available few cottars could aspire to a virgate. For a family unit as a whole to profit from additonal land, they had to have sufficient family labor to work it or money to hire paid labor. In the fifteenth century the conversion of former arable land to pasture permitted families and individuals to accumulate considerable land-holdings without being concerned about finding laborers to cultivate it. Herding was much less labor-intensive. Thus a shift in agricultural practices brought new opportunities to those who could rent land and had the capital to invest in livestock.

Advantageous marriages could also increase landholdings and status in the community. Since daughters could inherit the family holding if they had no brothers, these heiresses were much in demand for marriages. Widows also might be considered highly desirable marriage partners, although, as we shall see, they were less attractive after the Black Death, when more land was available. Marriages could bring prosperity even if the bride was not an heiress. John Love, for instance, wanted to enter a vacant holding but could not afford the £3 entry fee. Agnes Bentley offered to pay the fine if John married her daughter. John's name was, perhaps, derived from reputation, because the marriage was not allowed since he had had sexual relations with a kinswoman of the bride. The wealthy widow or heiress would probably be married to one of the prominent village families, for she would expect a substantial dower to match her inheritance.[28]

Another avenue to greater economic benefits was to seek skills or influential offices that would enhance economic opportunities. One time-honored tactic was to educate one son, often the eldest, so that he could move into a management position on the manor. Family fortunes that have been traced, such as the Cellarer family already mentioned, indicate how many benefits could accrue to the whole family if a son became a bailiff or manorial official. These men knew when pieces of land would be available and how the price of grain and livestock was doing in the market. Also, they usually received gifts for good service. On the manor of Newark-on-Trent such gifts were routine, as no doubt they were on other manors. Walter Shayl, a reeve on the bishop of Worcester's manor of Hampton Lucy, cultivated both his own yardland and a second one that belonged to the demesne but for which he paid very little. Thus, like the Reeve in the *Canterbury Tales*, he turned a nice profit working for the lord.[29]

Domination of village offices, such as juror, capital pledge, ale taster, and so on, not only offered social prestige but gave the office-holder a greater opportunity to manipulate competitors and further his own ends. In case of arrest, the officeholder could use his ties to ensure acquittal. In addition, some money could be made in petty corruption. So important were these positions that the primary village families jealously guarded access to these village offices and became village oligarchs.[30]

Finally, pursuing legal cases, particularly debts, could bring great advantages without great losses. It cost little to bring a land or debt case into the manorial court, and if the plaintiff won, he gained considerable profit, perhaps as much as a whole inheritance of land. Losing meant only a small outlay for a fine to have the case tried. Furthermore, if one's friends and relatives among the primary villagers were on the jury, the chances of an advantageous decision was higher. Prosecution of debt cases in Writtle, Essex, in the fifteenth century brought a profit to eight out of ten plaintiffs. About a third of the debt litigations indicate that primary villagers pushed some of the less fortunate villagers into a position of dependency by extending credit to them. Thus they established a vertical dependency that ensured them labor and also profit on their unused plow teams and other capital.[31]

Peasant families' strategies to supply basic needs and perhaps accumulate a bit extra were multifarious. Every avenue that could be pursued was. Thus their economy appears much more complex than that of a simple wage earner. A few examples will help to clarify the interplay of the different strategies above and beyond simply tilling the soil. William was the son of Stephen Algor and probably a teenager in 1290 when he and his mother Douce were presented for subletting land without permission. William and his widowed mother apparently could not work all their land and so resorted to leasing part of it for a short term, until William was grown. Later they were in mercy for not bringing tithing money to court, an attempt to stint on dues to the lord. William was an adult when he paid a tallage of 12d. with other customary tenants in 1303. He married and had three sons: Reginald, John, and Simon. Simon followed his father's strategy of improving his economic position by reducing dues he owed the lord. He refused to pay toll at the mill; he got the tithingmen to question the right of the lord to require service on land that he acquired and he defaulted on services. He finally improved his position by paying a 20s. fine to marry a widow and acquire the third of a virgate that she held in dower.

The Scaly family consisted of three competitive brothers, Stephen, Walter, and John. Stephen inherited the messuage and eighteen acres and did a certain amount of lending. He died in 1313, leaving a widow and a daughter. Walter bought three acres of land from a freeman with his settlement from the family. But he was eventually forced to alienate land and was fined for not keeping up the dower house on his property. He was envious of his brother John, who married a woman from a neighboring village, and slandered John's father-in-law. John had his own shrewd ways of cheating, and when required to plow for the lord, he substituted another ox for his own in the plow team.[32]

This chapter provides an outline for understanding the different economic strategies that the various status groups in the village used in pursuit of a livelihood and perhaps some economic betterment. Subsequent chapters in this section flesh out the bare outline presented here. Wealthy families had prosperous inheritances and, because of better diets, had more children to work their land, or they hired labor. They participated in supplemental economic activities, both legal and illegal, and were at an advantage in having capital to purchase additonal land, make lucrative marriages, and invest in some industry such as milling or brewing. They could also participate in the local credit market and be assured of winning court cases because of their influence as jurors.

Middling villagers faced a more difficult economic situation. Their lands and family labor could provide a livelihood, but distributing family wealth to all children could leave some of the younger ones deprived of full shares. The middle-status villagers relied more heavily on reciprocity with neighbors and credit arrangements to tide them over difficult seasons. They, too, participated in hunting and gathering and occasional petty theft. Some areas for economic improvement were open to them, such as a good marriage, renting bits of land, and pursuing lawsuits. They were not, however, likely to be jurors and receive the added advantages that being a village oligarch brought.

The cottagers were in a somewhat disadvantaged position, but not necessarily so if they successfully pursued a trade or craft in addition to cultivating their few acres of land. The small holders were in the worst position in the early fourteenth century, but with labor being highly paid during the population slump, their opportunities increased.

8

The Husbandman's Year and Economic Ventures

The husbandman's year had both honest and romantic qualities for those who wrote poetry and illustrated books of hours. The plowman became a symbol of good in such works as *Piers Plowman,* and the various tasks of the husbandman's cycle of labor appeared in sculpture and illuminations. The men who made their living by pen and brush could admire the husbandman's expertise in using his plow and sickle. In "How the Ploughman Learned His Paternoster" the skills and tasks of successful husbandry were outlined:

> He cowde eke sowe and holde a plowe,
> Both dyke, hedge, and mylke a cowe,
> Thresshe, fane, and gelde a swyne,
> In every season and in tyme;
> To mowe and repe both grasse and corne
> A better labourer was never borne; . . .

In addition, he could plow with ox and horse, shear sheep, strip hemp, graft trees, fell wood, thatch a roof, and daub a wall.[1] But these skills were only part of the various economic activities in which peasant men participated. They also sold goods in market, made loans to one another, and worked for wages either selling their skill as husbandmen or practicing some other craft.

The agricultural calendar imposed a strong seasonal pattern on men's work that influenced the course of their lives. A poem on the occupations by months sums up the activities:

> Januar   By thys fyre I warme my handys;
> Februar   And with my spade I delfe my landys.

124

Marche	Here I sette my thynge to sprynge;
Aprile	And here I here the fowlis synge.
Maij	I am lyght as byrde in bowe;
Junij	And I wede my corne wel I-now.
Julij	With my sythe my mede I mawe;
Auguste	And here I shere my corne full lowe.
September	With my flayll I erne my brede;
October	And here I saw my whete so rede.
November	At Martynesmasse I kylle my swyne;
December	And at Cristemasse I drynke redde wyne.[2]

If one looks at adult males' activities and places of accidents, January was a period when they spent more time at their hearths and in play. While activities involving leisure-time pursuits and games usually only accounted for 3.7 percent of men's accidents, they were involved in 23 percent of them in January. (See Appendix, Table 2.) In January as well, men were less likely to have accidents related to agriculture and construction, but the ordinary work around the house, getting fire wood and turves, and personal activities continued as usual. Of the adult males whose ages are recorded, January was the most dangerous for those over forty-five years old. (See Appendix, Table 3.) They were more likely to die from exposure or to stumble and fall into bodies of water.

Plowing was the peasant man's task. [The British Library, Lutterell Psalter.]

The spring months of February through May were times of plowing, planting, and tending to crops and garden. In February the husbandman delved the land and set out his crops—first the spring grains of oats and barley and then peas and beans. Plowing was difficult labor, requiring considerable skill and long hours. The husbandman worked behind the plow while his son, wife, or hired boy goaded the oxen. The soil might also be prepared with manure and with marl. Preparing marl was heavy work and digging in marl pits contributed to accidental deaths during this period of the year and also in the autumn, when the winter wheat fields were prepared for planting.[3] For the most part, however, plowing and planting were not dangerous activities for the husbandman. Plows and harrows occasionally injured men, and accidents involving animals and carts began to increase in March. But there were few risks in casting seeds from apron or seed lip. Weeding, chasing away birds, and other activities occupied the rest of the time.

The heavy labor of the agricultural year came in June and continued through the first part of September. Forty-seven percent of all men's accidents occurred from June through September. The greatest increase in accidents was in agriculture, but construction work, transportation, crafts, and even work around the home increased in those months as well. The whole process of harvesting, carting, and storing crops was dangerous, and the men worked such long hours that they were exhausted from their labors and careless of their safety. For women, as well, the harvest season was the most exhausting and dangerous, for they also worked in the fields in addition to their other tasks. In June and early July the husbandmen and laborers cut the hay and stacked it in their closes or in barns. Late July, August, and early September kept all hands busy with the harvest of wheat, peas, beans, barley, rye, oats, and mixed grains.

The use of the scythe and reaping hook took great skill, and occasionally a person received a fatal cut from one. The reaper, usually the father, gathered the grain in bundles and accumulated these until he had a sheaf, which the women and children tied up. A well-off peasant would hire labor to help with the harvest. The crops had to be tended to immediately. Once cut, grains had to be stacked or turned and could not be left in the field overnight or one day too long or they would shed or mold. Carting the grain from the field was also a skill. The wagons had to be loaded correctly or they would overturn. The sheaves, hay, or straw were piled on and ropes thrown over and tied to the sides of the wagon. The loads were so high that ladders were used to put on the last sheaves. Because of the height of the load, men who fell from ladders or the top of the load frequently broke their necks. Apparently, the workers

Both men and women worked to bring in the harvest. [The British Library, Lutterell Psalter.]

took great pride in their skills, for one case said that a man had fallen from the top of a load "out of vanity" as he was tying it.[4] Another skill was driving the heavily loaded cart across the furrows without overturning it. Sixty-eight percent of the carting accidents occurred between June and September and almost 50 percent of all carting accidents occurred in August and September. Accidents involving animals were higher in harvest, so that over a quarter of them occurred in these two months.

A few examples give something of the flavor of the harvest field. During a break from work on August 29, 1368, John, son of John Gallerer, and Edith Fohester were sleeping in a field at Wynneslegh and he had a scythe under his belt. When Edith woke up, she cut her arm against John's scythe and bled to death.[5] A Wiltshire man was trying to tie up a wagonload of straw. In pulling the cord he broke it, and the cart overturned on him. The loads were not only tricky to tie but also to ride. Thus a thirty-year-old man who was riding a cartload of peas from the field, fell off during harvest in Norfolk. Once the cartload had been safely brought from the field, the straw or hay had to be stacked in the close. The straw was stacked around a rick pole, and the stacks were high enough that one needed a ladder to work on the top. The ladders were often unstable and the stacks themselves very slippery, so that many accidents occurred at this part of the harvest. Finally, the grain had to be separated from its stalk with flails and from the husks by winnowing.

The grain was separated from the stalks with flails. The flail was a man's implement. [The British Library, Lutterell Psalter.]

Peasants stored their precious grain in barns or, more often, in their houses in solars or in sacks in the rafters.[6]

By Michaelmas the harvest was over and the preparation of fields for winter wheat began. As the poem says of October, "here I saw my whete so rede." November, and St. Martin's day in particular, was reserved for butchering, salting, and smoking meats. December again brought a lull and a time for relaxation, and with luck some "redde wyne" or at least some heavy ale from the barley harvest.[7] While most accidents involving males occurred outside the home, there was some increase in accidents in the home in December and January. The drinking and general conviviality, in addition to the dark, inclement weather, led to increased accidents while walking and traveling, especially to those over forty-five.

In addition to seasonal labor the husbandman had tasks that he tended to throughout the year. Collecting wood for the fire or digging peat turves, where it was available, were not only winter occupations, for fuel was needed in the summer months for cooking. Drainage ditches had to be dug in fields even during harvest in a wet season. The care of the larger farm animals such as horses and oxen was the task of the men in the family. And repairs on houses and outbuildings also occupied the men's attention.[8]

The husbandman rose early to go about his tasks; 20 percent of the fatal accidents involving adult males occurred at dawn before breakfast.

To men fell the task of gathering wood by hook or by crook. [Bodleian Library, MS. Douce 24, fol. 2.]

After a midmorning decrease they rise again at noon (17.7 percent), when workers were tired and hungry, and dropped to 7.5 percent in the afternoon, suggesting that they took a nap following the big meal of the day, as nineteenth-century farm workers often did. Working into the evening, their accidents went up to 18.9 percent around vespers. Blundering about in the dark, however, was most dangerous, and 33.9

percent died of accidents at night. But few people were about at
midnight, and so only 2.4 percent lost their lives in accidents in the
middle of the night.

Wage laborers, if they were engaged in agrarian work, had a
seasonal work pattern similar to that of the husbandman. Pay for field
labor varied considerably with the demographic trends and regional
demands. For instance, in a comparison of wages for threshing and
winnowing on Winchester and Westminister manors, laborers near
London commanded a higher wage than those in the country. Wages
rose in 1310–1319 because of famine and again in 1349–1359 because of
plague. Wages continued to rise in Winchester until 1409, when they
stabilized at a high rate; but in Westminister they fell gradually until
1399, when they again rose. Wages doubled with the plague, and the
demand for unskilled labor was so great that while in 1300–1309 a
carpenter's wage was twice that of a laborer, by the fifteenth century it
was only a quarter more. Comparative wages did not return to the
earlier proportion until the early sixteenth century. In addition to daily
wages the laborer might get a meal, the right to sleep on the barn floor,
or a sheaf of wheat.[9] Wage labor could be a profitable supplement, and
many skilled laborers and townsmen put down their tools and worked at
harvest to increase their income. Living by agrarian wage labor alone,
however, was hard in the years prior to the Black Death because the
work was seasonal and competition for wages high. With the precipitous
population decline, however, living by wage labor became more desirable and harvest work could be supplemented with other jobs during the
winter.

Laborers were hired in several ways. Manor bailiffs or prosperous
smaller proprietors including wealthy peasant cultivators, would hire
servants and laborers by the year. A manor would hire plowmen,
carters, stablemen, a dairymaid, and some domestic servants. Such
people could expect wages in food and money and often slept on the
premises. They were not necessarily youths (who will be treated in more
detail in a later chapter), but might be married and have their own
cottage. Simon of Langnoe, who was servant to the prior of Caldwell
and milked the priory cows, was described as a "cottager and clerk of the
chapel." People who worked as servants for a major establishment
would spend their lives in this capacity and might do quite well in their
jobs, eventually setting up their children in land or education. But most
laborers were hired for briefer periods. Outside harvest time an
unskilled man took what work he could find. A pauper accepted a job
gathering wood and driving a cartload of it with broken-down horses.
The cart overturned. Another labourer, Arnold of Tyringham, stood at

a cross in Bedfordshire to indicate that he was available for hire. It was January, and the best job he could get was carting manure to the fields. He was married, and his wife was the one who later found him under the overturned cart. Such temporary positions were paid for by the piece rather than by the day.[10]

Villages contained a variety of people pursuing an occupation in addition to agriculture. Pursuit of another craft accounted for 3 percent of men's fatal accidents. Most villages had a mill that employed a miller and some lads as assistants. The mills were dangerous and caused thirty-three fatal accidents (1 percent), but as they were used year-round the accidents did not accumulate in harvest season. Millers got caught up on the sails of windmills and dropped, fell from mills while repairing them, drowned in mill ponds, and, worst of all, got pulled into the gears and mill wheels.[11] But the miller was a necessary member of the community and the pay and opportunities for profit were very good, as Chaucer's Miller in *The Canterbury Tales* indicates.

Carting was also a common occupation for villagers. The local lords and religious houses kept carters in their pay regularly, but other men

Men did most of the carting and carrying and worked with the horses, oxen, and mules. In this illustration a man is carrying sacks of grain to the water mill. [Bodleian Library, MS. Bodley 764, fol. 41 verso.]

made their living by carrying loads of sea coal, casks of oil, wine and beer, logs and lumber, and other such bulky items. Various forms of transportation accounted for 43 percent of men's fatal accidents, and a quarter of the accidents involved carting specifically. Carting was done year-round, but, as we have seen, harvest brought a precipitous increase in accidents. Even for people who made their living as carters, accidents were common. Thus Robert of Swynarton, who was charioteer to the prior of the Hospital of St. John, was driving the carriage and six horses to the rectory when a shaft broke and the carriage overturned, killing him. Experienced carters were not immune from the risks of getting stuck on the road. One man who was using a beam to get a wheel out of a rut overturned his cart, and the casks he was carrying rolled off and crushed him. Other carters took advantage of the slow, monotonous journeys and napped, only to fall off their carts and under the wheels.[12]

In areas that had water, boating replaced carting and many men carried goods by punting in Norfolk and Cambridge and sailing larger vessels on the Humber in Lincolnshire. In a classic accident recognizable to anyone who has punted a boat, a forty-year-old man was boating on a river when he got his pole stuck on the bottom. Clinging to the pole as the boat drifted on, he slid down it to his death. In the larger boats people were swept off by sails, rudder handles, and storms.[13]

Selling ale out of the home and other products out of market stalls were occupations that could be done commercially to supplement the income. Women dominated home brewing, but in some communities men brewed as well.[14] Alehouses, however, were usually run by men. All manor courts kept the provisions of the Assize of Bread and Ale, which regulated price and quality as well as measures. Carshalton manor court explicitly regulated the selling of ale. A post or ale staff had to be put up and ale could only be sold from the home. The men had to sell ale in measured containers not in cups and bowls. Baking was done in much the same way as the brewing with women predominating in production but with men also participating. Rather than selling out of the home, some men bought or rented market stalls to sell both their own household produce and that of their neighbors. William, son of Nicholas Carter, had a market stall at the fair of Woodkirk and supplied it with twenty gallons of beer, worth 2s. 6d., cheeses worth 12d., a sack work 8d., and utensils to contain these items. He sued the man who over- turned his stall for 40s. in damages.[15]

Fishing and poaching were useful side occupations to combine with agriculture. As we shall see, boys fished with lines, but men used nets and weirs in mill ponds, rivers, and the sea. John Ball of Pynchbeck used a fish weir in a ditch to get fish in 1375. In manors that abutted onto forests, such as Bridgestock in Northamptonshire or Wakefield in Yorkshire, poaching was a routine part of men's provisioning for the family.[16]

A number of other craftsmen such as tinkers, carpenters, potters, and blacksmiths could service several villages in a locality. Pottery was a useful trade, whether it was for a local market or for a regional one. Most of the pottery was for cooking and eating, but tiles for roofs, at least around the vent for the fire, and floor tiles were also made. Bricks came into use in the mid-fourteenth century and became increasingly popular as a filler, replacing wattle and daub for walls. Until the advent of brickmaking, the heavy work of potting was digging the clay from pits. Like marl pits and turveries, the sides could fall on the potter or his laborer.[17]

Construction of various sorts occupied men with specialties in carpentry, masonry, thatching, and wattle-and-daub work. Eleven percent of men's fatal accidents involved construction. Then, as now, construction followed the weather and more accidents occurred in the summer months than in the winter. There were dangers stepping off scaffolding, sawing planks, getting timber, digging in gravel and sand pits, and cutting stone. Some of the quarrying was rather sophisticated. One laborer was trying to raise two stones with a wheel and cable when his arm got caught in the wheel and broke.[18]

Preparing hides for tanning and tanning itself were also side occupations for some villagers. A Lincolnshire man who lived on the coast took a cartload of hides to the sea to wash them in preparation for tanning. The waves came in and washed away him and his cart.[19]

Cloth production increasingly moved to the countryside during the late fourteenth and early fifteenth centuries. Women, of course, had always done the initial preparation of the thread, but they had usually sold it rather than turn it into cloth. Men dominated the cloth industry. The chief dangers in the pursuit of the craft came in dyeing the lengths of cloth. Large vats of water were brought to a boil before the dye and cloth were added, and dyers and their apprentices occasionally fell into the boiling water and were scalded.[20]

Mining was a regional side occupation. In Cornwall almost all tenants in the tin-producing region had some connection with mining and tin production, even if it only consisted of subleasing small parcels of land to miners and their families. Some tenants made rather large fortunes acting as middlemen in the tin industry.[21] In the north of England coal and iron mining provided supplemental occupations. The coal and iron near the surface was easily removed, but by the late fourteenth century pit mining was being employed.[22]

A number of other occupations and casual chores fleshed out the agricultural income. Bell ringing, for instance, was highly skilled but hardly paid enough to be anything other than supplemental. One case, in which the bell ringer took his servant to the church to pick up some meat, suggests that he may even have been paid with food rather than money.[23]

Some examples of how and why a peasant successfuly combined his agricultural enterprises with other occupations might clarify the import-ance of a diversified economy for the peasants. The agricultural season had periodic lulls when the husbandman's attention was not taken up by cultivating the soil. While animals needed continued care, as we shall see, women and children took over this task. The head of the household and grown sons, therefore, had some seasonal time to pursue other occupations. In Cornwall the size of landholding per family was relatively small (five acres or less), and consequently some supplemental occupations were needed for survival. Tin, lead, and silver mining, in those regions with ore, provided an obvious side occupation that could be engaged in on a temporary basis. If there was a boom in tin, many men from the region temporarily moved to the mining districts. Tenants of the duchy of Cornwall who had some of the largest landholdings— such as John de Pengelly, with one messuage and thirty-one acres plus twenty acres of waste, or the Bloyou family, with seven messuages and ninety-six acres—were also involved in the tin industry.[24]

For those with capital, such as the Bloyous, investments and management of resources were of the utmost importance. Like the less wealthy peasants who diversified their labor investment between agri-culture and a side occupation, the wealthy peasants sought to diversify the way they utilized their capital assets. Thus, in Cornwall, tenants with large landholdings might invest in tin mining and also make short-term leases to the workers for either a few acres of arable or pasture rights. They might also invest in livestock and perhaps buy part of the rights to a mill. Economic diversification was typical of peasants' investments. A group of four men jointly invested in a mill in Wakefield and agreed to pay 73s. 4d. for the mill; in another case eight men paid 20 marks for a mill. Others invested in livestock, particularly following the Black Death. Still others bought the expensive brewing equipment to set their wives to work in a lucrative trade. A brewer's inventory from a will showed that he had £14 10s. 11d. tied up in brewing equipment.[25]

One avenue of investment was loaning money or goods to fellow villagers. Substantial cultivators in Writtle, Essex, were creditors in 18 percent of the loans. These men lent their less fortunate neighbors plow teams, animals, tools, and even rented them parcels of land. As security they could demand labor or pasture rights from the small land-holder. The terms were unequal, for the creditor demanded three times the going rate for labor in exchange for extension of credit. Thus, when the pay for threshing was 4d. a day in the fifteenth century, the creditor required more than one day's work and in fact was requiring closer to 12d. in work. The arrangement assured the successful cultivator of labor when he needed it and kept the small cultivator continually in his debt. In the event of a complete default, the large cultivator might claim animals or land for settlement.[26] Through these unbalanced credit relationships, the wealthy peasant could take advantage of the new economic conditions of the fifteenth century because he was able to exploit the limited labor supply. The imbalance meant that the rich peasant got richer and poor poorer during the course of the century.

Land was another capital investment that a peasant might consider. Often the fluctuations in landholdings coincided with phases in a man's life cycle. A young man did not need extra lands until his children were teenagers. He would then have a sufficient work force to help him provide for the family. After the children left home, a man might divest himself of the extra rented acres and retire. Two generations of this cycle may be seen at Kempsey. Thomas Bate, at his prime in 1450s, had a variety of holdings that amounted to eighteen acres, but by 1456 he was not working part of that land and twelve acres were declared forfeit. When he died eight years later he had only six acres to leave to his widow. Walter Bate, his son, was eighteen in 1456 when he took over the twelve acres that his father forfeited. In 1470 he took the six acres that had supported his widowed mother. He added other pieces from demesne leases when he was between the ages of thirty-two and thirty-nine, as his family grew and he needed more land. As his children left home he too divested himself of the extra land, and when he died in 1500 at the age of sixty-two he had only six acres for his immediate support.[27]

Land was a valuable asset, and some peasants accumulated it even though they were not providing for a growing family. Land could be made to turn a profit in a variety of ways. Those who were sufficiently wealthy to rent substantial acreage subleased it to other peasants. In the fifteenth century, when population was low and land readily available, people accumulated land without the intention of cultivating it, but instead profited by putting large herds of sheep and cattle on it. On the other hand, those substantial cultivators who had made loans in exchange for labor could be assured of the cultivators they needed. Village studies have indicated that very few of the small holders were able to take advantage of the open land market in the fifteenth century.

In Holywell-cum-Needingworth those few small holders who increased their lands were related by marriage or blood to the larger village holders and, therefore, had some help in acquiring more land. The land market of the fifteenth century again underscores the advantage of the rich peasant even in improved economic conditions.[28]

One of the most effective ways to get an edge in the acquisition of land was to work as a manorial official. Such a position not only gave the official advanced information about land coming onto the market, but also the lord often made very advantageous terms for a valued servant. Richard Bakhampton, steward of the Cornish estates, not only rented tenements but got leases for life. Other officials also did very well at land transactions on the duchy lands.[29]

In addition to the major supplements to family income, peasant men pursued a number of less substantial additions. Some supplemental activities, as we have observed, were outright thefts, but most were small encroachments on neighbors or the lord. Subterfuges of this sort seem endlessly varied, when one reads complaints in manorial court rolls, and are a credit to the cleverness of the peasants. A few examples will suffice. At the most petty level of theft were the men who sheared another's sheep in the field. Other activities brought greater rewards. Simon de Bothes, for instance, had a field without a fence. When cattle strayed onto it he impounded them and thus was effectively charging a levy. The court eventually ordered him to put up a fence as his neighbors had. The lord, who could legally impound animals that trespassed on his property, found that some of his tenants not only fed their cattle at his expense but were brazen enough to rescue them from the impounding. Encroaching on the village common land or on the lord's waste was another common ploy. Master Robert Carpenter of Wakefield, for instance, enclosed a piece of meadow with a ditch and palings so that the men of Thomes and Snaysethorp no longer had the right of common there. Sometimes the encroachments went beyond petty advantage. At Carshalton twenty-one men were charged with having horses, cows, pigs, oxen, and sometimes up to two hundred sheep on the lord's pasture. The trespass was well worth it for the peasants because the fines were only 2d. to 4d.[30]

The maneuvers for advantage in court cases were also a way of settling disputes and may explain why there was so much theft directed against neighbors. For instance, a man in Wakefield came into court on a charge that he had stolen a cow worth 4s. He claimed, however, that he had taken it because the plaintiff owed him 4s. Thus some of the thefts were illegal ways of rectifying reciprocity arrangements that had gone awry and in that respect were akin to credit arrangements and debt litigation. But the litigation could go beyond settling old scores and become a form of aggression. For instance, William Wether complained that Thomas of Thodholm had seized from him land fourteen plowlengths long and three wide. Thomas denied the charge, but the jurors found him guilty. Thomas could certainly have afforded to rent the extra land, for in the same court he leased three and a half acres, but he would have gotten free land if he had succeeded in taking William's. His venture only cost him a fine of 6d. and so the risk was worth it.[31] Although men had greater access to the court and usually pursued family matters there, women, as we shall see in the next chapter, also used the court to protect their rights.

The pursuit of economic advantage could easily move beyond self-help and become a malicious attack on another villager. When one first meets Roger, son of Amabel, in the Wakefield manor court in 1315, he appears to be one of those villagers who continually lived on the other side of the bylaws. He was charged with the escape of two swine, for taking 10d. from one man and 20d. from another, and bribed his way out of an indictment for killing a doe. The same court session a group of men charged that he had burgled a house ten years earlier and had not been arrested; that he had kept the chattels of a brother who had been hanged as a felon; and had made enclosures to the damage of his neighbors. He was forced to make a large fine of 53s. 4d. and find pledges. He countered these charges in a later court, having had the record searched to prove that the charge of burglary had been malicious when it was raised twenty years before (not ten as his accusers charged) and that he had been "solemnly" acquitted at that time. He sued his persecutors for £40 in damages and the court agreed to award him 100s. He had a hard time collecting the money.[32] With neighbors such as these it is easy to see why men turned readily to assaults and homicides in the struggle for economic advantage.

As we mentioned in the last chapter, peasants were locked into manipulating their assets and seeking small economic advantages within the system unless they were able to decrease expenditures. Ceremonial expenses, as we indicated, became more burdensome after the Black Death, but the dues paid to lords decreased substantially as peasants both bought their way off the manor and refused either to work the lord's land or pay a monetary substitute. A study of manors in East Anglia outlines the process of change. Before the Black Death the lord relied on his bond tenants at least to do the harvest work, although he commuted plow services and other occasional labor. But there was no indication that serfdom or labor rents substituting for actual work was undermined. By 1378, however, some 250 acres of land that had been in the hands of tenants paying labor services was let to different tenants for a term of years or by the year and without payment for labor services. Both the death of tenants from plague and the flight of tenants from the manor explains the erosion of serfdom. Before the Black Death only two tenants had waived their tenements, and they did so because of weakness or poverty. But following the plague there was a steady erosion of tenants, particulary from those tenements most heavily burdened with labor services. In other words, peasants were willing, following the Black Death, to leave the family lands that were encumbered with serfdom and seek their fortunes elsewhere.

From the lord's point of view, serfs became less valuable. By the end of the fourteenth century half the demesne land was rented and the chief profits came from this rent. Serfs, however, were still useful in repairing demesne buildings, but chiefly because they still paid merchet and various other dues.

Flight from the land in East Anglia was gradual. The leases for a year or a term of years were at the lord's will and did not include the traditional guarantees of inheritance that went with bond land. Those who left early usually had small holdings requiring heavy service. Those who remained after 1373 had large holdings with light services. Furthermore, they were among the people who leased the demesne. Thus in 1400 there were at least sixteen servile families with large landholdings still on Forncett manor. By 1500 the number was reduced to eight, and by 1575 serfs ceased to exist on the manor.

The experience of some tenants in this period of flux appears in the records. The Brakests were a large family in 1400. Three men and three women already lived outside the manor by 1406, and three more bondmen relinquished their land in 1409. Orders to seize the fugitives failed to produce them. William Brakest stayed on his messuage and fourteen acres until he died in 1428, leaving the land to his brother and heir, Richard. But Richard alienated it to a different family. He stayed on in Forncett for a few years and then moved to Metfield, Suffolk, where he paid the chevage to remain abroad. When he left Metfield, however, he no longer paid, and the family disappeared from the records. The Hillyng family, on the other hand, stayed on the land throughout the fifteenth century. One branch held $13\frac{1}{4}$ acres in 1433, $18\frac{1}{2}$ acres in 1469, and $20\frac{3}{4}$ acres in 1493. These acres represented only the holdings on that particular manor, for when the last male of the line died in 1509 his will stated that he had 25 acres in Forncett but also had land on five other manors. The Houlot family did very well indeed by staying on the manor. When Robert Houlot died in 1401 he left his daughter 160 acres, but that was only part of his wealth. Apparently he had sublet 236 acres of land on questionable leases and the lord seized it.

Not all who remained prospered in the fifteenth century, and some died very poor and without heirs on their few acres.

Because the serfs who left were required to pay chevage for being off the manor, we have some idea of the experiences of this group as well. Of the serfs who left Forncett between 1400 and 1575, 126 had migrated to sixty-four different places. The largest number went to villages within a radius of ten miles, another 30 percent went to villages ten to twenty miles away, and 17 percent went farther afield. Norwich, about twelve miles from the manor, attracted twenty-two of the serfs. Of those whose occupations are known, some became weavers, tailors, saddlers, and other craftsmen. Others became agricultural laborers or took up tenements in other manors.[33]

Working as a laborer had great attractions following the Black Death, as the complaints of violation of the Statute of Labourers makes abundantly clear. Wage labor had always been an important part of the peasant economy and laborers were obviously carefully attuned to the value of their labor on the market. As soon as laborers realized that their labor was in demand following the first wave of plague, they immediately responded to the market and raised their wages. The king's council responded almost immediately in the spring of 1350, trying to keep the wages at the 1347 level. Like most attempts to legislate against the law of supply and demand, their ordinance and the later Statute of Labourers in 1351 failed. The complaints against laborers that appear in violations of the statute indicate the type of recompense that laborers wanted. They foremost wanted freedom to move about to procure the best wage that they could. They did not want to be tied to the manor and have to work for free or at a lower price than the going rate in another region. They preferred to work by the day rather than take a yearly wage; and if they did so, they demanded a very high yearly wage to make up for losses they would incur by not moving to a higher-paying job in the winter. They also preferred to have all their wages in money rather than in the old style of meals, grain, and money.[34]

Even with the dramatically changed economic opportunities that permitted higher wages and the possibility of throwing off the servile status, the results of the peasants' different strategies were mixed. Some of the bond tenants who remained on the land acquired vast landholdings and subtenants. Others died poor. Those who left the cumbersome servile ties behind gained independence, but not necessarily fortunes, as craftsmen and laborers. Those who moved to other manors may or may not have made fortunes as freemen. But it is quite apparent that peasants were willing to take the risk of leaving family land and traditional holdings as freemen rather than remaining bondmen. Not every peasant family emerged in the fifteenth century as yeomen, but those who did made their position well known to their less fortunate neighbors.

Amidst such major changes as the demise of serfdom, much remained the same. Peasant men competed for an edge by trespassing and relied on each other for aid and loans. Poaching and gathering still provided supplements to the diet, and wives added their share by brewing, spinning, and doing the housework. Heiresses were, as usual, valued as marriage partners. Whether free or villein the husbandman's year remained the same, as did many of the other economic strategies. The new econimic conditions did not change the calendar of agriculture and men still tilled the soil as they had before. A man's daily routine was succinctly summarized by his neighbors in a coroner's inquest. William the Red and John of Goldingdon had a disagreement concerning sheep and had attacked each other with axes. But they recovered from their wounds and were reconciled at the time that John died of a fever. The jurors told the coroner that in the interval between the fight and his death John "went to his work in the fields, to markets and to wrestling matches" as was usual.[35]

9

Women's Contribution
to the Home Economy

A women's work is never done, we say, and yet we do not know what work rural women did in the late Middle Ages. The hours must have been very long and the work hard, for the only literary piece that speaks of the peasant woman's day with envy is that old saw of the tyrannical husband who taunts his wife into changing places for a day because he thinks her work is easier. He, of course, learns his lesson.[1] Since the basic unit of economic production and consumption was the peasant household, a woman's contribution was made within the context of her family. Because medieval English peasant families were not normally extended with many female kin to lend a hand, a household relied heavily on the wife's contribution to the home economy. But what was the nature of her contribution? The tyrannical husband of the ballad argues: "And sene the good that we have is halfe dele thyn,/Thow shalt laber for thy part as I doo for myne."[2] Two areas are traditionally assigned to the wife: the daily running of the household and raising and training the next generation. But women performed a variety of other tasks, including the classical occupation of spinning, that supplemented the routine management of house and family by bringing in extra earnings.

The problem for historians has been to find evidence on how married couples divided the economic responsibilities of the household. Men's contributions emerge more quickly because they frequently appeared in the manorial court rolls in cases related to their work and landholding or in the account rolls where their wages were recorded. Women's work was more often directed toward the private household economy than the public one of the manor. One might take the excellent

141

studies that have been done of early modern and modern peasant women and project their picture back into earlier centuries, but the early modern economy was different in many ways from the medieval one. Women in early modern Europe had many more opportunities to work in cottage industry or to sell their labor in the rapidly expanding cities.[3] The economy of the thirteenth through late fifteenth centuries in England was still largely centered around the exploitation of individual holdings on manors. Manorial records do contribute something to our knowledge of women's work, and information can be gleaned from wills, poll tax returns, and coroners' inquests.

Most rural women would eventually marry, because they could find few positions outside the household economy. Peasant women would not become nuns and the position of servant was usually a temporary one within the teenage years of the life cycle. The other options for unmarried peasant girls were not entirely attractive. They could stay at their brother's home and work for his family; they could hope to find work in an urban center or on a manor as a servant; or they could become prostitutes. J. C. Russell's work on the 1377 poll tax showed that, in villages with populations up to eight hundred, 75 percent of the women were married. This percentage tended to decrease in boroughs. The figure represents all women over fourteen years of age (the taxable age) but does not indicate widows or those who would eventually marry.[4] As we have seen, determining the number of men and women who remained single is difficult but has been estimated to be 7 percent of the population in the mid-sixteenth century. Thus the number of permanently celibate women was very low.[5]

A woman's first contribution to the household economy, therefore, was the money, goods, animals, or land that she brought to the marriage in her dowry, dower from a former husband, or inheritance in her own right. These possessions came from a variety of sources, but wills give the most detailed information. One must remember, however, that they are a biased source since they tend to overrepresent the wealthier elements in the community. Since men left the vast majority of wills, women appear as beneficiaries of husbands, fathers, grandfathers, godfathers, and masters.

A father dying without a son to inherit could will his property to his daughters. In the customary law of the manor and in common law, as we noted in the section on inheritance, the property would be divided equally among the surviving daughters. A will gave a man of property an opportunity to divide the inheritance himself, so that he could favor one daughter, usually the eldest, and keep the family lands intact. Of the 319 married men leaving wills in Bedfordshire in the late fifteenth and early sixteenth centuries, 44 of them, or 14 percent, had only daughters as heirs.[6] Sometimes the daughter was already married and the will makes clear that the son-in-law would have control over the land, but the right to the land remained to the issue of the marriage. Since heiresses were much sought after in marriage, the father would have carefully selected the son-in-law. After all, the father might retire and live with them. Other fathers died young and left the lands in care of their widows until the daughters were of marriageable age.

Even if the daughter was not the chief heir, she could claim some part of the family wealth, usually payable in animals, grain, household goods or money. These inheritances might have been in addition to an earlier dowry or they might be a provision for it. Only 9 percent of the wills specifically mention that the bequest to a woman was for her marriage. Henry Davy, a prosperous man, died with two daughters still unmarried. He left them both considerable grants of land that they were to receive on their marriage.[7] Monetary bequests for dowries ranged from 13s. 4d. to £40. John Derlynge, who left his daughter 20s., was fairly typical of the humbler will makers.[8] Other relatives might also contribute toward a girl's marriage. An uncle on the father's side was the usual source, but one grandfather generously gave each of his grand-daughters £10 toward her marriage. In the poem "How the Good Wife Taught Her Daughter," the mother meets her obligations to her daughter's dowry by collecting household goods for her as soon as she is born.[9]

Dying men also raised the issue of their wives' remarriage and made provision for them accordingly. Of the 319 married men leaving wills, 74 percent were survived by a widow. Common law allowed a widow a third of the husband's property for life and would permit her to take this land into a new marriage.[10] Wills, however, gave husbands greater flexibility, and most chose the more generous provisions of customary law that gave the wife life interest in the tenement or control until the son reached the age of majority. Some other dower would be settled on her when she relinquished the land to their heir. The husband might also stipulate that the dower was hers only if she did not remarry. Other husbands left their widows clear title to some property that they could take with them if they married, but not the family land. Thus John Heywood provided his widow with £20, a number of animals, grain, and the household goods she had brought with her as dowry. These were to be given her "wit owt eny grugge . . . of my children."[11]

The women of whom we have been speaking received sufficient property from fathers, husbands, or other kin to make them sought-after marriage partners. Society did not dictate a specific value for the dowry in order to marry; that was a matter of individual negotiations. But if family could not provide, how could a single woman hope to accumulate a dowry or supplement a meager one?

Servants received bequests from dying masters or mistresses in addition to wages. The typical bequests included items of clothing, sheep, a small sum of money, or malt.[12] Occasionally, a favored servant would inherit a substantial bequest; Elizabeth Lamkyn was given 26s. 8d. "to her profeccion."[13] Since servants were often the social equals of the masters, some of these gifts may have been part of a social network of village mutual support. Thus servants were rather like godchildren and received similar types of gifts in wills.

Female servants also converted wages into bits of land of an acre or two that they could add to their dowry, as indicated by the entrance fines they paid in manorial court.[14] In the tight land market of preplague England even a woman with only an acre of land would be an attractive marriage partner. The living that such a small dowry could provide was not much and would probably be matched by a groom with equally meager resources, but five acres could support a couple in good years. Undoubtedly some young people even married without a cushion of land or savings, and had to rely on their labor for survival.[15] When fathers or brothers did not provide dowries, the young women tended to choose their own husbands, as we shall see later. They had no need of parental consent, as they were not part of the family's economic strategy.[16]

The dowry having been contributed to the new household, the bride settled into her other roles of providing her labor, reproductive capacity, and childrearing to the economy. The literature and folklore of the Middle Ages are decisive in dividing the men's sphere from the women's both in physical environment and types of work. John Ball's revolutionary jingle on class consciousness is well known: "When Adam delved and Eve span/Where then were all the gentlemen." It is instructive that Ball found nothing wrong with the sexual division of labor, only that in the beginning there were not class distinctions. Men and women were also distinguished by the symbols of their particular spheres of work, and these are common identifying characteristics in art and literature. The poem "The False Fox" provides a classic example:

> The good-wyfe came out in her smok,
> And at the fox she threw her rok [spindle].
>
> The good-man came out with his flayle,
> And smote the fox upon the tayle.[17]

The accidental-death patterns in the coroners' inquests and manorial court evidence confirm the sex-specific division of labor in rural England.

Women's work and their general round of daily activities was much less physically dangerous than men's; women comprised only 22 percent of the 2022 adults (over the age of fourteen) in the accidental-death cases in the coroners' inquests. Compared to the men, women's accidents indicate that they spent much more of their workday around the house and village: 29.5 percent of the women victims compared to 11.8 percent of the men died of accidents in their houses or closes. (See Appendix, Table 1.) Apparently they spent more time than men visiting and working with their neighbors: 5.8 percent of the women's fatal accidents were in a neighbor's home or close compared to 3.8 percent of the men. When women did venture from home, it was often in connection with their domestic duties. Thus 5.9 percent of the women victims drowned in a public well compared to 1.6 percent of the men, and 9.7 percent of the women died in a village ditch or pond compared to 4.9 percent of the men. Men were much more likely than women to die in fields, forests, mills, construction sites, and marl pits. The place of death, therefore, confirms women's chief sphere of work as the home and men's as the fields and forests.

The time of accident was given very roughly in the inquests, but nonetheless a definite pattern of greater and lesser risks for men and women appears as they pursued their daily routines. Both rose at dawn, but women had only 4.2 percent of their accidents then, compared to 9.8 percent for men. The morning work was more risky for women, with 15.6 percent of their fatal accidents occurring at that time, compared to 9.8 percent of the men's. Noon was high-risk for both, as they tired of their labor and became hungry: 20.8 percent of the women's fatal accidents occurred then and 17.7 percent of men's. Women might have had a slightly higher number of accidents because they were involved with cooking at noon. For both sexes afternoon represented a lull in activities leading to fatal accidents (4.2 percent of female deaths and 7.5 percent of male deaths, and may indicate a postprandial nap. But evening saw another increase (15.6 and 18.9 percent for females and males, respectively). Night was truly hazardous for both sexes at 39.6 percent for women and 33.9 percent for men.

When one looks at the causes of women's accidental deaths and the places they occurred at these hours, the round of daily work becomes apparent. The morning, noon, and some evening deaths are connected with fetching water from wells for washing and preparing meals.

Working with large animals and brewing also appear in the morning and at noon. The afternoon deaths were from laundry or seasonal fieldwork. The high number of deaths at night resulted from dangers in the home, usually house fires or walls falling on unsuspecting sleepers, or from wandering about at night without candles. There were, as we have observed, many bodies of water and pits and wells that one could fall into and drown after nightfall.

The seasonal pattern of women's and men's deaths were parallel, except that women had a significantly higher percentage of fatal accidents in May (12.9 percent, compared to 7.7 percent). This is puzzling. The cause of death indicates that women were more prone to falls and drowning during May, but their work does not seem to be particularly seasonal. It is possible that more women were pregnant or recovering from pregnancy, but sixteenth-century data indicate that births were most frequent in February and March.[18] The two high months for men's accidents, June and August, can be readily explained by harvest and other heavy fieldwork.

The division of labor by sex was set early in a child's life. As we shall see, by the age of two or three the accidental-death patterns of children reflected that of their respective parents.[19]

Women's work in peasant households has been largely misrepresented by modern historians who tend to equate peasant women with pioneer women. Medieval peasant women did not spend much of their time producing from scratch the basic necessities for their families. Instead, most households availed themselves of specialists in weaving, tailoring, and even brewing and baking. A second misconception that must not be allowed to stand is that women's work involved fewer hours than men's or that, because women had fewer accidents, their work was not as strenuous.[20]

Women's daily household routines are very well summed up in the "Ballad of the Tyrannical Husband." The goodwife of the poem had no servants and only small children, so that her day was a full one. She complained that her nights were not restful because she had to rise and nurse the babe in arms. She then milked the cows and took them to pasture and made butter and cheese while she watched the children and dried their tears. Next she fed the poultry and took the geese to the green. She baked and brewed every fortnight and worked on carding wool, spinning, and beating flax. She tells her husband that through her economy of weaving a bit of linsey woolsey during the year for the family clothes, they were be able to save money and not buy cloth from the market. Her husband insists that all this work is very easy and that she really spends her day at the neighbors' gossiping. But she retorts:

Soo I loke to our good withowt and withyn,
That there be none awey noder mor no myn,
Glade to pleas yow to pay, lest any bate begyn,
And for to chid thus with me, i-feyght you be in synne.[21]

The housewife's first task in the morning was lighting the fire. She had to go into the close to get kindling or straw to light the embers and get the wood started. One woman, we are told in a coroner's inquest, went out early in the morning to get kindling, climbed into a tree leaning over the common way, and fell. A housewife who was over seventy went to her straw sack to get straw to start a fire, as she had done for many years, but fell from her ladder on this occasion.[22] The fire started, the housewife heated the morning porridge and other food for breakfast.

Cleaning house occupied very little of a woman's time. As we observed in Part I, the houses were small and furniture rudimentary and the peasants owned few pans and dishes. The floors were covered with straw, and chickens, pigs, cats, and dogs wandered in and out at will. But the primitive nature of housing should not lead one to conclude that the housewives were slovenly and cared nothing about cleanliness. As archaeological evidence has shown, floors were swept frequently enough that the brooms left U-shaped depressions on house sites.

Of the 237 women whose activity at the time of death is specified, the cause of death of 37 percent of them related directly to work around the house. The most dangerous task was drawing water from wells and pits (17 percent). The water was for cooking, washing, and drinking. Either the housewife or the children got water for the household. Doing the laundry was also a dangerous activity, with 3 percent of the women either drowning or being scalded. The earth around wells, ponds, and ditches became treacherously slippery with water splashed on them, so that it was easy to slip in. Thus one woman washing linen cloth by a ditch in December 1348 slid into the water and drowned. Other accidents involving work related to maintaining the house included cutting wood, baking, cooking, taking grain to the mill, and general housework.[23]

Women's routine work for the household also included agricultural work. The women milked the cows and helped at calving time. They also kept the poultry: geese, hens, and maybe doves. The pig was in their charge, as was the garden in the close that produced vegetables and fruits. When their help was needed in the fields, they hoed, weeded, turned hay, tied sheaves, and even reaped. They gleaned when the harvest was over, a back-breaking task of picking up stray grain. One old woman was so tired after her day's gleaning that she fell asleep among her sheaves and failed to put her candle out.[24]

Women had charge of the domestic animals, including milking and butter and cheese production. [Bodleian Library, MS. Bodley 764, fol. 44.]

In making our economic boundaries too rigid, we assume that peasants did not hunt and gather. Women picked nuts, wild fruits, herbs, and greens from the woods and roadways and if they lived near the shore, they also gathered shellfish. They collected firewood, carrying fagots of sticks from the woods on their backs. Although men usually did the heavy labor of cutting turves from peat pits, occasionally women did as well. One woman, over forty years of age, went to cut turves for the family fire when a piece fell on her.[25]

One of the most significant contributions a wife could make to the household economy was the bearing and training of children. Children were an asset in the peasant economy; by the age of seven they could already be a help to the housewife in her daily round of chores. The early years were difficult, however, as the woman in the "Ballad of the Tyrannical Husband" pointed out. During that time the housewife added the burden of caring for young children to her other chores. But the production and training of the new work force was essential for a successful peasant household; otherwise one had to hire servants.[26]

Women could also diversify their labor to bring more cash into the family economy. In addition to the usual egg, butter, and cheese production, some women engaged in fairly large-scale beer and bread making. Both these occupations required investment in large vessels or ovens. In Broughton the wealthier peasant families tended to be the chief producers of beer on a large scale.[27] Brewing was an arduous and

Women processed the wool to make into thread. [Bodleian Library, MS. Douce 6, fol. 101 verso.]

rather dangerous activity, since it involved carrying twelve-gallon vats of hot liquid and heating large tubs of water. Five percent of the women in the coroners' inquests lost their lives in brewing accidents, usually by falling into vats of boiling liquid or spilling the hot wort on themselves.[28]

Spinning was the traditional supplemental economic activity for women. The spindle could be taken anywhere to occupy idle minutes. The woman may or may not have turned the thread into cloth. Most likely, she sold it to a weaver unless she was making rough material for daily wear and sheets.

Women could also work as wage laborers to aid the family economy. In a poor household supported by very little land, both the husband and wife would have to hire out their labor. We do not know

The wool was turned into thread with a spindle. The spindle was the woman's most characteristic implement. She could carry it with her to work on thread making in her free moments. [Bodleian Library, MS. Ashmole 1504, fol. 34.]

yet if women received equal pay for equal work. The matter will require considerably more study because of the problems of assessing the nature and difficulty of tasks performed. For instance, a thatcher received 2d. a day in the thirteenth century, but his female assistant received only 1d. Her work was gathering the stubble and handing it up to him while he did the more skilled labor. In general, manors hired female laborers and boys for such unskilled agrarian tasks, and consequently their pay was low. The work of picking over seed grain, however, was a highly skilled occupation in which women excelled and, therefore, tended to be paid more. When men and women did the same work, they received equal pay. Thus, although women did not normally work for the lord by either hoeing or stacking hay, when they did so they received the same pay as men.[29]

Some historians have maintained that with the decline of population after the Black Death women's wages became competitive with those of men.[30] More systematic data will have to be accumulated to demonstrate this, however, for the statutory information indicates that women were supposed to be paid less than men. A statute of 1388 decreed that female laborers and dairymaids should earn 1s. less a year than the plowman. In 1444 women servants would receive 10s. annually for their work compared to 15s. for the men, and in 1495 women's labor was still to be reimbursed at only 10s. annually, but men's had climbed to 16s. 8d.[31]

The village credit and land market as well as fairs and regional markets attracted women.[32] A variety of sources show women aggressively engaged in market activities. For instance, Mabel the Merchant was charged in 1294 in Chalgrave court with taking ash trees. Women made loans to other villagers that are recorded in the court rolls. And there is even a case in the coroners' inquests of a woman who went out to negotiate a debt, leaving her nine-month-old baby alone in the house, so that it died of a fire in its cradle.[33] Since women could inherit property and buy it as well, they played a fairly active role in the village land market even after marriage. Married women sometimes sold land they had brought with them to the marriage to help the family through a difficult time, or they might buy or inherit land that would eventually go to a child's marriage portion. Women were somewhat disadvantaged in the marketplace because, while they could bring suit on their own, they had no access to magisterial roles and seldom even used attorneys. Their pledges had to be men, although one woman tried to use all women in her case.[34]

One can easily overlook the extralegal contributions women made to household ease and even survival. Olwen Hufton has emphasized the economy of makeshift that both peasant and urban women practiced in preindustrial France. These petty illegalities, or tolerated transgressions, were usually a source of additional food. In France the rioting for bread was the woman's provenance.[35] In medieval England illegal gleaning was the most common way for a woman to get extra grain for her family. Gleaning after the main harvest, as observed earlier, was limited to the old and decrepit, but it was so profitable that wives of even prominent villagers did it. Reaping could pay only 1d. a day for women, but gleaning would bring in considerably more. Even being caught and fined was worth the risk because the fines were so low. The illegal gleaners appear in the coroners' inquests where they are caught in the act and a death ensued. Amicia, daughter of Hugh of Wygenale, died warding off an illegal gleaner. She had been hired by Agatha Gylemyn to guard her grain. During the night Cecilia, wife of Richard le Gardyner, came to steal the grain and threw Amicia to the ground when she tried to stop her. Three illegal gleaners got their punishment through an "act of God." They became frightened during a bad storm as they were gleaning illegally and hid in a haystack. Lightning struck them.[36]

The only limit to these illegal, petty economic gains was the imagination. It was common to graze animals on other people's crops, to reap grass illegally, to dig turves and collect nuts and wood in prohibited areas. In Yorkshire Alice, daughter of Adam, the son of William, dug a pit for iron and another woman dug up the high road for coal. Occasionally women were even accused of bleeding a cow for blood sausage or clipping sheep in the pasture for their wool. Isabel of Abyndam came to the fields of the abbess and took three pounds of wool from four sheep there. When the shepherd found her, she fought him off so that he was forced to hit her in the legs with his staff in self-defense. She was taken into custody but was so frightened that she refused food and drink and died of hunger.[37] Poultry theft and other petty thefts also appear frequently in manor courts.

In clearly felonious activities women also showed their concern for provisioning the family. They stole sheep and poultry rather than larger animals and stole proportionately more household goods and foodstuffs than did men. In the period of famine in the early fourteenth century, the number of females indicted for crimes increased to 12 percent and dropped to 9 percent after the period of dearth.[38]

When the day was done, it was the woman of the house who tucked in the family and turned out the light. We know about this sex-specific role because of the times that a housewife forgot to blow out the candle and it fell onto the straw on the floor, setting the house afire. For instance:

> On Tuesday [April 24, 1322] a little before midnight the said Robert and Matilda, his wife, and William and John their sons lay asleep in the said solar, a lighted candle fixed on the wall by the said Matilda fell by accident on the bed of the said Robert and Matilda and set the whole house on fire; that the said Robert and William were immediately caught in the flames and burnt and Matilda and John with difficulty escaped with their lives.[39]

We have argued that the woman's sphere of activity centered largely on production for the home, both in providing food and supplementary earnings for the household economy. She also reared the children and put them to work in the house and close at an early age. We have yet to investigate the value that the society placed on this contribution. Two historians, Joan Scott and Louise Tilly, have argued that "the separate spheres and separate roles did not, however, imply discrimination or hierarchy. It appears, on the contrary, that neither sphere was subordinate to the other."[40]

But we must still ask who wore the breeches in the medieval peasant family. Were economic decisions joint ones, with both husband and wife participating, or did the husband take the role of economic planner? Was it only a shrew who could don the breeches and control family investments? Literary sources are not neutral on their opinion of women. The clergy did not have a monopoly on the antifemale traditions, and popular lyrics often fault women who gossip, cheat, and scold:

> Sum be mery and sum be sade,
> And sum be bosy, and sum be bade;
> Sum be wilde, by Seynt Chade;
> Yet all be not so,
> For sum be lewed,
> And sum be shrewed;
> Go, Shrew, wheresoeuer ye go.[41]

Others praise women for their constancy and counsel and advise men to place their trust in their wives:

> ffor by women men be reconsiled,
> ffor by women was neyer man begiled,
> ffor they be of the condicion of curtes grysell [Griselda]
> ffor they be so meke and myled.[42]

Even the tyrannical husband indicated that the wife's work was half the productivity of the household and whatever the personal attributes of a wife, laziness would have been the most disastrous.

Sources other than literary are better for assessing appreciation of the wife's contribution because the latter are so steeped in a misogynist tradition that they are difficult to use. Wills are perhaps the best source. As a man lay on his deathbed he often considered how he could ensure his family's well-being and reward all for their contribution to the household economy. Wills showed that the men entrusted their wives with considerable responsibilities and rewarded them generously for their contributions during their lifetime. Most men (65 percent) made their wives executors. Others indicated through specific phrases the reliance they placed on their wives. One man left his son a bequest if he would obey his mother; others made the wife responsible for choosing a profession for a son; and one Yorkshire father went to great lengths in his charge to his wife: "that my wiffe have a tendire and faithfull luffe and favour in brynging uppe of hir childir and myne, as she will answer to God and me." He went on to direct her to "reward them after her power for us both."[43]

Most men leaving wills, therefore, trusted their wives to raise a family of young children and run both the house and lands. The widow with young children thus had an increased burden for maintaining the household. She would either have to hire labor in the fields, rely on other family members for aid, or remarry. It was not tradition alone that kept women from doing the plowing themselves, but rather their already full work load. Although women tended to outlive men and were more likely to be widowed, widowers were also left in dire straits in managing the household economy. They also would have to hire servants or rely on kin to rear young children and take care of routine household chores. In the poll tax the great majority of cultivators were married couples, because it was the most efficient unit. It is rare to find households composed of father/daughter or mother/son.

Although wills clearly establish the value and trust a man placed in his wife on his deathbed, they do not indicate how or if he expressed these sentiments during his lifetime. The economic contributions may have been equal, but decision making may not have been. The moralist writing "How the Good Wife Taught her Daughter" recommended that women not gad about the town or get drunk on the money they made from selling cloth, thereby implying that they had control over their butter and eggs money.[44] The law protected women's rights to their dowry and lands they inherited from their family, so that a husband could not legally demise it without the wife's permission. But more than one woman came into court complaining that she had not been consulted about the sale of land, because she feared to cross her husband. Joan, wife of Hugh Forester, was typical. She demanded and won the rights to one and a half acres that her husband demised without her permission because she was "not able to gainsay it in his lifetime."[45]

The argument for a partnership in the peasant marital economy, however, is a persuasive one, even if some husbands were tyrants. Many of the decisions that would have to be made during the course of the marriage would be ones in which mutual expectations or mutual needs would determine the course of action. Both partners shared the common assumption that children should receive a settlement from the accumulated family wealth. The couple would also share assumptions about investment in seed, tools, and household equipment. The needs of the economic unit were common to both. If the couple survived to retirement age, they would have a mutual interest in making arrangements for their support. Land transactions in manorial courts indicate a strong practice of mutual responsibility and decision making. When a villein couple married, it was common for the man to turn the land back to the lord, taking it again in both his name and that of his wife. Husband and wife also appear in manorial court purchasing or leasing pieces of land either for themselves or for their children or acting in concert in other business matters as well. While men appeared more frequently in economic transactions, they were not necessarily acting unilaterally. After all, a man would not leave his wife his executor if he had not gained some respect for her economic judgments during his lifetime.

The peasant family economy was based firmly on the contributions of both sexes with their separate skills and their separate domains. The initial goods and capital of the woman's dowry set up the household, and her labor and supplemental economic activites helped keep it going. The marriage was an economic partnership in which gender ordinarily determined the division of labor, but in which the goal of both partners was the survival and prosperity of the household unit. The mutual dependence of a couple on each other's economic contribution encouraged remarriage if one partner died and discouraged intrafamilial violence and homicide.[46]

10

Children and Servants
at Home and in the Fields

The economic contributions of children and servants had much in common. In the larger sense of the word *familia* that was employed in the Middle Ages, children and servants were dependents of the householder and his wife. They were young and took their sustenance and discipline at the husbandman's table. They might, in fact, be one and the same person in the household, for the poll taxes of the late fourteenth century sometimes list an individual as "daughter (or son) and servant." Their chores in the household and about the fields were similar, but they were the sort of tasks that seldom needed to be recorded in official records. Manorial court rolls sometimes mention servants of peasant families and also the permanent servants on the manor. Children occasionally appear in the manor court rolls, but usually only when they trespassed. The poll taxes of 1377, 1379, and 1380–1381 are the only sources that give something approaching a systematic listing of servants. With such sparse sources, the coroners' inquests become invaluable for describing the working life of children, teenagers, and servants.

The nature of children's and servants' work is of vital importance to the investigation of medieval family life. Earlier we argued that their contribution was essential to the smooth functioning of the peasant economy and asserted that for this reason children had a high value in the society. Illegitimacy was not the taint that it would have been in a society in which labor was not welcomed, and infanticide would have been more frequent if children were viewed as simply encumbrances. Furthermore, we must come to grips with the problem of fostering or sending children out to other households to work. For the upper classes it was common for children to be placed in another household after they reached the age of seven or eight, and in apprenticeship agreements a child might also leave home at this relatively early age. Was it common for medieval peasants to place their children in the homes of others? And would young people in their late teens expect to spend four or five years of their lives as servants? Although in the early modern period it was common for young people to be fostered or serve as agricultural servants living in another person's home, we must take care not to project such evidence back on to the fourteenth and fifteenth centuries, for agrarian conditions changed substantially in the sixteenth century. The famous description of English attitudes toward children made by an Italian observer, although widely quoted, cannot be accepted as decisive evidence. He observed only the upper classes and the upwardly mobile, and had no interest in what peasants did:

> The want of affection in the English is strongly manifested towards
> their children; for after having kept them at home till they arrive at
> the age of seven or nine years at the utmost, they put them out, both
> males and females, to hard service in the houses of other people . . .
> and few are born who are exempted from this fate, for everyone,
> however rich he may be, sends away his children into the houses of
> others, whilst he, in return, receives those of strangers into his own.
> And on enquiring the reason for the severity, they answered that
> they did it in order that their children might learn better manners.[1]

Thus, although the evidence is scattered, we must take up the difficult questions of children's work and the role of service both for the household economy and for a young person's life-cycle experiences.

Young children—infants and toddlers—could not contribute to the household economy and were, in fact, a drain on the time of the housewife. By the age of two and three, however, children's identity with their parents' work began to emerge in the pattern of accidental deaths. Little girls are already becoming involved in accidents that paralleled their mother's routine working with pots, gathering food, and drawing water (17.2 percent of their fatal accidents), even though these accidents only involved playing at these tasks. (See Appendix, Tables 6 and 7.) For instance, a two-year-old girl tried to stir a pot of hot water but tipped it over on herself.[2] The boys were more actively involved in play and observation of men working. One three-year-old boy was following his father to the mill and drowned; another was watching his father cut wood when the ax blade came off the handle and struck him.[3] The division of labor by sex thus began very early in a child's life and was part of their early identification with the roles of their parents.

By four and five work appears in children's accidental-death pattern. They were often assigned to baby-sit and go for water. For instance, a one-year-old boy was left in care of his five-year-old brother, but because the older boy was such a poor custodian, the inquest says, the cradle caught fire. Even if children of four and older were simply sitting and observing their parents work, they were beginning to learn some tasks such as cooking, brewing, milking, and digging.[4]

During the years six through twelve, children began to have real chores around the house, aiding both their parents in work and contributing to the supplemental income of the household through fishing and gathering food (6 percent of their fatal accidents involved such activities). From five to twelve fishing was a common pastime for boys. Those who lived by the coast searched for shellfish and those who lived near ponds, rivers, and streams, fished for eels and freshwater fish. William, son of Nicholas Baly of Spalding, aged twelve, was collecting cockles on the coast at Multon in March 1357 when a wave caught him and washed him out to sea. One five-year-old boy was looking for eels in the Humber and drowned. And in July 1348 two boys, one twelve and the other eight, went to a pile dam on the river in Cambridgeshire and fell in.[5]

Boys were useful for gathering various items for the family's use. One six-year-old drowned while gathering reeds in a Cambridgeshire marsh, and a seven-year-old, who was sent to get peat, died when a turf fell on him. In the manorial court rolls children were frequently fined for collecting dry wood, wild fruit, nuts, ivy, and so on.[6]

Herding was the traditional occupation for boys between the ages of seven and twelve and accounted for 7 percent of their fatal accidents. Herding geese was a task that young lad could do easily. A seven-year-old boy was guarding a neighbor's geese in May 1335 at vespers. The geese were on a green near a pond and the boy, playing while he worked, drowned. Boys often whiled away the time with various games and other diversions rather than watch their flocks and herds. Two boys, aged nine and ten, were watching sheep and playing with staffs. John, son of William le Wyte of Wilden, twelve years old, was watching his father's lambs in late April when he took off his clothes to bathe in a stream and drowned. Herding was pleasant enough in the summer, but in the winter it could be cold, miserable work. John Wayhe, aged twelve, was a swineherd on a manor. He was so cold one morning in December 1348 that he went into the manor's bakery and climbed into one of the huge ovens to keep warm and burned to death.

The pasturing and especially watering of horses also fell to the boys. They would ride the horses to the water and let them drink. Often the horse would want to head for the deeper water and the boys, riding bareback, would be swept into the river; or they took the horses to pasture in the evening and the horses took fright or the boys foolishly encouraged them to run and were thrown off. Their recklessness with horses accounted for 8 percent of their fatal accidents.[7]

Although the boys could be unskilled and even foolhardy, they were an important part of the economy for their household and for the village and manor in general. They could take the place of women as thatcher's assistants or as binders of grain at harvest, and at only half the wages. They could be used for errands and for carrying torches at night. They began to be of economic use as assistants to parents or employers. Play, however, was still predominant in their accidents. Furthermore, their tasks, if one may judge from the accidental-death cases, centered on chores rather than on work in the fields or on a trade or craft which accounted for only 2 percent of their fatal accidents, respectively.[8]

Girls from six to twelve also began to contribute to the household economy. They did much of the fruit picking, and nut, herb, and wood gathering. They picked apples, pears, and cherries in the closes or in the wilds. They also collected shellfish along the coast. Such activites resulted in 5 percent of their fatal accidents. Much of their work, however, aided their mothers in their daily work routine. They fetched the water, built fires, and helped with the cooking. Drawing water accounted for 32 percent of their fatal accidents, and cooking, laundry, and so on accounted for 14 percent. And, of course, they continued to baby-sit for their younger siblings, although often their carelessness led to the death of their charges. The youngsters tended to run off and play with the other village children rather than keep a watchful eye on the baby in the cradle. For the most part their tasks were not as dangerous as those of boys the same age and began to resemble the pattern for adult females. Occasionally, however, their work was beyond their physical abilities. A ten-year-old girl went to a neighbor's pit to fill up her water bowl, but when filled, it was too heavy for her to lift and she fell in.[9]

Some children learned adversity at a young age. Joan, a poor five-year-old, had risen early to beg bread. On returning home she failed to negotiate a bridge and fell in. Joan was a local villager and had a home, but one inquest stated that an eight-year-old boy had been found drowned in a pit in March 1341. He was a stranger to the place and was described as a vagabond who had been wandering at night.[10]

From the ages of thirteen to nineteen, the pattern of work and other activities came increasingly to resemble that of adults. For adolescent males agricultural activites caused 18 percent of their accidental deaths, essentially the same as for adult males. (See Appendix, Table 3.) Adolescents played less of a role in the skilled labor of construction and crafts than did men and continued to work on supplemental economic activites such as fishing and gathering wood and food, 23 percent of their fatal accidents arising from these ventures. For instance, Roger, son of Walter le Muth, ascended the church steeple at night to get pigeons when he fell and broke his neck.[11] Working with horses and carts involved 26 percent of their fatal accidents.[12]

The places of accidents changed as the youths matured. At four and five the boys still had a large portion of their fatal accidents at home, but from six to twelve their accidents were spread among home, other people's property, public and work areas (11 to 17 percent), with only deaths in bodies of water predominating with 43 percent of the accidental deaths. (See Appendix, Table 4.) But between the ages of thirteen to nineteen accidents at home accounted for 21 percent; on private property, 7.7 percent; in public areas, 17.9 percent; and in bodies of water, 31 percent of accidental deaths. The largest jump of all involved accidents in the work place (15.7 percent). On the other hand, their accidental-death pattern had not yet come to resemble that of adult males entirely. They still had 11 percent more fatal accidents in the home and 6 percent fewer fatal accidents in work places than adult males.

The high number of accidents in the home is important for two reasons. First, contrary to Ariès's claim that teenagers behaved like adults in the Middle Ages, their accident pattern shows similarities to those of both children and adults. They still lived and worked around the house and spent time fishing and gathering rather than following the pattern of their fathers in working primarily in the fields or at a craft. Second, the large percentage of those involved in accidents in the home suggests that teenagers did not routinely live in another person's house as servants. This latter problem is one that we must investigate further in this chapter, while Ariès's assumptions about medieval teenagers will be discussed in a subsequent chapter.

Because females were involved in fewer accidental deaths, information on their ages is scanty. The meager evidence on the age and activity of females (22 cases with age given for those six to twelve; 11 cases for those thirteen to nineteen; and 180 for adult females of unspecified age) indicates that females settled into their mothers' patterns more rapidly than males into their fathers'. While play and personal activites still occupied much of a girl's life from age six to twelve, she was also increasingly doing tasks about the home. From the ages of thirteen to nineteen their accidental-death pattern closely resembled that of the adult female. Most of their accidents involved household tasks, walking or other transport, supplemental economic activities, and some agricultural work. The places of death also show an essential similarity. Teenage girls went for water and wood and would often be left in charge of cooking.[13] (See Appendix, Table 5.)

The closer resemblance of girls' work to that of their mothers, compared to boys taking up their fathers' routine, suggests both the earlier maturity of girls and the usefulness of boys and adolescent males in helping out with supplemental economic activites and caring for animals. A boy's youth, like that of his sister, was largely spent on relieving the burden on the housewife, perhaps so that the latter could do some supplemental activity such as brewing. Since their strength and agrarian skills were only just developing, their full participation in men's work was delayed until the late teenage years.

Learning the skills of household work, husbandry, and crafts took place primarily during adolescence, either at home under the tutelage of parents, or as servants, apprentices, and occasionally as students. Experience in fieldwork came from watching and helping at an early age. Boys served as ox goaders at plowing, helped weed and hoe, and made the bands that women used to tie sheaves at harvest. As teenagers they graduated to plowing, casting seed, learning to use scythe and reaping hook, and loading and driving carts. Teenagers who worked at mills repaired sails and adjusted the mechanism of the mill. One fourteen-year-old boy in Norfolk was working on the sails when a wind came up, turning the sail and throwing him to the ground. They were also left to guard the mill when their father or master was absent. Thus William, son of Ralph Sucel, a serving boy of twelve, was left at the mill at lunchtime when a man came in and wanted to grind some maslin. Although William forbade him to do it, the man ignored him and got caught in the wheel and cogs and was killed.[14]

Teenagers were sometimes apprenticed to learn a craft such as dyeing cloth. At noon in April a dyer took his twelve-year-old helper with him to wash newly dyed cloth in a pit. The master was swinging the washing beaters when by accident he struck the legs of the boy because they were caught in the cloth. Another boy of the same age was apprenticed to a tailor. He was sitting cross-legged on the table in the tailor's shop when, wanting to cut thread, he leaned back against the scissors.[15]

Some peasant sons received an education. The lord exacted a fine of 6d. to 1s. for permission to attend school and sometimes imposed the stipulation that the boy could not take clerical orders or receive a tonsure. The lords had two motives for keeping peasants from ecclesiastical service. One was the desire to keep cultivators on the land and the other was that the lord himself needed trained secular clerks for his estate management. Those educated young men who did enter the lord's service had a great advantage in raising their social status and that of their families. A foresightful family would find investment in a son's education well worth the expense. Three boys from one manor sought education in 1348, and at Norton over a three-year period, 1331 to 1333, nine boys went to school. Fathers sometimes made provision in wills for a son's inheritance to include schooling or a craft.[16]

Other youths went into service in a manor, religious house, or private house, performing a variety of tasks such as getting water, fetching boats, doing errands, and learning to cook. William, son of Herbert atte Still, aged ten, was standing in the prior of Newnham's kitchen cutting up vegetables with a knife. The knife dropped, cutting a tendon of his foot. His mother, who was nearby and probably also a servant, carried him to their house, but he died of the bleeding.[17]

Young women learned brewing and a variety of other tasks at home from their mothers or in service. A housemaid's lament indicates the work:

> I must serve the old women, I must learn to spin, to reke, to card, to knit, to wash buckes, and by hande, to brew, bake, make mault, reap, bind sheaves, weed in the garden, milke, serve hoggs, make cleane their houses, within doores make beddes, sweep filthy houses, rubbe dirty ragges, beat out old Coverlettes, draw up old holes: Then to the kitchen, turne the spit, although it was but seldome, for we did not at meat often; then scour pottes, wash dishes, fetch in wood, make a fire, scalde milk Pannes, wash the Charne and butter dishes, ring out a Cheese clote, set everything in good order.

The servant girls' work was also dangerous. Amice, daughter of Robert Belamy, and Sibyl Bonchevler were carrying a tub full of grout between them in Lady Juliana de Beauchamp's brewhouse. As they were trying to dump the grout into a vat full of boiling water, Amice fell in and was scalded. And Emma, a washerwoman, fell into a large vat of boiling water.[18]

We must turn now to the question of the prevalence of servants in medieval peasant households and the likelihood of a teenager spending a few years in service. While we may rule out our Italian observer (see p. 157) as an objective source for peasantry, studies of early-modern sources have indicated that young peasants ten to twelve years of age were sent to other people's houses to work until they were in their twenties, when they would marry. Alan Macfarlane has leaped to the conclusion that, because there were servants in medieval rural England, it could not be called a true peasant society. According to his definition, peasants only use family labor, not hired labor.[19]

A few definitions are in order before we begin the discussion. *Serviens* had various meanings during the fourteenth century and included both domestic servants and agricultural laborers.[20] No doubt the confusion arose because often the hired help worked at a variety of tasks, both domestic and agrarian, and some were hired for piecework and others were year-round employees. For our purposes let us define laborers as those who supplemented their small landholdings with wages from agrarian work or milling or who rendered labor in connection with their holding a particular cottage and a bit of acreage. Servants, on the other hand, would be those who were hired year-round and did a variety of tasks as the season and need arose. They may or may not have resided with the family for whom they worked. That some sort of distinction existed in the minds of fourteenth-century administrators is apparent, for laborers are listed separately from servants in the poll tax lists.

Although servants could be found in households of both lords and peasants, it is difficult to find much specific information about them. Wages and work occasionally appear in the manorial court and account rolls and the title *servant* appears in records. For instance, Alice, daughter of William of the Grene, appeared in Wakefield court against William Gothe. She complained that when she had "gone out of the country on service" five years ago, she had given him the keeping of a cow and he would not return it.[21] The poll taxes of the late fourteenth century are the only systematic listing, and they are deficient because many servants, particularly female servants, were hidden from the tax collectors. Poll taxes and manorial records do not indicate whether servants lived with their employers and what their lives were like. The coroners' inquests, therefore, provide some of the best insights into the servants' lives.

None of the sources permit us to establish with any accuracy the percentage of people in society who were laborers or servants, or what their ages were. We cannot show, as has been done for the early modern period, that 60 percent of the youth from fifteen to twenty four were servants.[22] As we mentioned in an earlier chapter, communities varied in their composition, and that variation meant that the number of laborers and servants also varied. Taking the poll tax of 1379, the craftsman town of Skipton had seventeen servants who were unmarried, thirty-one married laborers, twenty-four married tradesmen or craftsmen, and only two cultivators. But the primarily agricultural community of Kettlewell had eleven servants, three craftsmen, one cattle buyer, and thirty-four agricultural laborers. Servants, therefore, comprised about a quarter of the village population in the Gloucestershire survey. In Kempsford, where the poll tax was taken twice because of evasions, the first tax listed thirty servants out of a population of 118, but the second

tax collection produced thrity-nine more servants who had been concealed. Servants, therefore, actually accounted for 44 percent of the
residents. The 1381 poll tax for the Hundred of Thingowe in Suffolk
showed that servants comprised about 40 percent of the population,
laborers 39 percent, craftsmen and tradesmen 14 percent, cultivators 7
percent, and gentry 1 percent. Again, the percentages of population in
the different categories varied greatly from one village to another. One
may conclude, therefore, that servants played an important part in the
work force, even if we cannot be sure of the percentage.[23]

While sources for the early modern period can answer decisively
that the servants were young, unmarried, and lived with their
employers, the medieval records are not conclusive. The handmaidens
who were accused in manorial courts of taking nuts or dry wood in the
lord's woods were probably young, for they are listed along with the
village youth. In the few cases where both age and occupation are given
in the coroners' inquests, however, servants might be any age. Some
people have used the high proportion of single people among the
servants in the poll taxes as an indication that the servants were young
and unmarried. Such information is suggestive rather than conclusive.
To be sure, most of those listed as cultivators were married (94 percent
in Thinghowe Hundred), as were most of the craftsmen (77 percent)
and laborers (84 percent), whereas only 54 percent of the servants were.
In market towns such as Mildenhall or Stowe, however, none of the
servants were married. For some youthful servants, the period of service
was probably a temporary one, but the evidence is hardly overwhelming.

Likewise, it is difficult to find conclusive evidence on whether or not
the servants lived with their masters in the same household. Hilton has
devoted considerable attention to this problem, even comparing a rent
list with a poll tax that listed people by household, but he still felt that
the evidence was inconclusive. At Buckland, in the Avon Valley, he
found thirty households of cultivators. Half of these had adult sons and
daughters resident and five had live-in servants.[24] Poll taxes add to the
confusion about the residence of servants, for it is not uncommon to find
sons or daughters listed as servants in their father's house. Thus John,
son and servant of John Wysman, or Isabel, daughter and servant of
John Shortnekke, are listed. In accidental-death cases teenagers, like
children had a large percentage of their accidents at their father's home
but a rather lower percentage at the homes of others, figures that suggest
that they were not living with a master.

Detailed coroners' inquests provide some information on live-in
servants. In cases of night burglaries all the residents of a house may be

named. For instance, at bedtime on November 15. 1369, felons and thieves came to the house of Edmund le Mastref of Clifton, broke in and entered it, tied up Edmund, his wife, Maude, and the housemaid Sarah. They went on to Agnes Colburne's house and wounded her servant, John le Toutere, and a neighbor woman, Beatrice le Sarreman. Margery Tailor was a servant in the house of Johanna del See and had her room in the solar.[25]

The evidence for live-in servants is hardly overwhelming. Hilton has estimated that in the Cotswolds perhaps one in eight families had servants, but this does not mean that more did not rely on hired help. Peasants had a variety of options for procuring workers if familial labor was insufficient and, consequently, did not necessarily need servants. Laborers gladly worked for piecework. Arnold of Tyringham was desperate for work and stood at the market cross in Bedford to indicate that he could be hired.[26] Some prosperous cultivators, as we have seen, had credit arrangements that provided them labor from their debtors. Reciprocity arrangements with neighbors could also help, particularly among the middling peasants. Whether the hired help lived in or not was probably a negotiable option in a labor contract. Robert, son of Thomas, for example, complained that Adam Trub owed him money for work because he had lived with him to his damage of 3d. This was obviously a labor contract in which part of the pay was in housing.[27] During harvest it was customary to provide sleeping arrangements for the harvest crew, but these were for temporary laborers who may have been migrating with the harvest.

On balance the evidence is against the practice of either having live-in servants or arranging for the majority of young people to undego a period of servitude. While not unknown, neither was a firmly established tradition for medieval English peasants. What we now know of economic and social conditions suggests the hypothesis that servitude and agricultural help might have undergone a substantial change during the late Middle Ages. In the first part of the fourteenth century the surplus of labor would have made the position of servant a very attractive one for it guaranteed meals, wages, and perhaps a roof over one's head. Noninheriting sons and daughters would have found such an arrangement attractive and so might a son who was waiting to inherit the family property. Following the Black Death, however, laborers changed their attitudes about receiving pay in food and housing and instead demanded monetary payment and tried to avoid working on year-long contracts. With low population continuing through the fifteenth century, laborers continued to prefer freedom from binding contracts and payment only in money. Furthermore, housing through the period was cheap to construct and readily available. A laborer with wages could have his own cottage; and the inheriting son of a cultivator would have his own land even before his father's death or retirement because of the ready availability of land. Fathers of the yeoman and cultivator groups probably preferred to keep their children at home until they were adults, so that they could have the benefit of their labor rather than hiring expensive laborers. Good wages and cheap housing may also explain why about half of the servants in the Suffolk poll tax were married.

In the late sixteenth and seventeenth centuries, however, the labor supply again outstripped demand and once again the postponement of marriage and the live-in arrangements for servants became a very attractive option for young people. Housing had also changed by this time and the more substantial stone and brick houses had separate rooms for the master and the help, so that the master could have live-in servants without depriving himself of privacy. Wattle-and-daub huts were still built, but may have been less attractive to young people entering service than a room in a substantial, modern house.

While most aspects of a servant's life are difficult to document, the relationship between the master and servant do surface in both literary and official records. One aspect of the relationship that concerned both sides of the contract was its permanency. A fifteenth-century poem warns "squier, yeman, and page" that "service is not heritage" and that "lordes love chaungeth oft." But a carol advised lords to treat their old servants with generosity "and elles must thou drink as thou dost brewe."[28] Both good and bad relationships between employer and employed are described, and servants varied in their competence. One imagines that Emma Coleville was distressed with her carter, Reginald Carter, when he lit a fire in her stable to keep warm at dawn in December 1342. The conflagration killed not only Reginald but eight cart horses, eight oxen, and destroyed carts.[29] Some masters inflicted extreme punishment for lapses in work. Warren Polehanger, a miller, accused his servant Walter of stealing a bushel of flour. He hit Walter with an ax and killed him.[30]

Murders of servants by masters were fairly rare, as were the opposite, and one is struck by the great loyalty of servants to their master's property and person, even when such loyalty meant risking their own lives. Sir Nicholas Peyvere's servant boy Gerleys came to the rescue of his master and the rector of Pertenhall, who were being threatened by a man with a sword. The assailant then attacked the servant, who shot him in self-defense. On the master's side, there was often familial concern expressed for servants who disappeared. Bertran

Polet left his master's courtyard at vespers in November to guard his master's wood. When he did not return "the household were troubled and searched for him for a whole week" until they found him.[31]

Unless the laborer who worked for the household was a casual one who did piecework, his or her relationship to the family would have been a close one whether or not he or she lived in the household. While the servant was not equal to the children of the family and would not inherit family land, bequests often indicate great affection. John Thrale of Lutton was a wealthy man who apparently had no children. He left the bulk of his lands to his wife and brother, but also left eight acres and a close to his servant, John Colyn, to use when he became twenty-eight, with the provision that he keep the obit. John's father's will is also recorded and it indicates that he was not a wealthy man and had done well to settle one son with a prosperous and well-disposed neighbor. In another example, Elizabeth Lamkyn received 26s. 8d. to pursue a trade from a grateful master. The more typical bequests included items of clothing, sheep, a small sum of money, or malt, Such gifts were the usual sort of token bequest reserved for godchildren, grandchildren, nieces and nephews and may have indicated a similar place in a master's or mistress's affections.[32]

Sometimes a servant was able to marry into the family. Thomas, who was a servant of Lettice, sued for half a bovate of land that his uncle sold out of court to Thomas's loss. The jurors found that Thomas had the just claim to it. The next time he appeared in court, he was Lettice's son-in-law.[33]

Children and servants were an indispensable part of the household economy, lending a hand at both men's and women's work in the close and field. Unless orphaned, children spent most of their leisure and working hours in the home or around the village until they were ten or twelve. Then they herded, gathered, and fished. Teenagers lived at home for the most part, helping their parents with their tasks. Some worked for other villagers or on manors as servants, particularly if the family had more labor than it needed, but they would not necessarily move in with their master. Some young people may also have chosen to work as servants for a period of time in order to earn sufficient money to marry. These would be younger sons and daughters or children from poorer families, who could not expect an attractive marriage settlement from their parents. The number of youth becoming servants is not known, but it appears that it was not yet a well-established routine for them to spend part of their life cycle in service in another person's house before they married. Socialization and training for work occurred within the domestic economy for those pursuing traditional careers.

From the earliest years children began to imitate their parents at work. Girls quickly identified with their mother's tasks while boys worked at both household chores and some field labor. By the time boys and girls were seven, they began to make routine contributions to the home economy, such as fetching water and herding. Young people did not take on the full work load and responsibilities of adults until their late teenage years, when they possessed sufficient strength and skills. Their accidental-death pattern indicates that they were between children and adults in their behavior, a subject that will be explored further in the next section.

IV

Stages of Life

11

Childhood

So much of recent historiography has centered on children. For almost every period of history and in every culture the young of our species have been studied for their play, developmental stages, and parental attitudes toward them. Philippe Ariès, in *Centuries of Childhood*, denied that people in the Middle Ages had a concept of childhood and argued that the sentimentalized view of childhood as a special phase of life did not exist until the modern period. Because medieval peasants kept no diaries and wrote no letters, it appeared that their childhoods would elude historical research and Ariès's view could stand; but the coroners' inquests open up the world of medieval peasant children. The cases tell about provisions for child care, the clothing and feeding of children, games and pastimes, and the exploration of their environment both alone and with adults and other children. A remarkable aspect of these vignettes of childhood is that medieval peasant children's behavior patterns fall into modern observations of child development; both their motor skills and their relationship to their environment develop within the stages that are familiar to us. This similarity of child development in the Middle Ages and in modern observations suggest, I argue, a strong biological basis for child development as opposed to decisive cultural influences. Although, as we shall see, medieval childrearing practices could be considerably different from modern ones, parents in both periods provided for their children's basic biological and psychological needs and thus the early years of maturation were similar.[1]

Leaving aside all Freudian ideas of birth trauma, for which there is no medieval information, we can, however, observe children in the early hours of their lives. The birth process itself belongs more properly to the woman's life experience, for it was a female ritual exclusively, and will be considered in a subsequent chapter. Once born, the child was prepared for baptism. The midwife washed the baby in warm water or perhaps used oil, salt, or rose petals to clean the baby and straighten its limbs. She also tied the umbilical cord. When the coroner asked witnesses about a dead baby girl, a half-day old, who had been found in the Thames, they told him that they did not know whose child it was but they knew that it had not been baptized because the umbilical cord was not tied.[2]

The first washing of an infant had a powerful sentimental importance in medieval culture that appears in poetry and ballads. Sympathy for the Christ child's poverty at his nativity is aroused in carols such as the famous "Cherry Tree Carol" by stating that he had to be washed in water rather than in milk or wine. In ballads fathers direct that their children be taken up and washed in milk and wrapped in silk. For a child born in the wilderness, a crystal-clear stream had to suffice.[3]

The role of the father in the folkloric tradition was important and reflects pre-Christian ideas about an infant's survival. In the medieval Scandinavian tradition the father decided whether the baby would live. If he took it into his arms, put water on it, and gave it a name, its mother could suckle it. Until this ceremony was completed the child could be abandoned or exposed, but afterward it would be considered murder to do so. In the Roman tradition as well the baby was laid on the earth before the father and would be allowed to live only if he picked it up. In medieval literature such as the Breton lays, when a child is abandoned it is done immediately after birth, as is the case in both "Sir Degaré" and "Le Freine."[4] Such customs indicate that before the ritual cleaning and naming, the child was considered dispensable and perhaps less than human.[5]

Christianity reinforced folklore in its insistence on rapid baptism, for the Church feared that the child would die in a state of original sin. Thus on the day of birth or the next day the child underwent the baptismal and naming ceremony. If a newborn baby appeared on the verge of death, the Church empowered lay people to baptize it so that it would not die in original sin. Preference was given to a layman, but the midwife could also perform the ceremony. Indeed, if the mother died in childbirth, the midwife was urged to cut her open, and extract and baptize the baby. The rudimentary baptism was to repeat, "I baptize you in the name of the Father, the Son, and the Holy Ghost."[6]

After the midwife washed and bundled up the newborn child at home, it was ready for its spiritual cleansing. The baptismal ceremony was elaborate. The father sent off messengers to get the godparents to come to the church posthaste. The godmother or midwife carried the baby to the church, perhaps as part of a joyous procession. At the church door the priest inquired after the sex of the child and whether it had been baptized before (there was great concern about baptizing twice). The ceremony at the church door included blessing the child, putting salt in its mouth to symbolize the reception of wisdom, and exorcizing demons lurking in it. The priest read passages from the Bible and ascertained the child's name and the godparents' qualifications for their spiritual task.

Following the ceremony at the church door, the party moved inside to the baptismal font where again the assembled party prayed and the priest anointed the child, immersed it in the font, and named it. The godparents raised the cleansed child from the font and the godmother put the child in a special white christening garment. The priest touched the infant on top of the head with chrism. A parish church window, now at Missenden Abbey, represents a child in its christening garment and with a bishop pronouncing a benediction over it.[7]

Baptismal water was not always clean. Directions to the clergy cautioned against changing this holy water frequently and instructed that if the child defecated in the water it should be thrown out, but if it only urinated the water should be used again. After the godparents raised the child from the font, they washed their hands, not because of the filth of baptismal water but to avoid the possibility of an inadvertent second baptism.

The ceremony was still not complete, for the new Christian was now taken to the altar for the profession of faith. The godparents, of course, made the responses for the day-old child. Finally, the party returned to the parents' house for the traditional gift giving and feasting.[8]

Such a long ceremony was hardly a pleasant experience for a newborn child, who had to endure hunger, salt, drafts, and immersion in water. In the proofs of age for the nobility, witnesses sometimes recalled how miserable the child had been. One witness said that another baptism had delayed that of the baby he had come to see baptized and the girl had become very unhappy and cried through the ceremony. Another witness said that he saw the priest sprinkling water excessively on the infant's face so that the child became angry. In a bit of fourteenth-century psychologizing he attributed the subsequent hatred the young man bore for this priest to the baptismal ceremony.[9]

The name a child received at the baptismal font was most often the name of his or her principal godparent, the one who raised the child from the font. The custom appears in priests' instruction manuals and was so ingrained that one godfather started a scuffle at the baptismal font when the child was named after someone else. In the various sources that name a godparent and godchild, this pattern predominates. In wills, for instance, one finds examples such as William Walle, vicar of Houghton Regis, who named three godchildren as beneficiaries, all of whom bear the name William; in two of these cases the father's name was Thomas. In the proofs of age among the nobility, 87 percent bore the name of the godparent. In the proof of English citizenship in York, 65 percent of the godsons bore the same name as one of their godfathers.[10]

The simplicity of the English naming pattern has been overlooked bcause people failed to investigate the baptismal process. One historian confidently maintained, for instance, that it was customary to give the child the father's or grandfather's Christian name in Halesowen.[11] Custom on this manor may have been different, but since no listing of godparents exists in manorial records, one cannot be confident that names descended from father to son. If one looks at serf lists, which are more reliable for naming patterns than are families reconstructed from manorial records, no strong pattern of naming children after parents appears. The coincidence of child's name with that of the parent is highly likely in a society such as that of late medieval England in which a relatively small pool of Christian names was drawn upon repeatedly. It was also possbible for parents to choose godparents who had the same first name as they themselves did.[12] Thus the appellations of *senior* and *junior* appear in the court records with some degree of regularity as a distinction between father and son.

Another perplexing problem that the baptismal naming resolves is that of two children in the same family having an indentical Christian name. Because of high infant mortality, some historians have assumed that two children bore the same name because parents could thus secure the perpetuation of a favorite name.[13] But with the limited number of popular names it was very easy for the godfathers of two brothers to have the same Christian name. While the practice confuses historians trying to reconstruct families, people at the time resolved the problem officially by calling the elder "major" and the younger "minor." In practice, however, nicknames probably distinguished the two.

The name that a child would bear from the thirteenth century on would have been a Norman one rather than Anglo-Saxon, and usually that of a saint. The variety was rather limited. In late-thirteenth-century serf lists only thirty-six different male names and twenty female names appeared in three villages. In tenant lists in a village in the fourteenth and fifteenth century there were only eleven male names and ten female names. Naming the child after the godparent tended to perpetuate the limited number of Christian names, keeping the pool of possible names small. John did not gain its predominance as a popular name until the fourteenth century, and even then shared its popularity with William, Thomas, and Robert. Favorite female names were Matilda, Margaret, Emma, Alice, and Agnes. They used other names as well, and some of the Anglo-Saxon ones, particularly Edward, continued in popularity.[14]

Surnames became common in England by the end of the thirteenth century, but it was not until the middle of the fourteenth century that a child would be expected to adopt the surname of its parent. The child might be identified by either the father's or the mother's surname, so that matronymics were not uncommon. The use of the mother's name was not reserved for illegitimate children, but, on the contrary, was common when the mother was chief inheritor of her family's land.[15]

The named and baptized new Christian returned from church in a baptismal gown, but exchanged it for swaddling clothes, so that the godparents could take the gown back to the church. A thirteenth-century Englishman, Walter de Bibblesworth, advised that the child be swaddled as soon as it was born and laid in a cradle to sleep.[16] The child spent a considerable part of its first years of life in a cradle by the fire. Since a swaddled baby could not creep about, it could be left alone. When the child was out of swaddling clothes it might be tied in the cradle to keep it out of trouble when no adult was present to mind it. Robert, son of Walter, one and a half years old, was left tied in his cradle. A fire started and he could not get out.[17]

Swaddling and tying infants in cradles may have prevented some accidents, but cradle fires were the leading cause of accidental death among infants. Of the fifty-eight children under one year of age appearing in the coroners' inquests, 33 percent died in fires in their cradles. The percentage drops to 14 for one-year-olds and to only 1 percent for two-year-old children. Unattended babies who were not in cradles also died in house fires; 21 percent of their deaths occurred in this circumstance. These fires are frequently described as being caused by chickens. Chickens pecked about the open hearth for food and either picked up a burning straw or twig and dropped it into the cradle or perhaps their feathers caught fire and they flailed around, setting the cradle or house afire. Since the children were wrapped in linen, linsey-woolsey, or wool, the fire was a smoldering one. The smell of burning cloth, if not the cry of the child, would call attention to the accident if an adult were in the house. The extent of the burns, in one case the child's entire legs, indicates that adults were far away. Cases sometimes

A typical family scene before the open hearth. The pot sits on a trivet, and a little boy uses a bellows to keep the fire hot. The mother has her hands full tending both the pot and the baby. [Bodleian Library, MS. Douce 6, fol. 22.]

mention where the parents were when their child died. In one case the father was in the fields and the mother had gone out to the well; other times the parents were at church.[18]

The time and seasonality of accidental deaths for babies through one year of age illustrates when the babies were most likely to be left on their own because their parents were too busy with other chores to watch them. No one day predominated over another for accidental deaths, even though both parents were likely to be at church on Sunday. Babies were most likely to have fatal accidents during the busiest part of their parents' day: 21 percent occurred in the morning and 43 percent at noon. During these times women would be looking after animals and doing other errands while the men would be in the fields. The months of May through August, when all able-bodied adults had to turn their attention to the fields, were the most risky for infants: 47 percent of all fatal accidents suffered by babies occurred during these four months. Because of the necessity of ensuring a good harvest, babies often had to be left in less than optimal circumstances. It was common in many peasant societies for the parents to take swaddled children to the fields with them when they worked, where they were put in trees or laid on the ground. Although no coroners' inquests mention this practice, in the

"Song of the Husbandman" the children are with the parents in the field:

> And at the londes ende lay a litell crom-bolle,
> and there on lay a little childe lapped in cloutes,
> And tweyne of tweie yeres old opon a-nother syde, . . .[19]

Babies taken to the fields may have had fewer accidents, but their presence interfered with work. The poor husbandman of the poem had to ask them to keep quiet while he and his wife got on with the plowing.

The deaths of infants in fires and other accidents, however, indicates that the babies spent much time alone and passive in the cradle. Five percent died from animal bites suffered when a pig wandered into the house and mauled the child, and in 4 percent of the cases walls or other objects fell on them as they were lying or sitting by them. A year-and-a-half-old boy was in his cradle by the fire when a red pig wandered into the house and mauled him; and a year-old girl was in her cradle by the fire when two small pigs who were in the house tussled and overturned the cradle into the fire. In both cases the parents were elsewhere.[20]

Abundant evidence from the coroners' inquests indicates that parents did not like to leave their children alone and that villagers did not approve of the practice. Villagers' censure is apparent in the wording of inquests. For example, a child wandered outside its father's house and "was without anyone looking after him" when he drowned, or a two-year-old died when she was "left without a caretaker." Often, however, the caretaker was ill equipped to mind the child. Maude, daughter of William Bigge, was left in the care of a blind woman while her mother was visiting a neighbor. When her mother returned, she found her daughter drowned in a ditch. Parents often entrusted the care of their babies to other children. Thus a thirty-week-old child was left in the care of a neighbor's three-and-a-half-year-old son. The attention span of other children in tending to their young brothers and sisters was obviously limited. William Senenok and his wife went to church on Christmas Day 1345, leaving their infant daughter, Lucy, in a cradle and in the care of their daughter Agnes, who was three. Agnes went out into the courtyard to play and the younger child burned. In another case the villagers commented that a five-year-old boy who failed to take adequate care of his brother was a "bad custodian."[21]

As the condemnations indicate, such negligence in arranging child care was not typical. Coroners' cases indicate that women tended each other's children or hired women or girls to baby-sit. On a February day when William Suger was at the plow, his wife wanted to bake bread in an oven in their close, so she hired a village girl, Maude, daughter of Ellis Bate, to sit with their daughter Rose, who was in the cradle. The mother drowned getting straw. In other cases the child was left with a baby-sitter in the sitter's house. John, son of John Bullok, was left with Anicia Porter, a neighbor, and William de Herford, one year old was left in the care of Cecilia de Wrynbe in the house of John Stanner.[22] Overall, however, babies apparently did not spend the majority of their time in child care. Only 16 percent of male babies' fatal accidents (see Appendix, Tables 4 and 5.) and 12 percent of female babies' occurred at other people's houses. The overwhelming majority of fatal accidents involving infants up to one year old occurred at home: 60 percent of the boys' and 79 percent of the girls'.

Accidents happened to children even when the parents were doing their best to attend to them. One mother had an epileptic fit and the child she was nursing slipped into the fire. The Church took a great interest in the care of children and spelled out in penitential literature the problems that were likely to arise in childrearing. They warned against cradle fires, scalding from hot liquids, and overlaying. They were certainly correct to be concerned with the first two, but only one case of overlaying appeared in the coroners' inquests. Robert, son of John Brown, was in the care of Isolda (possibly a wet nurse), who took Robert to bed with her and around 11 o'clock at night rolled over and crushed him.[23]

Babies were not continuously swaddled. Even Bibblesworth recommended the child be allowed to creep about before it learned to get up on its feet.[24] The mobility of one-year-olds shows up in both the type of accident and the place of accidents. All fatal accidents occurred to infants in the home, either of their parents' or that of another person, but the adventurous one-year-olds, particularly the males, often wandered into public streets and into their parents' work area. One little girl, aged one, crept into the street and was crushed by a passing cart.[25] As soon as they could creep, the infants' curiosity led them to play with fire, fall into ditches, and be scalded in pots and pans of hot liquid.

Although upper class women put their children out to wet nurses, the peasant women nursed their own, if they had milk. The image of Mary breast-feeding Jesus was a popular one in statuary and in literature. Folk poems express the earthiness of the scene:

> As she him took all in her lap.
> He took that maiden by the pap.
> And took thereof a right good nap [grip].
> And sucked his fill of that licour.[26]

Children were nursed for two or three years, although baby girls might have been weaned sooner. Peasant babies were probably not fed on demand, since, as we have seen, they were left alone much of the time.[27]

Peasants turned to wet nurses when the mother died or when she had no milk. Johanna, daughter of John of Burgoyne, was six months old when she died of burns. She was in the care of Beatrice Paysele, who nursed and took care of her. Beatrice, however, went off to church with a neighbor and left the child in the cradle by the fire. Other cases also explicitly indicate that a child had a wet nurse and suggest that it was placed in the nurse's home. These children were not foundings, for the father is always mentioned, and in one case the father seems to have initiated the inquest because he suspected foul play on the nurse's part.[28]

Some lullabies sung to medieval children have been preserved. Traditionally, we think lullabies are supposed to reassure the baby, singing of good things that will happen and protective people and surroundings; but not so the medieval versions. The songs put into Mary's mouth, as she comforts the Christ child, are grim predictors of his eventual death on the cross.[29] Similarly, peasant children first learned of the world's cruelties as their mothers rocked them. As a descendant of Adam, the world could only be a vale of tears:

> Child, thou nart a pilgrim byt and uncouth gest
>
> Child, if bitide thou shalt thrive and thee [prosper],
> Think thou was a-fostred upon thy modres knee;
> Ever have synde in thyn herte of tho thynges three—
> Wan thou comest, whan thou art, and what shal come of
>   thee.[30]

Unlike American lullabies that place the child in a separate fantasy environment, the medieval version integrated it immediately into the common worries of survival of both individual and family.

From the mother's viewpoint, such songs seem to have two functions: they express the mother's mixed feelings about childrearing and the time and trouble it takes.[31] They also speak of the extreme sorrow and frustration of raising a child who might be carried off by disease or accident before maturity. In lullabies and, as we shall see, in other songs about motherhood, a very strong emphasis is placed on the gratitude the child should feel to its mother for having reared it. The relationship betwen Mary and Jesus was a powerful and consoling social ideal and was held up for ordinary people to imitate.

The completion of the first year of life marks the first stage in child development. Problems of feeding, warmth, and attention dominated the child's life. Although 32 percent of children described as one year

old still died in cradle fires and while sleeping, 46 percent of the victims
were described as playing with water, pots, fire, and with other children
and 13 percent were described as walking when the accident occurred.
As in modern accidental-death statistics for children of this age, the
baby boys tended to be more active and aggressive at play (63 percent of
boys' compared to 54 percent of girls' accidents). (See Appendix, Tables
6 and 7.) Thus during their first year children began to enter the second
phase of child development, which is characterized by motor development and the reception to outside stimulation.

The second stage of child development and the second readily
definable accident grouping occur in the second and third years, when
children develop their motor skills and take a lively interest in their
environment.[32] The prevalance of cradle fires as a cause of children's
fatal accidents dropped to 3 percent, and the number of accidents
involving play and other activities indicates that the toddlers were in the
process of exploring, reaching out to the world around, and imitating
adults. Various types of play accounted for 65 percent of their fatal
accidents, and an additional 16 percent involved walking. As noted in
the chapter on children's work, little girls tended to have more accidents
in the home, such as when playing with pots in imitation of their mother,
and little boys wandered farther afield observing their father's work
around the close. The places where accidents occurred also indicate the
toddlers' new experiences and interests. The majority of fatal accidents
(49 percent) still occurred in the child's home, but 18 percent occurred
in another person's home, 20 percent in public places, and 12 percent in
bodies of water.

Examples from the coroners' inquests present vivid pictures of these
perambulations. Agnes, daughter of William Wryhte of Fordham, aged
two, was tagging along with other children and playing in the king's
highway. She tried to follow the others across a stream and drowned.
Another toddler was sitting in front of his father's house playing with
other children when a man came up on horseback to view a cloth for an
amercement (fine). The man's horse trampled the boy. A girl of two and
a half came out of her father's house with a piece of bread in her hand
when a small pig came up and tried to take it from her, pushing her into
a ditch. A little boy of two was watching men constructing a wall when a
ladder fell on him. The pot on the hearth was a great fascination.
Sometimes the toddlers tried to ladle out hot food to eat when pot fell
over on them. Other times the children were simply curious and looked
into cauldrons of hot groat and fell in.[33]

The play of some children indicates that they lacked sufficient
motor skills to carry through games they started. One little boy was

trying to get water in a pit, but the dish fell into it and he could not get it out. A three-year-old girl tried to pick watercress flowers in a neighbor's ditch, but overreached herself and fell in. A boy of one and a half was clever enough to throw his cap in the ditch but could not retrieve it successfully. And another child, tempted by a white feather floating on a brook, leaned over to get it.[34]

Accidental-death figures need to be put into a comparative framework in order to assess the experiences of medieval toddlers. In modern American accidental-death figures, the period of infancy showed a high frequency of accidents, with a sharp decrease by the time children reached the age of two and three;[35] but the medieval pattern shows 38 percent more fatal accidents happening to toddlers than to infants. The swaddling system may have kept down the number of accidents in the first year of life, but for unswaddled, active toddlers the medieval peasant home and close area was fraught with hazards. It was impossible to child-proof the peasant environment.

Were medieval parents negligent of their children's safety by leaving them unattended or inadequately surpervised? Sometimes they certainly were careless about their children, but often they had to be away from home and could not find adequate child care. The seasonality of toddlers' accidents was similar to that for babies; the planting and harvest seasons were the most dangerous because parents were busy away from home. Furthermore, if a child did wander into a ditch or well, the parents might not be able to save it, because they too could not swim. And one should not underestimate the mischief that toddlers could get into even when normal care was provided. While a father was eating lunch, his son, aged one and a half, wandered out doors and drowned in the well. In another case William, son of William Faunceys, aged three and a half, fell into Robert Waeng's ditch when his mother went in to get a pot of ale to take home.[36] It was, perhaps, the unpredictable nature of children's play and wanderings at this age that gave rise to the folkloric tradition of changelings being aged two or three. Elf children were exchanged for human children at this age.[37]

The behavior of the boys and girls continued to exhibit the differences that appeared in the first year of life. Boys were more aggressive in their investigations of their environment and consequently had more accidents. More of their misadventures involved play and walking than those of girls. But the place of the accidents showed a similar pattern for both, with home still predominating. Fields played a relatively minor role in their lives, although the village streets and neighbors' closes were familiar to them in their perambulations.

Parents of these active two- and three-year-olds were obviously able

to instil some sense of caution into their wandering children, for the
number of accidents dropped dramatically for both boys and girls after
they reached the age of four. Of the 945 children whose ages are given in
the coroners' rolls, 25 percent died in the first year of their life, 48
percent when they were two to three, and only 11 percent when they
were four to six. Even by age three accidents began to diminish,
testifying to a greater degree of motor control and training for coping
with the environment. By four children discover infantile sexuality, but
the coroners' rolls, of course, contain no evidence that children suddenly
took their fingers out of pots and put them on their genitals instead.
Such behavior, however, did not escape the careful scrutiny of the
clergy, and in the *Handlyng Synne* Robert Mannyng warned that parents
should not allow children to lie together as they grew older, for often the
worst sins are committed by children and such lechery may continue
with them into adulthood.[38]

At the ages of four to six and beyond, parents could discipline
children and train them for their adult lives. Books on morality and
advice had a great deal to say about the parents' responsibility in
disciplining a child, mostly along the lines of "spare the rod and spoil the
child." The "Proverbs of Alfred" was typical:

> Thus quoth Alfred:
> Wise child is Father's bliss.
> If it so happens
> That thou hast care of a bairn,
> While he is little teach him men's manners.
> Then when he grows older he will turn thereto.
>
> But if thou lettest him rule,
> In his growing time,
> When he is older
> Thou canst not control him,
> He will despise thy command
> And make thee often sad at heart.
> Better that he had not been born.
> For better is a child unborn
> That unboxom [disobedient].[39]

Discipline was proper, but cursing a child was a terrible mistake. In the
poem "How the Good Wife Taught her Daughter," the mother is of the
opinion that a rebellious child should not be cursed but rather beaten
smartly until it cries for mercy and understands what it has done wrong.
Robert Mannyng tells a moral tale that underlines the risks of curses. A
mother asked her daughter to have her clothes ready when she finished
her bath. The daughter did not bring them immediately and the mother

wished her to the devil. The devil took the daughter very willingly.[40]

Recorded cases indicate that corporal punishment was normal in dealing with children who misbehaved, but that extreme reprimands came to community attention, although not necessarily their condemnation. The wife of William Puncie hit Agnes, daughter of Matilda Foletby, with a stick when she found her in her garden doing damage. Anges died five weeks later of an illness unrelated to the beating, but the neighbors brought it to the attention of the coroner nonetheless. When a boy stole a parcel of wool by taking it under his hat, the wife of the shop owner chastised him by striking him under the left ear with her hand. The blow was fatal, but the jurors felt that the punishment was just and the death accidental, and no indictment for homicide was brought.[41] Although manorial courts sometimes interfered with husbands who beat their wives severely, no one has reported a case in which the jurors intervened in the case of children. Yet in the coroners' inquests a child was occasionally described as being beaten to death. A mother whipped her ten-year-old son so severely in a fit of anger that he died from the wounds.[42]

Discipline alone, however, did not bring about a reduction in children's accident rate between the ages of four to six. Ironically, in peasant society children seemed to have had more adult supervision during this period than they did from infancy through three years old. Contrary to Ariès's assumption that chidren were only valued when they began to contribute to the home economy, the greater supervision came because children's mobility made it possible for them to be with adults more. Their accident pattern indicates that, rather than suddenly becoming more productive, they were still spending most of their time playing. As we have seen, the work that they did perform was rather minimal. So, the activites of childhood predominate in coroners' inquests. A litte girl of four was holding a duck in her hands and wanted to put it into the river, but she fell in and drowned. William Annotson, four and a half years old, went to a well and saw his face reflected in its water. When he tried to reach down and touch the face, he fell in.[43]

The most striking change in a child's life in its progress to adulthood seems to have come at ages eight through twelve. During this period children began to show independence from adults and were given useful tasks of their own to perform for the family. They still lived at home for the most part, contrary to the assumption of Ariès and others, that all children older than seven were sent to live in another person's home. Their chores show that they were moving into adult life and were being trained for the work they would eventually perform as adults. Their accident pattern in both work and play became closer to that of adults. Boys no longer chased feathers or played with ducks; instead they were learning to have mock fights with staffs and to shoot at targets with bows and arrows. And girls began to take up female occupations.[44]

The coroners' rolls show that the children growing up in the medieval household went through distinct biological stages of development recognizable to us today. In addition, the inquests tell us something about the emotional climate in the home. One would assume that the inquests would reflect only negative feelings within the family, since they record homicides and violent death, but intrafamilial homicide was rare in the medieval family, as already observed, and within that category homicide involving parents and children was very rare indeed. Husbands and wives and siblings were more likely to be involved in the homicidal drama.[45] Cases of child abuse ending in homicide were rare. One woman put the hand of her eight-week-old daughter in boiling water and the child eventually died of the burn. Another mother beat and dismembered her daughter. The record of this case is graphic, explaining that the woman had become insane and with her own hands "dispoiled and dismembered her daughter Agnes." Another mother tied her four-year-old daughter to a doorway and struck her with sharp sticks. The child died from wounds at sunrise and the jurors said that the mother was insane at the time she did the deed. Pleas of insanity required the jurors to present a history of mental illness so we may believe that these cases were ones of genuine insanity.[46]

But to argue that medieval parents had a sentimental attitude toward their children we must find more than a forbearance in killing or mutilating them. We would expect emotional outpourings from parents upon finding a dead child. The rolls, unfortunately, stop short of the parent's lament. But to the extent that the relationship of the first finder to the victim demonstrates love and concern, this information from the coroner's inquests is instructive. About a third of children's bodies were found by members of their family. In the case of little boys, 43 percent were found by their fathers and 45 percent by their mothers. An additional 5 percent were found by siblings and 7 percent by other kin. The age of the little boy did not make a difference in whether the mother or father found the body. For little girls, however, only 33 percent were discovered dead by their fathers compared to 59 percent by their mothers. When the age of the female victim was three and younger, mothers far outweighed fathers as first finders of their bodies. Even though male toddlers were more active than their sisters and followed their fathers around, most of the fatal accidents still occurred in the home. The fathers apparently took a keener interest in the welfare of their male children, particularly during their early years of life, than they did in the female children. An occasional case shows a father's concern. For instance, Reynold, son of Thomas Tempsford, came home from St. Neots market and immediately asked where his son Richard was and searched for him.[47] The data could suggest that mothers and fathers had an equal concern for sons but the mothers had a heightened concern for their daughters.

Parents were willing to give their lives to save their children and often expressed anger at the loss of a child through murder or negligence. Medieval parents did not take the casual attitude toward the loss of children that historians of the modern family have ascribed to them:

> On Friday last [Aug. 9, 1298] John Trivaler and Alice his wife were in a shop where they abode in the parish of St. Mary late at night, ready to go to bed, and the said Alice fixed a lighted candle on the wall by the straw which lay in the said shop, so that the flame of the candle reached the straw before it was discovered and immediately the fire spread throughout the shop, so that the said John and Alice scarce escaped without, forgetting that they were leaving the child behind them. And immediately when the said Alice remembered her son was in the fire within, she leapt back into the shop to seek him, and immediately when she entered she was overcome by the greatness of the fire and choked.[48]

A ten-year-old boy who was shooting at a dunghill with his bow and arrow missed his target and hit a five-year-old girl instead. The jurors said that it was an accident, but that the boy had fled because he was afraid of the father's anger.[49]

The records give few glimpses of how parents viewed their roles and responsibilities vis-à-vis their children, be they young or adult. Fathers usually appeared in manorial court rolls furthering the material interests of their children, but occasionally disputes surfaced. One angry father, John Manning, described himself as "enfebled" and "decrepite" with age, but he was alert enough to detail his reasons for disinheriting his son. In folk literature and works such as that of Robert Mannyng the father's role was limited to providing an inheritance for his children and disciplining them, but it did not extend to nurturing them.[50]

The mother's role, on the other hand, received considerable emphasis in song and advice manuals. Analogies to Mary as the ideal mother were constantly drawn in story and statuary. A poignant glimpse of mothers with their children comes from a lament of Mary that other mothers can enjoy their children but hers, alas, is dead:

> Of all women that ever were born,
> That bear children, abide, and see

How my son lieth me forore,
Upon my knee, ta'en from a tree.
Your children you dance upon your knee
With laughing, kissing and merry cheer.

O woman, woman well is with thee.
The child's cap thou puttest on,
Thou combest his hair, his colour see . . . .

After grooming, the mother fastens a caplet on the child and "with great solace" takes the child by the hand, saying, "Sweet son, give me a stroke."[51] Such a sentimental picture of motherhood could not have been completely removed from reality, even for the hard-working peasant woman. Although there was much misogynistic literature in the Middle Ages, the role of women as mothers received respect.[52]

In return for the patrimony of their father and the nurturing of their mother children were instructed to obey their parents and keep them when they were old. Wills often provide insight into the continued process of parents trying to force their children to obey. A genuine feeling of partnership in childrearing emerges in these final injunctions. Fathers will provide inheritances for a son provided "he be good to his mother," of "yff he please hys modr well," or if he "wyzely behave hymselfe . . . with owte any vexyng or troblyng" his mother. Daughters would be given dowries only if "they will be counselled by their mother" or "ruled and be advysyd by their mother in ther marying."[53]

Coroners' inquests and literary remains show parents tending to the needs of their children, providing for their future, and exhibiting love and concern for them, but they do not indicate the sentimental attachment to the state of childhood that according to Ariès, distinguishes the modern family from the medieval one. Some clues to a sentimentalization of childhood do, however, appear. Medievalists have pointed out that, contrary to Ariès's claims, medieval artists quite frequently depicted real babies rather than little adults and have observed that by the end of the twelfth century there were stories about the special innocence and delights of childhood.[54] In a fifteenth-century work, *The Miracles of Henry VI*, half the miracles attributed to Henry consist of curing children and raising them from the dead. This hagiographic work is of particular interest because the cases read like coroners' inquests.[55]

Perhaps the most striking testimony to a medieval sentimentalization of childhood comes from the stories of martyred children. St. William of Norwich was supposedly crucified by the Jews in 1144. He was about eleven or twelve years old at the time. A cult immediately grew up around him and made Norwich a great center of pilgrimage.

There followed a rash of martryed young boys in many of the major cathedral towns. Toward the end of the trend, about a century after William, Lincoln got its martyr in St. Hugh, who became the most famous of all thanks to the "Prioress's Tale." The martyred child was a natural subject for sainthood because he presented strong parallels to lyric poetry about young Jesus and the biblical story of the Slaughter of the Innocents. People in the Middle Ages did sentimentalize and venerate childhood, but in the way that they knew best—they made saints out of them.[56]

Medieval sentimentalization of childhood, however, did not reach the proportions that it does in modern Western culture. Childhood was, however, a recognized, separate period in life. Because so much of the maturation process is biological rather than cultural, medieval peasants could not bypass this stage. In going through it, the behavior of medieval children very much resembled that of modern children as they go through the stages of child development. Medieval parents, perhaps, had less time to devote to childrearing, but they did manage to attend to their needs, teach them to talk and work, and discipline them. As the children grew up the parents continued to provide for them to the best of their abilities, arranging marriages, purchasing pieces of land, and trying to establish them in their own households and families.

12

Growing Up and
Getting Married

Conflicting myths and images surround love, sex, marriage, and adolescence among the peasantry and have done so since the Middle Ages. One view, that of the great analyst of love, Andreas Capellanus, held that peasant girls could not be won by sweet words but that a prospective lover from the upper class should simply take them by force. But other medieval authors associated romance precisely with young peasants and wrote pastoral poetry and plays, such as *Le Jeux de Robin et Marion*. Writers have assumed that young peasants were lusty, carnal, and attractive or, conversely lewd, bestial, and unattractive. Modern writers have added their overlay. Ariès has argued that the Middle Ages did not accord to teenagers a period of adolescence, with its games and flirtations, which we consider appropriate to that age group. And Edward Shorter has denied the peasants any romance at all before the nineteenth century.[1] One would like to answer definitively what adolescence, love, and the formation of marriages was like for peasant youths, but such information is elusive. However, even such sparse information as is available dispels Ariès's dreary view of children passing directly into adulthood without experiencing adolescence or having their teenage years recognized as a separate phase of the life cycle. The patterns of work and play, the rather late age of majority, and premarital sexual flirtation all point to teenage years not unlike our own. While we cannot reconstruct the pimpled faces, the other biological characteristics of teenage sexuality are abundantly apparent. As in the case of childhood, the stages of biological development must be given their due and cannot be entirely culturally suppressed.

A Middle English poem, "The Mirror of the Periods of Man's

Life," is primarily a vehicle for moralizing, but it also divides life in its stages by year. The period of infancy lasts until the seventh year when, the writer declares, the infant has become a child. By the fourteenth year "knowliche of manhode he wynnes" (or puberty). The period through the early twenties is one of struggle between the seven virtues and the seven sins. Reason dictates an education, but lust has other ideas:

> Quod lust, "harpe & giterne there may ye leere,
>   And pickid staff & buckelere, there-with to plawe,
> At tauerne to make wommen myrie cheere,
>   And wilde felawis to-gidere drawe.

Music, drink, mock fights, and wild companions give way to pride, anger, gluttony, westling, and lechery as the man passes into adulthood. At forty and at fifty conscience begins to counsel him and health becomes a worry, but it is only at sixty that he thinks of mending his ways.[2]

Medieval parents and priests were not unobservant and realized that teenagers were not yet adults and were still in training for adult responsibilities. Criminal law directed that children over the age of twelve must be in a tithing group and could be held responsible for their criminal acts because they knew and comprehended the wrongfulness of their felonious deeds, but that age plateau did not apply to matters of inheritance. We should have little trouble understanding a legal system that makes young people legally culpable for criminal acts but does not bestow other responsibilities (such as voting) until later. Among the nobility twenty-one was well established as the age of majority for inheritance, but even among the peasantry formal entry into a tenement usually was delayed until the young person was at least twenty. At Halesowen an heir had to be at least twenty, and at Chalgrave and Wakefield twenty-one was the usual age. John, son and heir of Jordan of Tebworth, demanded his father's land because he was heir and of full age. The court found that he was twenty-one years old and could inherit. Sale of land was only legal when the holder had reached the age of majority. Thus Wakefield found that since Cecily, wife of John the Miller, was twenty-one when she sold land, the transaction was legal and her husband could not regain it. But as we have seen from wills, a parent might stipulate inheritance in the middle or, occasionally, late twenties. Youths also did not enter into village governance until they were in their twenties, and probably did not become jurors or reeves until about thirty.[3] Legal responsibilities, therefore, delineated a period between childhood and adulthood.

The accidental-death pattern both at work and at play shows that the teenage years were a time of transition. The youths, as we have seen, were learning adult occupations in husbandry and crafts, but their activities fell into the categories of both adults and children. At play, as well, though youths were learning adult games, they were not participating in adult contests. Thus a boy of thirteen was playing a game with the other village boys in which the object was to make an arrow glance off the ground. One arrow glanced up and hit him in the stomach. Other boys played with staffs, at mock fights, and at random target practice. But many youths often simply amused themselves, as children did, by playing in the water, either swimming, fishing, or trying to cross bodies of water by pole-vaulting or swinging on ropes. Henry Chirston of Sauston, aged fifteen, and Richard Almar of Sauston, thirteen, went to the river on a Sunday afternoon in late June 1337 and jumped into it to cool off. They were pulled downstream by the current.[4]

Teenagers played at ball games as well. William Fitz Stephen, writing in 1183, reported that the youth of London went out into the fields to play ball games and that the older men came out on horseback to watch "and after their fashion recapture their youth in the young . . . partaking of carefree joys."[5]

Games and other pastimes tended to be played only within a village age cohort. Teenagers, unless they were eighteen or nineteen, did not participate in adult games of archery, wrestling, and gambling. Although children and adolescents were not denied drink, all of the accidents involving drunkenness in which the age of the victim is mentioned show them to have been adults.

The destructive rowdiness of teenage males also appears in records. The first appearances of young males in manorial court rolls is usually for a trespass, assault, or property damage. For example, four young villagers of prominent families in Broughton were charged with a spree of vandalism including breaking a neighbor's windows and pushing open doors. The jurors were outraged at their behavior and called them "vagabonds," a completely inappropriate term but indicative of community censure.[6]

Although relations between siblings were a common matter at all stages of a person's life, the adolescent years often presented serious conflicts as concern over inheritance and sexual interests came to the fore. One exasperated widow, who had been married twice and had eight chidren, singled out two children for chief inheritances and made cash and goods settlements on the others with the provision that "if any are not satisfied with their share, their portions to be divided among they that be content."[7]

The widow had a good idea of the sorts of rivalries that could arise among siblings over inheritances, for countercomplaints of cheating were common in the courts. Typical is the case of Agnes, daughter of Juliana, who claimed that she deserved part of the oxgang that her father had settled on Juliana for her life and had directed to be divided among their surviving children on her death. Only two children survived, Agnes and Thomas, but Thomas claimed that when he was young his father took him to manorial court and transferred ownership to him. The court said that he was wrong and divided the land between the two siblings according to the dead father's wishes.[8]

Arguments over inheritances festered and could lead to violence. Since the reading of their father's will, Robert and Thomas le Parker had been arguing over a piece of land that their father had left to Thomas. Robert decided to force Thomas into a settlement. Taking two of his kinsmen to Thomas's house, he abducted Thomas to his own house, locked the door, and began to threaten him with a knife. Thomas tried to escape, but finding the door locked, he seized the knife from Robert and killed his brother in self-defense. Evidence from the manorial courts give a background to this particular type of dispute. For instance, in a Ramsey village the Porthos brothers, John Major and John Minor, were identified not only as belonging to one of the main families but as having had disputes with each other that appeared in manorial court. In 1333 these disputes between the brothers finally ended in an attack in which one brother was killed.[9]

Sibling rivalries could go beyond the struggles over inheritances. Ballads emphasized the small amount of property that could lead siblings to fatal fights. In one case two brothers argued over a willow wand. Such rivalries were not the stuff of legend alone, as in the case of two brothers who argued over a half-penny and fought until one brother killed the other. Another common ground for disagreement was selection of marriage partners. In some ballads a young sister marries before the older, uglier sisters, and this upsetting of birth order causes friction; or a brother is not consulted about a marriage. On Chalgrave manor John Saly took a wife against the will of his brother Walter. Walter defamed his brother to his wife's father "and said many outrageous things to the grave damage of the said John," for which John sued him.[10]

Another risk in sibling relationships is that they can be too intimate, even incestuous. We have noted that preachers urged parents not to allow brothers and sisters to sleep together as children for fear that they would get into incestuous habits. But actual prosecution of such cases was rare. Since incest was a moral matter, such cases fell to the jurisdiction of the bishop's court rather than manorial or royal courts. The possibility of committing such a deadly sin, either between brother and sister or parent and child, seems to have been somewhat of a preoccupation, if we may judge from literary references. In the *Breton Lays*, which enjoyed a broad popular audience, three of the stories involve mistaken identities and near-misses with incestuous relationships. Usually some garment indicated the true identity of the intended spouse before actual consummation of the marriage. In the ballads, however, incest did occur, and always with dire consequences. In "*The Sheath and Knife*" a brother gets his sister with child. Because of the shame involved, they go out to a deer park for the birth of the child, where both mother and child die in childbirth. In another popular ballad three girls on their way to church are accosted by a robber who demands sexual intercourse. The youngest says that she has a brother in the forest who will avenge her. The robber realizes that he is the brother and kills himself.[11] The literary interest in incest, however, did not spill over into reporting local cases to bishops.

Flirtation was very much a part of young people's lives and a subject of humor and condemnation in popular poetry. The writer of "A Little Sooth Sermon" complains about "those proud young men" and maidens who go to church and market "and talk light love and sly." When they are in church, they look around at each other and pay no attention to the mass or matins but think only of Wilkin and Watkin:

> Robin will Gilot
> Take to have ale:
> Sit there together
> And tell her a tale.
> He will pay for her drink
> And see to his game,
> At eve to go with him,
> She thinketh no shame.
> Her sire and her dame
> Threaten her to beat:
> She'll not forgo Robin
> For any threat.

But the poet says that "when her body showeth that childing is nigh," Robin will make excuses and not come near her.[12]

The poems emphasize both the joys of young love and the risks of being jilted or becoming pregnant. Occasionally they give a direct account of the sexual slang of the day, as does the poem "Our Sir John" (*Sir* was a title of respect for a priest):

ser Iohn loues me and i loue hym;
> the more I loue hym the more I maye

he says, "swett hart, cum kys me trym"—
> I have no powre to say hym nay.

ser Iohn to me Is proferyng
> for his plesure ryght well to pay

& in my box he puttes hys offryng
> [I have no powre to say hym nay.]

ser Iohn ys taken In my mouse-trappe
> ffayne wold I haue men bothe night and day.

he gropith so nysleye a-bout my lap,
> I have no powre to sa[y hym nay].[13]

The advice for the man who complained of being 'fagged out'' from too much sex was rest.[14]

The physical ideal of young beauty also appears in poems. A young girl speaking of her boyfriend, who is a servant, praises his clothing and appearance and comments that "his face yt is so lyke a man." His kiss is worth "a hundred pownde." In one poem a woman's physical beauty was described as abundant brown hair, black eyes, a slender and well-turned waist, and a lovely face.[15]

The flirtations and sexual activities among the village youths appears in records as well as poetry. A Berkshire squire of the early seventeenth century noted in his account book that he had gotten less malt from his barley than usual. He then recalled that one of his servants had been in love with Alice, the maid in charge of making malt. The distraction made her inefficient.[16] Coroners' inquests record the activities of young couples as well. Christine, over twenty years old, and Nicholas were joking together in the highway and throwing his knife back and forth between them when it came out of his sheath and stabbed her.[17]

Village rituals institutionalized flirtatious behavior. The youths of Croscombe in Somerset belonged to gilds called the Younglyngs, for young men, and the Maiden's Gild. The Maiden's Gild blocked the thoroughfares of the village and made the young men pay for passing. On the next day the Younglyngs did the same to the maidens. The proceeds went to support the parish church.[18] May Day was a fertility festival for youth. Village youths chose a king and queen of the May and performed the Morris Dance and the Robin Hood Games. In his moralizing, Robert Mannyng condemned the festivals in which young women gathered in fields, wearing garlands as crowns, and selected the fairest maiden. In his view, they were gatherings for lechery and pride. Caroling and dancing formed part of the youth celebrations, as one case from the Hundred Rolls shows. Some boys and girls were caroling for the prize of some doves. One of the boys singled out one of the girls as the best singer and gave her the doves. But the two men who had put up the prize disagreed and beat the boy.[19]

A vignette of daily interactions among village youths is preserved in two late-thirteenth-century coroners' inquests in Radwell and Chellington in Bedfordshire. After vespers on a November evening a group of young men and women—Edith, daughter of Thomas the Fisher; Geoffrey, son of William of Chellington; Thomas, son of John le Hode of Chellington; Agnes, daughter of Daniel Atwell; Alice, daughter of Hugh the Fisher; and Agnes, daughter of Walter the Miller—gathered by the river. Edith wanted to take them by boat across the river to her father's house. The boat was old, however, and sank when the four women got into it. The young men were able to pull out all the girls but Edith, who drowned. Alice, daughter Hugh the Fisher, was perhaps married by the next year, or at least had a separate house, for her brothers Simon and Richard, were coming from her house on the night of March 30, 1270, on their way to their father's house. They cut across the courtyard of Robert Ball of Radwell and apparently surprised two lovers, Simon, son of Agnes of Radwell, and Juliana, daughter of Walter the Fisher, in a haystack there. Simon rose out of the haystack and struck one of the brothers over the head with an ax.[20]

The dalliances could also lead to jealousies. Adam of Karlile of Peykirke and John Threscher argued over a serving girl whom John claimed to be his concubine. Adam killed John with a sword.[21]

It was not murder, however, that worried moralists about these flirtations and fornications, but rather the future of the sinners' souls. Robert Mannyng warned about "foule kissing" with the authority of one experienced in the art:

> Some maner [of] kissing is full of great vice
> And women's hearts to sin will tise
> And who so dalieth him therein
> Women to folly for to win.

He thought that the devil was behind such kissing.[22]

Assessing how widespread premarital sex was among village youth would seem initially an easy task, since lords fined young women for having intercourse before marriage or producing a baby out of wedlock. The first of these offenses brought a fine called legerwite (or lecherwite) and the second, childwite. Different manors and different bailiffs on the same manor administered these fines inconsistently. In Broughton the fines were collected fairly routinely, and thirty-four of the fifty-six fines of young women were for fornication or babies born out of wedlock (eight fornications and twenty-six babies). In Wakefield, on the other hand, legerwite was a rare fine except for one court session in January 1316. In this session it appears that all the young women were rounded up and fined for either being deflowered or married without license. Thus one finds entries such as "Juliana daughter of John Sibbeson, a neif, was deflowered before she was married and has not yet paid lechewytt nor merchet, 2s. Alice daughter of the same John, a neif, has been deflowered." The cases enumerate all pubescent girls in each family and amerce them. But this court session was unique and related to the lord's need for funds rather than a sudden decay of the moral fiber at Wakefield. In Halesowen legerwites, rather than birth out of wedlock, was the only fine. In seventy-eight years before the plague there were 117 legerwites but the number dropped to only 9 in the thirty-seven years following it. The dramatic drop is possibly attributable to earlier marriages and, hence, fewer cases of premarital sex, but it could also be a reporting phenomenon brought on by the general tendency of peasants to abandon the old fines that indicated servile status.[23]

In Broughton women accused of sexual lapses were concentrated in the upper and lower status groups. But in Halesowen daughters of the middling and particularly the poor families predominated in the charges of legerwites. The differences could be either regional or result from differing research methods in assessing a family's status. In any case, such data are difficult to interpret. Fornication can represent sex as a prelude to marriage, or it might indicate that these young women had to delay marriage, if not sexual activity, until they were better situated financially.[24]

Ecclesiastical court cases suggest that society took a casual attitude toward premarital sexual encounters. In one case, for instance, a woman was cited as having had sexual relations with three different men. An ecclesiastical inquiry found that Stephan Gobat had agreed to marry Juliana Bigod in accord with a sentence by the bishop. But he later claimed that he could not marry her because of an affinity arising from Juliana's early sexual relationships with William Attemore. Stephan claimed he was related to William by a prohibited degree of consanguinity. Almost a year later another young man, Stephan Pertefeu, claimed that he had a marriage contract with Juliana. Meanwhile, however, Gobat had decided that his marriage to Juliana was legal, that he was not related to William Attemore, and that his marriage predated Juliana's contract with Pertefeu. Juliana's marriage to Gobat was nullified on the grounds of his affinity to Attemore, and Pertefeu was her legal husband. It was also not uncommon for two women to claim sexual consummation of a marriage with the same man.[25] Although virginity before marriage was a common concern of moralists, it apparently did not worry prospective husbands.

The number of premarital pregnancies and illegitimate births among medieval English peasants is also impossible to know. In Broughton, if the courts accurately reported all children born out of wedlock, twenty-six cases appeared in fifty-two years. Studies of the sixteenth century, based on parish registers, indicate that premarital pregnancies were relatively infrequent (13 to 26 percent of all marriages) and that bastardy was uncommon. The researchers have concluded that teenagers were less promiscuous in the sixteenth century than they were in later centuries. Later studies have also shown that for most of these women a premarital pregnancy was a prelude to marriage and that conception may, indeed, have been necessary for the marriage to take place. Children were so important to the economy that a couple wanted to be sure of fertility before entering into a marriage. But some women had two or more illegitimate children, suggesting that a small subset of village women routinely engaged in illicit sex.[26] The stigma of an illegitimate birth for either the mother or the child need not have been very strong in peasant society.

A coroners' inquest preserves the community sentiments toward one unwed mother. Johanna, daughter of Alice of Fordham, was "secretly pregnant" and gave birth in the middle of the night to a female infant. The infant died without baptism, but there is no hint from the jurors that it was killed. What they did object to was Johanna's subsequent action. She "shamefully took the infant and put it at the door of Thomas King in his croft." He was apparently the father, but the village found her way of indicating that fact reprehensible.[27]

Ballads, however, illustrate some of the problems of premarital sex and pregnancy for young women. In "Gill Brenton" the young bride was worried on her wedding night because she was not a virgin; she had had previous sexual relations with a man in the forest. She tried to substitute her maid for herself but was discovered. The groom's mother, however, found out that her son was the one who raped the bride in the forest and that she was already with child by him. The couple were happily united and expecting their first child. In "Willie's Lyke-wake" Willie had been unable to get his sweetheart to marry him, so his understanding mother suggested that he pretend to be dead. The sweetheart came to the wake and he grabbed her and put her between himself and the wall (a sexual position that appears in other ballads as well). She begs that he desist, but he maintains that he will not send her home until she is with child. He left her few options to an eventual marriage. But some of the young women in ballads gave themselves to their lover only to be told afterward that he had a wife and five to seven children at home. The number of is offspring is always large, thus demonstrating his sexual prowess and the hopelessness of her position.[28]

Young peasants going through their adolescence had one foot in childhood and one in adulthood. They were still tied to their families, for the first finder was still usually a parent. By their late teens they engaged in flirtations and, the evidence suggests, in sexual contacts. For peasant youth who would come into property marriage was a more serious matter and the free love of adolescent years had to be put aside for more serious considerations of a suitable match. Whether rich or poor, male or female, the most important *rite de passage* for peasant youth was marriage.

Discovering who the young men and women married is as difficult as finding out their age of marriage. Did they marry within their villages? Did they make their own choices or accept the dictates of their parents or a lord? The manorial court rolls usually only indicated that a merchet (fine to the lord for a woman's marriage) was paid toward the marriage of a peasant woman, and only rarely does the prospective husband's name appear. The *Liber Gersumarum* of Ramsey Abbey gives some indication of marriage arrangements. Of the 194 cases in which the husband is known and his residence given, 41 percent were outsiders. Ecclesiastical court cases, which list both names in a disputed marriage, do not provide conclusive evidence on the percentage of endogamous compared to exogamous marriages but indicate that perhaps as many as two-thirds could be from the same village.[29]

The popular poetry of the day discouraged freedom of choice in marriage. "Mutatis Mutandis," a fifteenth-century poem, deplored that

> Self-will is taken for reason,
> True love for fancy chooseth
> And no man thinketh shame.[30]

Such moralistic preaching against freedom in marriage selection is a sure sign that a noticeable number of young people were choosing their own mates. But the prevalance of youth selecting their own spouses must have been limited, even though the Church argued that both parties had freely to consent to a marriage.

In developing the consensual theory of marriage, it would appear that the Church was offering a theory of matrimony that left to the individual the final choice of a marriage partner and excluded the control of family, feudal lord, or king. The consensual theory stated that

a marriage could only be considered canonically valid if both parties
freely consented to it. It was a short step from consensual theory to
accepting private or clandestine marriages as valid. The dangers of
abuse were apparent, and sermons and synods spoke against secret
marriages contracted against the wishes of responsible parties. The
solution was to require that the parish priest read the banns at an
interval before the marriage (three weeks in England) so that nyone
who had objections to the marriage could raise them. The usual
objections were consanguinity, prior contract, or marriage of one of the
parties. If no one raised objections after the banns were read, the priest
married the couple at the church door. The advantage of the banns and
ceremony at the church door was that the marriage could be publicized
and thereby curb some of the abuses of clandestine marriage, such as
bigamy.[31]

Clandestine marriages, however, were canonically valid, for all that
was needed was for both parties to agree to the marriage. Thus one
comes across such pathetic cases in the consistory court as that of John
Borewelle and Margaret Stistede. John claimed that he promised to
marry Margaret if his family (*parentes*—but on another questioning he
used the word *amicorum*) agreed and they then had sexual intercourse.
Margaret affirmed that he had promised marriage and that they had
had sexual intercourse, but denied that he had put any condition on the
marriage agreement.[32] With such informal arrangements constituting
legal marriage, young people could easily contract marriages without
parental consent, and sometimes contracted them to their regret, as
bigamy cases indicate.

Family and friends, however, did play a major role in arranging
marriages, especially if land and other wealth accompanied the union.
The parents and other siblings in the families had a concern in the
marriage, and the lord also wished to keep some accounting of village
marriages. In cases where the marriage was part of the family's
economic and social strategy, careful planning by the whole unit was
needed, for a good marriage could bring considerable economic benefits. The prospective bride and groom also had an economic stake in a
marriage contract, because it would determine not only who their life
partner would be, but also how well they could expect to live. To marry
for love without land or chattels could assure nothing but a life of
penury.

Because the family had such strong vested interests in marriage,
strategy became all important. A good example is Alwin of High Easter,
a half-virgater, and his placement of his five sons. He managed to marry
two of them to heiresses inheriting half-virgates. Another son married a

widow with a dower of half a virgate, and the fourth son took over the paternal holding. While Alwin paid the merchet for the marriages, he had to purchase land for only the fifth son. One does not imagine that these sons protested their father's efforts to find them wives who brought them land. Fathers of daughters were also willing to make comfortable marriage arrangements for them at considerable expense to the family. Richard Young in Berkshire held thirty-eight acres in the common fields in addition to other pieces of land. He had four children who had to be provided for out of family capital. One son, of course, inherited. A second son was sent to school and returned in the exalted position of steward. A daughter, Felicia, was given a large dowry of nine marks and married off the manor. In the next generation the pattern repeated, with one son becoming priest, a daughter making a very favorable marriage, and the land passing on to another son. Fathers of heiresses had even greater reason to select their sons-in-law with care, because they would take over the family land and perhaps care for them in their old age. Even poorer families with only a few acres made the best marriage arrangements they could for their children. If the parents were dead, it was incumbent upon the inheriting son to arrange marriages for his siblings.[33]

Marriage contracts involved detailed planning. Sometimes they would be planned far in advance, with ernest money put down toward keeping the terms. The delicate negotiations could come to naught because the young man had sown his wild oats with a kinswoman and the marriage could not take place because of consanguinity. John Love, for instance, wanted to take up a vacant holding, but could not afford the entry fee of £3. Agnes Bentley offered to pay the fine if he married her daughter Alice. He had to turn down this attractive offer because he had already had sexual intercourse with one of her kinswomen. Another woman, Agnes Smith, was so desirable a marriage match that John Tolle gave her 24s. to reserve herself for marriage to him. He claimed that she agreed to return the money if there was an impediment to the marriage. But when it transpired that he had sexual relations with one of her kinswomen, she refused to return the money and the marriage was not permitted. In a breach of promise case, however, the partners to the contract expected the earnest money to be returned, and Alice Sourhale successfully challenged Henry Poket for detaining 4s. 8d., which he had promised her if she withdrew from the marital suit.[34]

With the family making as generous provisions as they could toward the marriage of their children and providing them with a standard of living they had become accustomed to at home, one would expect that most of the young people consented to the arrangements and probably took part in them. If one looks at ecclesiastical court cases, very few cite force and fear as a grounds for divorce. In the eighty-four divorce cases in a study of the Ely diocese courts from March 1374 to 1384 only three people claimed that they were forced into their marriages. Force and fear were also rare grounds for divorce in Canterbury and York. One daughter complained that her father said that he would break her neck if she did not agree to marry the young man of his choice. Another was threatened with being taken by her ears and thrown into a pool if she did not consent to an arranged marriage. Sometimes there was every indication of impending violence. One woman complained that her family brought staves to the marriage contract ceremony, but her family maintained they had only used them for getting over ditches on the way to the ceremony. On the whole, the courts were not lenient in such matters and tended to uphold the validity of the marriage.[35]

Not all young people, however, had marriages arranged for them. Some were from poor families who had nothing to negotiate and hence would either not marry or marry whom they pleased. Others were younger sons and daughters and not part of the family's economic strategy and, therefore, had a greater independence. It is even possible that in times of land shortage, family interference in marriage was less common because they had nothing with which to bargain. Thus the Irish peasants before the potato famine did not make elaborate arrangements for marriages because they had little property, and children married whom they wished. After the migrations and deaths from famine, elaborate negotiations for marriage became common.[36]

The merchet payments from Ramsey Abbey's *Liber Gersumarum* show the peasant marriage market at work. While the document does not record all marriages between 1398 and 1458, and is therefore not complete, the 426 merchet cases recorded present the broad outline of interested parties in marriages and the amounts they paid for merchet. The bride's father paid in 33 percent of the cases, and the bride paid the merchet in the same percentage of cases. The bridegroom paid in 26 percent of the cases, and another person, such as the bride's mother, paid in 8 percent of the cases. Four categories of licenses appeared in the records. The most typical (37 percent) was for a naif (villein) of the village to marry another naif of the same village. Licenses to marry people outside the village comprised 26 percent, and marriage to a freeman constituted 16 percent. In all these cases the groom was specified. But in 21 percent of the cases only a general license to marry was purchased.

When the father paid the merchet, he had probably arranged the marriage and used family funds for both the merchet and the daughter's dowry. In only 28 percent of these cases did a father pay the merchet for a general license for his daughter to marry whom and when she pleased. Bridegrooms, of course, paid for licenses to marry specific women, who were apparently heiresses or were bringing large dowries with them, for the bridegrooms tended to pay a higher merchet for their brides. But of the women purchasing their own merchets, 54 percent purchased general licenses. These general licenses that women procured for themselves cost less than the fines that their fathers paid, indicating that a large dowry was not involved. Furthermore, the fact that the young women were asked to produce pledges to guarantee that they would pay the merchet indicates that their credit standing was not very good. These young women did not rely on their families to select their marriage partner, or even asked for family money to pay the merchet, but used money from wages they had earned independently as servants.

The evidence suggests that while most young women had marriages arranged for them, one-third may have had free choice in selecting husbands. If one looks at the types of licenses these independent young women purchased (with a few exceptions, these women were not widows but making first marriages), they show considerable initiative. Only 22 percent paid to marry a naif of the same village, compared to 40 percent among those whose fathers paid; 18 percent of these women married outsiders, compared to 31 percent when the fathers paid; and 28 percent paid to marry a freeman, compared to 15 percent in marriages arranged by the father. The rest bought general licenses.[37] Apparently the young women sought independence not only from family but from the village. They probably met the freemen in the course of their employment away from the family.

The marriage to freemen might have been a revolt against the other party who claimed control over marriages, the lord. The lord's control over marriages and the charging of merchet has been the subject of much recent debate. The origins of the fine need not detain us here, but it is important to know who or what was taxed. Some scholars have argued that it was a tax on people marrying, while others have argued that it was a tax on goods and land transferred at marriage. All agree that it did not constitute an effort on the lord's part to intervene in the marriage arrangements of his peasantry. What appears from these surveys of merchet on various manors is that it was a levy that was not routinely applied to all villein girls, for some were too poor to pay. The levy tended to be higher when the peasant was wealthier, and in these cases the explicit transfer of land was frequently mentioned. Thus the merchet was a combination of a marriage tax and land transfer fee.

Since the tax varied, it is possible that it depended on the value of dowry, but such evidence is difficult to find explicitly in the records. On the whole, the amount of tax was not high, 3d. to 4s. being typical, but it was certainly an annoying encumbrance on the family economy at a time when they were also dividing family wealth. It was, further, a reminder of their servile state and the power of their lord. Like many other onerous fees of serfdom, merchet gradually disappeared in the fifteenth century.[38]

A crucial question, however, is whether or not the lord extended his power beyond a simple pecuniary charge on marriages and large dowries to dictating or approving a choice of marriage partner. The lords had reason to be interested in the marriages of their tenants' daughters and widows. If a daughter married outside the manor or married a freeman, the lord stood to lose a potential worker and producer of serf children. If an heiress or widow married, the lord might well be interested in the quality of the man who was to take charge of her land, for he would lose profits if the land was not productive. The Ramsey Abbey materials indicate that when land was involved in the dowry, the merchet was higher and usually the groom paid it.[39] But evidence of a lord's direct intervention in a tenant's marriage plans are rare. One finds the lord urging marriage on a tenant, usually a bachelor or widow, but not directing whom the person should marry. In one case a lord required a man to marry a particular widow, but the man found the situation so distasteful that he left the manor. Whatever the lord's intervention in peasant marriages, it seemed to have been largely confined to financial exactions rather than actual impositions of his choice of partner.[40]

Marriage for love has traditionally been assumed to be the dubious privilege of those without property. The lord would not bother to impose a merchet, parents would have no property to bestow and thus have no control, and the Church would not dissolve a marriage even if all the young couple did was to agree to marry while lying together in a haystack. When a young woman, through her initiative and wages, managed to accumulate a bit of chattels and land and paid her own merchet, she could choose her own marriage partner. But the freedom in choice of marriage partner may have been a larger phenomenon, going far beyond those without property. Evidence from the Ely bishop's court may indicate a widespread acceptance among the populace, as well as the clergy, of a more individualistic interpretation of the rules of free consent in marriage. Thus, while historians have traditionally given parents and lords decisive influence over marriages, the cases coming before the consistory court seldom mention these authority figures but concentrate instead on the individual's actions and decisions.[41]

Medieval culture was largely an illiterate one, and public ceremonial, symbols, and celebrations did not simply provide entertainment but also publicized important events such as marriage. Even in clandestine marriages, the couples reported some sort of ceremony and ritual, usually in the presence of witnesses. Thus when Alexander Wrighte and Isabel, daughter of Joan of Wisbech, were brought to the consistory court for marrying without benefit of clergy, they reported their marriage ceremony. Alexander asked Isabel if she would be his wife and she responded affirmatively. He pledged to marry her and then they joined hands. He endowed her with a kerchief and a little chest. Other couples mention that the groom placed a ring on the bride's finger. Witnesses attested to the marriage contract and the ceremony that united the couple.

If the family and the couple chose to do the ceremony under the auspices of the Church, however, the families of the bride and groom would make the financial arrangements, and when both sides were satisfied, a betrothal took place. Next the banns were read in the parish church. After the three weeks' delay to allow for objections, the couple, their families, and friends would proceed to the church doors. At this stage, dower and dowry would be announced. The dower usually guaranteed the wife rights to a portion or the whole of her husband's property after his death, while the dowry that the wife brought to the marriage was usually money, chattel, or small pieces of land. Ritual words would solemnize their marriage. The vows have a familiar ring, but the woman's is explicit about the sexual duty of marriage:

> *Man:* I take the N. to my wedded wif, to haue and to holde, fro this day forwarde, for bettere for wors, for richere for pourer in sycknesse and in hele, tyl dethe us departe, if holy chyrche it woll ordeyne, and thereto y plight the my trouthe.

> *Woman:* I take the N to my wedded housbonde, to haue and to holde, fro this day forwarde, for better for wors, for richer for pourer in sicknesse and in hele, to be bonere and boxom, in bedde and atte bord, tyll dethe vs departhe, if holy chyrche it wol ordeyne, and therto I plight the my trouthe.

The rings are then blessed and exchanged and the words "with this ring I thee wed and with my body I thee honor" are spoken.[42] If the priest could persuade the wedding party to partake of a bit more religious ceremony to sanctify the marriage sacrament, they proceeded into the church and heard mass. But the clergy complained that peasants would not take the further and unnecessary ritual.[43]

Marriages were festivals, and although we have no descriptions of marriage feasts and revels, contemporary moralists often provide a clue to the usual proceedings:

> Further we enjoin that marriage be decently celebrated, with
> reverence, not with laughter and ribaldry, not in taverns or at
> public drinkings and feastings. Let no man place a ring made of
> rushes or of any worthless or precious material on the hand of a
> woman in jest that he may more easily gain her favours lest in
> thinking to jest the bond of marriage be tied. Henceforth let no
> pledge of contracting marriage be given save in the presence of a
> priest and of three or four respectable persons summoned for that
> purpose.[44]

The warning was justified, for in at least one case members of the
wedding party got into a brawl during the postnuptial festivities. Among
the guests at the wedding feast might be a representative of the lord as a
symbol of his rights over marriages.[45]

One reason wedding feasts became boisterous was that they occurred in the flush seasons or during months of revelry. The most
popular months were January (the saturnalia month of fertility rites)
and October and November (the harvest and butchering feasts).
Summer months when the new crops were coming in were also popular.
In general, agrarian communities tended to tie marriages more closely to
the agricultural calendar than the woodland or pasture communities.
The Church prohibited marriages during Lent, Rogationtide, and
Advent through Christmas. This eliminated about eighteen to twenty
weeks, or about a third of the year. Early sixteenth-century data show
that both marriages and conceptions were less numerous during these
weeks, indicating a fair degree of compliance.[46]

And so the young people are led to the marriage bed, the final stage
of this *rite de passage*. They are probably in their twenties when they
contract this first marriage, and they probably have some land, even if it
is only a few acres, or they have a trade or employment as manorial
servants. They have known a period of adolescence and they have had
their flirtations; they may very well have had sexual experiences before
marriage and might even be expecting their first child. They may have
married for love, but probably not if land and property were involved.
Some of their friends and siblings who participated in the celebrations
might remain celibate all their lives, but probably not many if they
stayed in the village community. After all, marriage was so easy to
contract that lusty young people had to be careful not to make more
than one marriage commitment.

13

The Partnership Marriage

Marriage moved young people into the adult word of childrearing and establishing a family economic unit centered on the labor of husband and wife—a marriage partnership. But in addition to these practical matters of married life, medieval people of all ranks discussed, theorized, advised, and analyzed what made good and bad marriages and what virtues and vices husbands and wives might have. No stage of life attracted so many moralizers, satirizers, misogynists, and old wives with their store of tales than did matrimony. Discussions of childhood and old age paled in comparison. The lore of marriage with all its platitudes and theological implications receives a brilliant and humorous summation in Chaucer's "Prologue to the Wife of Bath's Tale." From the wit of Alison we learn the male proverbs and diatribes against the fickleness of women, their shrewish tempers, and the bottomless pit of their lust. But the Wife of Bath also knows the women's proverbs, such as "lies, tears and spinning are the things God gives by nature to woman, while she lives," and adds some advice on how to use at least the first two to control husbands.[1] No doubt this vivid pulpit and folk wisdom influenced attitudes toward marriage, but it probably came to the fore in people's lives only when a shrew, a wife beater, or a faithless spouse in the village exemplified the lessons. In investigating peasants' actual experiences with marriage, both case studies and folklore will occupy us in this chapter. Most married couples, occupied with the problems of daily living, had little time to analyze the happiness of their union. To have sufficient daily bread, raise worthy children, avoid sickness, and put by a bit for retirement would make most marriage partners feel blessed.

Two dominant traditions on marital relations emerge from the folk and ecclesiastical literature and remain with us to this day. One is the war between the sexes as described in the Wife of Bath's prologue. Women bring to the battle their abilities to intimidate and manipulate men through scolding, crying, and withholding sexual favors. Faced with the wiles of women, a husband's resource was physical brutality— wife beating:

> ... a woman to regrayne is not posybyll
> With wordes, except with a staffe thou hyr intrett;
> For he that for a faut hys wyff wyl not bett
> Wherein sche offendyt hym very mych,
> That gyder of hys hows mus nedes wer no brych.[2]

Other poems advocate a reversal of roles, with the wife beating the husband. The weaponry and battles in the war between the sexes always had a comic side, a recognition that such marital discords occurred but that they were neither the most desirable nor very common. Thus the carvings of wives beating their husbands that appear on misericords are meant for good fun rather than instruction.

Admonitions to practice physical and emotional bludgeoning were amply balanced in poems and books of advice by the second tradition, recommending good judgment and mutual respect. Myrc's *Instructions for a Parish Priest* suggests that the priest ask his parishioner in confession if he has helped his wife and "meyne" when they have needed it and refrained from causing strife with his wife.[3] Such lessons also appear in instructional poems such as "How the Wise Man Taught His Son." The father advises his son not to marry for money but to make enquiry about his prospective wife to find out if she is meek, courteous, and wise. If you find such a woman, he says, you should cherish and not burden her, for it is better to eat homely fare in peace than have a hundred fine dishes served with strife. Likewise, a husband should not anger his wife or call her bad names, but correct her faults with fairness and gentleness. He should take his wife's side when she has a complaint, but not until he has examined the matter, for if he acts too swiftly they may both regret it. The companion piece, "How the Good Wife Taught Her Daughter," echoes the advice. A woman should not scorn proposals, but should consult with her friends about the marriage. The key to a happy marriage was to love and honor one's husband above all earthly things and meet his moods with "fair" and "meek" words. Beyond these basics the good wife recommended being cheerful, faithful, respectable in public, and managing the household tasks and servants with good order and firmness.[4] In short, the good wife would have condemned the Wife

A common perception of the middle ages is that men beat their wives, but the usual illustration was the reverse of the stereotype. Medieval people found these inversions of roles amusing. [The British Library, Lutterell Psalter.]

of Bath's recommendations on all points except managing money well.

Literature and manuals of morality speak of both marital strife and accommodation, but if we want to know about the actual behavior, we must go to the court records. Some caution is in order when looking at court records, for the cases that tend to stand out after a casual reading are those of brutality and adultery. When a salacious reading informs researchers, we get such books as *Before the Bawdy Court* and *Wanton Wives and Wayward Women.*[5] The vast majority of cases appearing in manorial courts, however, are those that show husbands and wives in cooperative activities. They are the inheritance cases that we have already observed of the husband ensuring the wife's right to his family holding by surrendering it to the lord and taking it back again in both his name and hers; or it is a case of the bridegroom paying the merchet for his new wife; of wills in which the wife is left the executor of the estate. In economic matters we have seen the husband and wife working for the family unit in house and field, and coroners' inquests have depicted husband and wife at their tasks or taking their evening meal together when a child drowns or an accident befalls them.

The very routine nature of these cases, revealing a mundane life for husbands and wives, lulls the reader into ignoring them; thus the relatively few cases of marital discord tend to stand out. In the criminal court cases, however, only 0.7 percent of all felonies involved indictments of one family member committing a crime against another. In homicides alone in the coroners' inquests, family was suspected in only 8 percent of the cases. Husbands and wives were the most common familial relations cited in such cases and accounted for half of the intrafamilial cases, or only 4 percent of all cases. Husbands predominated as the killers in such cases. Even the argument that familial disputes were more likely to stop short of criminal actions does not find support in court records, for in manorial courts family accounted for a low percentage (2 percent) of recorded discord. While assault predominated over debt and trespass as charges against members of the same family, it was brothers rather than spouses who tended to come to blows or litigation.[6]

Communities tried to exert pressure on the wife abuser and the scold, because they disturbed the peace of the village. Thus, in Wakefield in 1332, the jury directed Richard Childe to find pledges that he would "receive his wife in his house and treat her agreeably and provide for her faithfully and courteously to the best of his ability." Other times it was the family of the wife that intervened. Thomas Assholff sued John de Scoles, saying that they had agreed for half a mark of silver that John would find Thomas's daughter Ellen food and clothing. But John drove her out of the house and beat her, so that she could not remain. John countersued, saying that she had taken all the goods and chattels with her. In a coroner's case a battered wife called out to her brother to stop her husband from beating her. The brother rushed into the house and permanently stilled her husband's upraised fist with a blow from a hatchet. Help was not always so forthcoming for the battered woman. One man beat his wife severely with a staff on the arms, legs, back, and head. He waited to see if she would die from the beating, and when she did he fled to his father's house in Salisbury.[7]

Jealousy and infidelity also brought discord to family and community. Robert Mannyng urged men and women not to indulge in jealousy, for it was sure to cause strife. But adulterers had to be punished. The Wakefield manor court summoned John Kenward of Hepworth to account for living adulterously with Alice, daughter of Simon de Hepworth, and driving his wife from his house. The matter was obviously one demanding severe community sanction, for he paid a heavy fine of 6s. 8d. for not appearing in court. Another man accused of living with a harlot paid 40s. Women as well as men were cited for their wayward lives. The wife of Thomas de Langsfeld not only committed adultery with John del Risseleye but also fled the village with goods belonging to her husband.[8]

Sexual infidelities are a classic scenario for murder. John Edwyne of Weld and Emma, the former wife of William le Carpenter and concubine of John, were convicted in Huntingdonshire of murdering William. They were not poor, for the crown confiscated 13s. 6d. in chattels from him and 27s. 5d. from her. It was more common, however, for the husband to kill the wife and/or the lover. Robert le Bauserman killed John Doghty when John came to his house at night while Robert was asleep and had a secret rendezvous with Robert's wife. When Robert awakened and found his wife was not at his side but with John in the other room, an argument ensued in which John was killed.[9]

Long-standing incompatibility and the problems of separation and child support entered into homicide cases as well. Often when records mention separate residences for husband and wife, it is an indication that they had been living apart before the murder. In a few cases the problems were more explicitly spelled out, as in this argument over child support:

> On the night of 29 March 1271 Walter le Bedel of Renhold came to the house of his wife, Isabel daughter of Reynold, in Ravesden and asked her to come with him to Renhold to get a bushel of wheat which he wished to give her for her boys, and she went with him. When they reached "Longmead" meadow, he immediately struck her over the left ear apparently with a knife, giving her a wound three inches long and in depth to the brain.

He threw her body into a ditch afterward.[10]

Although economic necessity forced many a man and woman to put up with an ill-tempered spouse, there were, in fact, few ways to rid oneself of a lazy or disloyal mate. The Church courts regulated divorce within a very narrow interpretation of the law. The bond of matrimony, while less valued than virginity and celibacy among the ecclesiastical theorists, was not easy to break. As Helmholz observes in his discussion of divorce, "the most striking fact about divorce litigation is how little there was." Only six grounds for divorce appear in the English ecclesiastical court records. We have already seen that marriage among children and marriages in which one party claimed force and fear as a reason for dissolution of marriage were rare, probably a sign that the society shared the Church's repugnance for such alliances. The difficulties of proving consanguinity and affinity discouraged people from using them as grounds for divorce. A man and woman who lived adulterously while one or both had a living spouse could not marry, and if they did so, the Church divorced them. Such cases, however, rarely appeared in the church court records. But the possibility of bigamy and precontract, when consent was the only requirement for a valid marriage, led to considerable confusion and grounds for divorce.[11]

Precontract was by far the most frequent ground for divorce or investigation of the legality of a marriage. The ecclesiastical court carefully investigated such cases, because opportunities for collusion were obvious. One party would enlist the help of a third party to swear to prior contract in order to get the marriage dissolved. In one blatant case in Ely, William Chilterne, who had been married to Amicia Nene at the church door two years before, claimed that he was already married and his marriage to Amicia was not valid and had been inspired "from malice towards her that had grown in him." Joan Squire colluded with him in the archdeacon's court, claiming both precontract and children from the union, and the court annulled the marriage between William and Amicia. As it later came out, however, Joan soon married another man. The court then reversed itself and declared the marriage of William and Amicia valid from the first.[12]

Consent made a marriage valid, but if the parties could not consummate a marriage, divorce could be granted. After three years of marriage, one of the couple could bring suit. Because of the possibility of deceit, the court might require a physical examination of the woman by "honest women" to see if she was a virgin. In York and Canterbury records, seven "honest women" were instructed to test the man in the suit. One witness "exposed her naked breasts, and with her hands warmed at the same fire, she held and rubbed the penis and testicles of the said John." She embraced and kissed him in an attempt to arouse him and admonished him that he "should then and there prove and render himself a man." But she told the court that the whole time the penis remained a mere three inches long. She and her six female companions then left, after cursing the man for his failure.[13]

The Church, for the most part, tried to preserve marriages and ensure marital validity of sexual unions between a man and a woman. In the matter of prostitution, however, the Church could only condemn. Robert Mannyng admonished men to take only one woman and not a woman who takes many men. A curious practical warning accompanies this advice, that one can get "meseles" (in the original French version it was leprosy) from prostitutes.[14] In view of the controversy over the Old or New World origins of venereal diseases, one wonders exactly what these sex-linked diseases were, but perhaps the moralist was simply threatening sinners with a pox.

In cases of concubinage, the Church acted to legitimate the union if there were no impediments. Usually such cases were decided in court and the couple were either declared married already or they were told to make suitable arrangements. But the parties could be recalcitrant. In March 1376 Thomas Barbo and Joan Seustere, his mistress, were summoned to Ely for an inquiry about consent to marriage and subsequent intercourse. Joan claimed that they were married the previous year at Stourbridge Fair and asked that Thomas be declared her husband. Thomas disputed her story. He said that before the feast of the Exaltation of Holy Cross at the fair, he had told her that their affair was over. When he learned that she was going away, however, he was so depressed that he wanted to kill himself. He came in tears to Joan and the court recorded his version of the conversation. "Joan, if you will stay here, I will be true to you," he declared, and Joan replied that she wanted to stay. Then Thomas said, "Joan, I give you my word that I wish to have you," and Joan replied that she was content. They then had intercourse as before. But Thomas maintained that he did not intend a contract of marriage, but only to have her as a mistress. The court arranged a compromise, getting Thomas to swear that if he had intercourse with her again he would have her as a wife. Twenty-five months later, Joan won her case. Thomas apparently could not live without her.[15]

Although dedicated to preserving the sacrament of marriage, the Church realized that adultery, cruelty, and heresy could make a marriage intolerable for one or both partners and that a judicial separation might then be in order. Acting in this capacity the clergy were more like marriage counselors trying to arrange amicable settlements, than judges. Few cases of separation appear in ecclesiastical courts, an indication that the Church's net was not a wide one. Take, for instance, the case of Robert Handenby and his wife, Margaret, who came to the York court in 1390. She sued for separation on the grounds of cruelty, but the court arranged that they try a reconciliation and "that [if] the aforesaid Robert shall in the future treat the same

Margaret badly, and this can be proved by two legitimate witnesses, then the aforesaid Margaret may effectively secure a divorce with respect to bed and mutual servitude between herself and the same Robert." The court often required the husband to guarantee his promise of good behavior with pledges or with goods and money. But not all cases ended in reconciliation. John Colwell and his wife asked the court for a separation because they lived in daily fear of their lives and would rather live in prison than together. When a separation was allowed, the Church would arrange a division of wealth and support for children of the union.[16]

Individual solutions to marital incompatibility eluded Church control even when they were blatant, so that the ecclesiastical courts are not a complete guide to marital discord. Hawisa, daughter of William, the son of Alexander, grew up in Sherington as the daughter of a well-to-do peasant. Her father married her to a man from another village and endowed her with property at that time. She deserted her husband, however, and lived with Thomas de Shirford. They had an illegitimate son, Richard, and then married and had another son and two daughters. Strictly speaking, the marriage was not licit because the couple were adulterers, but they ignored the reprimand of even such a great church leader as Robert Grosseteste. Lay authorities also ignored the irregular status of the marriage and permitted her son to claim her estate as legitimate heir.[17]

Although no one would argue that Margery Kempe had entirely normal views of sexuality, her autobiography does provide an intimate view of discontentment and mismatch in a marriage. She was the daughter of the mayor of Lynn and, therefore, from a well-to-do family. Her husband was of a lower status. Married at just over twenty years of age, she immediately became pregnant. Her pregnancy was difficult and she complained of being sick and having a very bad labor. These conditions appeared with the pregnancy of each of her fourteen children. Her husband was evidently a lusty man, continually seeking "fleschly comownyng" and "medelying with" her. She apparently did not enjoy his sexual advances and was tempted to have an affair with a man she loved. Gradually, however, her religious meditations led her to visions and she asked Jesus for help with her husband's sexual advances. The vision suggested that she fast on Fridays, which would give her one night off a week. Then, on Wednesday in the week of Easter, when her husband approached her, she said "Jesus, help me," and that stopped future intercourse.

Giving in to her religious enthusiasm, her husband accompanied her on a series of pilgrimages. As she explained it, they reached an agreement on chastity on "Friday in midsummer even in right hot weather as this creature [Margery] was coming from York bearing a bottle with beer in her hand and her husband a cake in his bosom." Her husband asked her if she would rather see him dead than let him "comown kendly" and "medele with" her again. She said that she would prefer to see him dead and reminded him that they had not had sexual relations for eight weeks. He claimed that it was because he was afraid of her. They stopped at a roadside cross and continued the discussion. He "clasp his wife unto him" and said "Margery grant me my desire and I will grant yours." His conditions for granting her permission to take the vow of chastity were that they should share the same bed, eat together on Friday, and she would pay all his debts. She consented; but finally they lived apart until he was old and senile and she took him in and nursed him.[18]

As if the difficulties betweeen husband and wife were not bad enough in-laws could create problems as well. In folklore and literature the mother-in-law dominates and oppresses her daughter-in-law. Rather typical is the Breton lay "Emaré." The husband goes off to service, leaving his pregnant wife in the care of his mother. His mother finally puts Emaré and the baby in a boat and sets them adrift in the sea. The motif reflects reality to the extent that the husband's mother would be the person most likely to be left living with a grown son and his family. But, as we shall see, such arrangements were distasteful to both parents and children, and the parents lived on their own as long as possible. The problem of in-laws seldom arose in court records and did not figure among homicides. Margery Kempe, for all her problems with marriage and her husband, was a kind mother-in-law. A son married a woman in Germany, but was devoted enough to his mother to bring his wife home to meet her. When the son died a month after their arrival, Margery kept her daughter-in-law and eventually traveled with her back to Germany, because she thought it inappropriate to let her travel on her own.[19]

The language of divorce and separation cases provides some insight into the roles that husband and wife were supposed to assume in marriage:

> Thomas Waralynton appeared and was sworn to treat Matilda Tripes his wife with marital affection with respect to bed and table, and to furnish her with those things which are necessary in food and other materials according to his ability. And the woman was sworn to obey him as her husband. . . .

The wife's duty to obey, and the husband's right to ensure that she did, was a cornerstone of the ideal marriage. One woman asked for a separation on the grounds that her husband had twice attacked her with a knife and inflicted wounds and a broken arm. The husband maintained that he had been reasonable and honest and had acted solely for the purpose of "reducing her from errors." The court agreed.[20]

The husband's responsibility to correct his wife was legally ensured. At the Chalgrave manor court the jurors "presented that Margery Himgeleys is a malefactor of the corn of others and henceforth her husband will punish her."[21] Law upheld the husband's commanding role over his wife, for the punishment meted out to a wife for killing her husband was that for treason rather than felony. She would be burned at the stake for killing her lord and master.

The exalted position of the husband, however, carried responsibilities with it as well. He had to be a good provider, within the limits of his wealth, and to treat his wife with affection. He must also be her defender. For instance, a woman on Wakefield manor asked damages from a man because he beat her. He did not deny the charge but said that he did so because she insulted his wife. Another man killed to defend his wife. Philip le Miller of Killyngworth broke into the house of Adam Rose at Navesby, raped his wife and abducted her to a field. Adam came to the rescue and killed Philip with a pitchfork. Robert Mannyng concluded his advice to men on how to treat a wife with the observation that there was no greater solace under heaven than having a loving wife.[22]

That marital discord occurred among the English peasantry is not disputable, but its extent cannot be known. In official records, both lay and ecclesiastical, marital problems play a surprisingly small role even compared to the sixteenth century. It is entirely possible that a wife or husband took a hard knock from a spouse from time to time, and that the neighbors would not complain as long as the situation was not routine. That the male was given a dominant role over his wife in law, and over women in general through office holding, does not automatically imply that he used his additional powers arbitrarily or viciously. Nor can we argue that marriages were short and perhaps brutish affairs terminated within ten years by the death of one partner. A person in his or her early twenties could expect to live twenty-five more years. Thus, while we might expect to see few fiftieth wedding anniversaries, the twentieith wedding anniversaries would be common. With that many years of potential commitment and with the importance of maintaining a smoothly functioning economic unit, it behoved the couple to get along with each other.

As is true of traditional peasant societies, a primary expectation of medieval peasants was that marriage would produce children who could eventually contribute to the household economy and, if the parents were fortunate, take care of them in their old age. Medieval peasants, as noted in the discussion of birth control, had at least an accurate folk knowledge about the process of conception and possibly contraception as well. Indeed, a repeated theme in popular verse was the dilemma of Mary:

> Mary Mother, well with thee!
> Mary Maiden, think on me!
> Mother and maid was never non,
> Together, lady, but thou alone.[23]

Mary was obviously a perplexing case, as was the rest of the Holy Family:

> Thou woman without peer,
> Didst thine own father bear
> Great wonder 'twas
> That one woman was mother
> To father and her brother—
> So never other was.[24]

In a society with vertical and horizontal kinship systems, the Holy Family appeared to have a circular one.

The more bawdy popular literature made the male's role quite clear, as in the poem about chapmen "who be light of foot and foul of ways":

> Damsel buy some ware of me
> I have a pocket for the occasion
> Therein be two precious stones
> Damsel had ye tried once.
>   Ye would rather go with me
> I have a jelyf of God's sending
> Without feet it can stand
> It can smite and hast no hand
>   Ask yourself what it may be.
> I have a powder for to sell
> What it is I cannot tell
> It maketh maiden's wombs to swell
>   Thereof I have a quantity.[25]

But some confusion about conception remained, for one folk belief was that if a woman had twins, she must have a lover in addition to her husband.[26]

Following conception of the child, the father had a small role, for childbirth was a women's ritual. Men were excluded from the birth chamber, and hence it is that the medical treatises and encyclopedias dealing with gynecology contain no actual descriptions of the birthing process. At most they mention breach births and cesarean sections.[27]

Folkloric sources are virtually the only ones with information on childbirth. They illustrate the taboo on having a man present and the anxiety of both sexes at breaking it. In the *Leesome Brand* the father offers to help with the birth, saying that he will bind his eyes, but the eleven-year-old prospective mother sends him off for water and bemoans the absence of a midwife when she gives birth in the forest. Normally a midwife would be present, as may be seen in various illustrations of the birthing chamber following birth.[28] The position of the woman during birth is moot. Sixteenth-century manuals suggest the use of a special chair (birthing stool) in difficult births to put the woman in an upright position. Two ballads, "*The Cruel Mother*" and "*Fair Janet,*" suggest a more primitive method used for births in the woods when there was not an attendant midwife. In "*The Cruel Mother,*" the mother-to-be went out to the woods and leaned with her back against a tree. In some versions she put her foot to a tree or to a stone. In "*Fair Janet*" she directs her lover as follows:

> Ye'll do me up, and further up
>   To the top of yon greenwood tree;
> For every pain myself shal hae,
>   The same pain ye maun drie.

It may well be that the birthing tree or a semicrouched position was used in medieval England even when the delivery did not take place in the wilderness. A medieval English treatise depicts a woman in labor pulling on a cord fixed to a beam above the bed.[29]

The first book directed at an audience of women appeared in England in the early fifteenth century. It is possible that it was written by a woman and certain that it was written for women because it preserves the secrecy of the ritual of childbirth, declaring that a man should only look at the book if he must aid in a birth. It describes a natural birth as one in which the child comes out, head first, in twenty pangs or within those twenty. It also gives detailed and, on the whole, practical instructions on procedures for difficult childbirth and recommends the proper herbs, baths, and so on for a variety of gynecological problems.[30]

Childbirth was a risk for women, particularly if the mother was ill or the child lay in the wrong position. A forty-year-old woman appeared in the coroners' rolls because she died some time after her son was born. The neighbors told the coroner that she had had a difficult labor but had lived to be churched. She remained debilitated and died shortly thereafter. Because of the difficulties of labor and birth a number of folk customs grew up around childbirth to aid the woman. Childbirth, people thought, could be aided by opening chests, doors, or windows, unlocking chests, or shooting an arrow, all symbols of opening the womb. But in spite of the risks of childbirth, most women appeared to survive it, for the wills indicate that the overwhelming majority of men were survived by wives, usually their first.[31]

Following a birth, the Church honored the Old Testament rule that a woman was impure for six weeks and prohibited her from attending church. The churching of a woman was the final ritual of childbirth allowing the woman back into society. As Mary became increasingly central to religious ceremonial, the Feast of the Purification of Mary, or Candlemas, in early February became a major celebration and one particularly associated with married women.

Medieval records to not indicate that women were continually pregnant, nor do the folkloric sources contain laments on having too many pregnancies as they did in France. Some hints of problems come from Margery Kempe, who complained in her autobiography of her frequent and difficult pregnancies (fourteen children). Her experiences may have influenced her views of sexuality and her decision to take a vow of chastity. The cumulative number of children for married women aged twenty to forty-four for 1550–1599 was 6.53 but it is difficult to know if this figure is also representative of earlier centuries.[32]

Other than producing children, married life mostly meant hard work in the woman's space of the home and the man's space of the field. But there was time for conviviality and games. As we have seen, some of these activities were divided by age cohort and, often, by sex as well. Archery contests and bull baitings were pastimes for adult males; and a tightrope walker who was balancing on a rope tied between two trees was described as being a man over forty. Only adult males participated in organized wrestling matches, and men of the village had football games as well. Thomas Sharp of Easton, for instance, was playing football with the other men on a Sunday in January 1367 when he accidentally fell on the knife of one of the other players.[33]

In addition to physically active games, men in villages played games of cards and dice. Sumptuary legislation in the early fifteenth century tried to prohibit handball, football, dice, "coytes," stone throwing, skittles, and so on. Furthermore, there was to be no betting on football, cock fighting, and on the occasion of marriages.[34] Manorial courts tried to enforce the legislation. At Carshalton in 1446 Thomas Buxale and Robert Mordema were fined 12d. each for playing handball. Buxale did not desist and, along with eight other men, was fined at another meeting of the court. In 1447 eleven men were fined for playing ball. At Broughton three men were fined for play *alepenypricke* when they should have been performing their week-work for their lord.[35]

Accidents related to pastimes involving relaxation or play were rare, but men and women appear to have been equally at risk. Among men these accounted for 3.8 percent of their accidents, and among women, 4.4 percent. Needless to say, many of the pastimes and games were harmless and do not appear in the coroners' inquests.

Not all leisure activities kept the sexes separate. A number of private and village functions required the husband and wife to participate as couples. Gild membership and gild feasts, for instance, always involved husband and wife as well as their adult children. Religious festivals were times for the couple to relax together as a social unit. And there were the many dinners exchanged with neighbors. Medieval marriage partners did not live in that harsh world of separate social spheres that Stone has ascribed to plebs of sixteenth-century England and Shorter has shown for eighteenth-century France.[36]

In analyzing peasants' marriages, as we have, from the viewpoints of economic interdependence of the couple, legal prescriptions on marriage (both ecclesiastical and lay), folk theories, and actual practice, the modern descriptions of marriage in traditional society appear to be distortions. The majority of marriages do not fit Shorter's dismal picture of the "Bad Old Days" in which wives were dispensable or, at best, servants to their husbands. Hufton's work on eighteenth-century France dispels the notion that the wife's economic contribution to the household was considered unimportant. The coroners' inquests show medieval husband and wife sitting down at the table to eat together, and while the wife put the food on the table, she was not acting as a servant and did not stand behind her husband while he ate.[37] Husband and wife walked side by side in fifteenth-century England, as Margery Kempe and her husband did while discussing their irreconcilable differences. Nor is marriage among the plebs as devoid of companionship as Stone describes it. The separate spheres of work in home and field and the sex-specific games did not exclude couples from a range of mutual leisure activities. A married couple was not simply an economic unit in the eyes of society, but also a social and convivial one. One cannot measure the amount of affection between spouses from medieval evidence except that court cases show an absence of malice and a strong tendency to provide and support a wife's interests. Wills indicate a high degree of trust and even affection.

The patriarchal model of marital relationship is also not entirely applicable. To be sure, the law made it treasonous for a wife to kill her husband, but since the event was such a rarity the law must be viewed as an abstraction. The separate space for men's work and women's work did not denigrate the input of the wife relative to that of the husband, nor is there evidence that medieval peasant men thought so. In folk literature both husband and wife expressed the opinion that they worked harder than the other partner. Furthermore, a predominant father figure does not appear in suggestions on childrearing even though there was a golden oportunity to elevate paterfamilias to such a position in instruction books and homilies on the commandment to honor one's father and mother. Instead, the mother, like the Virgin Mary, was chiefly identified with childrearing.

The marriages, however, do not fall into the categories suggested for the modern marriage pattern. They were not the "companionate" ones Stone describes as characteristically modern nor the scenes of "domesticity" Shorter identifies. Husband and wife did not seek marriage for entertainment and consolation. They were not looking for some ideal of domestic bliss, even though their romantic stories also ended with "and they lived happily ever after."[38] But, equally, medieval peasant couples could not afford to go their separate ways in the marriage.

Partnership is the most appropriate term to describe marriage in medieval English peasant society. The partnership was both an economic and an emotional one. Marriage began with a contract outlining the economic benefits of the partners; the traditional roles for work guaranteed the effective functioning of the household unit; and the necessity of planning for the children's eventual marriage and, finally, the retirement of the couple made mutual planning desirable. Not all partnerships worked well, of course. In some the husband dominated to the wife's disadvantage, and in some, one or the other party failed to meet expectations; but the exceptions were not so numerous as to modify the ideal that couples should contribute their share to their partnership. It is not necessary to paint a foul picture of traditional peasant marriage in order to suggest that marriage is somewhat different in the modern period. Certainly, our high divorce rate gives us no grounds to consider the modern mode of marriage superior. Rather, we should look on the institution of marriage as a remarkably flexible one that adapts to meet the needs of the economic and social conditions prevailing at different times.

14

Widowhood

Medieval society ascribed few viable roles to single people. After childhood and adolescence most people would marry; the category of spinster, defined as an unmarried woman, was not a medieval one, and bachelor likewise carried a different meaning from its modern one. In the village context the two most notable categories of single heads of house would be widows and the local priest. One might wonder why widowers are not included in this category, but demographic studies and property-holding surveys make it quite clear that, then as now, women were more likely to outlive their husbands and less likely to remarry than men. An old peasant proverb noted that the household could survive without the husbandman but not without the good wife, and most men rushed into remarriage. For widows, however, the death of the husband brought a variety of new options and new independence, both economically and emotionally, that women could not achieve in any other phase of their life cycle. Widows were thrust into a new position, legally and personally, which gave them a greater role in planning their own future and that of their children. A widow could enter into land contracts on her own, could decide on marriage alliances for children, could make her own decisions about remarriage and whom she would marry. The new-found freedom, however, was not welcomed by all widows; some flourished and others suffered. But what is of interest to us is how peasant widows coped with this unique phase in their life cycle. We will leave aside elderly widows until the subsequent chapter and investigate here the lives of those women, still young or in their prime, who must manage as only half of the former partnership.

Medieval literary sources would lead us to believe that widows were poor and vulnerable. We are all familiar with Chaucer's portrait of the poor widow in the *Canterbury Tales*. But other writers also expressed disapproval over the poverty of widows and those who tried to deprive them of their rights. One lyric advised that a knight should "mayntene trouth and rightwysnes/And Hole Cherche and wedowes ryght."[1] As we have already seen, widows were very common in medieval England, and so the writers had reason to be concerned about them. But were they poor and vulnerable?

As we saw in the chapter on inheritance, widows could demand a third of their husband's property as dower or the husband could make more generous provisions for her through manorial court arrangements or through wills. Men could make several broad types of provisions for their widows: (1) give the widow all or part interest in the family landholding for life, (2) endow her either in a will or by dower with some land, housing, and goods, or (3) make provision with sons or others to see that the widow was honorably kept.

Nowhere is the mutual respect and sense of partnership in marriage better demonstrated than in men's provisions for their wives in manorial court or in wills. Through these directives they left the perpetuation of mutual responsibilities to their helpmate, and the majority did so with obvious trust. As we have seen, the wife was the most frequent executor of her husband's will, and moralists had no warnings against putting the wife in such a capacity, as they did against trusting offspring of the marriage. The variety and generosity of legal provisions for the continued maintenance of widows indicates that not only husbands, but society as a whole, regarded a wife's contribution to the home economy as highly significant and well worth rewarding after the death of her spouse.

In manorial court rolls one frequently reads that a husband and wife reverted their tenement to the lord and made fine with him so that they could hold it again in joint tenancy. When the husband died, the wife could continue on the tenement for the rest of her life. She would be expected to continue providing the labor services, working the land, and paying rent. On some manors, as we have seen, she might have to relinquish the land when her sons reached the age of majority. In these cases some further provision would be made for her well-being.[2]

Wills present the full range of options that a man with property could make for his widow. Of the 326 wills of adult males surveyed, 235 had surviving wives. Sixty-three percent of these women received the home tenement for life, 3 percent had the tenement only until the oldest son reached majority, 3 percent were allowed the house but not the lands and 3 percent were allowed a room in the main house. Other provisions for the widows included a dower of one-third of the property (2 percent), return of the dowry (5 percent), land other than the home tenement (15 percent), and a separate house (5 percent). In addition, widows were left money, animals, household goods, and the residue of the property after the debts were paid (52 percent). In general, the provisions for widows were generous, with husbands preferring to give their wives the greater benefits possible under customary law as opposed to the third allowed in common law.

Those provisions that gave the widow a room in the main house or some guaranteed source of support in food or money were common when the main holdings were already distributed to the heirs or the heirs were adults and ready to take charge of the land. These benefits were in addition to the dowry that she had brought with her at marriage and that she would have returned to her unless she had given it to her children. The wills indicate a wide range of possible accommodations. The widow might have the main house for a number of years and then move to a dower cottage; she might be guaranteed room in the family house and a place at the hearth; or she might be given lands and house separate from the family holdings. The coroners' inquests in which widows appear as accident victims show that all of these options were used.[3]

Sometimes the dying husband would instruct in his will that the son should provide for the surviving widow, and the amount was often explicitly stated. Such wills usually indicate that the husband and wife were already retired and he was making arrangements for her final years. The actual provisions of these settlements are a more fitting topic for the following chapter, on old age.

While the material comforts must have varied consideraby, the wills and manorial court cases make it clear that widows always had some provision made for them. We must look beyond the legal settlements, however, in order to see how well widows coped with their new life and, perhaps, considerable new responsibilities for cultivating the land and rearing their children alone.

Quite frequently widows were left with young children who had to be raised and provided for in adulthood. In Halesowen the ages of five husbands can be established at the time of their death. Their ages ranged from twenty-three to forty-four and most had young children. The wives paid fines to become guardians of these children and keep the family holding for them.[4] In the wills husbands left wives explicit guardianship over the children and often made property settlements for them, should they grow up. A husband might give his wife extensive control over the children, including the right to disinherit them. Thomas

Clay of Potton directed that his tenement and lands in Potton pass to his son Richard after his wife's death "on condition that in the future his behavior improves to the satisfaction of his mother and the executor [Richard's uncle, John the Chaplain]." Only one husband felt that his wife was unfit to care for his children because of her insanity: "she shall kepe my childerne or els she shall not enter . . . and if so be she have not her witts," the executors are to do what they think best.[5]

One can trace the careers of some of these young mothers in the manorial court rolls. For instance, Agnes of the Land did fealty for the family tenements in 1286 and carried on the cultivation of the lands until 1306, when her son Richard was twenty-one and took over the lands. She received as dower a third part of the land and Richard paid 20s. for entry and the right to marry. By 1313 Richard had married and increased the family landholding. Often the mother took the land in both her name and that of her heir, so that the succession would be automatic. In the case of the heir being a daughter, the mother usually surrendered the land when the daughter married.[6]

A widow left with land and a young family to care for must have found the responsibilities taxing. Widows remaining single had to arrange for the cultivation of the land, but these contracts could go awry. For instance, Eve, formerly wife of William de Colley, sued John Payne because he failed to plow and sow for her. In some communities the widow cultivated the land only until her sons reached the age of majority. Isabell, widow of Patrick, for instance, surrendered her rights to her land to her son John. She arranged that he would give her 15s. 4d. by Whitsuntide and pay her 6s. 8d. a year maintenance. A study of inheritance and land-use patterns in the Chiltern Hills shows that the widow usually released her life interest to the inheriting sons and then held her dower lands jointly with them. Another common solution widows chose was to rent out the land for a specified period until the children came of age. Thus Alice, widow of John of the Mere, rented land to a man for a period of twenty years. When that time was up, the land was to revert to the heirs of her husband.[7]

Widowhood, however, did not have to be a period of just managing to cope in the face of great odds. Many widows appear to have flourished in their new-found freedom. They no longer faced the encumbrance of pregnancies, and the legal controls of the husband over the family finance had ended. Thus the manorial surveys show widows holding full tenements as well as simply cottages. In manorial courts one sees widows actively buying land and pursuing trades. Johanna, widow of William of the Bothes, arranged for her minor son to take over the eighteen acres and the buildings of his father, but to remain with his lands and person in her custody. She then purchased two acres of new land for herself and her heirs. Clare de Blakewode and Matthew, her son, acquired four acres of additional land. Matilda, widow of Elyas, did well enough in her economic management to sue another couple for 7s. 4d. worth of flour she had sold them. Widowhood released women into a legal category that left them free to pursue economic enterprises denied to single women or wives.[8]

Not all widows, however, chose to remain on their own, and some sought to solve the problem of managing the land and children through remarriage. In the thirteenth and early fourteenth centuries, widows remarried rather rapidly because they were often well-endowed marriage partners and their responsibilities required a man to work the fields. A similar pattern was observed for the sixteenth century. The marriage market for widows, however, appears to have fluctuated depending on the availability of land. In the tight land markets of the early fourteenth and sixteenth centuries widows were in demand. The marriage patterns on the late thirteenth-century Winchester estates has been described as a marriage fugue. On manors on which there was no vacant land, young men sought old widows for marriage partners. They lived on her land until she died, and they then perhaps remarried younger women, thus establishing a fugue pattern of a young man marrying an older widow, remarrying a younger woman who, when she is widowed, will marry a younger man.[9]

Looking at the marriage patterns over more than a century on the Crowland Abbey estates the historian Ravensdale correlated the marriages of widows with the population density and availability of land. In the late thirteenth and early fourteenth centuries, when land was in considerable demand and a very active land market in small plots was prevalent, widows were sought-after matches. The widow's dower lands could support the new husband and perhaps a new family at least for the lifetime of the widow. If the widow wanted to retire and not remarry, there were plenty of nonkin as well as kin who were willing to cultivate the land in exchange for an agreement to support the widow until her death. During the period of land hunger the lords encouraged widows to remarry because they could then collect money from the marriage fines. After 1349, however, when land was in plentiful supply, many widows refused to take their husband's lands because they could find neither a new husband nor laborers to work the land. Young men with land were choosing to marry younger women. Thus widows were no longer desirable in the marriage market. Other court roll studies have since shown a similar pattern in widows' marriages.[10]

The percentage of remarriages is difficult to determine accurately.

In the sixteenth century 25 to 30 percent of the widows remarried; for widowers it was higher. Widowers had a harder time managing the tenement alone than did widows, and if they had young children at home a wife would be most helpful. Remarriage was fairly rapid, with almost half of those remarrying doing so within the year. Canon law required no mourning period in such cases.[11]

Judging from wills, first husbands had a range of feelings about the remarriage of their widows. Some explicitly mentioned that the amount of lands and goods would be diminished if the wife remarried, or that she would get a greater amount "providing that she does not remarry."[12] Other husbands purposely endowed their widows with land or goods that they could take with them to a subsequent marriage. For instance, William Spenser gave his wife four acres and three rods of land that she held in clear title and could alienate. Another huband generously instructed his son to keep his wife, but that if she married or moved she was to have half of the movable goods.[13]

Wills and manorial court evidence indicated that widows were well provided for both by custom and by individual arrangements of their husbands. But there remains the question of their ability to collect these benefits. In the Bedfordshire wills surveyed, 197, or 65 percent, of the nonclerical males made their former wives executors, so that they had some control over the dispersal of the goods and lands. Widows often appeared in the court rolls, however, trying to regain payments and dower lands that were rightfully theirs. On Chalgrave manor a mother sued her son and had the court roll searched to prove that he had taken an acre of land that was rightfully hers.[14] Usually it was the son or the husband's brother who was at fault in denying the widow dower rights.[15]

Widows appearing in manorial courts and wills had lands and goods to transfer or to sue for, but an unknown portion of the widows were left penniless when the chief breadwinner died. They relied on charity to see them through, hoping for occasional work and begging for their bread and housing. If they had young children, their reliance on the generosity of neighbors would be very great indeed. Such a one was Matilda Sherlok of Pinchbeck, a beggar, who had two sons, John and six-year-old William, and a daughter. They lived in a house in Spalding that John Herney lent to them. When they went to bed Matilda placed a candle on the wall and forgot to extinguish it, so that it fell, causing the house to burn and killing Matilda and her family.[16]

We are left with the problem of assessing the community's opinion of widows, but finding such information is always difficult. We know that poets felt that widows should be protected. But remarkably little of the folk poetry or the writings of moralists deals with widows. The omission is particularly striking when one considers the volume of comments on marriage and the noticeable presence of widows in society. Even though Alison had been a widow five times, she is the Wife of Bath not the Widow of Bath. Widows are generally assigned one of two roles in society: respectable or disreputable. If we may judge from wills and literary remains, the assumption in medieval peasant society was that most widows would fall into the first category. There were, of course, some widows who did not. Such widows did take lovers and some became prostitutes. Isabel Edmond, a tenant in Cleeve Prior, took a lover, but he paid an entrance fine for her lands and the banns were read. But Lucy Pofot, widow of Thomas of Houghton, was at a tavern on the evening of November 30, 1270. After returning home at night, "a ribald stranger came and asked for entertainment and Lucy entertained him." She was found dead in the morning with five knife wounds in her heart. Sarra, a widow forty-six years old, one evening entertained three men at her house who killed and robbed her.[17]

We need not end on a gloomy note, however. Since most widows did not rush into remarriage, a fair proportion of them must have taken up their new responsibilities as steward of the family fortunes with serious dedication and perhaps even relish. By not remarrying, they could preserve their own authority while benefiting their children by not introducing a new husband who would try to lay claim to the land or, worse, starting a new family to erode the rights of the children by the first husband. Widowhood, therefore, could bring both personal power and preseve family harmony. The years of widowhood, even for elderly widows, need not have been lonely, for, as we shall see in the next chapter, some of them died surrounded by loving children, grandchildren, nieces and nephews, friends, and fellow villagers.

15

Old Age and Death

Concern about aging is not new. Both literary remains and court records speak of problems that are all too familiar to us: the physical decline of the body, the lack of dignity and respect that advanced age brings, and the anxiety of guaranteeing continued care when one cannot provide for oneself and when the society in which one lives does not venerate the aged. The harsh reality of the problem is succinctly summed up in the medieval story of the divided horse blanket. The son has inherited the family house and land and is raising his own family, but his old father lives on as another mouth to feed. It is winter and the old man, shivering with cold, asks his son for a blanket. The son directs his son to get the horse blanket and give it to his grandfather. The grandson returns with half the blanket, and when asked why he cut the blanket in two, he replies, "I will keep the other half until I am a man, and then use it to cover you."[1]

Care of the aged produces a far greater variety of societal adaptations and solutions than do other stages of life. While childrearing must take into consideration such biological imperatives as feeding, clothing, and teaching children the rudiments of survival, and marriage is, in most preindustrial societies, an institution of economic and biological perpetuation, aging brings about such culturally extreme responses as veneration and parricide. Anthropologist Jack Goody, in "Aging in Non Industrial Societies," has surveyed, cross-culturally, the basic problems that the aged face in securing their material survival and respect in their social milieu. Concerns with shelter, clothing, and food dominate the list of needs, but participation in household decisions, assurances of political and religious inclusion, and the guarantee of a "decent" burial are important psychologically as well. Above all, the older generations must have cultural institutions that will ensure that provisions for their old age will be maintained even when they become impotent.[2]

If the war between the sexes was cause for comment, so too was the clash between young and old. Moralists not only repeated homilies about the callousness of children toward aged parents, but also warned fathers not to use their children as executors, for, as Robert Mannyng observed, children would not carry out the provisions of a will because they would stand to lose the most from bequests not directed to them. He shrewdly comments that you should make neither your heir nor your doctor an executor.[3] A persistent tension existed between the possessors of land, goods, and power and their heirs. Once the old person retired and passed on these accoutrements of adult life, he or she could be left at the mercy of the younger generation. From the younger generation's viewpoint, the aged pose problems. They no longer worked equivalent to the amount they consumed; they stood in the way of the young adult's advancement; their appearance offended the aesthetics of their juniors. A young man might have to wait until his father died or retired before he could marry and set up his own household. If old men married younger women, then they were taking potential wives of young men in the community. A young man might marry an older widow to get her rights in dower and thereby deprive a village girl of a desirable marriage partner. The young, therefore, had ample reason for not regarding old people as benign, and their prudent elders sought legal safeguards for retirement rather than relying on cultural precepts about honoring father and mother and respecting the aged.

But how serious was the problem of coping with old people in late-medieval England? To answer that question we must know how large the problem was and the ways in which the aged functioned in society. The age at which people were specified as old in the Statute of Labourers was sixty. Beyond that age the statute's provisions did not apply. Ecclesiastical sources indicated that anyone aged fifty or more could be called *senex* (old),[4] but peasants would not necessarily have been aware of the ecclesiastical divisions of life stages and even the scribes in manorial and royal courts did not use the word *senex* to describe the elderly. Indeed, neither the statute nor the ecclesiastical descriptions could have had practical application, for people had only a vague idea of their ages since they never recorded births and were seldom called upon to give their age. When an adult's age was given in the coroners' inquests, it was always rounded off with the statement *et amplis* (and more). The description of a person as aged was based on his or her physical appearance and general health, not simply on calendar years.

We may never know the percentage of old people in the medieval English population, but we must not be misled into thinking that because life expectancy was about thirty-three years of age there were few old people. High infant mortality rather than adult deaths was the chief contributor to the low life expectancy. Analysis of bones from medieval English burials indicates that 10 percent of the people were over fifty.[5] Late sixteenth- and seventeenth-century parish registers show that roughly 8 to 16 percent of the population was over sixty.[6] And in fourteenth- and fifteenth-century Tuscany 6 to 15 percent of the rural population was over sixty.[7]

Although 10 percent or more of its population was over fifty and conflicts between the needs of the old and the aspirations of the young could produce tension, parricide in medieval England was extremely rare.[8] Instead, either the old people themselves, their families, or the community made arrangements for the aging. These accommodations varied considerably in the material comfort and satisfaction they provided, but there was a range of options open to the aged.

Retirement contracts are one of the most apparent of these arrangements because they appear frequently in manorial court rolls. In essence, these contacts provided that the retiring peasant would relinquish the use of his buildings and lands in exchange for food, shelter, and clothing from the person, whether a kinsman or not, who took up the contract. While wills mostly describe arrangements men made for their aging wives,[9] manorial records are a rich source on the lot of both sexes.

The historian Elaine Clark has studied 200 maintenance cases largely from fourteenth-century East Anglia and has provided an insightful discussion on retirement.[10] Her conclusions may be extended back to the late thirteenth century and to other regions of England as well. Maintenance contracts could be made in three ways. First, the lord and the community could impose a contract on a tenant who became too old and impotent to work the land and pay the rent. In such cases the community leaders met in manorial court and made arrangements for someone else to take the land in exchange for providing for the person. By so acting, the community made way for a younger person to establish him or herself while still guaranteeing care for an aged neighbor. The lord encouraged such arrangements so that he could get rents from the land. Thus, for example, in Chertsey Abbey court John Atte Wyle's mother was described as "of great age and *non compos mentis* and it seems useful to the court that John shall be admitted."[11] The court could settle the senile or impotent person's affairs with a neighbor, if there was no kin or if the kin were not interested in taking over the tenement.[12]

In most cases the retiring tenant made his or her own arrangement through a contract. A father might make such an agreement with a son when he relinquished the family land to him or with a daughter at the time of marriage. Richard Loverd of Northamptonshire put his cottage with appurtenances into the lord's hands, and Emma, his heir, did the same. Her prospective husband paid the lord 5s. to enter the tenement, agreeing at that time that he would marry Emma and provide her father with food and clothing.[13] In another case, a kinsman of Ralph Beamonds took over the tenement because Ralph was impotent. The kinsman promised Ralph that he would have a cottage and a curtilage along with, yearly, a garment valued at 2s. 6d., a pair of linen hose, a pair of shoes worth 6d., a pair of woolen hose worth 6d., four bushels of fine white wheat, and four bushels of barley. As in court-dictated settlements, the agreement could be reached with someone not related to the pensioner. When Hugh took over Simon's tenement, he agreed to recondition the property and "to look sufficiently after Simon's wife Alice, his son and all his children and Simon was to have food and drink when Hugh acts as host to his wife."[14]

And third, the dying tenant or peasant proprietor could make provision for his wife and family by recording his provisions or will in the manor court. These were often deathbed scenes with the bailiff coming to record the final arrangement or, as in one case, the whole manorial court came. On his deathbed John Whytyng surrendered his messuage and land to Simon Wellyng with the provision that Simon provide John's widow with food, drink, and sixteen bushels of barley. He also had to maintain for her use one cow, six hens, and one goose and cultivate and seed an acre of arable in every season of the year. He was to provide 3s. for clothing annually as well as a pair of shoes each Easter. She was to be allowed to continue to live in her late husband's house, although she was only guaranteed entry, a place by the fire, and a bed.[15]

In the cases that we have looked at so far, the retirees have all been sufficiently well off that they exchanged only their land and buildings in return for specific arrangements for their comfort. But what of cottars who might find it hard to get good terms because they had so little with which to bargain? With two to three acres being considered necessary for the support of one person, these people found it difficult to attract a caretaker. Cottars often made further concessions in order to ensure care, such as promising the caretaker not only the use of the land but also making him or her the chief beneficiary of the will. In practice this meant that all of their household equipment, clothing, and other movables would go to the person who agreed to provide for them in their old age.[16]

The retirement contracts show great care in planning and indicate that the individuals making them tried to cover all possible contingencies. Rather than leaving to chance the food, clothing, and shelter that they would receive, the pensioners spelled it out in detail. Modifications in the house plan might be specified so that a solar, hall, or chamber be added for the retiree. Sometimes separate houses were built. In 1281 Thomas Brid agreed to build for his mother a house thirty feet long and fourteen feet wide and having three doors and two windows.[17] In addition, some asked for the regular laundering of clothing, horses for riding, gardens, fuel, tools of their trade, and other such benefits. Psychological needs were also stipulated in the contracts. Provisions were made for regular visits from friends when the pensioners were on their sickbeds and for funeral processions and prayers for their soul when they died.[18]

To protect the agreement and ensure that the terms of the contract would be met, the pensioner always transferred the land conditionally. If the terms were not met, the land reverted to the pensioners. Custom as well as the binding nature of the contract protected them, for the community or the lord could insist on the reversion to the pensioner if the contract was broken. Furthermore, when the contracts were recorded in the manorial court, the son or other contractee swore he would uphold its obligations. He had to produce kin and friends who were to act as surety or guarantors that he would abide by his oath or they would be personally responsible.

The reversion clause served another purpose as well. The contractee might die before the pensioner. In the century and more following the Black Death, this eventuality was a real risk because mortality from disease was so high. The contract could specify that heirs of the original caretaker would have to take up the tenement along with the continued support of the pensioner. Sometimes the original caretaker decided to sell his or her rights in the land and the contract changed hands. The person taking up the land had to agree to the old terms and continue to provide for the pensioner in order to hold the land.[19]

Clark's study permits some generalizations about the preferences and concerns that retiring peasants shared. Whether married or widowed, they wished to continue living on their own property. In the manorial cases the norm was for coresidence with their contractee; only one in twelve had the luxury of a private residence. Second, even after the population decline of the late fourteenth and fifteenth centuries made land readily available, 50 percent of the retirees had small holdings of less than 5 acres. While few pensioners mention the issue of how long they expected to live, those who did anticipated that they would live another six to nine years. All sought the most binding legal protections in making their contracts so that their comfort would be ensured. Perhaps the most interesting of Clark's findings is that only one-third of the pensioners negotiated contracts with their own children.[20]

These conclusions are provocative and deserving of further analysis. Should there have been a census taken in the fourteenth century it would have shown that households with old people present would not necessarily be stem families, but, rather, the old person could be a pensioner unrelated to the current head of the house. Manorial records, however, may tend to overrepresent this type of nonkin arrangement. One may assume that some parents and children had amicable agreements that did not have to be guaranteed in manorial court. More well-to-do peasants, as we shall see, chose to make their arrangements by will or established their children in separate holdings before their death. The manorial cases, therefore, may represent people with fewer resources or without close kin. An alternative hypothesis is that the contracts with nonkin were second retirements, that is, peasants who had already distributed their land to their children but had retained a cottage and a few acres. They were thus making arrangements for final illness. In any case, these households probably did not constitute a large percentage of the population, if we may infer from later studies where population information is available.[21]

The position of aging single people was not necessarily worse than that of married people with family, provided they had some land that they could negotiate into a maintenance contract. In Clark's figures only 36 percent of the pensioners were married, while 43 percent were women alone and 21 percent were men alone.[22] The predominance of single people suggests that retirement contracts were normally negotiated when the person or persons felt that they could no longer cope with providing for their own living, particularly after the loss of a spouse.

It is curious that a cottage and a few acres encumbered with the care of an old and sick person was in demand at all, since land was readily available following the Black Death. One can easily imagine that such an arrangement would be much sought after in the land hunger of the early fourteenth century, but it would appear to be undesirable if one could get land free of an aged tenant. Unfortunately, manorial records do not permit a comparison between the number of contracts recorded before the plague of 1349 and those afterward. One might conclude, looking at Clark's study, that the incidence increased following the depopulation, but her data were not collected in such a way as to permit a comparison. Missing records from the early part of the century could easily explain the disparity. Nevertheless, the continued popularity of the retirement contract from the contractee's viewpoint needs further investigation.

An unpleasant explanation is that entrepreneurs bought up these retirement contracts simply to get the land and might even have hastened the death of the pensioner through neglect. A breakdown of those taking land with pensioners on it suggests a different motive: 44 percent were couples, 5 percent were single women, and 51 percent were single men.[23] While entrepreneurs cannot be ruled out completely, it appears that some of these may have been young people whose families had not yet provided for them, or could not, and who were planning to set up households on their own. Even in the land glut of the early fifteenth century, people put a premium on land that had traditionally belonged to a family. The people taking up the contracts were, therefore, being "adopted" by the retiring peasant and could enter the land with the same claims to it that the old person had.[24] The cottage and few acres became "family land" rather than rented lands and gave the contractee a secure tenure on it.

Simply knowing the provisions of the maintenance contracts, however, does not indicate the standard of living and treatment of the aged. Did all of the legal ploys at least safeguard the promised material standards? Complaints of contract violations indicate that the unscrupulousness suggested in the story of the divided horse blanket did occur. A Wakefield manor court case underscores the problems entrepreneurial caretakers created. The community charged in 1286 that William Wodemous drove out Molle de Mora and her son from her house, killed her dog, and carried off ten ells of linen. He also took a cloak of hers and did not meet his obligations to repair her house. When the community had to intervene in these cases, they meted out suitable punishment to the offender. When John Catelyne evicted Elena Martyn from her house and tore it down, the jurors of Wistowe ordered him to rebuild the house and find a suitable residence for her until it was done. When a son failed to honor the terms of his contract with his aged mother, the jurors fined him and gave the land back to her, banning him from holding it during her lifetime.[25]

A complication related to contracts was that they could be sold by one contractee to another. Such a transfer of a contract must have been a great disruption to the elderly. For instance, a cottar died in 1415 and made provision that his wife should have the cottage and acre conditional to her caring for his enfeebled sister for her life. After six months the widow left, making arrangements with a local man that he take up the obligations and live in the house. After a year he too moved

out, selling the contract to another villager.[26] Once a person was unable
to cope with the courts, the village community would have to be the
watchdog on broken contracts, and in all likelihood neighbors would
only intervene in cases of flagrant neglect and maltreatment.

Wills present a somewhat different picture of retirement than do
the contracts arranged in manorial courts. People at the upper end of
the village social scale were more likely to make wills, and thus they
represent the arrangements of people who are more likely to be well off.
Furthermore, unlike retirement contracts, wills usually entrusted the
care of the old person to close kin rather than to strangers.

When wives were aged, husbands might make provisions in wills
similar to those made in manorial courts, spelling out in detail the care
for the old woman. In such cases a son was the most frequent person
assigned to carry out the terms of the will. Again, the careful peasants
tried to anticipate failures to honor the arrangements. One man
expressed his suspicion of his son and stated explicitly that his wife
should have one-half of the crops for the first year and three acres of
grain the following years along with an old horse to carry her grain sacks
to the mill. Other times the husband made contingency plans. The
mother and son should live together, but if they were not able to get
along, the mother would be given a separate house or be guaranteed a
room in the house. Another man worried that his son might sell the
property and instructed that whoever holds the property left to his son
John shall provide a chamber in the house for the testator's wife to dwell
in, and also meat and drink such as he "ettythe and drynkes" for life.[27]

One foresightful husband tried to cover all the possible contingencies in providing for his widow and his mother. He left his eldest son,
John, the family holding with the provision that "he pay the testator's
mother £4 per year for life and to find her meat and drink if she wants
to live with him." His wife was to have a place with the second son and
receive 20s. from each of the three younger sons when they reached the
age of majority. If the wife was not satisfied with the annual payment,
she could have her dower as provided by law.[28] Husbands also appealed
to finer sentiments in wills. One stepfather provided for the daughter of
his wife and instructed his own son to keep his wife "during her lifetime,
as he would have kept his own mother."[29]

The men leaving provision for widows in wills had, for the most
part, lived a comfortable life. Those who lived their span to the fullest
had already distributed the family tenement to a son but had retained a
house, some land, and possessions for themselves. The majority of men
leaving wills (72 percent) had wives and their own homes. But Thomas
Smyth intended to sojourn at his son's hearth and rewarded the kindness

of his son and daughter-in-law. His will was, in fact, a retirement contract. He left his daughter-in-law all the goods in the house that still belonged to him and two bushels of malt. As long as he lived he would give his son 40s. at Christmas for board and "for his good attention to him and his labours" another 40s.[30]

The extent to which kin were relied on for care in age is difficult to determine. If we may again use later studies as an inference, it would appear that living with children, other kin, or strangers was not the preferred arrangement for retirement. In rural Austria, where there were legal and customary mechanisms for stem families, they were still rare in the seventeenth through nineteenth centuries. In early modern England only when all else failed did an aged parent live with an offspring.[31] All medieval evidence suggests that this was already an established pattern: People lived on their own as long as they could manage (usually as long as they had a spouse alive and were healthy), and even when they were driven to maintenance contracts only a third made them with kin.

Another solution that the aging person might pursue was hiring a caretaker to come and live in the house. Thomas Cyne, for instance, had become very prosperous, as had his two brothers and a sister whom he mentioned in his will. He appeared to have no wife or children but left money to a woman whom he described as his "keeper." Katherine Vyncent, a widow, had no children but remembered her "wench" and her "keeper" in her will. Aging parish priests often hired caretakers for their old age, although there were hospitals that specialized in the care of aged clergy.[32]

For the most part, peasants would not have had access to hospitals or monasteries for their retirement and final sickness. They did, however, form voluntary associations of their own that provided some benefits to the aged and impotent. Of the 507 gilds that returned descriptions of their charters in 1389, about a third of them (154) provided their members with benefits during disaster or old age. In a fifth of the gilds the benefits were a weekly allowance and perhaps clothing in the event of disaster. The average weekly allowance was 7d., only enough to buy a loaf of bread a day. An additional 7 percent offered to bury a brother or sister who was too impoverished to pay for interment.[33] Since the time of payment was limited to a few months or a couple of years, the dole from the gild was obviously not meant to support a prolonged retirement and may only have helped the indigent members or those terminally ill.

The gilds were significant, however, in providing psychological comfort to aged brothers and sisters, one of those important aspects in the treatment of the aged that Goody has identified. Testators (48 of the 389 Bedfordshire wills) left money, malt, and sometimes land to their gilds. The gilds were in some respects an extension of family, for they provided gild feasts, visitors to the sickbed, and a chaplain, or at least prayers, for their members.

The people we have considered so far had some property with which to negotiate care and perhaps respect. But what of those who had little or no land and had lived on wages earned by the sweat of their brow or those whose ungrateful children actually threw them into the streets? These people often appear, as is the case today, in a coroner's inquest where they are described as having died of exposure or some accident relating to their poverty. Alice Berdholf of Donyngton, a beggar seventy years of age, was drunk and near a well in the highway. She saw a straw and fell in the well trying to get it.[34] Alice was known and died near her home, but often the person is simply described as an old stranger such as one who was found dead of cold and exposure in a cowshed in December 1362.[35] The impoverished elderly were sometimes forced to beg even when they had adult children living in the village:

> On 14 January 1267 Sabina, an old woman, went into Colmworth to beg bread. At twilight she wished to go to her house and fell in a stream and died by misadventure. The next day her son Henry searched for her, and found her drowned.[36]

This was not an isolated incident, so that the warning of the homilies to beware of children mistreating their parents was not entirely misplaced.

Wanderers were dependent on community charity for their meals, food, and space in the cowshed. If the person was known in the community, he or she might fare moderately well at begging; but strangers were regarded with suspicion. The village bylaws permitted the very young, the old, and the impotent to glean in fields after harvest. But as we have observed, gleaning could only provide grain for several weeks and assumed that the old person was still sufficiently able-bodied to do the arduous, backbreaking labor of gleaning. Religious houses and parish priests were expected to give charitable contributions of food and perhaps clothing for the poor, including the aged poor, and gilds and private individuals often made alms part of the burial ceremony. Such aid, however, was sporadic and could not be counted on every day.

Old age and possibly retirement upon them, how did the elderly spend their days? While coroners did not normally record the ages of adults, in eighty cases we are either given an age over fifty or the person was described as old. Even such a small number of cases is suggestive of these peoples' lives. First, their accidents occurred either as they were working around their homes or when they were in transit. Twenty-two percent of their accidents occurred in their homes and crofts while forty-four percent occurred in some public place such as a ditch, highway, river, or stream. This pattern is quite different from the distribution for adults in general, who had more accidents in fields, barns, neighbors' closes, forests, and marl pits. John Ballard, who was described as old and debilitated when he died on the highway in early January 1368, was returning from West Acton. Mariot, the widow of a reeve, was living with another family, perhaps on a retirement contract. While the rest of the family went about their morning chores, she lay in bed, being old and infirm. Becoming thirsty, she rose from her bed and took a pitcher to the well to get water but fell in because of her feebleness. The accidents, in general, show that the aged remained as physically active and as involved in daily work as they were able. Even an old blind woman could be pressed into baby-sitting during harvest. We know of her role because the child in her charge drowned.[37]

The causes of old people's deaths have a familiar ring. Thirty-eight percent died from falls, compared to 15 percent of adults in general. For instance, Isabella, wife of John, the son of Margery of Bodekesham, was described as an old woman but she rose early in the morning and took a ladder to get straw from a stack to start the fire. She must have done that every morning, but in October 1334 she fell from the ladder and died. Another woman, at least sixty years old, went to collect fruit by a well. When the tree limb on which she stood broke, she fell in. Here the old woman seems to have taken up again the tasks assigned to girls in their early teens.[38] Considering the instability of the aged, it was unfortunate that their retirement quarters were sometimes in a solar that could only be reached by a ladder.

While old people were no more likely to drown than adults as a whole, they were 4 percent more likely to be described as drunk when they drowned. This higher pecentage could indicate alcoholism after years of drinking ale, but is just as likely to be attributable to a more general lack of surefootedness, as in the cases of falling. They were also more susceptible to dying from excesses of heat and cold. Thus, when one looks at the distribution of their deaths by season, they have a higher mortality in January, February, March, and August than do adults in general. In winter bad weather led to deaths among beggars and travelers in this age group, and in the summer they died at harvest overexerting themselves in the heat.

Inattention or physical weakness made them 3 percent more likely to die by fire than adults in general. One old woman had returned from gleaning at harvest and had retired to her solar to count her grain. She feel asleep without putting out the candle and died in the ensuing fire. A vicar over sixty years old had also gone to bed, probably a more comfortable one than the old woman's pallet, but he too forgot to blow out the candle.[39]

To the extent that the first finder of the dead person indicated who was concerned about the individual, old people resembled adults in general: 15 percent were found by close relatives. Sons and daughters were somewhat more likely to be first finders of the aged.

Senility and its problems, as well as the usual frailties of old age, were well know to medieval people. Margery Kempe explains in her autobiography that she cared for her husband during his decline. He was "of great age passing three score years" when he fell down some stairs and broke open his head. Athough it was sewed up again, he was enfeebled and could not take care of himself. She provides a classic description of senility: "in his last days he turned childish again and lacked reason that he could not do his own easement to go to a sege [latrine], or else he would not but as a child voided his natural digestion onto his linen cloths." She complained that she was kept busy washing and wringing and had to keep a fire in her cottage to keep him warm.[40]

The literary image of the aged was overwhelmingly pessimistic. In folklore age was associated with evil for both men and women.[41] In more formal poetry such as the "Proverbs of Alfred," old age was commensurate with the departure of worldly goods, friends, and health.[42] An early fourteenth-century poem on old age speaks derisively of the loss of hair, good fortune, love, eyesight, and the acquisition of repulsive mannerisms that come with aging:

> I stunt, I stomere, I stomble as sledde,
> I blind, I bleri, I bert in bedde,
>   such sond is me sent;
> I spitte, I spatle in spech, I sporne,
> I werne, I lutle, ther-for I murne,
>   thus is mi wel i-went.[43]

But a fifteenth-century poem describing the general degeneracy of the times deplored the scorn for old men.[44]

If literary references and accidental-death cases tend to impose a gloomy hue on the everyday life of the aged, wills with their bias to the propertied can present a surprisingly happy and optimistic picture. Widows' wills reveal a great deal about the village networks in which they participated and show them surrounded by kin, servants, neighbors, and friends. Since they did not have extensive lands to give away but wished to reward those who had shared their days, they took great care in distributing their household goods, clothing, and other movables among those they held dear. One widow, who lived with her son, rewarded not only him but a servant who took care of her. She also left bequests to two grandsons and three relatives.[45] Alice Tichemarch was the second wife of a man with a number of connections in Bedfordshire. In her will she honored his wishes to leave the household goods to his daughters by his first wife. She also left a variety of dishes, spoons, sheets, and household goods to nieces, nephews, and godchildren. She belonged to the local parish gild and left her gild brothers and sisters money as well.[46] Finally, one widow must have endeared herself to the village young people, for she left 6d. to all of marriageable age.[47]

Old men also appear surrounded by material comforts and their circle of family. One will presents a particularly homely picture of an old man's comfortable last days. He had a young grandson of whom he was very fond and to whom he left all the contents of his house except that which he reserved for his wife. The house was commodious by peasant standards, having at least four rooms and being furnished with beds and bed linen, pots and pans, candlesticks, and even wall hangings with religious pictures painted on them.[48] One also reads occasionally that the skill of the older workman was particularly valued. In Upwood in 1411 a plowman described as "ancient William" was paid more than younger men because of his greater skill in plowing.[49]

The aged were preoccupied through the last years of life with dying and with the fate of their souls. Those who lived to old age had seen many die before them of illnesses, accidents, and perhaps even a homicide. But the sudden violence depicted in our sources should not mislead us into believing that most people died away from home. On the contrary, most people died at home in their own beds. A typical deathbed scene appears in manorial records. Philip Barnabie was lying in his bed in "grete sicknesse," surrounded by friends including John Wyndover. At about ten or eleven o'clock at night John was sent over to the bailiff's house because Philip wanted to settle his estate. John went to the bailiff's chamber where he found the bailiff too sick to come to Philip, but he commissioned John to take the deposition for him saying, "John, thou art a trew man." By the time John got back, Philip could not speak comprehensibly. Another man, knowing that his end was near, got a blanket and placed his back against a venerable tree where he died peacefully. Others, of course, were not as fortunate. John de Bristowe had falling sickness (epilepsy) in church. He lay near a pillar from morning to midday, when he finally died. The inquest observes that "many [people] were passing by and praying" but none stopped.[50]

If a person had reached the age of sixty, he would enter into what

was considered the last stage in the "Ages of Man" and prepare himself
for death:

> The last age of mankynd is called decrepitus;
> Whan man lakkith reason, than deth biddith hym thus:
> Owt of this world his lyf to pas with mercy of Jhesus;
> Death strykith with sword and seyth, "Man, it shal be thus."[51]

Death was most likely to occur from January through April, the cold
dreary months when food might be short and a variety of respiratory
diseases were rampant.[52] The pattern was very different from the
accidental deaths which peaked in summer when labor was difficult.

Graphic descriptions of physical death indicated very few pleasant
illusions about the process:

> eyes get misty
> ears full of hissing
> nose cold
> tongue folds
> face goes slack
> lips blacken
> mouth grins
> spittle runs
> hair rises
> heart trembles
> hands shake[53]

And so the person was dead and ready for burial amid the pealing of the
parish church bells.

The burial place was the sunny side of the churchyard. It would not
be a lonely grave, but one crowded with ancestors and neighbors. At
Wharram Percy there were up to four levels of burials. New graves were
cut into the old ones, with the bones of various generations mixing
together. However, the layout was orderly, going from east to west, and
graves must have had some marker to facilitate adding new ones.[54]

The passing of a family member and neighbor, did not go
unobserved. Indeed, the ceremonies surrounding death were some of the
most expensive for the family budget. The two big expenses were to the
lord and the Church; the best beast went to the lord as heriot and the
second-best beast to the Church as mortuary. Failing animals, goods or
money was demanded. These death dues were an onerous burden and
severely handicapped the person taking over the tenement. Feasting and
drinking were the ceremonial debts owed to the community. The family
held a wake for the dead, even though the Church tried to discourage
such revelry. At a wake in Bedfordshire two boys, John, son of Hugh de

Lodey, and Henry, son of Thomas of Duloe, apparently accompanied the adults to the vigil of a dead man in the hamlet of Duloe. They went outside to play and both fell into a pit and drowned.[55]

The spiritual welfare of the departed Christian's soul also cost the family a pretty penny. Perhaps because of the gloom cast by the high mortality, preoccupation with death and dying increased in the late fourteenth and fifteenth centuries. Fears about purgatory or worse were enhanced through graphic depictions on the church walls and popular stories. For instance, in the visions of Child William, a boy of fifteen:

> He saw grown-up people placed in caldrons and boiled till they became, in size and shape, to all appearances newly-born babes. And after being taken out with burning flesh-hooks, they recovered quicky their former aged appearance and were again boiled, and this same process was continually repeated.[56]

If this dreadful rendering of the soul was purgatory, one could only shudder at what hell was like. A person would have to take precautions, at least at the end of his or her life, to avoid the prospect.

Prayers, masses, and a fine funeral were prescribed for the escape from the worst of purgatory. The testators were scrupulous about making provisions; 67 percent put aside some of their wealth for prayers and Masses for their souls. At their most extreme, the funerals could be very expensive. The will of a gild chaplain indicates how elaborate even a village funeral might be:

> ... to the rector and high alter 3s. 4d.; fabric of cathedral church 6s. 8d.; fabric of parish church for burial of body in church 6s. 8d.; upkeep of altar of St. John the Baptist 3s. 4d.; altar of Holy Trinity 3s. 4d.; St. Mary 3s. 4d.; to parish church in Lympne in Kent 40s., to each chaplain at burial 8d.; to each clerk, same, 4d.; to each clerk who reads lesson 2d.; to each poor scholar, 1d.; each bell ringer 2d.; fees for bells 12d. ...[57]

As we have seen, some laymen went to extremes and essentially mortgaged their family's future well-being by an excessive bequest for prayers for their soul. The testators expressed great anxiety that their children would not keep their obits or not have the masses said at their funerals. Many instructed the executors that children were not to have land or goods unless they honored the prerequisite observances.

Gild membership could provide both financial and psychological comfort in this time of dire need. One of the primary functions of the social-religious gilds was to give members a fine funeral procession and the correct masses. Further, the brothers and sisters would routinely pray for dead members on the anniversary of their death. Since the membership fee and the annual dues guaranteed this service, the member could spread the cost for these ceremonial expenses throughout his lifetime, and not dilute the bequest to his family. Furthermore, if he doubted that his ungrateful children would forget about his soul, he could be assured that his gild brothers and sisters would not forget. Gild membership was the best insurance against purgatory that money could buy.

The evidence from a broad range of fourteenth- and fifteenth-century English sources indicates a considerable tension between the young and the old. The young were desirous of gaining control of the family resources while the old wished to secure care and comfort. In the absence of a binding cultural norm of devoting family resources to caring for the aged, such as is found in China, English peasants restorted to contracts and wills when they doubted that their families would provide adquate care. How one fared in such contract negotiations depended then, as now, on the personal resources one had amassed in a lifetime. Peasants with land and goods could negotiate for their care either with kin or with other parties. Those with nothing depended on private charity. Retirement arrangements were flexible. The aged persons showed a marked preference for staying in their own homes even if it meant that they would have to share it with nonkin. But sharing a home was a choice imposed by economics and not by preference. In addition to anxieties about material comfort in old age, peasants worried about their funeral and prayers for their soul. Again, rather than trusting to family completely for these offices, they formed voluntary associations—surrogate family—that would ensure safe passage through the hereafter.

V

Surrogate Family

16

Surrogate Parents and Children

In the preceding sections and chapters we looked at the close-knit unit that the nuclear family formed in its residential patterns, in its household economy, and in the emotional reliance of its members on one another. A few loose threads remain, however, in the fabric of the argument for the cohesive nuclear family. One is the argument of Ariès, Shorter, and Stone that in the rural hinterland of medieval Europe community meant more to peasants than family did. As Stone has put it, the family was "porous" and friends and neighbors could easily enter it or draw out family members into close relationships. A second thread left dangling is the hypothesis stated in the introduction that while family tended to meet adversity by regrouping into new nuclear units without experiencing permanent structural change, the relationship of individuals and family to the community did change. And, finally, the reader must be wondering what happened to kinless men, women, and children. Was their plight as bad as that described in the Anglo-Saxon poem "The Wanderer"? These are the themes that we must bring together in this final section to make our argument of whole cloth.

The individuals that immediately come to mind as needing surrogate families are children left orphaned or otherwise neglected. Who was to shelter the child bereft of parents or suckle an infant whose mother died in childbirth, and who would attend to their spiritual welfare? Not being a callous, indifferent people, medieval peasants had ways of coping with these very pressing problems. Laslett has suggested that in preindustrial England the number of children left orphaned was as great as it is in the modern United States, even when one includes in the recent figure children from broken homes.[1] Provision had to be made for such children.

Children who came into this world alive had godparents. We have noted the urgency with which children were rushed to the baptismal font to ensure that their souls would be saved. But once these godparents were acquired, what role did they play in children's lives? The Church, of course, had special instructions for the godparents and set them out in manuals for priests. Godparents were not simply to name the child, but were to undertake the spiritual upbringing of their charge. They arranged for confirmation and taught the child its "Pater Noster," "Ave Maria," and "Credo." Because one could not be sure that the godparents knew these prayers, the instructions urged parents not to accept as godparents anyone who did not. The obligations of godparents included a shared responsibility for the physical well-being of the child until it was seven years old. They were admonished to keep the children from such accidents as being run over by horses and, like the biological parents, they were not to sleep with the child, for fear of overlaying, until it was able to manage by itself.[2]

The Church was also concerned about the possiblity of the relationship becoming too intimate. Robert Mannyng, in the *Handlyng Synne*, discussed at length the evils of sexual abuse of godchildren. He related a story from Pope Gregory I about the godfather who invited his goddaughter to spend the Easter holidays with him and then seduced her. His just punishment from on high was to die a week later and have his body burn up in his grave. The taboo on such sexual relations was particularly strict in the Middle Ages, and a marriage between godparent and godchild was considered incestuous. Godparents were linked with parents in the commandment to honor one's father and mother.[3]

The initial relationship between the child and the godparents was, symbolically at least, a close one. The mother was still in bed during the baptism, and, even if well, she would have been prohibited from going to church. The whole naming and spiritual cleansing ceremony was in the hands of the baby's godparents. A further tie, this time a material one, was a gift to the child from the godparents.

The role of godparents in children's lives after the baptism ceremony is difficult to determine. In three centuries of inquisitions postmortem in Yorkshire, only 12 percent of the witnesses on proof of age were godparents, and the number acting as guardians was minuscule.[4] This source represents only the upper class, of course, but may also indicate a laxity of feeling about the role in general. If one turns to the more ordinary people who left wills in late fifteenth- and early-sixteenth-century Bedfordshire, only 15 percent remembered godchildren in their wills. Usually the bequest was 4d., a sheep or lamb, or a bushel of barley, the standard type of token bequest that we have seen before for grandchildren. Only one favored godson received land. William Tychmers left one bushel of barley to each godchild, but specified that William Goldisborowe was to get two sheep. Young William had apparently endeared himself to his godparents because when widow Tychmers died the next year she also left him land.[5]

The pattern of bequests in wills indicates that godchildren became more important as the person aged. Young men provided only for their immediate families when they died, but older men and women left money to friends, servants, and grandchildren in addition to immediate family. The broader range of bequests indicates less concern about the future of their families, who have already been established, and more sentimentality about the companionship godchildren, grandchildren, and friends provided in their last years. Another curious aspect of bequests to godchildren is that they were seldom referred to by name. Since the executor was often the wife, and the parish priest often wrote the will, the testator could presume that they knew who the godchildren were.

A clue to the functions of godparents may be found in looking at the people chosen. For a female child two women and a man acted as godparents, and for males, two men and a woman. Care was taken not to select close kin or anyone who would be a potential marriage partner. Thus the selection of godparents enlarged the kinship circle rather than drawing upon those already in it.[6]

A unique source yields some information on godparents. In late-fifteenth-century York hostility to the Scots had reached such a pitch that people who were suspected of being Scots were forbidden to practice their trade. Tradesmen authenticated their English parentage by producing certificates citing their place of birth, parents, and godparents. For instance, Bartram Dawson was a draper in York. His certificate showed that he was born in Warmeden and that his god-fathers were Richard Craucester, gentleman, and Bartram Fenkyll of Newham, yeoman. His godmother was Margaret Hudde of Shoston. Bartram's father had selected godparents either within or above his social rank. Of the seventeen such certificates extant, only one had a godfather and godmother with the same surname as the godson. In the eight cases where the social class of the godparents was listed, these York craftsmen all had at least one godparent who was a gentleman and, therefore, of a higher social class than they were. One father had selected his employer as spiritual guide for his son.[7] The selection of a higher-status individual to be at least one of the godparents suggests that the parents hoped the sponsor would help the young man when he was looking for places and preferment. The other godparents might be closer friends of the parents and might be expected to take a greater role in rearing the child than the local gentleman.

Pulling together the scanty information available, it is difficult to argue that godparents were a major substitute for family. They often gave their names to the children, gave them gifts at birth, and may have remembered them in a rather perfunctory way in their wills, but a more active role beyond those cannot be established. We do not even know if they taught the youths their prayers. When a godparent appears in folk literature, the role is usually that of a *deus ex machina*, intervening in a bad situation rather than acting as surrogate parent.

In the period of extraordinary mortality that we have been studying, the likelihood of one or even both parents dying before a child reached maturity was fairly great. Families had to be prepared to meet such eventualities, and a number of children would have been reared by a stepparent, single parent, or even a court-appointed guardian. The experiences of one family in Halesowen illustrates both the frequency of disruption and the ways in which the family coped with it. Thomas Richard was in his late teens when his father, a yardlander, died in 1348. Philip Tompkyns, a wealthy villager from the same township, took him and his holding into his custody and married him to his young daughter Juliana. But Thomas also died of plague, leaving his wife with a newborn son. The Tompkyns family were the next to fall victim, with Philip and his elder son dying in quick succession. This left the Tompkyns family with a minor son, an elder married daughter, and the widow of Thomas Richard and her son. The elder daughter and her husband got the family land and took in the surviving remnants of the family.[8]

Fathers dying when they had minor children left the rearing of them to their widows. The arrangement was so common, as we have seen, that the one testator who had doubts about his wife's mental health felt it necesary to explain why he was departing from the usual procedure. The sentiments of these young fathers are expressed well in Ralph Sneuth's will: "that my wife have a tender and a faithful love and favour in bringing up of her children and mine, as she will answer to God and me." He left to her discretion the way they would be reared and the final settlement of property on them.[9]

Other fathers made more elaborate arrangements for the care of the children. Thomas Wales died, leaving five minor children. His wife was to have the tenement for sixteen years provided that she raised their children "tyll thei can helpe themselves." Then the property was to go to the eldest sons, who were to give their brother 10 marks and their sisters 40s. when they married. Another man gave the land in trust to his wife until the children were twenty-four years old. By that time he expected her to remarry and their sons to enter the land. Fathers had to balance the right of each child to have a share of the family goods and also keep the family land intact. To accomplish this dual purpose some fathers chose to sequence the holding. Thus a Bedfordshire man left his tenement to his wife for seven years. By that time his eldest daughter would be an adult and allowed to hold it five years. After her term her sister was to hold it five years until, finally, the young brother would be of age to take over the tenement.[10]

Single parents on their deathbeds sought other solutions to the care of young children remaining at the hearth. Fathers often pressed the older children into the role of caring for their younger brothers and sisters by making bequests contingent on their meeting their obligations to the young ones. One father gave his eldest son the home tenement provided he make payments to his younger brother; but the father wanted to go beyond this monetary arrangement, "desyryng also the same Thomas to be frendly to his said brother." In another case the older sons were to administer land left to the younger brother and with the proceeds they were to send young George to school or to learn some useful craft. If there were no older siblings, grandparents, uncles, and aunts were left with the rearing of minor children.[11]

Alice Alyne of Kempston, a widow, turned to the local vicar and her brother to oversee her children. She charged Hugh Burton to keep her son at school until he came of age and to disperse her goods other than land to her two daughters when they married. Having taken care of the final distribution of the property, she left it up to the vicar and her brother to find someone to rear the two girls. They were to "hand [the goods] to whoever shall be caring for the girls during this time."[12]

A father whose wife died in childbirth faced the problem of finding a wet-nurse for his infant. While there are no records dealing specifically with wet-nursing, the wet-nurse appears in scattered cases in the coroners' inquests. There were two ways of retaining a wet-nurse. John de Burgoyne placed his infant in the care of Beatrice Paysele, who took care of the child in her own home. John Bronn also left his son John at the home of the wet-nurse, but Robert Asplon had Isabel, wife of Nicholas le Swon, come to his house to nurse his son. One cannot generalize on the basis of one case, but it is possible that family harmony was better maintained if the child were kept with the wet-nurse. Nicholas le Swon was so jealous of his wife spending "too much time" at Robert Asplon's house that he killed her with a sword as she was bending over to make up their bed.[13]

An obvious solution for the single parent was to remarry, and many medieval children were raised by stepparents. The wicked stepmothers of fairy tales and folklore are not simply the stuff of myth. Stepparents could easily disinherit a child by the first marriage either by alienating the family land or producing children who could challenge the inheritance rights of the first family. It was not uncommon to find a stepchild suing a stepparent for rights to land and chattels.[14]

Occasionally the hatred spilled over into homicide. Emma Mabyll belonged to a prominent family in the Midland village of Wigston. She first married John Baker and had a son by him named Richard. When she married Adam de Sutton, she had inherited a piece of freehold property. Adam must have persuaded her to sell the freehold rather than pass it on to Richard. On the night of November 13, 1390, probably in front of his mother's house, Richard lay in wait for Adam and killed him with a staff before his mother's eyes.[15] Sometimes the first family ganged up on the new wife. One night in October 1273 Robert le Tailur and his children, Eve and Raymond, killed Emma, wife of Robert and stepmother to the children. They cut her throat and shins and buried her in a dung heap outside their house.[16]

A coroner's inquest recounts an unsavory family scene involving a short-tempered stepfather. George Stokeley, six months old, was suffering from a severe fever and was in his mother's arms. His father, William, was about to correct his stepdaughter, Mary Borowe, "by beating her with a 'wymble.'" George and Mary's mother interposed herself between her husband and her daughter and by accident the head of the "wymble" flew off and hit the baby.[17]

Not all relationships between stepparents and stepchildren were disagreeable or violent. Wills often indicate evenhanded treatment of stepchildren, and even affection. For instance, John Luffe gave his three children a bullock each and gave the same bequest to his wife's three children from her first marriage. John Lyght left substantial gifts of livestock to his four stepchildren, and when his wife died she left all the children equal gifts, including items of gold and silver.[18]

When a child was orphaned and the parents had made no plans for its care, the village community, through the manorial court, would make arrangements. The land of the tenant was given to someone who would house and feed the children until they reached the age of majority. Thus a man who took the guardianship of three girls had the use of their land for six years, at which time the eldest girl was to marry a specific young man and they would take over the tenement. Occasionally the wardship of the land would go to one person while the custody of the heir went to another. The terms of the wardship were often agreed on, just like retirement contracts, and specified the amount of food and type of housing that the child could expect. One man asked permission to build an addition on his house to accommodate his ward.[19]

Guardianships, whether established by the community or through a will, did not always work out well and, as in retirement contracts, communities had to be the watchdogs. Other times it was the children themselves, when they were old enough to appear in manorial court, who brought charges against a guardian who cheated them out of their proper bequests.[20]

Children with inheritances were sure to find people in the community willing to raise them in exchange for the use of their land and chattels or a marriage contract with one of their children. But what of the landless orphans, illegitimate children, and foundlings? An illegitimate child was raised in its mother's house, if he or she had one. Felicia, daugher of the tailor John Gotter, and her mother, whose name was unknown, lived in the home of John Best when Felicia died of a cradle fire while her mother was getting water; and Alice Saddler and her son Ham, six months old, lived with Christine Rumbold, where Alice carried on her work of making harness. The immediate compassion of neighbors for orphans came to the fore in a case that must have been a fairly normal one for a community to face. A mother and her two-year-old were in their house when it caught fire. The mother burned, but the neighbors took in the orphan, who subsequently died of burns.[21]

It is difficult to determine if rural society had many foundlings. Abandoned children were a romantic theme in the *Breton Lays*. For one reason or another, the child of a noble was considered inconvenient to have around, and it would be bundled off with some symbol of its noble birth that would serve to identify it for its dramatic reappearance. In "Sir Degaré" the child was left with a hermit who baptized the little boy and took it to his sister to raise. In "Le Freine" the child is deposited at the door of a nunnery.[22] But such standard foils of the storyteller are not good clues to the presence of foundlings in society at large.

Although the Order of the Holy Spirit, founded in France in 1160, was intended to take care of foundlings and orphans, the orders in England appear not to have played a large role as surrogate parents. English nunneries took in girls, usually of gentle birth, to educate them and teach them other virtues, but they did not take in poor children.[23]

A few hospitals and eleemosynary institutions specialized in the care of abandoned children. St. Katharine's in London took in waifs and strays of society, and other asylums were dedicated to them as well. Because, as one such institution indicated, "certain orphans are placed in danger through the negligence of their friends, and deserted, ... [they] are brought into the hospital of St. Sepulcre, guarded and educated there." Hospitals that took in poor women during childbirth cared for their children if they died and also took in foundlings. Ages were often mixed in these institutions, with young and old treated alike. Another type of hospice for the young was for those who attended grammar school in a town. They could have a bed and board while they pursued their studies. They might sing in the choir of the sponsoring religious establishment as well.[24] Such hostels, however, were not for poor and abandoned boys. Even those few institutions that were available to care for abandoned infants and children could accommodate very few; hospitals often had only twelve beds.

Evidence of community care for destitute infants and children is difficult to find. A few cases in the coroners' rolls indicate that the children were taken in by other village families. Possibly the rector took some role in the placing of orphans, because very young children sometimes died of accidents at the rectory. For instance, Simon, son of Hugh of Clyne, was one week and four days old and was lying alone in the rectory of Trumpington when a sow came in and bit his throat.[25] Villagers were generally concerned about the homeless, children as well as adults, and offered charity. Roger, son of Agnes of Maulden, a poor boy of eight, sat in the road opposite the house of Reynold le Wyt and cried because he did not have a house. When Reynold came out and tried to comfort the boy, thieves attacked and killed him.[26]

Adoption, which modern readers would regard as the obvious solution for caring for orphaned children, was not used in medieval England. Goody has identified three reasons for adoption: to provide homes for orphans, bastards, and foundlings; to give childless couples social progeny; and to provide heirs for property.[27] Aside from the last consideration, English peasantry did not feel the need to make formal arrangements. Parentless children appear to have been taken in by family and community without a formal adoption procedure. Since surnames were not stable in the early period and not a point of family pride, medieval peasants had no feeling, as people do today, of having a child to carry on the family name. Childless couples do appear among those leaving wills, but they compensated for their lack of immediate family by forming closer bonds with siblings and their children, godchildren, and friends. For the purposes of passing on property, however, a type of adoption was formally practiced. When, as we have seen, a peasant retired, he or she often made a contract with another person that essentially made that person his or her heir in return for support in old age. The advantage of this "adoption" was that it gave the person taking up the land the same family inheritance rights that the former tenant had. The "adoption" could also be done without a retirement contract. Isabel, daughter of William le Blac, gave 1s. to the lord that she might be the heir of Walter the cowherd.[28]

Although the upper classes practiced fostering and apprentices were characteristic of urban life, there is little evidence of systematic fostering among the peasantry. One might argue that the brief period of acting as servant in another person's house was fostering, but it was not done routinely and, when done, appears to have been pursued out of economic necessity and not for the purposes of training a youth.

We have discussed in a previous chapter the retirement contracts that old and sick people made for surrogate family to minister to their last needs, and we have in this chapter discussed the parent substitutes who provided for children. But we have addressed only obliquely the institutions for the poor and sick and the general attitude toward charity in rural society.

Historians have estimated that there were some five hundred to seven hundred hospitals in late medieval England, but only a few specialized in caring for the aged, poor women in childbirth, maimed soldiers, and the "deserving poor." The shelter that most of these establishments provided was temporary and there were not enough of them to serve adequately society's needs. Most were rather small establishments holding a dozen people; others would only take people for one night. The situation was so bad by 1509 that Henry VII described the problem thus:

> ... there be fewe or non such commune Hospitalls within our Reame, and that for lack of them, infinite nombre of pouer nedie people miserably dailly die, no man putting hande of helpe or remedie.[29]

He hoped to build hospitals "to lodge nightly 100 poor folks," but did not carry out the project.

One reason why the hospitals became increasingly inadequate arose from abuses of their founding charters. Patrons sometimes insisted that their retired servants be lodged at the hospitals rather than the deserving poor. The case of the hospital at Bury St. Edmunds illustrates the problem well. Initially, the hospital was founded to provide food and clothing to the indigent and give the sick and aged a place in the monastic hospital. The establishment had only seven beds in the thirteenth century but grew into a complex of buildings. By the fourteenth century the abbot decided who would reside there and began charging people as much as twenty-six marks for the privilege of spending their old age in the hospital. Eventually, the space reserved for aged women was used for aged monks and clergy and ultimately most of the hospital's clientele was clergy or paying guests.[30]

Life in one of the almshouses or hospitals was not to everyone's liking. The inmates had to follow a modified monastic rule. Their treatment could be so bad that they sometimes rebelled against their keepers.[31]

The population expected that clergy and monastic establishments would provide charity, but this charity could take the form of food and clothing and not necessarily shelter. Parishioners expected their parish priest to dispense about a third of his income in alms and might have felt that he should organize charity in the village.[32] Monasteries regularly gave out food. The abbeys might provide other services as well. Four unknown paupers asked the abbot of Sawtry's servant to ferry them across the river out of charity, but the boat sank because of the current and the servant lost his life, although the paupers made it safely to shore.[33]

Local people also called on lay lords for aid, and these routinely gave distributions of alms and food. The trencher on which a wealthy person ate his meal was made of an inferior bread. At the end of the meal these were collected and distributed to the poor, complete with the juices and gravy that had seeped into them. The lord and his officials also forgave fines of those who were too poor to pay them in manorial court.

While medieval peasants themselves tended to be charitable, especially to people they knew, more general aid was sporadic at best. One widow's will is a particularly good illustration of the very local focus of pious bequests. She wanted all of her wood to be distributed to poor neighbors. She also desired that every poor person in Goldington be given 12d., and named in her will these ten poor men and women.[34]

The coroners' inquests present the beggar's story in sad detail. For instance, on an evening in June 1273 Joan Fine of Milton Bryant came to Houghton Regis and sought hospitality from door to door, carrying her son, aged two, in her arms. She was allowed to spend the night in Richard Red's barn. Her son wandered out and drowned. Since she was unknown in the village, she could not find pledges and was delivered to the bailiff. Emma of Hatch had been begging from door to door on a cold day in January when, unable to find lodging of the night, she died of cold in a field. Beatrice Bone begged from door to door in October and finally fell down and died on Amice Mordant's threshold. People of all ages begged for food from their neighbors, sometimes even when they had a house and family in the village. Alice Coke, a poor woman, lay ill in a small house she shared with her sister Agnes. At twilight her sister went out to beg milk for her. While she was gone a fire broke out and Alice died. Both Alice and Beatrice were found dead by kin.[35] Begging was a hard life that often ended tragically.

Giving charity, however, could be risky, particularly if one did not know the people. One couple took in a man and his wife for the night, but they turned out to be two men who killed them and took their goods.[36]

The various formal institutions of charity and the informal one of begging left much to be desired in both material and emotional comfort for the proverty-stricken, orphaned, old, and sick. They were poor substitutes for having wealth adequate to procure decent care.

We have discussed surrogates for dependent children and adults, but we have yet to investigate the emotional bonds people formed in the absence of familial ones. Priests' wills provide some of the best insights into the friendships and ties that consoled single people. A priest dying in Bedfordshire in 1516 put aside a large part of his estate for prayers for both himself and his parents. He left the bulk of his estate to his sister and brother-in-law and gave each nephew and niece a silver spoon. He remitted the debt of a tenant and gave his wife some beads. His books went to fellow clergymen. The man who had been his keeper in his old age was given 6s. 8d. He gave 3s. 4d. to a promising young man, whose mentor he had been, if he eventually became a priest.[37] His will is typical of the networks of affection that the unmarried built into their lives.

We also catch an occasional glimpse in coroners' inquests of a local priest involved in friendly interactions with their parishioners. One priest, on a visit to a family, took the ten-year-old boy of the house for a ride on his fancy horse. When he tried to set the boy down, the boy fell.[38]

Pet animals may also have consoled medieval peasants, as they did the upper classes, and provided them with surrogates for children. Chaucer has provided us with a classical example, the Prioress in the *Canterbury Tales*, of a childless woman's affection for her little dogs:

> And she had little dogs she would be feeding
> With roasted flesh, or milk, or fine white bread.
> And bitterly she wept if one were dead
> Or someone took a stick and made it smart;
> She was all sentiment and tender heart.[39]

Noble women were often painted with lapdogs, and there was even a satirical song about women who fed delicacies to their dogs while the servants went short of food. To the nobleman as well, dogs were constant companions.[40]

Only a few hints about affections for pets emerge from our records.

In a court case in 1294 "William Yngeleys complains against John Saly and Christina his sister because they detain a certain cat to William's damage, which damage he would not willingly have borne for 6d."[41] Whether he lost the services of a good mouser or the companionship of a prized pet is unclear. Dogs, while generally forbidden in manorial custumals, were common to the villagers. We read in manorial court rolls of men and boys illegally hunting with dogs and of dogs mauling and biting people. But that dogs had an importance beyond hunting is shown in a manorial court case previously cited in which the man who abused a maintenance contract for Moll de Mora not only stole goods from her and did not keep up her house, but also killed her dog. Another indication is archaeological. In the dig at Upton the full skeleton of a dog was found with a knife in its body, the victim, archaeologists believe, of the final abandonment of the homestead.[42]

Childless couples probably took in orphans or nieces and nephews when a brother or sister had too many children to provide for, but, if so, it was not done through formal adoption. Most orphaned children would be cared for by a relative or someone in the community. The person who usually offered shelter was a man who hoped to marry a son or daughter to the orphan and gain access to the orphan's land, or someone who hoped to profit from a wardship. For those children, adults, and old people without land or relatives, charity from clergy and the community would have to suffice, because hospitals and almshouses could take only a few. With greater mobility and new economic opportunities, the old community ties loosened and the welfare functions it had performed began to deteriorate along with the bonds that had held neighbors together.

17

Neighbors and Brotherhoods

Emotional surrogates for family must be our final consideration. In Shorter's "Bad Old Days" the ship of family had gaping holes in it that permitted the community to stream in; Ariès saw emotional ties to the community as more important than those to family for the medieval peasant; and Stone has portrayed the community as a continual irritant that prevented affective ties from developing within the traditional pleb family. In the final analysis, then, did the community so intrude on family life that the emotional bonds that we associate with the nuclear family could not develop or were the close, sentimental ties with the community rather than the family? The matter is not a trivial one. If, in committing homicide, one is more likely to kill a person with whom one has close bonds, then the murder pattern among the peasants of medieval England would suggest that they were more emotionally involved with their neighbors than with their families. Intrafamilial homicide was very low compared to the number of neighbors who were victims. Furthermore, medievalists have always emphasized the importance of community for medieval people and speak of the "Christian community," "the monastic community," "the community of the realm," and "the village community." In so doing they have taken their cue from medieval records themselves.

To investigate the problem, we want to know both the extent to which community intruded into family and those relationships in the community that provided services and emotional support that we normally associate with family. We will want to discover if godparents formed closer bonds than family, if the shared emotions among neighbors were stronger than those among family members, and if parish

257

gilds were more important to people than their family. We want to know what change, if any, population depletion and mobility made in the sense of community, for, as we have seen, family remained stable. A fundamental question in considering the emotional attachments of medieval peasants is whether or not an individual is capable of more than one type of emotional bonding. Ariès and Shorter have implied that the individual either relates to the family or the community, not to both.

We will begin with the problem of the community's intrusion into family life. Stone has described the preindustrial peasant community in terms of a generalized spy network that peered into people's windows and charged them with the immoralities and infringements of rules that they saw therein. This omnipresence of neighbors prohibited the development of intimate emotional lives within the family.[1] The testimony of witnesses in LeRoy Ladurie's account of life in Montaillou also leads a reader to suspect that one could not have a secret with such aggressively curious neighbors.

When one reads court records, it is very easy to see all life as bickering, slander, and gossip, without looking at the other personal interactions that occurred. What may appear at first to be prying may also be interpreted as an effort to protect and preserve family rather than interfere with it.

Most of the material relating to family in manorial courts was concerned with either adjudicating family disputes or keeping family intact. Only a tenth of all manorial court cases dealt with family, and most of these involved property and debts. A very small proportion of the intrafamilial cases involved violence or even adultery.[2] Marital problems were not a routine part of court business. In general, the neighbors appear to have intervened only when the community was disturbed or there was an accompanying infraction of bylaws. While the lord and neighbors might require a bachelor or widow to marry or pay a fine, they did not tell the person whom to marry. Their chief concern was that the house and land be maximally productive. Furthermore, it was not prurient interests that led to the legerwite. The lord used the fine on young women who were deflowered to raise money, and the neighbors might impose it to keep lines of descent beyond dispute.[3] Inheritance problems came into court only when the peasant proprietor died intestate or when there was a dispute over the settlement. In all the cases related to family the court's object was to protect and encourage family, not harass the institution.

The neighbors, through the manorial court, could also be the best protection that an individual from a truncated family could have. In wardship arrangements and retirement contracts it was the community who could intervene if the terms of the contract were not met. The community, then, became the general guardian of such people. The community, however, did not want to know about problems through idle talk and punished those of its members who gossiped "to the grave nuisance of the countryside." Thus Matilda Bowees, Agnes Mulleward, Isabell Ingelfon, Samina Kyinde, and Agnes Andrewe were distrained for being *communes garulators* and William Barbor was fined for gossiping with neighbors.[4]

If neighbors did not inhibit the development of emotional bonds within the family, they might have formed more significant ties with each other than those between one family member and another. The extrafamilial bonds of godparents with the parents of the godchild (coparents), for instance, might replace familial ones. While the significance of the godparent/godchild relationship appears to have been minimal, some historians have argued that the relationship of the coparents was of great importance. In studies of godparenting in Mediterranean countries, and even in LeRoy Ladurie's study of Montaillou, coparents formed a network of mutually beneficial ties. The assumption is that the men and women officiating at the baptism were linked together in a type of kinship tie that promoted cooperation in ventures other than the spiritual welfare of their mutual charge. The relationship was reinforced by ecclesiastical prohibitions against marriages contracted between people who had entered into coparentity.[5] If such a network of mutual cooperation even existed in England, it remains obscure and the very lack of reference suggests that it was relatively unimportant. Testators do not leave bequests to people identified as coparents. Folklore, which reserves a role for godparents in aiding a godchild, has no similar tradition for coparents. The only hint that the relationship may have produced significant ties is linguistic. The common use of *gosse* (*compater*) and *gossep* (*comater*) left us the word *gossip* as a form of address and a derogatory label.

Historians working on village studies have used pledging as an indication of the strength of intervillage ties and the lines that these ties took. A person who was fined, directed to appear at a future session of court, or entering into some form of contract would have to find people who would answer for him if he failed to meet his obligations. These pledges were fined if their pledgee defaulted. Sometimes a person could have such a bad reputation that he could not find a pledge. One man who neglected his tenement on Chalgrave manor to the damage of 100s. could find no one who was willing to stand surety for him, so his land was confiscated.[6] Studies of pledging have introduced conflicting interpretations of its importance for village cohesiveness. All are in agreement that, with the possible exception of husbands standing as pledges for their wives in brewing fines, kin were not called on as pledges. In Redgrave in Suffolk, as we have noted, those groups that relied most heavily on their neighbors were the middle and upper-middle wealth groups who called on each other for pledging and other favors. In Broughton and Holywell-cum-Needingworth there was also evidence of cooperation, but the upper group of villagers played a more active role in pledging for lower-level villagers. Such intergroup pledging could be either a sign of village cohesion or an indication of the dominance of the upper status group over the lower one.[7] As such, it is not an unalloyed example of village emotional ties and loyalites.

Other clues to cooperation among villagers appear in manorial courts. The court could encourage concords and "love days" between community members who were in dispute, so that community harmony could be restored. Community members who were close to each other exchanged pieces of land, worked together in the fields, and lent goods and animals to each other. Again, in the Huntingdonshire villages the main village families tended to predominate in the use of this reciprocity.[8]

Villagers cared enough for each other to risk their lives helping a friend. The coroners' inquests have numerous cases of men who died helping a neighbor free wagons stuck in the mud, put out house fires, catch animals, or secure a boat. Thomas Teddy of Chesterton lost his life helping his neighbor Henry de Becahe put out a house fire. Other people lost their lives standing up for neighbors in quarrels or pursuing a fleeing felon (the hue and cry) in defense of the community peace.[9]

Shared leisure activities accompanied the shared work in the village community. Games, sporting events, drinking, and religious ceremonies brought neighbors into emotional contact. Bull baiting, wrestling matches, and archery contests drew people together, as did the various games of football.[10] The tavern was a social center for both men and women, as we have seen, and people seemed to spend evenings at the local as well as stopping in during the day. Such drinking was not discouraged in Catholic England and, as we have also seen, church ales helped to provide for the upkeep of the parish church.[11] One testator saw the community drink as an opportunity to have prayers said for his soul. He left three acres of meadow and one acre of arable to hold "one drynkynge evermore to be kept the twysday in the rogacon weke at Pekworth Crosse to the Intent to be prayd for ever more and to be parte taker of prayers and suffragis there sayd."[12] His bequest would have provided a generous quantity of beer.

The calendar was also filled with a variety of festivals, both Christian and pagan remnants, that brought the community together. In Croscombe in Somerset, in addition to the youth gilds that we have mentioned, the Archers, who impersonated Robin Hood and Little John, held an archery contest, and the Webbers, Tuckers (fullers), and Hogglers (field laborers and miners) all had performances. The village also performed plays, had a Play-King, and held mock courts in summer and autumn.[13]

Viewed across the centuries, the traditional festivities of peasant communities have an innocent appeal and they were a major contribution to entertainment and socializing among neighbors. They were among many institutions that encouraged community identity and cohesion. The judicial system, based on community arrest and vigilance over bylaw violations, required the participation of all members; the annual beating of the bounds and football matches with neighboring villages contributed to a sense of identity; and the very inevitability of daily contact ensured that good neighborliness would be cultivated. While one would call such neighborly ties emotional, they are not the same as those that we have seen within the family.

Wills show other types of affection and loyalty to communities. Of the 389 people leaving wills in late fifteenth- and early sixteenth-century Bedfordshire, 65 left bequests to repair roads and 32 to repair bridges. Many of the testators, of course, also left gifts for the parish church.

All of these examples of community bonds are exactly what we would expect to find in a world of neighbors, but they are not familial bonds and not a substitute for them. We must turn from the more general ties in the community and look at attitudes toward particular friends.

Friends played a more important part in wills than did extended family, with 419 receiving bequests. Some of the male testators who had children still at home relied on friends to act as executors along with their wives and rewarded them in their wills. Money payments went to a quarter of the friends receiving bequests, animals to 22 percent, personal effects to 19 percent, household goods to 17 percent, and grain to 8 percent. Surprisingly, testators felt so strongly about some of their friends that 7 percent of friends receiving bequests were given land or a house. Others offered their friends the first option or a discount on buying the home tenement. In general, the value of bequests was greater than the ceremonial gifts to godchildren, grandchildren, and other kin. In other words, the wills tend to confirm the conclusion that neighbors and friends, rather than extended kin, played a significant role in daily life.

The wills of widows and older men are particularly informative about the importance of friendships, for they are voluntary arrangements by people who have had a long life of accumulated debts of gratitude. In Northhill in Bedfordshire, at the beginning of the sixteenth century, the wills of Christina Gylmyn, Simon Peyndell, William Tychmeers and his second wife, Catherine, John Taylor, Thomas Kenygall, John Gray, and Robert Harrison all overlapped in their bequests, indicating that they as well as other people they named were linked through mutual friendships. The Basse, Gere, and Hafurne families showed similar overlaps that included intermarriages and the passing on of land among their families.[14]

Social-religious gilds are good candidates for surrogate family, because in their very conception they adopted metaphors of family. Members called each other brother and sister and consciously performed some functions expected from family. They also agreed to submit themselves to the discipline of the head of the gild as they would to a father.

Gilds were multifaceted organizations with religious, political, economic, and social functions, but it is primarily their quasi-familial activities that shall occupy us here. In rural communities all adults who could afford to pay the entrance fee and annual dues belonged to the gild, and sometimes the fees were reduced for the deserving poor. In the village of Bardwell, for instance, there were thirty married couples, thirty single men either widowers or bachelors, and twenty-four single women six of whom were described as widows.[15] Their chief officer was an alderman who was selected from the wealthier members of the gild to serve an annual term.

Of those aspects of gild activity that could be seen as familial, the most apparent was the funeral procession and subsequent prayers for the soul of the departed member. In some respects gild members were surrogate family for the hereafter. Of the nearly five-hundred gilds responding to the writ of 1389 requiring gilds to register their rules, 74 percent told the royal government that funerals for members were of primary importance. The ceremonial expenses of religious observances, both for the public and individual good, were expensive. The funeral masses alone—*dirige, placebo,* and *requiem*—could cost as much as eight marks by the fifteenth century. Such expenses were better borne by a group than an individual. Corpus Christi of Lincoln offered its members four soul candles on the hearse, masses, soul alms from the membership, and the gild banner to be carried before the hearse with the brothers and sisters walking behind it. The gild also paid for bells to be tolled at the funeral.[16] This collective family could put on a more elaborate funeral than most of the individual families would be able to do.

Gilds brought psychological comfort as well as financial relief to members. One could not be sure that family would continue to pray for the dead person even though the will might make bequests conditional on keeping the obit, but gild members could be counted on to pray for former dues-paying members. After all, the members' souls would need the same services in the course of time.

In addition to providing a type of "salvation insurance," gilds offered their members companionate functions. The feast in honor of the gild's patron saint was not simply a religious event, it was a convivial occasion for brothers and sisters to eat well and, perhaps, drink too much. In small fraternities of neighbors the entertainment would fall to each couple in succession to provide the gild meal in their homes. Or the meal would be a simple one of bread, cheese, and ale—in one case, thirty gallons of ale.[17] The fifteenth-century accounts from the Bardwell gild cited earlier in the book give a good picture of how elaborate these village feasts could be. Common worship in the gild chapel, processions on the saint's day, and visiting sick brothers and sisters were all part of gild companionship.

Some gilds, such as that of Bardwell, were wealthy enough to construct a gild hall that could seat as many as 150 members at a communal feast. But smaller gilds relied on a tavern or church-house for their banquets.[18]

Gilds also imposed regulations directed towards socializing their members. Since a quantity of ale was served at the feast and the participants could become boisterous, rules required a solemn prayer at the beginning of the feast. Members who slept noisily or failed to pass the cup when it was set in front of them were fined. A dress code enjoined banqueters from coming in tabard or cloak, or bare-legged or barefoot. And they were to leave their caps and hoods off when they sat at table.[19]

Gilds went beyond the dinner table, instructing their members in general ethical and moral behavior. Thus one gild would exclude a member if "he lie too long in bed, is lazy, looses his goods through his foolishness." Other gilds had rules against brawling, gaming, gambling, talking beyond reason, or other inappropriate behavior. They expelled adulterers, lewd young men, and nonvirgins among their single sisters.[20] In short, they imposed rather puritanical values on their members.

Like any good family, members were required not to fight with each other and to maintain cordial relations with each other at all times. If disagreements arose, they were to go to the head of the gild for arbitration. The intent of all regulations was to achieve internal harmony, and some gilds explicitly drew an analogy to family. Gild members "must stand by a brother or sister charged with any offense such as homicide and in markets, with counsel and help, as if they were all children of the same father and mother."[21]

The gilds might also provide their members with economic aid and support in time of need. The gild account books show how the credit operations worked for members and how the gild, as a whole, profited from the investments. Loans might be in money but were more commonly in kind. In a Cambridge gild, for instance, dues were payable in quarters of malt. The gild placed a value of 4s. to 6s. on a quarter and lent it to members for brewing. The member borrowing malt returned its value plus 1s. 2d. to 1s. 4d. at the end of the year. The gild made over 25 percent on its investment and the member could make and sell beer without a large capital outlay for malt.[22]

Most rural gilds lent livestock. Gilds either purchased herds from the treasury or received them as bequests. Some gilds, such as Eyam in Derbyshire, lent out oxen for plowing. Agricultural historians have pointed out that only the wealthiest peasants could afford to own a full plow team and that others would have to borrow them. Gild ownership of herds permitted villagers to share the expense of purchasing and feeding the oxen.

Many gilds kept breeding stock including sheep, horses, cows, bulls, and so on. The animals were rented for the year and the leasee returned the animal with rent and the value of the offspring, if any.[23] In the fifteenth century, when labor was scarce and more and more land was being turned into pasture, the use of breeding stock would be of great value to gild members and help them to take advantage of the new economic opportunities. It is even possible that the gilds consciously purchased better animals in order to improve the stock of members.

A second economic benefit for members, which we noted earlier, was disaster insurance. Potential disasters were specified: poverty, sickness, old age, blindness, loss of limb, loss of cattle, fall of a house, making a pilgrimage, false imprisonment, aid in temporary pecuniary difficulties, and losses by fire, flood, robbery, or shipwreck. One gild even provided a midwife for the gild sisters.[24] In the 1389 gild returns, 19 percent of the gilds declared that they provided a weekly allowance and clothing in the event of misfortune. The average weekly allowance was only 7d. With a loaf of bread costing 1d., this was not a generous aid. Apparently, gilds did not consider poor relief as one of their main functions.

To avoid abuses, the gilds placed limitations on eligibility. At Ludlow, for instance, a member could only get relief in misfortune three times during his or her lifetime. The word *misfortune* was the key to eligibility, for a member could claim aid only if he were "overtaken by folly not of his doing." One gild would provide for widows "as long as they conduct themselves well and honestly."[25]

The fifteenth-century account book of St. George's Gild in Norwich gives some indication of the recipients of these benefits. This was a large gild and apparently expected to support several people a year because the members had to subscribe $\frac{1}{2}$d. a week for relief. The charity rolls included a brother who had once been wealthy and had even served on the city government. The more usual recipients were poorer members who also held such gild offices as beadsman, bellman, beadle, and so on.[26] In the returns of 1389 the urban gilds showed more concern about insuring members against destitution than rural ones: 46 percent of the urban gilds had provisions for poor members compared to 19 percent of the rural. The rural populace apparently expected to make personal arrangements, rather than use their gilds, in the event of old age or misfortune.

Of all the extrafamilial bonds that we have investigated—coparenthood, pledging, personal friendships, and gild membership—the latter comes the closest to being surrogate family. And yet gilds did not provide the same emotional functions that family did. In the final analysis they were voluntary associations, not family.

Another approach to assessing the strength of bonds between neighbors as familial substitutes is to look at what community did not do. If we begin with the very basic and biological, community did not reproduce the species. Most children were born in wedlock. The community was not the primary trainer of children; rather, parents took the major responsibility without seeming to have much recourse to godparents. And the selection of marriage partners was not a community decision, even when community urged marriage. When a child was scalded, it was not the community that called upon a saint to revive little Agnes, but Agnes's mother.

The basic unit of production was not the community but the individual household. All members of the household contributed work on the family land, and when they reached the age of majority all children expected some share in its accumulated wealth. The community did not decide what portions would go to which children in the family unless a father died without making his wishes known.

When a person lay on his or her deathbed and drew up a final will and testament, the priorities of emotional concerns were first for the salvation of his or her own soul; second, the division of family property among family members; and third (if the second had been done inter vivos), to remember friends and more distant relatives and godchildren. Only after having seen to these obligations did the testator leave goods to gilds, hospitals, and for roads and bridges.

Community could provide only a portion of the material and emotional needs of an individual. While important to the medieval peasant, it was rather limited as a surrogate for family. The argument of Shorter and Ariès suffers from a basic fallacy, namely, that humans have only a finite ability to form emotional bonds. They can either form these bonds with the family or with the community, not both. In traditional society, these authors argue, these ties were with the community, and in the modern period they shifted over to family. Humans, however, form a variety of emotional bonds that vary somewhat with the circumstances. A peasant's ties with his neighbors, while emotional, were of a very different sort from those with family, just as a modern college graduate might feel emotional ties to an alma mater that are very distinct from his or her ties to a real mother. One might argue that the modern world is poorer for having lost community bonds while not necessarily having gained more familial ones.

Perhaps the nostalgia for the past that has entered into our modern view is not for the loss of extended family and distant kin, but rather the closeness to neighbors and community cohesion. The close-knit community of the Middle Ages began to break down by the beginning of the fifteenth century. Gilds may have been formed to meet the perceived decline in community ties rather than as a substitute for family ties. Thus gilds were more properly surrogate community rather than surrogate family. The Poor Laws of the sixteenth century may be seen as an attempt to reinstitute the old community services with the force of law. Such laws tried to enforce community, not family spirit.

The plague and other diseases took their toll of the community in more than numbers of dead. Although family units tended to regroup fairly quickly, with more distant kin taking the place of family who died, they did not have the same socialization into the community that the former tenants had, the mutual cooperation and community cohesion that had been built on generations of interactions and trust. Of the old power structure at Overton in Huntingdonshire, for instance, only two of the main village families remained after the 1348. New families in the village tended to be more opportunistic and the older families could not keep the dominance they once had.[27] Attractive wages lured away people with less desirable lands, and new people, not even related by distant family ties, came into communities. The fifteenth century saw the development of greater differences in the wealth of community members. The primary villagers acquired more land and also a new title, that of yeoman, while the poorer villagers increasingly lost wealth and status relative to the yeomen.[28]

Although no one would argue that community suddenly ceased to play a large role in peasants' lives, the signs of breakdown were unmistakable. Pledging, the most apparent example of community cooperation in the court rolls, began to decline in the fifteenth century. Trespasses tended to increase, particularly the trespass of animals into a neighbor's crops, and violence among the higher-status peasants rose.[29] Another sign of the waning of community was the decline in importance of community policing and of manorial courts. The justices of the peace increasingly replaced the sheriff's tourn and gradually took over the slander, assault, debt, and trespass cases from the manorial courts. The rising peasant proprietors, the yeomen, participated in the change and identified increasingly with the gentry rather than with the lower peasantry who worked for them. The demise of serfdom meant that, even to the lords, manor courts ceased to be as important as they once had been.[30]

While families showed resilience and regrouped into nuclear units fairly readily, the community proved less robust. If there was a major change from the medieval to the early modern period it took place less in the structure and function of family than in community.

Epilogue

If the medieval peasants whose actions are recounted in these pages appear to behave in ways that are entirely comprehensible to us, and if their family life does not seem unfamiliar, perhaps we should not be surprised. We have more continuity with the lives of our ancestors than we normally assume. Historians are so dedicated to showing change over time and revolutionary breaks with the past that they often overlook historical behavior that does not change radically. Historians are also prone to making implicit value judgments about the past, looking back at earlier times with nostalgia for lost innocence or, alternatively, seeing in the past the horrors of a benighted time from which we modern people have fortunately escaped. Neither approach does justice to the lives of our peasant ancestors. We are not entirely like them, but they are not alien to us even though we are separated from them by five hundred years.

When considering an institution as basic as the family, the very biological necessities of perpetuating our species ensures that many aspects of medieval life must be similar to our own. The elemental care of children in their first years and the awkwardness of adolescence cannot be substantially modified simply through different cultural norms. The family is a particularly interesting social phenomenon to study, because it is an intersection of both the biological and the cultural. While suckling a baby is biological, other aspects of family life, such as treatment of the aged, is cultural.

The family has proved to be a remarkably flexible institution. People have adapted it to a number of severe economic swings, but it remains recognizable. The family has gone from the economy of hunting and gathering, through one of peasant cultivation, and is still a viable institution in the modern world.

268

Appendix: Coroners' Rolls

The office of coroner was created in 1194 in the counties of England as an aid to the royal administration, particularly the general eyres. Each county was to elect four knights to act as coroners, but in practice the number varied from two to four. The coroners' duties covered a range of adminstrative activities, but their chief function was to investigate all deaths that were unnatural, violent, sudden, or surrounded by suspicious circumstances. In practice this meant that they investigated all cases of homicide, suicide, and accidental death or misadventure.

When a body was found, the first finder (either the actual person who found the body or someone in the community who assumed this legal role) summoned the neighbors, who sent off for one of the coroners. The coroner was to come as quickly as possible, summon a jury from the vicinity, and view the corpse. He turned it over, noted wounds, and tried to determine the probable cause of death. The body was then buried and the inquest was held. The jurors had collected information among the community to determine the activities of the person before he or she died, the people present, the instrument that caused the death, the time of day, and so on. The instrument that caused an accidental death was assessed and the crown claimed the value of the object, the deodand. In the case of homicide, an indictment would be made and directions sent out to arrest the suspect. The coroner or his clerk kept a record of the inquest to present to the royal justices when they came to the county. When the justices demanded the records, a fair copy was made by the clerk for deposit with the justices.

While the eyres worked smoothly in the thirteenth century, the coroners' rolls were fairly routinely collected, but in the fourteenth century the collection of the rolls was more sporadic, so that few counties have continuous series of coroners' rolls. Furthermore, the quality of the rolls submitted varied considerably, with some being very complete reports while others gave only the bare essentials. In the fifteenth century very few coroners' rolls were collected and preserved.[1]

The rolls used in this study are from those counties in which the coroners kept fairly detailed records, even if only for a brief period. The most detailed of all the records are those of the late thirteenth century (1265–1276, 1300–1317) from Bedfordshire, 94 cases.[2] Cambridgeshire (Just. 2/17, 18, 21, 24), 418 cases, covers the years 1374 to 1376. Lincolnshire (Just. 2/64–93), 1115 cases, deals with the years 1349 to 1393. Norfolk (Just. 2/102–105), 261 cases, covers 1362 to 1379. Northamptonshire (Just. 2/107–127),

674 cases, has the most complete series, covering most of the fourteenth century (1301–1419). Wiltshire (Just. 2/193–204), 275 cases, includes rolls from the years 1341 to 1384. While the six counties are spread throughout England, the southeast and northwest are not represented.

In the current study I used only the misadventure cases, with a scattering of homicide cases for illustration of particular points. The misadventure cases presented a more accurate and detailed picture of people's daily life. Furthermore, the seasonality and victims of misadventures and homicides differed widely, so all the homicides are left out of calculations. Because of the sporadic nature of the collection of rolls, I made no attempt to look at trends in different types of accidents. My chief interest in the accidental-death cases was the incidental details of daily life. I have been more interested in the qualitative detail of the record than in accumulating quantitative information. Since the cases are not uniform, some contain more descriptive material than others. For this reason, not all of the material was even quantifiable. Some quantitative results, presented here in the form of tables, contribute to a greater understanding of patterns of daily routines for men, women, and children.

The material on children is particularly rich because the coroners recorded the age of children through the age of twelve. Until a child reached the age of twelve it was not legally responsible for criminal acts and did not join a tithing group. Fortunately, coroners recorded the ages of most children, even those who died of misadventure. The very act of recording these ages suggests that society noted the death of children in particular. The ages of adults were only occasionally given, with some coroner or his clerk taking an interest in providing such information. Norfolk and Cambridge coroners seem to have been most interested in ages.

The information contained in the rolls is of enormous diversity and, although the cases were coded into machine-readable form, the variety has been too great to reproduce here. Any number of objects could cause death, people engaged in a wide range of activities when they died, some died immediately and others lingered for months, and the places of death were numerous. The rich quality of these documents enhanced their value as a guide to everyday life, but that very richness is difficult to duplicate in a table. The grouping of information into categories means that some of the vividness of the record is lost. For this reason the tables have been put into the appendix for those who wish to have further information. So that the reader may form some idea of the detail in the records, I have included one table with the aggregate data on activities of the victim at the time of death.

Table 1. Adult Males and Females: Place of Accident

	Males		Females	
Home	118	11.8%	87	29.5%
Private property[a]	62	6.2	27	9.0
Public areas[b]	181	18.1	66	22.0
Work areas[c]	377	37.7	53	17.5
Bodies of water	262	26.2	67	22.0
	1000	100.0%	300	100.0%

[a] Includes neighbour's house or close, taverns, manor houses, etc.
[b] Includes greens, streets, highways, markets, churches, etc.
[c] Includes fields, marl pits, shops, etc.

Table 2. Adult Males and Females: Activity

	Males		Females	
Agriculture	203	19.1%	10	4.0%
Construction	119	11.2	0	0.0
Craft	32	3.0	12	5.0
Supplemental Economic[a]	78	7.3	24	9.0
Household Related	43	4.0	87	37.0
Tranportation[b]	465	43.7	70	30.0
Play and Leisure	39	3.7	18	8.0
Personal	79	7.4	16	7.0
Total	1058	99.4%	237	100.0%

[a] Includes begging, hunting and gathering, marketing, etc.
[b] Includes walking, horseback riding, carting, etc.
[c] Includes bathing, washing clothes, sleeping, visiting, being a bystander, etc.

Table 3. Adult Males: Activity by Age[a]

	13–19		20–30		31–45		46 +	
Agriculture	7	17.5%	7	16.7%	5	15.6%	6	17.6%
Construction	2	5.2	1	2.4	5	15.6	2	5.9
Craft	0	0.0	2	4.7	1	3.2	0	0.0
Supplemental eco.	9	23.1	7	16.7	3	9.4	3	8.8
Household	1	2.6	2	4.7	2	6.3	1	2.9
Transportation	10	25.6	17	40.5	12	37.5	19	56.0
Play	1	2.6	0	0.0	3	9.4	0	0.0
Personal	9	23.1	6	14.3	1	3.1	3	8.8
Total	39	100.0%	42	100.0%	32	100.0%	34	100.0%

[a] Sample of adult females with age given too small to tabulate.

Table 4. Place of Death by Age of Male Children

	Infant		1		2		3		4–6		7–12	
Home	15	78.9%	37	54.4%	62	47.7%	48	60.8%	15	35.7%	15	16.9%
Private property	4	21.1	10	14.7	26	20.0	6	7.5	9	21.4	10	11.2
Public areas	0	0.0	12	17.6	22	16.9	15	19.0	9	21.4	12	13.5
Work area	0	0.0	2	2.9	2	1.5	3	3.8	2	4.8	14	15.7
Bodies of water	0	0.0	7	10.3	18	13.9	7	8.9	7	16.7	38	42.7
Total	19	100.0%	68	100.0%	130	100.0%	79	100.0%	42	100.0%	89	100.0%

Table 5. Place of Death by Age of Female Children

	Infant		1		2		3		4–6		7–12	
Home	37	94.9%	40	67.8%	45	39.8%	27	51.9%	14	42.4%	7	25.9%
Private property	2	5.1	10	16.9	22	19.5	11	21.2	5	15.2	3	11.1
Public areas	0	0.0	5	8.5	29	25.7	6	11.5	4	12.1	7	25.9
Work area	0	0.0	0	0.0	5	4.4	1	1.9	0	0.0	2	7.4
Bodies of water	0	0.0	4	6.8	12	10.6	7	13.5	10	30.3	8	29.6
Total	39	100.0%	59	100.0%	113	100.0%	52	100.0%	33	100.0%	27	100.0%

Table 6. Activity by Age for Male Children

	Infant		1		2		3		4–6		7–12	
Agriculture	0	0.0%	0	0.0%	0	0.0%	0	0.0%	0	0.0%	11	12.9%
Construction	0	0.0	0	0.0	0	0.0	0	0.0	0	0.0	0	0.0
Craft	0	0.0	0	0.0	0	0.0	0	0.0	0	0.0	2	2.4
Supplemental eco.	0	0.0	0	0.0	1	1.3	0	0.0	0	0.0	6	7.1
Household	0	0.0	0	0.0	1	1.3	4	8.7	5	19.2	8	9.4
Transportation[a]	0	0.0	6	12.2	13	16.8	8	17.4	4	15.4	28	32.9
Play	2	11.8	25	51.0	52	67.6	30	65.2	14	53.9	20	23.5
Personal[b]	15	88.2	18	36.8	10	13.0	4	8.7	3	11.5	10	11.8
Total	17	100.0%	49	100.0%	77	100.0%	46	100.0%	26	100.0%	85	100.0%

[a] For all categories until age 7–12 walking is the chief mode of transportation.

[b] For infants and toddlers this category consists primarily of sleeping, but for the older children it may include washing in addition.

Table 7. Activity by Age for Female Children

	Infant		1		2		3		4–6		7–12	
Agriculture	0	0.0%	0	0.0%	0	0.0%	0	0.0%	0	0.0%	0	0.0%
Construction	0	0.0	0	0.0	0	0.0	0	0.0	0	0.0	0	0.0
Craft	0	0.0	0	0.0	0	0.0	0	0.0	0	0.0	0	0.0
Supplemental eco.	0	0.0	0	0.0	1	1.5	0	0.0	1	4.2	1	4.5
Household[a]	0	0.0	2	5.7	4	6.2	3	8.8	1	4.2	10	45.5
Transportation	0	0.0	5	14.3	8	12.3	8	23.6	2	8.3	3	13.6
Play	2	5.6	12	34.3	45	69.2	20	58.8	14	58.3	6	27.3
Personal	34	94.4	16	45.7	7	10.8	3	8.8	6	25.0	2	9.1
Total	36	100.0%	35	100.0%	65	100.0%	34	100.0%	24	100.0%	22	100.0%

[a] Most household accidents for the infants and toddlers involved playing with pots.

Table 8. Activities at Time of Victim's Death: Aggregate Numbers

Agricultural work
- 21 General fieldwork
- 120 Carting in field
- 8 Digging marl
- 1 Guarding crops
- 2 Harrowing
- 7 Harvesting
- 2 Haymaking
- 2 Plowing
- 18 Herding
- 45 Working with animals
- 1 Milking

Construction
- 41 General construction
- 3 Carpentry
- 14 Carting for construction
- 1 Cleaning structures
- 14 Cutting timber
- 5 Masonry
- 1 Painting
- 20 Quarrying
- 4 Thatching
- 1 Road work

Crafts
- 4 General crafts
- 17 Brewing
- 15 Milling
- 1 Tanning
- 6 Wool production
- 4 Carting goods

Supplementary economic activities
- 18 General
- 1 Baby-sitting
- 12 Begging
- 35 Cutting firewood
- 27 Fishing
- 17 Food gathering
- 2 Hunting
- 1 Looking for work
- 3 Marketing
- 3 Gardening

Housework
- 17 General
- 1 Cleaning
- 7 Cooking
- 51 Drawing water from well
- 41 Drawing water, general
- 16 Placing candle
- 11 Going to mill
- 12 Laundry
- 6 Storage

Travel
- 11 General
- 107 Boating
- 132 Carriage, carts
- 110 Horseback
- 154 Walking
- 18 Walking drunk
- 20 Fording bodies of water

Playing
- 261 General
- 6 Ball games
- 6 Drinking
- 5 Play with animals
- 3 Play with fire
- 5 Play with knives
- 2 Play with staffs
- 1 Private entertainment
- 5 Bow and arrow
- 7 Play in water
- 3 Wrestling

Personal
- 13 General
- 35 Bathing
- 15 Bystanding event
- 4 Eating
- 81 Lying in cradle
- 3 Relieving oneself
- 10 Sitting in close
- 28 Sitting in house
- 10 Sitting in public
- 43 Sleeping
- 2 Visiting

1205 Unknown

Notes

1. Michael Mitterauer and Reinhard Sieder, *The European Family: Patriarchy to Partnership from the Middle Ages to the Present*, trans. Karla Oosterveen and Manfred Horzinger (Chicago, 1982), Chap. 1. Recent historiography on the preindustrial European peasant family abounds with discussions of patrilineage, patriarchy, kinship, and family types. Since the purpose of the current study is not a historiographical essay but rather an attempt to discuss what we know about the medieval family, I will not attempt to provide a complete discussion of the various views, many of which are not relevant to this study. For recent evaluations of the literature, see: Jack Goody, *The Development of the Family and Marriage in Europe* (Cambridge, 1983), pp. 1–5, and Louise Tilly and Miriam Cohen, "Does the Family Have a History? A Review of Theory and Practice in Family History," *Social Science History* 6 (1982), pp. 131–180.

2. Alan Macfarlane, *The Origins of English Individualism* (New York, 1979), pp. 7–33.

3. R. H. Hilton, *The English Peasantry in the Later Middle Ages: The Ford Lectures for 1973 and Related Studies* (Oxford, 1975), Chap. 1, particularly p. 13. For a more abbreviated definition, see Eric R. Wolf, *Peasants* (Englewood Cliffs, N.J. 1966), pp. 1–4, and Theodor Shanin, ed., *Peasants and Peasant Societies* (Harmondsworth, 1971), pp. 11–19.

4. J. Ambrose Raftis, "Social Structure in Five East Midlands Villages: A Study of Possibilities in the Use of Court Roll Data," *Economic History Review*, 2nd ser., 18 (1965), pp. 83–100, and "The Concentration of Responsibility in Five Villages," *Mediaeval Studies* 28 (1966), pp. 92–118, were the two pioneering studies of the methodology. Edwin DeWindt, *Land and People in Holywell-cum-Needingworth* (Toronto, 1972), took the method farther. Edward Britton, *The Community of the Vill: A Study in the History of the Family and Village Life in Fourteenth-Century England* (Toronto, 1977), pp. 166–169, includes a discussion of the legal, as opposed to social, distinctions between villein and serf. Zvi Razi, *Life, Marriage and Death in a Medieval Parish: Economy, Society and Demography in Halesowen, 1270–1400* (Cambridge, 1980), used the same methodology but was more interested in demography than in social status indicators and social interactions.

5. The summary of demographic, economic, and social conditions in the fourteenth and fifteenth centuries has been brief and only meant to be a reminder of the major events and an aid to nonspecialists. Several excellent books provide more information. Hilton, *English Peasantry*, discusses the impact of these events on the manorial system and the peasantry. J. Z. Titow, *English Rural Society, 1200–1350* (New York, 1969), discusses the earlier period, the contributions of M. M. Postan, and the controversies surrounding Postan's Malthusian interpretation of late-thirteenth- and early-fourteenth-century demography. John Hatcher, *Plague, Population and the English Economy, 1348–1530* (London, 1977), assesses the effects of depopulation on the countryside. J. L. Bolton, *The Medieval English Economy, 1150–1500* (London, 1980), provides a convenient overview. For the effects of the depopulation on particular communities, see J. Ambrose Raftis, "Changes in an English Village after the Black Death," *Mediaeval Studies* 29 (1967), pp. 158–177, and DeWindt, *Holywell-cum-Needingworth*.

6. Edward Shorter, *The Making of the Modern Family* (New York, 1975), pp. 3–4, for analogy of family to ship; pp. 22–53 for more complete discussion. Lawrence Stone, *The Family, Sex and Marraige in England, 1500–1800* (New York, 1977), pp. 4–7, 87–93. Philippe Ariès, *Centuries of Childhood: A Social History of Family Life*, trans. Robert Baldick (New York, 1962), p. 368.

7. Macfarlane, *Origins of English Individualism*, pp. 87–197.

8. Ibid., p. 16.

9. David Herlihy and Christiane Klapisch-Zuber, *Les Toscans et leur familles: un étude des catasto florentin de 1427* (Paris, 1978). Diane Owen Hughes, "Urban Growth and Family Structure in Medieval Genoa," *Past and Present* 66 (1975), pp. 3–28. Randolph Trumbach, *The Rise of the Egalitarian Family: Aristocratic Kinship and Domestic Relations in Eighteenth-Century England* (New York, 1978), pp. 13–16 and in his introduction, tried to develop a model that distinguished between the lineage system of the aristocracy and the kindred system of the peasantry or lower classes. He based his generalizations largely on Diane Hughes's study of family in Genoa. When one comes to examine it closely, however, the distinctions begin to crumble and one is left once again with the dilemma that a Mediterranean city may not provide the best model for agrarian England.

10. Georges Duby, *Medieval Marriage: Two Models from Twelfth-Century France*, trans. Elborg Forster (Baltimore, 1978). Jacques Heers, *Le Clan familial du Moyen Age: Étude sur les structures politiques et sociales des milieux urbains* (Paris, 1974). Sylvia Thrupp, *The Merchant Class of Medieval London* (Chicago, 1948). These are but a few examples of a more extensive literature.

11. Ronald Blythe, *Akenfield: Portrait of an English Village* (New York, 1969), is a fine example of the use of oral history for reconstructing the milieu of village life. George C. Homans, *English Villagers of the Thirteenth Century* (Cambridge, Mass., 1941), p. 109. H. S. Bennett, *Life on the English Manor* (Cambridge, 1937), pp. 237–238.

12. *Select Cases from the Coroners' Rolls, A.D. 1265–1413*, ed. Charles Gross, Selden Society 9 (London, 1896), pp. 14–15. This volume contains sample cases with both the Latin original and an English translation and is a fine introduction to the coroners' rolls.

Chapter 1. Field and Village Plans

1. Trevor Rowley, "Medieval Fields Systems," in *The English Medieval Landscape*, ed. Leonard Cantor (Philadelphia, 1982), pp. 25–55. This essay contains a good summary of current knowledge about fields and their origins.

2. Howard L. Gray, *The English Field Systems*, Harvard Historical Studies 22 (Cambridge, Mass., 1915). Charles Orwin and Christabel Orwin, *The Open Fields* (Oxford, 1938).

3. W. G. Hoskins, *Leicestershire: An Illustrated Essay on the History of the Landscape* (London, 1957), p. 4. Historians of local and village history owe a debt of gratitude to Hoskins and his students for introducing landscape evidence.

4. Brian K. Roberts, *Rural Settlement in Britain* (Folkstone, Kent, 1977), pp. 87–88.

5. Ibid., p. 86.

6. Hoskins, *Leicestershire*, p. 17.

7. J. Ambrose Raftis, "Town and Country Migration," in *Studies of Peasant Mobility in a Region of Late Thirteenth and Early Fourteenth Century*, ed. Edward Britton and J. Ambrose Raftis (in manuscript).

8. Warren O. Ault, *Open-Field Farming in Medieval England* (London, 1972), p. 65.

9. W. G. Hoskins, *Local History in England* (London, 1959), pp. 46–47.

10. J. Ambrose Raftis, *Tenure and Mobility: Studies in the Social History of the Mediaeval English Village* (Toronto, 1964), pp. 18–20. J. Z. Titow, "Some Differences between Manors and Their Effects on the Condition of the Peasant in the Thirteenth Century," *The Agricultural History Review* 10 (1962), p. 3. He found that in Taunton, Wargrave, and Witney 56 to 74 percent of the peasants held fifteen acres and 5 to 12 percent held thirty or more acres.

11. Just. 2/113 m. 29.

12. Ault, *Open-Field Farming*, pp. 51–53.

13. Raftis, *Tenure and Mobility*, p. 97.

14. Barbara A. Hanawalt, *Crime and Conflict in English Communities, 1300–1348* (Cambridge, Mass., 1979), pp. 54, 99.

15. *Bedfordshire Coroners' Rolls*, trans. R. F. Hunnisett, Bedfordshire Historical Record Society 41 (1961), p. 99.

16. M. W. Barley, "Farmhouses and Cottages, 1550–1725," *Economic History Review*, 2nd ser., 7 (1954–1955), pp. 291–306. W. G. Hoskins, "The Rebuilding of Rural England, 1570–1640," *Past and Present* 4 (1953), pp. 44–59.

17. Roberts, *Rural Settlement*, pp. 122–128.

18. Peter Bigmore, "Villages and Towns," in *The English Medieval Landscape*, ed. Leonard Cantor (Philadelphia, 1982), p. 164.

19. J. G. Hurst, "A Review of Archaeological Research to 1968," in *Deserted Medieval Villages*, ed. Maurice Beresford and J. G. Hurst (London, 1971), pp. 125–127. Bigmore, "Villages and Towns," pp. 164–166, suggests that the Wharram Percy pattern is more typical of the north than the Midlands. In both Durham and Yorkshire, perhaps in response to destruction from raids, villages were replanned in a more regular fashion. But certainly this argument would have to apply more to the fourteenth than the thirteenth century.

20. Colin Platt, *Medieval England: A Social History and Archaeology from the Conquest to 1600 A.D.* (New York, 1978), pp. 38–39. Bigmore, "Villages and Towns," pp. 169–170, suggests that some village contractions, such as in the relatively high-altitude Hound Tor in Dartmoor, showed signs of attempts to deal with the worsening climate in the fourteenth century by building grain-drying facilities and converting deserted houses into barns. Conversion of deserted houses into barns appears to have been routine throughout England.

21. Hurst, "A Review," pp. 130–131.

22. Ibid., p. 127.

23. Ibid., pp. 128–129.

24. Ibid., p. 126.

25. Just. 2/104 m. 2, 2/73 m. 2d.

26. Just. 2/18 m. 46.

27. Guy Beresford, *The Medieval Clay-Land Village: Excavations at Glotho and Barton Blont* (London, 1975), pp. 46–47. Just. 2/85 m. 5.

28. Just. 2/104 m. 23.

29. Just. 2/18 m. 48d., 2/103, 2/71 m. 3, and many other examples.

30. Just. 2/195 m. 2.

31. Just. 2/91 ms. 4, 5, 6; 2/82 m. 5d.; 2/92 m. 2; and *Bedfordshire Coroners' Rolls*, p. 91.

32. Just. 2/18 m. 58d.

33. Just. 2/83 m. 1d. In Just. 2/66 m. 2d. a woman "went to church to see the sacrament."

34. *Church-Wardens' Accounts of Croscombe, Pilton, Latton, Tintinhull, Morebath, and St. Michael's Bath*, ed. Edmund Hobhouse, Somerset Record Society 4 (1890), p. xxi. Lawrence A. Blair, *English Church Ales* (Ann Arbor, Mich., 1940). Dorothy Owen, *Church and Society in Medieval Lincolnshire*, Lincolnshire Local History Society 5 (1971), p. 131.

35. Just. 2/82 m. 5.

36. Just. 2/18 m. 44. *Court Rolls of the Manor of Wakefield*, I, trans. W. P. Baildon, The Yorkshire Archaeological Society Record Series 29 (1901), p. 267, hereafter referred to as *Wakefield*, I.

37. *Bedfordshire Coroners' Rolls*, p. 46.

38. Ibid., pp. 50, 51.

39. Just. 2/67 m. 8d.

40. Beresford, *Clay-Land Villages*, p. 19.

41. Just. 2/195, ms. 4, 4d.

42. *Bedfordshire Coroners' Rolls*, p. 46.

43. Just. 2/17 m. 4d.

Chapter 2. Toft and Croft

1. George Homans, *English Villagers of the Thirteenth-Century* (Cambridge, Mass., 1941), pp. 72–74, 208–209,

2. Michael Mitterauer and Reinhard Sieder, *The European Family: Patriarchy to Partnership from the Middle Ages to the Present*, trans. Karla Oosterveen and Manfred Horzinger (Chicago, 1981), pp. 9–10. Emmanuel LeRoy Ladurie, *Montaillou: The Promised Land of Error*, trans. Barbara Bray (New York, 1978), pp. 24–37.

3. J. G. Hurst, "A Review of Archaeological Research to 1968," In *Deserted Medieval Villages*, ed. Maurice Beresford and J. G. Hurst (London, 1971), pp. 104–107, 114.

4. Guy Beresford, *The Medieval Clay-Land Village: Excavations at Glotho and Barton Blont* (London, 1975), pp. 12–13.

5. Hurst, "A Review," pp. 106–107.

6. Beresford, *Medieval Clay-Land Village*, p. 19. J. G. Hurst, "The Changing Medieval Village in England," in *Pathways to Medieval Peasants*, ed. J. A. Raftis (Toronto, 1981), pp. 44–48.

7. R. K. Field, "Worcestershire Peasant Buildings, Household Goods and Farming Equipment in the Later Middle Ages," *Medieval Archaeology*, 9 (1965), pp. 126–128.

8. *Bedfordshire Coroners' Rolls*, trans. R. F. Hunnisett, Bedfordshire Historical Record Society, 41 (1961), p. 98. Just. 2/67 m. 1d.

9. Hurst, "A Review," pp. 90–91.

10. *Bedfordshire Coroners' Rolls*, p. 12.

11. F. W. B. Charles, *Medieval Cruck Building and Its Derivatives* (London, 1967), pp. 16–32. H. M. Colvin, "Farmhouses and Cottages," in *Medieval England*, ed. A. Lane Poole (London, 1958), pp. 77–97. Eric Mercer, *English Vernacular Houses: A Study of Traditional Farmhouses and Cottages* (London, 1975). *Wheatley Records, 956–1956*, ed. W. O. Hassall, Oxford Record Society 27 (1956), p. 12.

12. Field, "Worcestershire Peasant Buildings," pp. 112–114.

13. Beresford, *Medieval Clay-Land Village*, p. 41.

14. N. W. Alcock, "The Medieval Cottages of Bishops Clyst, Devon," *Medieval Archaeology* 9 (1965), pp. 146–153. Just. 2/67 m. 34 cites a case where a cartload of tiles is being carried in Lincolnshire. And in 2/87 m. 3 a man who is sitting in his chamber was killed when a roof tile fell on his head.

15. *The Court Rolls of the Manor of Wakefield from October 1331 to September 1333*, ed. Sue Sheridan Walker, Yorkshire Archaeological Society, 2nd ser., 2 (forthcoming), pp. 37–38. The manuscript was lent to me courtesy of the author and will be noted in the text in further references as Walker, *Wakefield*.

16. Hurst, "A Review," p. 99.

17. Ibid., pp. 94–96. Beresford, *Medieval Clay-Land Village*, p. 20.

18. Alcock, "Medieval Cottages," pp. 147–149.

19. Field, "Worcestershire Peasant Buildings," pp. 125–126. *Chertsey Abbey Court Rolls Abstract*, ed. Elsie Toms, Surrey Record Society 21, part 1 (1937), part 2 (1954), pp. xx–xxi, for other examples.

20. *Court Roll of Chalgrave Manor, 1278–1313*, ed. Marian K. Dale, Bedfordshire Record Society 28 (1954), p. 33.

21. Just. 2/92 m. 4.

22. Beresford, *Medieval Clay-Land Village*, pp. 27–29. Hurst, "A Review," p. 99.

23. Just. 2/18 ms. 5, 42. In one case the straw on the floor came from shelling beans. In Just. 2/77 m. 4 a woman returned from a tavern at night with a candle in her hand. She put it on the straw on the floor by the bed.

24. Just. 2/92 m. 4d.

25. *Bedfordshire Coroners' Rolls*, p. 44.

26. Ibid., p. 37. Just 3/48.

27. Field, "Worcestershire Peasant Buildings," p. 111.

28. Just. 2/199 m. 6d.

29. Just. 2/93 m. 3.

30. Just. 2/18 m. 46, 2/104 m. 49, 2/195 m. 15d. The latter is a case of a servant woman working in a solar during harvest.

31. Guy Beresford, "Three Deserted Medieval Settlements on Dartmoor: A Report on the Late E. Marie Minter's Excavations," *Medieval Archaeology* 23 (1979), pp. 135–136.

32. Just. 2/67 m. 40, 2/87 m. 3, 2/194 m. 12. *Bedfordshire Coroners' Rolls*, pp. 92, 102.

33. Just. 2/203 m. 7.

34. Just. 2/201 m. 1.

35. Hurst, "A Review," p. 98. Beresford, *Medieval Clay-Land Village*, p. 44. S. Moorhouse, "A Late Medieval Domestic Rubbish Deposit from Broughton, Lincolnshire," *Lincolnshire History and Archaeology* 9 (1974), pp. 3–6.

36. Hurst, "A Review," p. 98.

37. *Court Rolls of the Manor of Wakefield*, I, trans. W. P. Baildon, The Yorkshire Archaeological Record Society Series, 29 (1901), p. 261.

38. Just. 2/104 m. 7. See also Just. 2/67 m. 14d.

39. *Bedfordshire Coroners' Rolls*, pp. 228, 236. Just. 2/67 m. 23, 2/18 m. 19d.

40. Just. 2/66 m. 2 and 2/93 m. 3 mentions a well ten feet deep. Some wells were covered to prevent accidents; Just. 2/77 m. 3d.

41. See, for instance, Just. 2/66 m. 2 for various examples. Beresford, *Medieval Clay-Land Village*, p. 44.

42. Just. 2/67 m. 19d., 2/68 ms. 1, 2.

43. Beresford, *Medieval Clay-Land Village*, p. 44.

44. Hurst, "A Review," p. 116.

45. James E. Thorold Rogers, *Six Centuries of Work and Wages: The History of English Labour* (London, 1884), p. 67.

46. *Bedfordshire Coroners' Rolls*, pp. 33, 92, 111.

47. Ibid., p. 73.

48. Beresford, *Medieval Clay-Land Village*, pp. 13–17, 45.

49. Just. 2/220 m. 5.

50. Just. 2/18 m. 2.

51. Just. 2/85 m. 6, 2/91 m. 8d.

52. W. O. Ault, *Open-Field Husbandry and the Village Community: A Study of Agrarian By-laws in Medieval England*, Transactions of the American Philosophical Society 55 (Philadelphia, 1965), p. 29.

53. Hurst, "A Review," p. 115.

54. Just. 2/17 m. 1d. See also Just. 2/84 m. 8, 2/71 m. 2d., 2/69 m. 3.

55. Beresford, *Medieval Clay-Land Village*, pp. 45–46.

56. Just. 2/88 m. 3.

57. Beresford, *Medieval Clay-Land Village*, p. 12.

58. Hurst, "Changing Medieval Village," p. 33.

59. The description of the uses of ditches is taken from numerous examples in the coroners' rolls. For an example of a boy pole-vaulting, see Just. 2/70 m. 7.

60. Just. 2/91 m. 3. The discussion of activities in the close is taken from many examples in the coroners' rolls. The activities of men, women, and children will be discussed more fully in other sections.

61. Just. 2/200 m. 8.

62. Lawrence Stone, *The Family, Sex, and Marriage in England, 1500–1800* (New York, 1975), pp. 6, 93. Edward Shorter, *The Making of the Modern Family* (New York, 1975), pp. 44–53.

63. Hurst, "A Review," p. 80.

64. R. H. Hilton, *The English Peasantry in the Later Middle Ages: The Ford Lectures for 1973 and Related Studies* (Oxford, 1975), p. 56; other examples in manorial court rolls.

65. Marjorie J. O. Kennedy, "Resourceful Villeins: The Cellarer Family of Wawne in Holderness," *Yorkshire Archaeological Journal* 48 (1976), p. 116.

66. Margot R. Adamson, *A Treasury of Middle English Verse Selected and Rendered into Modern English* (London, 1930), p. 87.

Chapter 3. Standards of Living

1. R. T. Davies, *Medieval English Lyrics: A Critical Anthology* (Evanston, Ill., 1964), pp. 71–73.

2. Geoffrey Chaucer, *The Canterbury Tales*, trans. Nevill Coghill (Harmondsworth, 1951), pp. 35–36.

3. R. K. Field, "Worcestershire Peasant Buildings, Household Goods and Farming Equipment in the Later Middle Ages," *Medieval Archaeology* 9 (1965), pp. 105–145.

4. Ibid., pp. 140, 145.

5. J. G. Hurst, "A Review of Archaeological Research to 1968," in *Deserted Medieval Villages*, ed. Maurice Beresford and J. G. Hurst (London, 1971), p. 141. Guy Beresford, *The Medieval Clay-Land Village: Excavations at Glotho and Barton Blont* (London, 1975), p. 53.

6. Beresford, *Clay-Land Villages*, p. 143.

7. R. H. Hilton and P. A. Rahtz, "Upton, Gloucestershire, 1959–1964," *Bristol and Gloucestershire Archaeological Society* 85 (1966), pp. 112–113. Beresford, "Clay-Land Villages," p. 77.

8. Barbara A. Hanawalt, *Crime and Conflict in Medieval English Communities, 1300–1348* (Cambridge, Mass., 1979), pp. 75–86.

9. *Court Roll of Chalgrave Manor, 1278–1313*, ed. Marian K. Dale, Bedfordshire Record Society 28 (1954), p. 10.

10. *Court Rolls of the Manor of Wakefield*, I, trans. W. P. Baildon, The Yorkshire Archaeological Record Society Series, 29 (1901), p. 85.

11. Just. 2/91 m. 3.

12. Just. 2/92 m. 4.

13. Just. 2/73 m. 7. Two sisters are described as sleeping together in one bed. Cases of husbands and wives in the same bed appear in homicide cases as well as accidental deaths. The position of the cradle is made amply clear from the numerous cradle fires.

14. *Harrison's Description of England in Shakespere's Youth, 2 & 3 Books*, ed. Frederick J. Furnivall, pt. I, the second book, The New Shakespere Society 6, 1 (London, 1877), p. 240.

15. *Testamenta Eboracensia: A Selection of Wills from the Registry at York*, III, Surtees Society 45 (1865), pp. 118–122.

16. A. F. Cirket, *English Wills, 1498–1526*, Publications of the Bedfordshire Historical Records Commission 37 (1956), p. 29. In Just. 2/195 m. 4 a fourteen-year-old boy burned down the family house when he put a candle on the wall before an image.

17. Thomas Wright, *A History of Domestic Manners and Sentiments in England during the Middle Ages* (London, 1862), pp. 406–407.

18. Just. 2/82 m. 1.

19. Just. 2/67 m. 40, 2/85 m. 8.

20. R. H. Hilton, *The English Peasantry in the Later Middle Ages: The Ford Lectures for 1973 and Related Studies* (Oxford, 1975), p. 42.

21. Just. 2/78 m. 2.

22. Just. 2/67 m. 19.

23. Hurst, "A Review," p. 142.

24. *The Court Rolls of the Manor of Wakefield from October 1331 to September 1333*, ed. Sue Sheridan Walker, The Yorkshire Archaeological Society, 2nd ser., 2 (forthcoming), p. 175.

25. Just. 2/67 m. 40d, m. 23d are cases where a servant was sent to get a cartload of peat. Just. 2/104 m. 3 describes the cases of a woman over forty and a boy of seven who went to get peat.

26. William Langland, *Piers Plowman*, ed. W. W. Skeat (Oxford, 1886), B. 11, p. 228.

27. Chaucer, *Canterbury Tales*, p. 233.

28. Just. 2/106 m. 1; 2/114 ms. 3, 7, 8, 18.

29. Wright, *A History of Domestic Manners and Sentiments*, pp. 250–251.

30. James E. Thorold Rogers, *Six Centuries of Work and Wages: The History of English Labour* (London, 1884), p. 67.

31. Hilton, *English Peasantry*, p. 42.

32. W. O. Ault, *Open-Field Husbandry and the Village Community: A Study of Agrarian By-laws in Medieval England*, Transactions of the American Philosophical Society, 55 (Philadelphia, 1965), pp. 25, 31–33.

33. *Bedfordshire Coroners' Rolls*, trans. R. F. Hunnisett, Bedfordshire Historical Record Society, 41 (1961), p. 11. Just. 2/109, ms. 1, 7.

34. Ault, *Open-Field Husbandry*, pp. 20–30. For pigs mauling children see, for instance, Just. 2/70 ms. 10d., 11; 2/67 m. 33; and 2/104 m. 8.

35. George Homans, *English Villagers of the Thirteenth Century* (Cambridge, Mass., 1941), pp. 61–62.

36. Just. 2/92 m. 4d, 2/104.

37. Hurst, "A Review," pp. 138–140. Horse bones at Wharram were 20 percent of all bones. This may indicate that horses were more common than thought, although horses provide a large number of bones per carcass.

38. Hilton and Rahtz, "Upton," pp. 139–143.

39. M. M. Postan, "Village Livestock in the Thirteenth Century," *Economic History Review* 2nd ser. 15 (1962), pp. 219–249. D. L. Farmer, "Some Livestock Price Movements in Thirteenth-Century England," *Economic History Review* 2nd ser. 22 (1969), pp. 1–16.

40. Jennie Kitteringham, "Country Work Girls in Nineteenth-Century England," in *Village Life and Labour*, ed. Raphael Samuel (London, 1965), p. 75–79.

41. Hurst, "A Review," pp. 138–140.

42. J. G. Turner, *Select Pleas of the Forest*, Selden Society 13 (London, 1901), pp. 8, 88.

43. Frederic W. Maitland and William Paley Baildon, *The Court Baron*, Selden Society 4 (London, 1891), pp. 54–55.

44. Just. 2/74, 2/82 m. 9, 2/67 m. 19d.

45. Just. 2/203 m. 13.

46. J. R. Ravensdale, *Liable to Floods: Village Lands Cope on the Edge of the Fens* (Cambridge, 1974), pp. 60–61.

47. Just. 2/74 m. 11.

48. Rogers, *Six Centuries of Work and Wages*, pp. 59–63.

49. William Ashley, *Bread of Our Forefathers* (Oxford, 1928), pp. 83–104.

50. Wright, *Domestic Manners and Sentiments* p. 158. The upper classes ate their meals on trenchers of inferior bread that were given to the poor as charity after the meal. Robert Richmond, ed., "Three Records of the Alien Priory of Gorve and the Manor of Leighton Buzzard," *The Publications of the Bedfordshire Historical Record Society* 8 (1924), p. 31.

51. John Gower, quoted in Ashley, *Bread of Our Forefathers*, p. 95.

52. William Langland, *Piers Plowman*, ed. W. W. Skeat (Oxford, 1886), c, vii, 201.

53. Just. 2/78 m. 2.

54. Ault, *Open-Field Husbandry*, pp. 19–20.

55. Ibid., pp. 12–16.

56. Just. 2/67 m. 33d.

57. Walker, *Wakefield*, p. 38.

58. A. R. Bridbury, *England and the Salt Trade in the Later Middle Ages* (Oxford, 1955). In Just. 2/105 m. 1d a child of three fell into a vat of verjuice in a neighbor's home.

59. Hurst, "A Review," p. 135.

60. C. Wells, "A Leper Cemetery at South Acre, Norfolk," *Medieval Archaeology* 11 (1967), pp. 242–248.

61. Rossell Hope Robbins, *Secular Lyrics of the XIVth and XVth Centuries* (Oxford, 1952), pp. 73–76.

62. Thomas Wright and James Orchard Halliwell, eds., *Reliquiae Antiquae: Scraps and Ancient Manuscripts Illustrating Chiefly Early English Literature and the English Language*, I,(London, 1841), p. 43.

63. Langland, *Piers Plowman*, B, V, 194; C. VII, 201; C, X, 72.

64. Fernand Braudel, *Capitalism and Material Life*, trans. Miriam Kochan (London, 1973), pp. 87–91.

65. Edward Miller and John Hatcher, *Medieval England: Rural Society and Economic Change, 1086–1348* (London, 1978), pp. 159–161.

66. K. L. Wood-Legh, *A Small Household of the XVth Century: An Account Book of Munden's Chantry, Bridport* (Manchester, 1956), and *Perpetual Chantries in Britain* (Cambridge, 1965), pp. 234–270. Peter Heath, *The English Parish Clergy on the Eve of the Reformation* (London, 1969), p. 23. E. H. Phelps Brown and Sheila V. Hopkins, "Seven Centuries of the Prices of Consumables, Compared with Builders' Wage-Rates," in *Essays in Economic History*, II, ed. E. M. Carus-Wilson (London, 1962), p. 180.

67. Rotha M. Clay, *The Medieval Hospitals of England* (London, 1909), pp. 167–170.

68. Homans, *English Villagers*, p. 261.

69. Ibid., p. 262. *Harrison's Description of England*, pt. 1, p. 162. *Robert [Mannyg] of Brunne's Handlyng Synne*, ed. Frederick J. Furnivall, The Early English Text Society 119 (London, 1901), p. 231.

70. Catherine B. Firth, "Village Gilds of Norfolk in the Fifteenth Century," *Norfolk Archaeology* 18 (1914), p. 185.

71. *Bedfordshire Coroners' Rolls*, pp. 55, 97, 98.

72. *Bedfordshire Coroners' Rolls*, pp. 69, 107. Just. 2/17 m. 7d., 2/18 m. 44, 2/102 m. 1, 2/104 m. 18, 2/85 m. 8, 2/109 ms. 1, 5. Walker, *Wakefield*, p. 267. Richard Leighton Green, ed., *The Early English Carols*, 2nd ed. (Oxford, 1977), p. 491. There are three versions of this carol.

73. Wright, *Domestic Manners and Sentiments*, p. 162.

74. Doris M. Stenton, *English Society in the Early Middle Ages, 1066–1307*, 4th ed. (Harmondsworth, 1971), p. 28.

75. Jacques Rossiaud, "Prostitution, Youth, and Society in the Towns of Southeastern France in the Fifteenth Century," in *Deviants and the Abandoned in French Society*, ed. Robert Forster and Orest Ranum, trans. Elborg Forster and Patricia M. Ranum (Baltimore, 1978), pp. 1–46. Hope Phyllis Weissman, "Why Chaucer's Wife is from Bath," *The Chaucer Review* 15 (1980–1981), pp. 12–35.

76. Just. 2/104 m. 8. *Bedfordshire Coroners' Rolls*, pp. 11, 51. Just. 2/82 m. 1; 2/69 ms., 7d, 8. See also Just. 2/81 m. 3, 2/76 m. 1, 2/74 m. 8d, 2/67 m. 22d, 2/194 m. 7.

77. Just. 2/69 m. 7d., 2/67 m. 22, 2/104 m. 43 d. *Bedfordshire Coroners' Rolls*, p. 5.

78. Francis Elizabeth Baldwin, *Sumptuary Legislation and Personal Regulation in England*, Johns Hopkins University Studies in Historical and Political Science 44 (Baltimore, 1926), pp. 75–76.

79. Just. 2/77 m. 3.

80. A. R. Bridbury, *Economic Growth: England in the Later Middle Ages* (London, 1962). R. H. DuBoulay, *An Age of Ambition* (London, 1970), gives a good label to the century.

81. Hanawalt, *Crime and Conflict*, pp. 168–171.

82. *Bedfordshire Coroners' Rolls*, p. 31.

Chapter 4. Inheritance

1. Jack Goody, "Inheritance, Property and Women: Some Comparative Considerations," in *Family and Inheritance: Rural Society in Western Europe*, ed. Jack Goody, Joan Thirsk, and E. P. Thompson (Cambridge, 1976), pp. 10–34.

2. A. E. Levett, *Studies in Manorial History*, ed. H. M. Cam, M. Coate, and L. S. Sutherland (Oxford, 1938), Chap. 4. Paul R. Hyams, *King, Lords, and Peasants in Medieval England* (Oxford, 1980), gives a detailed discussion of the history of villein holding and the law and is well worth reading for those interested in a complete discussion of the problem. I only briefly cover the material here as I am interested in its relationship to the family. Since a lord wanted to keep the land productive, he had no desire to deprive a tenant of his chattels, and hence he demanded heriot (the best animal or cash on a tenant's death) as a symbol of his rights: J. A. Raftis, *Tenure and Mobility: Studies in the Social History of the Medieval English Village* (Toronto, 1964), pp. 46–47.

3. Paul Vinogradoff, *Villeinage in England: Essays in English Mediaeval History* (Oxford, 1908), pp. 246–250.

4. George C. Homans, "The Frisians in East Anglia," *Economic History Review*, 2nd ser. 10 (1957–8), p. 191, supported the general conclusions about the division of champion and woodland that Vinogradoff had established.

5. *Chertsey Abbey Court Rolls, Abstract*, trans. Elsie Toms, Surrey Record Society 21, p. xiii.

6. Zvi Razi, *Life, Marriage and Death in the Medieval Parish: Economy, Society, and Demography in Halesowen, 1270–1400* (Cambridge, 1980), p. 96.

7. David Sabean, "Aspects of Kinship Behaviour and Property in Rural Western Europe before 1800," in *Family and Inheritance: Rural Society in Western Europe, 1200–1800*, ed. Jack Goody, Joan Thirsk, and E. P. Thompson, (Cambridge, 1976), pp. 98–99.

8. James B. Given, *Society and Homicide in Thirteenth-Century England* (Palo Alto, Calif., 1977), pp. 162–163. Barbara A. Hanawalt, *Crime and Conflict in English Communities, 1300–1348* (Cambridge, Mass., 1979), pp. 162–163.

9. Sabean, "Aspects of Kinship," p. 98.

10. Razi, *Halesowen*, p. 52. Zvi Razi, "Family, Land and the Village Community in Later Medieval Engalnd," *Past and Present* 93 (1981), p. 7, found that 60 percent of the inheriting brothers provided siblings with land in preplague Halesowen. Such arrangements also appear frequently in wills. Raftis, *Tenure and Mobility*, pp. 45–48.

11. Margaret Spufford, "Peasant Inheritance Customs and Land Distribution in Cambridgeshire from the Sixteenth to the Eighteenth Centuries," in *Family and Inheritance: Rural Society in Western Europe 1200–1800*, ed. Jack Goody, Joan Thirsk, and E. P. Thompson (Cambridge, 1976), pp. 156–159, discusses the effects of providing for siblings on the success of the inheriting son. She argued that the necessity of giving chattels to siblings or taking on their support could severely hamper the economic success of the inheriting brother.

12. Barbara Dodwell, "Holdings and Inheritance in Medieval East Anglia,"

Economic History Review 2nd ser. 20 (1967), pp. 53–66. George Homans, *English Villagers of the Thirteenth Century* (Cambridge, Mass., 1941), pp. 133–143, and "The Rural Sociology of Medieval England," *Past and Present* 4 (1953), pp. 32–43. Rosamond J. Faith, "Peasant Families and Inheritance Customs in Medieval England," *The Agricultural History Review* 14 (1966), pp. 77–86.

13. H. E. Hallam, "Some Thirteenth-Century Censuses," *Economic History Review*, 2nd ser. 10 (1958), pp. 345–348. He found a rather remarkable range of diversity among the villages he surveyed. In an area that generally practiced partible inheritance (among sokemen at least) anywhere from 13 to 55 percent of the tenancies were joint. The size varied from below five acres to thirty acres with the upper range being more usual. Dodwell, "Holdings and Inheritance," pp. 61–64.

14. A. R. H. Baker, "Open Fields and Partible Inheritance on a Kent Manor," *Economic History Review* 2nd ser., 17 (1964), pp. 20–21.

15. David Roden, "Fragmentation of Farms and Fields in the Chiltern Hills, Thirteenth Century and Later," *Mediaeval Studies* 31 (1969), pp. 232–237.

16. Hilton, *English Peasantry*, p. 99. Raftis, *Tenure and Mobility*, pp. 37–42, for a discussion of the succession of the wife. Eleanor Searle, "Seignorial Control of Women's Marriage: The Antecedents and Function of Merchet in England," *Past and Present* 82 (1979), p. 38, argued that giving a dower was a sign of freedom on the part of the husband and that the unfree peasants, who were bound by manorial customs, endowed the wife with half of the husband's tenements for life. In a strict legal sense such a conclusion might be correct, but the blurring of the lines between free and unfree tenants and the use of wills actually made the system more flexible; both free and unfree husbands tended to use the generous provisions of customary law.

17. Margaret Spufford, *Contrasting Communities: English Villagers in the Sixteenth and Seventeenth Centuries* (Cambridge, 1974), pp. 162–163. J. Z. Titow, "Some Differences between Manors and the Effects on the Condition of the Peasant in the Thirteenth Century," *Agricultural History Review*, 10 (1962), pp. 6–8. Titow has argued that on manors with land shortages the marriage of widows tended to make the direct descent from father to son meaningless, and that family holdings tended to "wander around."

18. *Court Roll of Chalgrave Manor, 1278–1313*, ed. Marian K. Dale, Bedfordshire Historical Record Society 28 (1950), p. 10.

19. *English Wills, 1498–1526*, ed. A. F. Cirket, Bedfordshire Historical Record Society 37 (1956), p. 46.

20. Roden, "Fragmentation of Farms and Fields," pp. 228–230.

21. *Chertsey Abbey*, p. xiii.

22. *The Court Rolls of the Manor of Wakefield From October 1331 to September 1333*, trans. Sue Sheridan Walker, The Yorkshire Archaeological Society, 2nd ser., 2 (forthcoming), p. 219.

23. *Chertsey Abbey*, pp. xiv–xv.

24. Ibid. See also Walker, *Wakefield*, p. 256. *Court Rolls of the Manor of Wakefield*, I, trans. W. P. Baildon, pp. 212–213.

25. R. H. Helmholz, "Bastardy Litigation in Medieval England," *American Journal of Legal History* 13 (1969), pp. 370–371. Searle, "Merchet," p. 36. Razi, *Halesowen*, p. 65.

26. Walker, *Wakefield*, p. 5.

27. W. G. Hoskins, *The Midland Peasant: The Social and Economic History of a Leicestershire Village* (London, 1957), pp. 28–55, shows free peasants passing family land from generation to generation for hundreds of years. Cicely Howell, "Peasant Inheritance Customs in the Midlands, 1280–1700," in *Family and Inheritance: Rural Society in*

Western Europe, 1200–1800, ed. Jack Goody, Joan Thirsk, and E. P. Thompson (Cambridge, 1976), pp. 126–131. Razi, "Family, Land and the Village Community," pp. 1–9.

28. Alan Macfarlane, *The Origins of English Individualism* (New York, 1979), pp. 85–86.

29. Howell, "Peasant Inheritance," pp. 123–124, 131.

30. Edwin DeWindt, *Land and People in Holywell-cum-Needingworth* (Toronto, 1972), pp. 167–183. Edward Britton, *The Community of the Vill: A Study in the History of the Family and Village Life in Fourteenth-Century England* (Toronto, 1977), p. 79, has less precise information but estimates that 75 percent remained before the plague and then the number declined. Razi, "Family, Land and the Village," pp. 20–21. Raftis, "Changes in an English Village after the Black Death," *Mediaeval Studies* 29 (1967), pp. 158–177. Generalizations in medieval peasant society are maddeningly difficult because of the marked regional differences. In the case of Cornwall, the tin industry led to greater mobility and consequently a greater turnover of tenements in the first half of the fourteenth century. The Black Death did have the usual dislocating effects, but by the end of the fourteenth century there was greater stability, with over three-fourths of the tenants renewing. This pattern held in the fifteenth century. John Hatcher, *Rural Economy and Society in the Duchy of Cornwall, 1300–1500* (Cambridge, 1970), p. 220. Faith, "Peasant Inheritance Customs," pp. 88–92. Faith found that while demand for family land was breaking down in general, widows continued to insist on their family right.

31. C. N. L. Brooke and M. M. Postan, eds., *Carte Nativorum: A Peterborough Cartularly of the Fourteenth Century*, Northamptonshire Record Society 20 (1960), Chap. 2.

32. A variety of studies have commented on the land market in the early fourteenth century. Anne DeWindt, "A Peasant Land Market and Its Participants: King's Ripton, 1280–1400," *Midland History* 4 (1978), pp. 142–158. Howell, "Peasant Inheritance," pp. 135–137. DeWindt, *Holywell-cum-Needingworth*, pp. 43–67. Britton, *Community of the Vill*, p. 86. E. J. King, *Peterborough Abbey, 1086–1310: A Study in the Land Market* (Cambridge, 1973). Faith, "Peasant Inheritance Customs," pp. 86–87.

33. Howell, "Peasant Inheritance," p. 125.

34. Andrew Jones, "Land and People at Leighton Buzzard in the Later Fifteenth Century," *Economic History Review* 2nd ser. 25 (1972), pp. 18–27. Christopher Dyer, *Lords and Peasants in a Changing Society: The Estates of the Bishopric of Worcester, 680–1540* (Cambridge, 1980), pp. 298–315. Razi, "Family, Land and the Village Community," pp. 18–22, correctly cautions that the decline in people of the same surname taking up properties does not necessarily mean that the same bloodline is not inheriting. The argument here, however, is that families and individuals did acquire new pieces of property to help their family placement strategies either by taking on a distant relative's tenement or purchasing entry into new lands. In doing so, they ignored the old customary rules of unigeniture or partible inheritance.

35. DeWindt, "Peasant Land Market," p. 153. Dyer, *Lords and Peasants*, p. 315, found much the same pattern by reconstructing the biographies of men from the middle to late fifteenth century who acquired land during the prime of their life and gradually dispersed it as they aged. He mistakenly regards this as a sign of the breakup of the family, for it is more reflective of the new land market. Indeed, further examples in Dyer's chapters also indicate the continued inportance of family inheritance. Howell's "Peasant Inheritance" and Spufford, "Inheritance Customs", pp. 156–157, indicate that the family remained strong.

36. Patricia Bell, *Bedfordshire Wills, 1480–1519*, Bedfordshire Historical Record

Society 45 (1966), pp. 11–12. Razi, "Family, Land and the Village Community," pp. 20–21.

37. DeWindt, "Peasant Land Market," pp. 152–153. *Chalgrave Manor*, pp. 63–64.

38. *Wakefield*, I, p. 208.

39. Ibid., p. 108. The court rolls abound with cases of the father setting up sons and daughters during his lifetime. For other cases, see ibid., pp. 85–88, 95, 97, 120, and Walker, *Wakefield*, pp. 40–41, 214, 288, 299, 301. Hallam, "Thirteenth Century Censuses," p. 351, found that such inter vivos settlements were rare in areas practicing partible inheritance. A father might be particularly careful to make an inter vivos settlement if he planned to have two sons take joint control of a tenement on a manor that normally practiced primogeniture. Thus William Lolyere and his two sons entered a covenant that he would grant the tenement to the two brothers and their heirs with the provision "that one of the aforesaid brothers shall not be allowed to alienate or sell the said tenement without consent of the other:" *Chalgrave*, p. 32. For similar cases, see *Chertsey Abbey*, pp. xiv, xxxvi.

40. *Wakefield*, I, p. 211.

41. *Bedfordshire Wills*, p. 6.

42. Howell, "Peasant Inheritance," pp. 141–143.

43. 8 percent, 6 percent, 4 percent, 3 percent, 7 percent, respectively.

44. 4 percent, 0.5 percent, 3 percent, respectively.

45. *Bedfordshire Wills*, p. 50.

46. Ibid., pp. 11–12.

47. *English Wills*, pp. 31–39.

48. Ibid., no. 149. In no. 156 the will of one of Hugh's sons is recorded and shows that the land he received from his father was divided between two sons.

49. Howell, "Peasant Inheritance," p. 141. In manorial courts, if the person died without kin the land was taken into the lord's hands and rented out again. Some effort would be made to find a person in direct descent to take the land, and sometimes the person would present themselves in court to claim the land. Razi, *Halesowen*, pp. 110–113 found that after the Black Death kin quickly appeared to take up land left vacant.

Chapter 5. Kinship Bonds

1. Bertha Phillpots, *Kindred and Clan in the Middle Ages and After: A Study in the Sociology of the Teutonic Races* (Cambridge, 1913), pp. 242–263. She argued that because the Anglo-Saxons migrated by boat as individuals or small family units, they lost kin identity earlier than continental tribes, who, in migrating overland, moved as a kin group. Some of the discussion of the open-field system has revolved around the early kinship systems, but as our period is later we may leave the matter aside. For a taste of the arguments, see Robert A. Dodghson, "The Landholding Foundations of the Open-Field System," *Past and Present* 67 (1975), pp. 3–29, and T. M. Charles-Edwards, "Kinship, Status and the Origins of the Hide," *Past and Present* 56 (1972), pp. 3–33.

2. Lorraine Lancaster, "Kinship in Anglo-Saxon Society," *British Journal of Sociology* 9 (1958), 236–239.

3. Ibid., pp. 366, 372. Jack Goody, *The Development of Family and Marriage in Europe* (Cambridge, 1983), pp. 18–19, 262–278.

4. Richard Helmholz, *Marriage Litigation in Medieval England* (Cambridge, 1974), pp. 77–87.

5. Kenneth W. Wachter, with Eugene A. Hammel and Peter Laslett, *Statistical Studies of Historical Social Structure* (New York, 1978), p. 159.

6. Helen M. Cam, *Liberties and Communities in Medieval England: Collected Studies in Local Administration and Topography* (Cambridge, 1944), pp. 124–135.

7. Zvi Razi, *Life, Marriage, and Death in the Medieval Parish: Economy, Society and Demography in Halesowen, 1270–1400* (Cambridge, 1980), pp. 147–149; "Family Land and the Village Community in Later Medieval England," *Past and Present* 93 (1981), pp. 22–27.

8. Michael Mitterauer and Reinhard Sieder, *The European Family: Patriarchy to Partnership from the Middle Ages to the Present*, trans. Karl Oosterveen and Manfred Horzinger (Chicago, 1982), p. 9.

9. A. C. Chibnall, *Sherington: Fiefs and Fields of a Buckinghamshire Village* (Cambridge, 1965), p. 95. *Chertsey Abbey Court Rolls, Abstract*, trans. Elsie Toms, Surrey Record Society (1937), p. xxxix. The use of the matronymic is thus consistent with the earlier practice that David Herlihy, in "Land, Family, and Women in Continental Europe, 701–1200," in *Women in Medieval Europe*, ed. Susan Mosher Stuard (Philadelphia, 1976), pp. 13–46, described for Europe.

10. M. F. Nimkoff and Russell Middleton, "Types of Family and Types of Economy," *The American Journal of Sociology* 66 (1960), p. 217.

11. Maurice Bloch, "The Long Term and the Short Term: The Economic and Political Significance of the Morality of Kinship," in *The Character of Kinship*, ed. Jack Goody (Cambridge, 1973), p. 86 and throughout.

12. Lancaster, "Kinship in Anglo-Saxon Society," pp. 368, 370. The duties of fictive kin are not spelled out either.

13. Keith Wrightson and David Levine, *Poverty and Piety in an English Village: Terling, 1525–1700* (New York, 1979), pp. 82–109. See also their comparisons to French studies and a modern British study.

14. Elaine Clark, "Debt Litigation in a Late Medieval English Vill," in *Pathways to Medieval Peasants*, ed. J. Ambrose Raftis (Toronto, 1981), p. 252. Richard Smith, "Kin and Neighbors in a Thirteenth-Century Suffolk Community," *Journal of Family History* 4 (1979), pp. 224–225. Edwin DeWindt, *Land and People in Hollywell-cum-Needingworth* (Toronto, 1972), p. 246, has similar results. See also Martin Pimsler, "Solidarity in the Medieval Village? The Evidence of Personal Pledging at Elton, Huntingdonshire," *The Journal of British Studies* 17 (1977), pp. 1–11.

15. Smith, "Kin and Neighbors," pp. 245–247.

16. Marjorie J. O. Kennedy, "Resourceful Villeins: The Cellarer Family of Wawne in Holderness," *Yorkshire Archaeological Journal* 48 (1976), pp. 107–113.

17. Judith Bennett, "The Tie that Binds: Peasant Marriages and Peasant Families in Late Medieval England," *The Journal of Interdisciplinary History* 15 (1984), pp. 111–129.

18. *Court Roll of Chalgrave Manor, 1278–1313*, ed. Marian K. Dale, Bedfordshire Historical Record Society 28 (1950), pp. 45, 47, 53–54, 64, and p. 15, in which an aunt of the inheritor is guaranteed a third of the land for life. For a complicated case from wills, see the arrangements of the Russel family in *Bedfordshire Wills, 1480–1519*, trans. Patricia Bell. Bedfordshire Historical Record Society 45 (1966) no. 149, 156, and 173. *Court Rolls of the Manor of Wakefield*, I, trans. W. P. Baildon, The Yorkshire Archaeological Society Record Series 36 (1901), p. 104. *Court Rolls of the Manor of Wakefield*, IV, trans. John Risler, Yorkshire Archaeological Society Record Series 57 (1917), pp. 10, 144, and p. 86, in which an uncle is the heir to his bastard niece—hereafter referred to as

Wakefield, IV. E. A. Wrigley, "Fertility Strategy for the Individual and the Group," in *Historical Studies of Changing Fertility*, ed. Charles Tilly (Princeton, 1978), pp. 135–154.

19. *The Court Rolls of the Manor of Wakefield From October 1331 to September 1333*, trans. Sue Sheridan Walker, The Yorkshire Archaeological Society Record Series 2 (forthcoming), p. 210. At Wakefield in 1332 the sons of William del Lyghthesles exchanged land in various parcels with Henry del Lone and his family, but they do not appear to be related in any apparent way. Razi, "Family, Land and the Village Community," pp. 8–29. Using somewhat more refined methods for detecting familial relationships than surnames, Razi has estimated that in Halesowen reliance on extended family was much greater than at first appeared, particularly in the period of population decline and stagnation. But his numerical data include nuclear family as well as extended and, therefore, are not useful in presenting a broader picture of reliance on more distant relatives. His point is well taken, however, about the problems of relying on surname evidence alone, but the arguments of the article are conflicting. All examples that he uses for relying on distant kin following the Black Death are inheritances and a debt that will finally be resolved through an inheritance.

20. *Bedfordshire Coroners' Rolls* trans. R. F. Hunnisett, Bedfordshire Historical Record Society 41 (1961), pp. 28–29. In another case the record said that the whole household was concerned and they had searched for the missing member for a whole week.

21. Wrightson and Levine, *Poverty and Piety in an English Village*, p. 83.

Chapter 6. Household Size and Structure

1. William Goode, *World Revolution and Family Patterns* (New York, 1963), p. 17, argued that even in the twelfth and thirteenth centuries in Europe, where he sees a great deal of mobility, the family structure did not change to a conjugal family system. He confesses that the lower strata of society "resembled conjugal families," but that the elders dominated family life and thus the real characteristics of such a system could not exist. Instead, with the Reformation, conjugal families began to develop. John C. Caldwell, *Theory of Fertility Decline* (New York, 1982), pp. 157–179, for a summary of his theory, and pp. 217–222 for problems with western European patterns. Caldwell's theory is that in all peasant economies high fertility and many children contribute to the family unit's prosperity. He argues that many hands lightened the load of home- and fieldwork and assured the senior couple that family wealth would continue to flow up to them as they aged and they could, therefore, be assured of a comfortable and prosperous old age. Caldwell himself admits that in the historical perspective, England and much of western Europe did not conform to this pattern in the preindustrial period. Since he would like to argue that Third World populations go through the same phases as that of western Europe, this admission proves somewhat damaging to his theory. First he assumes that the traditional family is extended and paternalistic, whereas the medieval peasant family was neither. He also assumes that family wealth and benefits flow up to the parents, whereas medieval English parents had constantly to worry about how they would distribute family land and wealth so that as many of their children as possible receive a portion. Among medieval English peasants family wealth flowed down, not up, and peasant parents faced the unhappy prospect that they might have an impoverished old age.

2. M. F. Nimkoff and Russell Middleton, "Types of Family and Types of Economy," *American Journal of Sociology* 9 (1974), pp. 219–220.

3. E. A. Hammel and Peter Laslett, "Comparing Household Structure Over Time and Between Cultures," *Comparative Studies in Society and History* 16 (1974), pp. 76–97.

4. H. E. Hallam, "Some Thirteenth-Century Censuses," *Economic History Review*, 2nd ser. 14 (1961), pp. 348–353.

5. Lutz Berkner, "Recent Research on the History of the Family," *Journal of Marriage and the Family* 35 (1973), p. 399; "Rural Family Organization in Europe: A Problem in Comparative History," *Peasant Studies Newsletter* 1 (1972), pp. 145–146; and Franklin Mendels, "Inheritance Systems, Family Structure, and Demographic Patterns in Western Europe, 1700–1900," in *Historical Studies of Changing Fertility*, ed. Charles Tilly (Priceton, 1978), pp. 209–223. Berkner has argued on the basis of his evidence from early modern Germany that stem families are typical of peasant societies. J. Krause, "The Medieval Household: Large or Small," *Economic History Review* 2nd ser. 9 (1957), pp. 420–421. George Homans, "The Frisians in East Anglia," *Economic History Review*, 2nd ser. 10 (1957), p. 192, argued that on a Norfolk manor between 1309 and 1329, 136 holdings were transferred to heirs during the tenant's lifetime and only 74 went to heirs after the tenant's death. The fathers, he argues, were retiring and the families lived on in the same house. Hallam, "Thirteenth-Century Censuses," p. 353, found only 4 three-generational households out of 252 mentioned in the thirteenth-century serf lists.

6. M. W. Barley, *The English Farm House and Cottage* (London, 1961), pp. 12–13. J. G. Hurst, "A Review of Archaeological Research to 1968," in *Deserted Medieval Villages*, ed. Maurice Beresford and J. G. Hurst (London, 1971), p. 113.

7. Just. 2/67 m. 40. *Bedfordshire Coroners' Rolls*, trans. R. F. Hunnisett, Bedfordshire Historical Record Society 41 (1961), p. 101, records a felonious attack on a household at night. In it were a husband and wife, the husband's mother and brother, and the daughter of another brother.

8. Cicely Howell, "Peasant Inheritance Customs in the Midlands, 1280–1700," in *Family and Inheritance: Rural Society in Western Europe*, ed. J. Goody, J. Thirsk, E. P. Thompson (Cambridge, 1976), p. 145, has concluded that peasant men married rather late, so that the period of three-generational families was short, about three and a half years.

9. Kenneth Wachter with Eugene A. Hammel and Peter Laslett, *Statistical Studies of Historical Social Structure* (New York, 1978), pp. 64, 80–90, 105–112, have suggested that the English case might be different and that in Russia, parts of France, Germany, and perhaps the Mediterranean area stem families would be more common.

10. David Herlihy and Christine Klapisch-Zuber, *Les Toscans et leur familles* (Paris, 1978), pp. 482–485. Jean-Louis Flandrin, *Families in Former Times; Kinship, Household, and Sexuality*, trans. Richard Southern (Cambridge, 1979), pp. 71–84.

11. Hallam, "Thirteenth-Century Censuses," p. 352.

12. Ibid., p. 348. R. H. Hilton, *The English Peasantry in the Later Middle Ages* (Oxford, 1975), pp. 99–100. Barbara English, *A Study in Feudal Society; The Lords of Holderness, 1086–1260* (Oxford, 1979), p. 191. In the Herlihy–Klapisch-Zuber study, *Les Toscans*, the widows headed 6 percent of the households (widowers 6.8 percent) in the countryside; the percentage was even higher in the city. Christiane Klapisch, "Household and Family in Tuscany in 1427," *Household and Family in Past Time*, ed. Peter Laslett (Cambridge, 1972), p. 273.

13. Peter Laslett, *Family Life and Illicit Love in Earlier Generations: Essays in Historical Sociology* (Cambridge, 1977), p. 13, has distinguished four characteristics of the Western

family: (1) the basic nuclear family, (2) the woman's rather late age of marriage, (3) the relatively small gap in age between marriage partners, and (4) the presence of servants in households and the importance of servitude as part of the life cycle of young people. Because the issue of servitude as part of the life cycle—and, indeed, their routine presence in households—is questionable, the matter of servants will be discussed in later chapters.

14. Jack Goody, "The 'Family' and the 'Household,'" *Domestic Groups*, An Addison-Wessley Module in Anthropology 28 (1972), pp. 5–9.

15. David Herlihy, "Population, Plague, and Social Change in Rural Pistoia, 1201–1430," *Economic History Review* 18 (1965), pp. 235–244. The drastic depopulation following the plague forced landlords to make capital investments in agriculture and allowances on the rent in order to keep their peasants. Carlo Poni, "Family and 'Podere' in Emilia Romagna," *The Journal of Italian History* 1 (1978), pp. 205–217, found that in nineteenth-century Italy the landholding was almost an unconscious control over family size. If landholding was small, so too was the family. There was an escape provision that if the number of people on a holding got too large, the lord could set up a new holding for a secondary family. But failing new land, the young men became servants. In the Herlihy–Klapisch-Zuber study of Tuscany they found relatively large households in the countryside in 1427. The mean varied from 4.4 persons per household in Arezzo to 7.5 in San Gimignano. Household size increased with wealth, although, by occupation, agricultural households averaged only 4 persons. Klapisch, "Household and Family in Tuscany," pp. 275–278.

16. Razi, *Halesowen*, pp. 32, 85–88, 93. He found that male replacement rate for poorer peasants was only 0.713, but higher for the wealthy. The mean was 1.220. Manorial records underrepresent women, so that, making the assumption that the ratio of women to men was 50:50 (a ratio that has been disputed), he suggests that between 1270 and 1349 the average number of a couple's offspring over twelve years of age was 2.8, with the rich having 5.1 children, middling peasants 2.9, and poor 1.8. Suffolk figures from R. M. Smith, "English Peasant Life-Cycles and Socio-economic Network," Ph. D. Thesis (Cambridge University, 1974), p. 104. Hallam, "Some Thirteenth-Century Censuses," pp. 340–354, 361, found an average household size of 4.86 in the late thirteenth century in Lincolnshire. He also found that larger holdings produced larger families. Thus those with zero to five acres had 4.33 persons per household, those with five to thirty acres had 4.78, and those with over thirty acres had 6.2. In some cases Hallam found that these people were routinely living on one to one and a half acres per family, but they were diversifying their economy with fish and game and pasturing. H. J. Habakkuk, "Family Structure and Economic Change in Nineteenth-Century Europe," *Journal of Economic History* 15 (1955), pp. 6–10, also argued for larger family size in areas of partible inheritance. Peter Laslett, "Mean Household Size in England since the Sixteenth Century," in *Household and Family in Past Time*, ed. Peter Laslett (Cambridge, 1972), pp. 133, 143–146. Josiah Cox Russell, *British Medieval Population* (Albuquerque, 1948), p. 24, used 3.5 as household size, but all modern estimates have moved that figure higher.

17. Robert S. Gottfried, *Epidemic Disease in Fifteenth-Century England: The Medical Response and the Demographic Consequences* (New Brunswick, N.J., 1978), pp. 167–175, 187–203, regretfully does not discuss number of children in a testator's will, which would have been a useful table to include, but his replacement rates of males is remarkably low and would seem to place the average household size closer to Russell than to other studies. But since children might be excluded from wills either because they were young

or they had already inherited, the wills are not very reliable for studying household size.

18. Flandrin, *Families in Former Times*, p. 53.

19. John Hajnal, "European Marriage Patterns in Perspective," in *Population in History*, ed. David V. Glass and D. E. C. Eversley (Chicago, 1965), pp. 113, 116–120. Russell, *British Medieval Population*, pp. 154–158. T. H. Hollingsworth, "A Demographic Study of the British Ducal Families," *Population Studies* 11 (1957–58), p. 14, and his *Historical Demography* (Ithaca, N.Y., 1969), pp. 382–383. The problem with the poll tax evidence is that there was widespread evasion, especially among the young people that one wants to be able to count. The information on the peerage is not a reliable index to the age of marriage of the population at large because the aristocracy frequently entered into earlier marriages if some diplomatic or economic alliance could be accomplished by betrothing children. E. A. Wrigley, "Family Limitation in Pre-Industrial England," *Economic History Review* 2nd ser. 19 (1966), p. 86, calculated the mean age of first marriage for males in the years 1560–1646 at 27.2 and for women at 27.0. The median was close to 26 for both and the mode was around 23. Michael Flinn, *The European Demographic System, 1500–1820* (Baltimore, 1981), pp. 19–29, concluded from looking at all the early modern data that 24 for women and 26 for men was more common. Herlihy and Klapisch-Zuber, *Les Toscans*, p. 207, also show that the age of marriage went down following the Black Death, but in Italy the women married in their middle to late teens and men in their thirties, so that the differences in ages of the partners was thirteen to fifteen years. Keith Wrightson and David Levine, *Poverty and Piety in an English Village: Terling, 1525–1700* (New York, 1979), p. 47, found men marrying at 25.3 and women at 24.6. Peter Laslett, *The World We Have Lost* (New York, 1965), p. 83, showed that in the early seveteenth century the age was 21.6 for women and 26.5 for men.

20. Richard Smith, "Hypothèses sur la Nuptialité en Angleterre au XIIe–XIVe siècles," *Annales Economies, Sociétés, Civilisations* 38 (1983), pp. 107–124, presents an assessment of Hajnal's argument as well as a discussion of the other European studies. Comparing the most reliable poll tax returns from 1377 and 1381 with records from 1599 and taking into account the various estimates of the number of males left out of the tax because they were legitimately exempt as beggars and clergy or were concealed, Smith has concluded that from 50 to 55 percent of the male population was married.

21. Edgar Powell, *The Rising in East Anglia in 1381* (Cambridge, 1896), Appendix A, contains a complete transcription of the poll tax for Suffolk.

22. Razi, *Halesowen*, pp. 47–63, 132–137. Wrigley, "Family Limitation," p. 92. David Levine, *Family Formation in an Age of Nascent Capitalism* (New York, 1977), p. 148. The marital response to plague and economic opportunity has been questioned for early modern England. Wrigley found that the visitation of plague in 1646–1647 brought later marriage and lower fertility. Levine found that although a farm laborer could earn the maximal amount that he would by age twenty, he did not marry because social pressures in the peasant community inhibited early marriage.

23. George Homans, *English Villagers of the Thirteenth Century* (Cambridge, Mass., 1941), pp. 133–176, argued that in areas of primogeniture sons waited until their father died to marry, and thus the age of marriage was high. Howell, "Peasant Inheritance Customs," p. 145. In support of his argument, Howell has written that the large number of widows granting land to their sons indicates that they did wait. But mere transfer of land does not necessarily prove that the son did not already have a family. Widows' rights varied considerably from community to community but need not have barred a son from working the land and marrying or being settled on other land with his new family.

24. Razi, *Halesowen*, pp. 50–58, 135.

25. H. E. Hallam, "Population Density in Medieval Fenland," *Economic History Review* 2nd ser. 14 (1961), p. 78, found 0.46 persons per square acre and households with one to one and a half acres. J. Z. Titow, "Some Evidence of the Thirteenth-Century Population Increase," *Economic History Review* 2nd ser. 14 (1961), pp. 218–224, found 3.3 acres per capita in 1248; by 1311 it decreased to 2.55. Razi, *Halesowen*, p. 30, found that 43 percent of the population lived on a quarter-virgate or less.

26. Elaine Clark, "Some Aspects of Social Security in Medieval England," *Journal of Family History* 7 (1982), pp. 307–320.

27. J. R. Ravensdale, "Deaths and Entries: The Reliability of the Figures of Mortality in the Black Death in Miss F. M. Page's Estates of Crowland Abbey, and Some Implications for Landholding," in *Land, Kinship, and Life-Cycle*, ed. Richard Smith (forthcoming). See also Titow, "Thirteenth-Century Population Increase."

28. Judith Bennett, "Medieval Peasant Marriage: An Examination of Marriage License Fines in the Liber Gersumarum," in *Pathways to Medieval Peasants*, ed. J. A. Raftis (Toronto, 1981), pp. 208–211.

29. *Bedfordshire Coroners' Rolls*, pp. 48–49.

30. Barbara A. Hanawalt, *Crime and Conflict in English Communities, 1300–1348* (Cambridge, Mass., 1979), pp. 104–107, 153.

31. *Robert [Mannyng] of Brunne's Handlyng Synne*, ed. F. J. Furnivall, EETS, o.s. 119 (London, 1901), p. 60. Richard Helmholz, *Marriage Litigation in Medieval England* (Cambridge, 1974), pp. 91–99. Darrel Amundsen and Carol Jean Dreis, "The Age of Menarche in Medieval Europe," *Human Biology* 45 (1973), pp. 363–368. The reported age of menarche was twelve to fifteen in the sixth through the fifteenth centuries.

32. Francis James Child, *The English and Scottish Popular Ballads* (Boston, 1883–1894), I, no. 7. In the Erlington group, no. 8A, there is also a bride theft in which Willie takes a well-guarded maiden but loses his life.

33. Rossell Hope Robbins, *Secular Lyrics of the Fourteenth and Fifteenth Centuries* (Oxford, 1952), p. 37. Thomas Wright, *Songs and Carols* (London, 1836), song xii. Richard Leighton Greene, *The Early English Carols*, 2nd ed. (Oxford, 1977), nos. 404, 405.

34. Just. 2/104 m. 49. Margery Kempe, *The Book of Margery Kempe*, ed. Sanford B. Meech and Hope Emily Allen, EETS o.s. (London, 1940), p. 6.

35. E. A. Wrigley and R. S. Schofield, *The Population History of England, 1541–1871: A Reconstruction* (Cambridge, Mass., 1981), pp. 257–265. Their figures were made on the basis of back projections. They have observed that "there is a general tendency in western societies for early marriage to be associated with low levels of permanent celibacy, and for late marriage to go with a higher level of permanent celibacy." Peasants in medieval England may have adapted depending on economic circumstances. The medieval record evidence for percentage of population marrying and the age of first marriage is unsatisfactory and perhaps too weak to overcome a hypothetical argument along the lines of the models suggested in Wrigley and Schofield's concluding chapter on the dynamics of population and environment (pp. 454–484). To argue that the early modern pattern of late marriage was simply a continuity of the medieval marriage pattern is to ignore major social and economic changes that could have had a profound influence on age of first marriage. If anything, the late sixteenth century with its large population would more closely resemble the early fourteenth century, but the pattern in between could have been radically different.

36. John Hatcher, *Plague, Population and the English Economy*, (London, 1977),

pp. 55–62. Sylvia Thrupp, "The Problem of Replacement Rates in Late Medieval English Population," *Economic History Review* 2nd ser., 18 (1965), pp. 101–119. Ronald Lee, "Models of Preindustrial Population Dynamics with Application to England," in *Historical Studies in Changing Fertility*, ed. Charles Tilly (Princeton, 1978), pp. 155–207, devised a model testing the effects of demands for labor on population change and found that between 1250 and 1700 it had little influence.

37. John T. Noonan, Jr., *Contraception: A History of Its Treatment by Catholic Theologians and Canonists* (Cambridge, Mass., 1965), pp. 202–203. P. P. A. Biller, "Birth-Control in the West in the Thirteenth and Early Fourteenth Centuries," *Past and Present* 94 (1982), pp. 3–26. J. A. Barnes, "Genetrix : Genitor :: Nature : Culture," in *Character of Kinship*, ed. Jack Goody (Cambridge, 1963), pp. 69–73. For the folkloric traditions, see Barbara A. Hanawalt, "Conception Through Infancy in Medieval English Historical and Folklore Sources," *Folklore Forum* 13 (1980), pp. 127–157.

38. Noonan, *Contraception*, pp. 210–217. *Calendar of Nottinghamshire Coroners' Inquests, 1485–1558*, ed. R. F. Hunnisett, Thoroton Society Record Series 25 (1969), p. 8.

39. Barbara A. Kellum, "Infanticide in England in the Later Middle Ages," *History of Childhood Quarterly* 1 (1974–75), p. 367.

40. Juha Pentikäinen, *The Nordic Dead-Child Tradition* (Helsinki, 1968), pp. 68–79, 94–95.

41. Child, *Ballads*, I, nos. 20, 21.

42. Hanawalt, *Crime and Conflict*, pp. 154–157, for a more complete discussion. The work on church courts is Richard H. Helmholtz, "Infanticide in the Province of Canterbury during the Fifteenth Century," *History of Childhood Quarterly* 2 (1975), pp. 382–390.

43. Don Brothwell, "Paleodemography in Earlier British Populations," *World Archaeology* 4 (1972), pp. 83–85.

44. Johannes de Trokelowe, *Annales (Chronica Monasterii S. Albani)*, ed. H. T. Riley (London, 1866), p. 94.

45. Barbara A. Hanawalt, "Childrearing Among the Lower Classes of Late Medieval England," *Journal of Interdisciplinary History* 8 (1977), pp. 9–14, for an expanded discussion.

46. Walker, *Wakefield*, p. 211. For the sixteenth-century figures and a general discussion of English illegitimacy, see Peter Laslett, *Family Life and Illicit Love in Earlier Generations: Essays in Historical Sociology* (Cambridge, 1977), pp. 102–155. For the low illegitimacy figures in Europe in general, see Flinn, *European Demographic System*, pp. 25–26. While illegitimacy rates were low, considering the delayed marriages, bridal pregnancies may have been high.

47. J. Z. Titow, "Some Differences Between Manors and the Effects on the Condition of the Peasants in the Thirteenth Century," *Agricultural History Review* 10 (1962), p. 4.

48. Just. 2/67 m. 40d. In Just. 2/33 m. 7 the two children are five and two and both are girls.

Chapter 7. The Family as an Economic Unit

1. A. V. Chayanov, *The Theory of Peasant Economy*, ed. D. Thorner, B. Kerblay, and R. E. F. Smith (Homewood, Ill., 1966), p. 1.

2. Eric R. Wolf, *Peasants* (Englewood Cliffs, N.J., 1966).

3. A number of models for household economy have been presented by historians

and anthropologists. A popular historical one is based on the life cycle. Glen Elder in sociology did some of the pioneering work on life cycle in *Children of the Great Depression* (Chicago, 1974); Tamara K. Hareven, "The Family as Process: The Historical Study of the Family Cycle," *Journal of Social History* 7 (1974), pp. 322–329, and Tamara K. Hareven and Maris A. Vinovskis, eds., *Family and Population in Nineteenth-Century America* (Princeton, 1978), are other examples. These studies rely heavily on modern census data and do not have the flexibility needed for different types of sources. More valuable for earlier periods is Franklin Mendels, "Industry and Marriages in Flanders before the Industrial Revolution," in *Population and Economics: Proceedings of Section V of the Fourth Congress of the International Economic History Association,* ed. Paul Deprez (Winnipeg, 1970), pp. 81–93. The life-cycle models are too static and only represent one variable. It assumes that peasantry are homogeneous. Davydd J. Greenwood in *Community-Level Research, Local-Regional-Governmental Interactions and Development Planning: A Strategy for Baseline Studies,* Rural Development Occasional Paper no. 9, Rural Development Committee, Cornell University (1980), pp. 11–16, has emphasized the importance of viewing peasant societies as heterogeneous. Other anthropological models include Teodar Shanin, ed., *Peasants and Peasant Societies: Selected Readings* (Harmondsworth, 1971); James C. Scott, *The Moral Economy of the Peasant* (New Haven, 1976); Samuel Popkin, *The Rational Peasant* (Berkeley, 1979); and Jack Goody, *Production and Reproduction: A Comparative Study of the Domestic Domain* (Cambridge, 1976).

4. Wolf, *Peasants,* pp. 1–17.

5. Olwen Hufton, "Toward an Understanding of the Poor in Eighteenth-Century France," in *French Government and Society, 1500–1800,* ed. J. Bosher (London, 1954), pp. 143–165, shows that the obligation of the community to care for local poor was a very strong custom. English wills also indicate that people left provision for poor men by giving clothing and bread, as I elaborate in Part V.

6. *English Wills, 1498–1526,* ed. A. F. Cirket, Bedfordshire Historical Record Society 87 (1956), p. 55.

7. George Homans, *English Villagers of the Thirteenth Century* (Cambridge, Mass., 1941), pp. 361–363.

8. M. M. Postan and J. Z. Titow, "Heriots and Prices on Winchester Manors," *Economic History Review* 2nd ser. 11 (1959), pp. 392–411, show that the poorer peasants died off during even minor peaks in the price of grain at the beginning of the fourteenth century and suffered considerably in the major famines.

9. J. R. Maddicott, *The English Peasantry and the Demands of the Crown, 1294–1341, Past and Present* Supplements 1 (Oxford, 1975).

10. Frances G. Davenport, "The Decay of Villeinage in East Anglia," in *Essays in Economic History* 2, ed. E. M. Carus-Wilson (London, 1962), pp. 115–116. Wolf, *Peasants,* p. 16, has suggested that acceptance of Protestantism in some parts of the world has had the effect of reducing ceremonial demands. In general, he sees a breakdown of authority as providing peasants an opportunity to reduce external payments, a condition certainly descriptive of fifteenth-century England.

11. H. E. Hallam, "Some Thirteenth-Century Censuses," *Economic History Review,* 2nd ser. 10 (1958), pp. 342–345.

12. Edwin DeWindt, *Land and People in Holywell-cum-Needingworth,* (Toronto, 1972), pp. 112–117.

13. W. W. Skeat, *Pierce the Plowman's Crede,* EETS (London, 1906), pp. 16–17. Beatrice White, "Poet and Peasant," in *The Reign of Richard II,* ed. R. H. DuBoulay and C. M. Barron (London, 1971), p. 70.

14. *Court Rolls of the Manor of Wakefield*, trans. W. P. Baildon, The Yorkshire Archaeological Society Record Series 36 (1906), I, pp. 86, 203, 219, and *passim*. *English Wills*, pp. 26, 60, and *passim*.

15. J. Ambrose Raftis, "The Concentration of Responsibility in Five Villages," *Mediaeval Studies* 28 (1966) pp. 117–119.

16. A. Raistrick, "A Fourteenth Century Regional Survey," *Sociological Review* 21 (1929), pp. 242–245. See also Edgar Powell, *The Rising in East Anglia in 1381* (Cambridge, 1896), Appendix I, for Suffolk poll tax information.

17. Christopher Dyer, "A Small Landowner in the Fifteenth Century," *Midland History* 1 (1972), pp. 13–14. Joan W. Scott and Louise A. Tilly, "Women's Work and the Family in Nineteenth-Century Europe," *Comparative Studies in Society and History* 17 (1975), pp. 36–64, point out that when women went off to labor in industry in towns, they did not necessarily send money home but kept it toward their own marriages. Judith Bennett, "Medieval Peasant Marriage: An Examination of Marriage Fines in the *Liber Gersumarum*," In *Pathways to Medieval Peasants*, ed. J. A. Raftis (Toronto, 1981), pp. 204–205.

18. J. R. Ravensdale, *Liable to Flood: Village Landscape on the Edge of the Fens* (Cambridge, 1974), pp. 48–62, surveys the various uses of fens and resources outside traditional cereal crops. The supplemental production of vegetables and various special items such as hazelnut oil was long a traditional occupation for French peasantry to help them through hard times. Carlo Poni, "Family and 'Podere' in Emilia Romagua," *The Journal of Italian History* 1 (1978), p. 214, found that in nineteenth-century Italy woman and children spent as much as ten hours a day during July and August working on the hemp.

19. Just. 2/17 m. 4d. Their boat capsized when a large wind came up. Isabelle drowned, but Paganus made it to shore. Elaine Clark, "Debt Litigation in the Late Medieval English Vill," in *Pathways to Medieval Peasants*, ed. J. A. Raftis (Toronto, 1981), p. 258 and throughout the article, discusses the various craftsmen and middlemen who enter into agreements with fellow villagers for goods and services.

20. *Bedfordshire Coroners' Rolls*, trans. R. F. Hunnisett, Bedfordshire Historical Record Society 41 (1961), pp. 117, 118. Just. 2/104 m. 9d.

21. *Wakefield*, I, pp. 89–91, 141, 158, 176.

22. *Wakefield*, I, p. 149. See also p. 117. *Court Rolls from the Manor of Carshalton from the Reign of Edward III to that of Henry VII*, trans. D. L. Powell, Surrey Record Society 2 (1916), pp. 23, 31. These types of cases represent some of the main business of the court rolls. W. O. Ault, "By-Laws of Gleaning and the Problems of Harvest," *Economic History Review* 2nd ser. 14 (1961), pp. 212–214.

23. Barbara A. Hanawalt, *Crime and Conflict in English Communities* (Cambridge, Mass., 1979), pp. 83–85, 166–183, for more detail on thefts and the relationship of neighbors in crime, pp. 58–59 for information on acquittal and convictions.

24. Barbara A. Hanawalt, "Community Conflict and Social Control: Crime in the Ramsey Abbey Villages," *Mediaeval Studies* 39 (1977), pp. 402–423, has a fuller discussion of the criminal activities of the three different status groups. See also Hanawalt, *Crime and Conflict*, pp. 128–134. For trespasses, see Edward Britton, *The Community of the Vill: A Study in the History of the Family and Village Life in the Fourteenth Century* (Toronto, 1977), p. 116.

25. Clark, "Debt Litigation," pp. 256, 267–71.

26. Richard M. Smith, "Kin and Neighbors in a Thirteenth-Century Suffolk Community," *Journal of Family History* 4 (1979), pp. 229–249.

27. Anne DeWindt, "A Peasant Land Market and its Participants: King's Ripton, 1280–1400," *Midland History* 4 (1978), pp. 142–159. She found that the small land transactions benefited both the large holders and the lesser holders. This currency in small strips was a fluid and adaptable system that met individual family needs. Only a few of the more prominent villagers were also actively accumulating increasingly more land, and some of them were becoming peasant landlords themselves.

28. Eleanor Searle, "Seigneurial Control of Women's Marriages: The Antecedents and Function of Merchet in England," *Past and Present* 82 (1979), p. 32. R. H. Hilton, *The English Peasantry in the Late Middle Ages* (Oxford, 1975), p. 59.

29. A. E. Levett, *Studies in Manorial History*, E. M. Cam, M. Coate, L. S. Sutherland (Oxford, 1938), p. 246. Hilton, *English Peasantry*, pp. 40–42. Marjorie Kennedy, "Resourceful Villeins: The Cellarer Family of Wawne in Holderness," *Yorkshire Archaeological Journal* 48 (1976), p. 114.

30. Britton, *Community of the Vill*, pp. 97–103.

31. Clark, "Debt Litigation," pp. 253, 267–271. The two groups most distinguishable as creditors were the wealthy villagers and craftsmen.

32. *Court Roll of Chalgrave Manor*, ed. Marian K. Dale, *Bedfordshire Historical Record Society* 28 (1950), pp. xxvii–xxviii.

Chapter 8. The Husbandman's Year and Economic Ventures

1. *Reliquiae Antiquae*, I, ed. Thomas Wright and James O. Halliwell (London, 1841), p. 43.

2. Rossell Hope Robbins, *Secular Lyrics of the Fourteenth and Fifteenth Centuries* (Oxford, 1952), p. 62.

3. Just. 2/194 m. 2, 2/195 ms. 7, 10, 10d. In an accident involving harrowing a field, the harrow turned over on the man's legs. Just. 2/200. For plowing accidents, see Just. 2/92 m. 4d. and 2/91 m. 4.

4. Just. 2/201 m. 2. David H. Morgan, "The Place of Harvesters in Nineteenth-Century Village Life," in *Village Life and Labor*, ed. Raphael Samuel, pp. 27–72, has excellent descriptions of the field labor at harvest. Some of his evidence came from newspaper accounts of harvest deaths that are equivalent to the coroners' inquest records.

5. In Just. 2/200 m. 1, 2/91 m. 4 a man hit himself in the leg.

6. Just. 2/194 m. 12; 2/104 ms. 32, 34d, 40; 2/105 m. 8; 2/71 m. 2d; and 2/69 m. 3 give a few examples among many.

7. For a more complete description of the agricultural year, see H. S. Bennett, *Life on the English Manor* (Cambridge, 1937), pp. 77–96, and George Homans, *The English Villagers of the Thirteenth Century* (Cambridge, Mass., 1941), pp. 353–381.

8. Wood was cut from limbs and put into bundles or fagots and carted across the fields. Accidents involved falling from carts, having limbs fall on workers, and some even sat on the limbs that they were cutting and, of course, fell with the limb. Just. 2/194 ms. 1d, 2; 2/195 for examples. Just. 2/194 m. 6 for digging drainage ditch. Working with horses was a frequent cause of death. The horses kicked people, threw riders, wandered into deep water to drink and the riders were washed off, or bolted at the sight of birds when they were being led to pasture. There are many examples throughout the rolls. See, for instance, Just. 2/194 m. 6, 2/104 m. 8. A man using a beam to prop up his house was crushed by the beam in Just. 2/195 m. 15.

9. William Beveridge, "Westminster Wages in the Manorial Era," *Economic History Review* 2nd ser. 8 (1955), pp. 20–26, and "Wages in the Winchester Manors," *Economic History Review* 7 (1936), pp. 22–43. A. Jones, "Harvest Customs and Labourers' Perquisites in Southern England, 1150–1350," *Agricultural History Review* 25 (1977), pp. 15, 98.

10. James E. Thorold Rogers, *Six Centuries of Work and Wages: The History of English Labour* (London, 1884), pp. 170–175. *Bedfordshire Coroners' Rolls*, trans. R. F. Hunnisett, Bedfordshire Historical Record Society 41 (1961), pp. 15, 106, 111. Just. 2/85 m. 8, 2/67 m. 40. Christopher Dyer, "A Small Landowner in the Fifteenth Century," *Midland History* 1 (1972), p. 13, for pay of various servants confirms Rogers's conclusion that the permanent servants could be paid very well indeed. A fishpond keeper and hedger got £3 19s. 6d. annually.

11. In Just. 2/92 m. 5 a man was sitting on the wheel of a horse mill when it started pulling and he was crushed. See also Just. 2/88 m. 2, 2/85 ms. 5, 8. In Just. 2/203 m. 5 a man was milling when his millstone broke and one of the pieces hit him in the back.

12. Just. 2/18 m. 45; 2/104 ms. 14d, 15; 2/67 ms. 3, 5d, 19; 2/195, ms. 13d., 16d. The roads themselves caused some of the accidents. One man was driving on the highway and hit a pothole that made the cart overturn: Just. 2/85 m. 5. Carting was by far the most dangerous occupation for men, either in connection with fieldwork, carting goods, or travel. Of course, some of the carters were drunk when they had accidents. See, for instance, Just. 2/195 m. 9d, 2/203 m. 3.

13. Just. 2/104 m. 15; 2/91 ms. 3, 4, 5; 2/88 m. 2; 2/92, ms. 2, 4. Another man who was punting a boatload of goods across the water got stuck and tried to push off with his pole. It catapulted him into the water and he drowned: Just 2/104 m. 13.

14. Judith Bennett, "Village Ale-Wives," in *Women and Work in Preindustrial Europe*, ed. Barbara A. Hanawalt (Bloomington, Ind. forthcoming in 1986), has argued that men brewed in woodland as opposed to champion country. But no one questions that women predominated in brewing. L. F. Salzman, *English Industries of the Middle Ages* (London, 1923), p. 187. R. H. Hilton, *The English Peasantry in the Late Middle Ages* (Oxford, 1975), p. 45. *The Court Rolls of the Manor of Wakefield*, trans. Sue Sheridan Walker, The Yorkshire Archaeological Record Series, 2nd ser. 2 (forthcoming), pp. 122–123.

15. *Court Rolls of the Manor of Carshalton*, trans. D. L. Powell, Surrey Record Society 2 (1916), pp. 9, 21, 23, 31–40. *Court Rolls of the Manor of Wakefield*, IV, trans. John Lister, The Yorkshire Archaeological Society Record Series 78 (1930), p. 3.

16. Just. 2/78 m. 6. See also Just. 2/104 m. 13, 2/91 m. 7, 2/17 m. 2d. *Carshalton*, pp. 23, 31. *Wakefield*, IV, p. 94. G. J. Turner, *Select Pleas of the Forest*, Selden Society 13 (1901), gives the villagers' activities in poaching in royal forests.

17. L. F. Salzman, *English Industries of the Middle Ages* (New York, 1913), pp. 114–132. The accidents with pottery came both from digging for clay and from getting the kiln so hot that it burnt the house. Just. 2/104 m. 26, 2/195 m. 6, 2/87 m. 3.

18. For examples, see Just. 2/93 m. 4; 2/91 ms. 8, 10, for masonry; in 2/67 m. 33d. a carpenter working on a house fell from his scaffolding; 2/82 m. 9 for driving cartload of beams; 2/194 ms. 7d, 8, for pulling beams out of old houses for reuse; in 2/199 m. 5 a man steps off a scaffolding while making a wattle-and-daub wall.

19. Just. 2/92 m. 4. Salzman, *Industries of the Middle Ages*, p. 171, suggests that although leather dressing was a widely diffused industry, it was not quite as common as Rogers suggested and would not be found in every village.

20. Just. 2/199 ms. 3, 5; 2/92 m. 4.

21. Hatcher, *Rural Economy and Society*, pp. 220–256.

22. Salzman, *Industries of the Middle Ages*, pp. 1–37. Accidents occurred in these pits similar to those in quarries and marl pits. They also tended to fill with water when not worked and people fell into them. In Wakefield the tenants could collect coal for their own use, but they had to pay for the right to do so.

23. *Just.* 2/67, 2/87 m. 2.

24. John Hatcher, *Rural Economy and Society in the Duchy of Cornwall* (Cambridge, 1970), pp. 222–243. *Bedfordshire Wills Proven in the Prerogative Court of Canterbury, 1383–1548*, ed. Margaret McGregor, Bedfordshire Historical Record Society 58 (1979), pp. 41–42.

25. *Court Rolls of the Manor of Wakefield*, I, trans. W. P. Baildon, The Yorkshire Archaeological Society Record Series 29 (1901), pp. 80–81. *Wakefield*, IV, p. 20.

26. Elaine Clark, "Debt Litigation in a Late Medieval English Vill," in *Pathways to Medieval Peasants*, ed. J. A. Raftis (Toronto, 1981), pp. 261–267.

27. Christopher Dyer, *Lords and Peasants in a Changing Society: The Estates of the Bishopric of Worcester, 680–1540* (Cambridge, 1980), pp. 305–315.

28. Edwin DeWindt, *Land and People in Holywell-cum-Needingworth*, (Toronto, 1972), pp. 117–126, 134–137. Cottagers were less likely to participate in the land markets than were the yardlander and half-yardlanders.

29. Hatcher, *Rural Economy and Society*, p. 236–238, 245, found that burgesses in Cornwall were taking land in the country and putting it to pasture.

30. *Wakefield*, I, pp. 91, 96, 117. *Carshalton Court Rolls*, pp. 3, 7, 17, 25, 29. *Wakefield*, IV, pp. 16, 18, 22, 94, 95. One man put his mark on trees in order to steal them. *Court Roll of Chalgrave Manor*, ed. Marian K. Dale, Bedfordshire Historical Record Society 28 (1950), p. 51.

31. *Wakefield*, I, p. 83. *Wakefield*, IV, p. 19.

32. *Wakefield*, I, pp. 12, 14, 30–32, 40. He had to give 6s. 8d. for aid in collecting the 100s.

33. Francis Davenport, "The Decay of Villeinage in East Anglia," in *Essays in Economic History*, II, ed. E. M. Carus-Wilson (London, 1962), pp. 112–124.

34. Nora Ritchie (née Kenyon), "Labor Conditions in Essex in the Reign of Richard II," in *Essays in Economic History*, II, ed. E. M. Carus-Wilson (London, 1962), pp. 91–111.

35. *Bedfordshire Coroners' Rolls*, pp. 6–7.

Chapter 9. Women's Contribution to the Home Economy

1. *Reliquiae Antiquae*, II, ed. Thomas Wright and James O. Halliwell (London, 1941), pp. 196–199.

2. *Ibid.*

3. See, for instance, Louise A. Tilly and Joan W. Scott, *Women, Work, and Family* (New York, 1978); and Olwen Hufton, "Women and the Family Economy in Eighteenth Century France," *French Historical Studies*, 9 (1975), pp. 1–22, and "Women in the Revolution, 1789–1796," *Past and Present* 53 (1971), pp. 90–108.

4. J. C. Russell, *British Medieval Population*, (Albuquerque, 1948), pp. 154–156.

5. E. A. Wrigley and R. S. Schofield, *The Population History of England, 1541–1871: A Reconstruction* (Cambridge, Mass., 1981), pp. 257–265.

6. The wills are taken from the full collection for Bedfordshire: *English Wills*,

1498–1526, ed. A. F. Cirket, Bedfordshire Historical Record Society 37 (1956) and *Bedfordshire Wills, 1480–1519*, trans. Patricia Bell, Bedfordshire Historical Record Society 45 (1966). In using the wills for these figures I have omitted all clerics' wills and those of the few men who were bachelors.

7. *Bedfordshire Wills*, p. 87.

8. *English Wills*, p. 33.

9. Ibid., pp. 9, 76. Frederick J. Furnivall, *Manners and Meals in Olden Times*, EETS, o.s. 32 (London, 1868), p. 46.

10. F. Pollock and F. W. Maitland, *History of English Law before Edward I*, new ed., II, (Cambridge, 1968), pp. 404–407.

11. *English Wills*, p. 80.

12. Ibid., pp. 17–18, 22.

13. Ibid., p. 70.

14. For women purchasing bits of land, see *Court Rolls of Chalgrave Manor*, ed. Marian K. Dale, Bedfordshire Historical Record Society 28 (1950), p. 22. *The Court Rolls of the Manor of Wakefield*, trans. Sue Sheridan Walker, The Yorkshire Archaeological Society Record Series, 2nd ser. 2 (forthcoming), pp. 152, 153, 162, 170. *The Court Rolls of the Manor of Wakefield*, I, trans. W. P. Baildon, The Yorkshire Archaelogical Society Record Series 29 (1901), pp. 81, 96, 106, 115, 122, 124, 174.

15. *Bedfordshire Coroners' Rolls*, trans. R. F. Hunnisett, Bedfordshire Historical Record Society 41 (1961), pp. 48–49.

16. Judith Bennett, "Medieval Peasant Marriage: An Examination of Marriage Fines in the *Liber Gersumarum*," in *Pathways to Medieval Peasants*, ed. J. P. Raftis (Toronto, 1981), pp. 208–211.

17. Rossell Hope Robbins, *Secular Lyrics of the Fourteenth and Fifteenth Centuries* (Oxford, 1952), p. 44. Ester Boserup, *Women's Role in Economic Development* (London, 1970), pp. 24–30, maintains that in all plow cultures, plowing is a male role and women seldom do it. There is in the folklore of plow cultures a male sexual connotation to the act of plowing.

18. Wrigley and Schofield, *Population History of England*, pp. 503–504.

19. Barbara A. Hanawalt, "Childrearing Among the Lower Classes of Late Medieval England," *Journal of Interdisciplinary History* 8 (1971), pp. 1–22.

20. Boserup, *Women's Role*, pp. 27–29. Carlo Poni, "Family and 'Podere' in Emilia Romagua," *The Journal of Italian History* 1 (1978), pp. 201–234, has shown that nineteenth-century Italian peasant women spent more time in the house from November to March, working largely on linen; from April to October their fieldwork surpassed their housework. Their day was often longer than the man's.

21. *Reliquiae Antiquae*, II, "Ballad of the Tyrannical Husband," pp. 197–198.

22. Just. 2/78 m. 2.

23. Just. 2/18 m. 19, 2/69 m. 7d.

24. Two percent of women's accidents came from dealing with animals. See, for instance, Just. 2/67 m. 40d., 2/70 m. 10, 2/86 m. 2. In the latter case a woman had put a ladder against the post of a barn to get straw down for her cows when the ladder broke.

25. Twenty-three percent of the women died in accidents related to supplementary activities such as gathering, fishing, and begging. See, for instance, Just. 2/18 m. 11, 2/104 m. 3.

26. Hanawalt, "Childrearing," pp. 14–18.

27. Edward Britton, *The Community of the Vill: A Study in the History of the Family and Village Life in Fourteenth-Century England* (Toronto, 1977), p. 88.

28. See, for instance, Just. 2/67 m. 23, 2/91 m. 4, 2/81 m. 8.

29. William Beveridge, "Wages in the Winchester Manors," *Economic History Review*, 7 (1934), pp. 33–34.

30. Ibid., p. 34. R. H. Hilton, *The English Peasantry in the Later Middle Ages* (Oxford, 1975), pp. 101–102.

31. F. W. Tickner, *Women in English Economic History* (London, 1923), p. 23.

32. Walker, *Wakefield*, p. 22. Hilton, *English Peasantry*, pp. 103–105. R. H. Britnell, "Production for the Market on a Small Fourteenth-Century Estate," *Economic History Review* 2nd ser. 19 (1966), p. 383. Elaine Clark, "Debt Litigation in a late Medieval English Vill," in *Pathways to Medieval Peasants*, ed. J. A. Raftis (Toronto, 1981), p. 252, found that 7 percent of the creditors were women. In Just. 2/17 m. 4d. a woman taking reeds to market, and in Just. 2/200 m. 7 a woman taking cheese to market. *Chalgrave*, p. 33.

33. Just. 2/18 m. 44.

34. Hilton, *English Peasantry*, p. 105. *Wakefield*, I, p. 194: "Sara, widow of Henry son of Robert de Hertesheved, came and waged her law with women, and the said John de Dychton sought judgement because she waged her law with women." She lost. A. E. Levett, *Studies in Manorial History*, ed. H. M. Cam, M. Coate, and L. S. Sutherland (Oxford, 1938), pp. 242–243.

35. Hufton, "Women in Revolution," pp. 92–95.

36. W. O. Ault, "By-Laws of Gleaning and the Problems of Harvest," *Economic History Review*, 2nd ser. 14 (1961), pp. 212–214. Just. 2/17 m. 3d.

37. Walker, *Wakefield*, pp. 28, 164, 169, 175. *Wakefield*, I, 91, 117, 149.

38. Barbara A. Hanawalt, *Crime and Conflict in English Communities, 1300–1348* (Cambridge, Mass., 1979), pp. 120–122.

39. Just. 2/106 m. 1. See also Just. 2/114 ms. 3, 7, 8, 17.

40. Joan Scott and Louise Tilly, "Women's Work and the Family in Nineteenth-Century Europe," *Comparative Studies in Society and History* 17 (1975), pp. 44–45.

41. R. L. Greene, *The Early English Carols*, 2nd ed. (Oxford, 1977), no. 401. See also nos. 400, 402, 403.

42. Robbins, *Secular Lyrics*, pp. 35–36. Greene, *English Carols*, no. 399.

43. *Testamenta Eboracensia: A Selection of Wills From the Registry at York*, III, Surtees Society 45 (1865), p. 203.

44. Furnivall, *Manners and Meals*, p. 39.

45. Walker, *Wakefield*, p. 264.

46. Fredricka Pickford Santos, "The Economics of Marital Status," in *Sex Discrimination and the Division of Labor*, ed. Cynthia Lloyd (New York, 1975), pp. 249–250. She further explored a model of Gary Becker, "A Theory of Marriage, Part I," *Journal of Political Economy* 81 (1973), pp. 813–846, and "A Theory of Marriage: Part II," 82 (1974), pp. s11–s26. Both writers explore the shared economic benefits that accrue to both partners in a traditional marriage. For a more theoretical discussion of women's economic contributions in preindustrial Europe, see Barbara A. Hanawalt, Introduction, in *Women and Work in Preindustrial Europe* (Bloomington, Ind., forthcoming in 1986).

Chapter 10. Children and Servants at Home and in the Fields

1. *The Italian Relation of England*, ed. C. A. Sneyd, Camden Society 37 (1847), p. 24. Ann Kussmaul, *Servants in Husbandry in Early Modern England* (Cambridge, 1981) has the most complete discussion of early modern servants.

2. Just. 2/113 m. 37. Other children looked into caldrons or tried to taste the contents: Just. 2/113 ms. 32, 33, 46.

3. Just. 2/109 m. 8, 2/106 m. 1d., 2/77 m. 3d, in which a child was watching construction work when a ladder fell on him.

4. Just. 2/200 m. 2.

5. Just. 2/67 m. 19d., 2/91 m. 6, 2/18 m. 21d., 2/104 m. 3d., 2/92 m. 8, 2/104 m. 3d.

6. Just. 2/92 m. 8, 2/104 m. 3. *Court Rolls of the Manor of Wakefield*, IV, trans. John Lister, The Yorkshire Archaeological Society Record Series 78 (1930), p. 193.

7. Just. 2/17 m. 2d., 2/18 m. 19d., 2/104, m. 39d., 2/195 m. 17, 2/199 m. 4, 2/109 ms. 1, 7. *Bedfordshire Coroners' Rolls*, trans. R. F. Hunnisett, Bedfordshire Historical Record Society 41 (1961), p. 11.

8. James E. Thorold Rogers, *Six Centuries of Work and Wages: The History of English Labour* (London, 1884), p. 170. *Bedfordshire Coroners' Rolls*, pp. 29–30, gives the case of William Fraunceys, who set out to get his cattle with his ten-year-old son.

9. Just. 2/88 m. 3; 2/82 ms. 4d., 9; 2/67 m. 40; 2/77 m. 9; 2/104 m. 27; 2/44.

10. *Bedfordshire Coroners' Rolls*, p. 82. Just. 2/195.

11. Just. 2/203 m. 13.

12. Just. 2/104 m. 42.

13. Just. 2/104 ms. 5, 27, 42.

14. Just. 2/104 m. 11. *Bedfordshire Coroners' Rolls*, p. 103.

15. Just. 2/104 m. 2., 2/91 m. 5.

16. A. E. Levett, *Studies in Manorial History*, ed. H. M. Cam, M. Coate, L. S. Sutherland (Oxford, 1938), p. 246.

17. *Bedfordshire Coroners' Rolls*, p. 54.

18. Ibid., pp. 13, 15, 52. Just. 2/85 m. 2. G. E. Fussell, "Countrywomen in Old England," *Agricultural History Review* 50 (1976), p. 176. "Three Records of the Alien Priory of Grove and the Manor of Leighton Buzzard," ed. Robert Richmond, in *Publications of the Bedfordshire Historical Record Society* 8 (1924), pp. 31–38, has information on the work that the various servants, men, women, and "lads" did on the manor.

19. Alan Macfarlane, *The Origins of English Individualism*, (New York, 1979), pp. 148–149.

20. Bertha Haven Putnam, *Enforcement of the Statute of Laborers during the First Decade after the Black Death, 1349–1359* (New York, 1909), pp. 79–80. Kussmaul defines laborers as those hired for part of the year and living separate from the employer, whereas servants are hired for the year and live with the employer: *Servants in Husbandry*, p. 7. Since medieval servants may not have lived with the employer, I have modified the definitions.

21. *Wakefield*, IV, p. 99.

22. Kussmaul, *Servants in Husbandry*, pp. 3, 11–12.

23. A. Raistrick, "A Fourteenth-Century Regional Survey," *Sociological Review* 21 (1929), pp. 242–246. R. H. Hilton, *The English Peasantry in the Later Middle Ages* (Oxford, 1975), p. 32. Edgar Powell, *Rising in East Anglia in 1381* (Cambridge, 1896), pp. 67–85.

24. Hilton, *English Peasantry*, pp. 31–33.

25. *Bedfordshire Coroners' Rolls*, pp. 22, 92. Often in these burglaries only one out of four or five burglaries will be of a house in which there is a servant present at night. In Just. 2/67 m. 33 a servant is killed by leaving a candle burning. Just. 2/93 m. 3.

26. *Bedfordshire Coroners' Rolls*, p. 111.

27. *The Court Rolls of the Manor of Wakefield*, trans. Sue Sheridan Walker, The Yorkshire Archaeological Society Record Series, 2nd ser. 2 (forthcoming), p. 318.

28. R. T. Davies, *Medieval English Lyrics: A Critical Anthology* (Evanston, Ill., 1964), p. 154. Greene, *English Carols*, no. 346.

29. Just. 2/18 m. 4.

30. *Bedfordshire Coroners' Rolls*, p. 23. In Just. 2/105 m. 5 a man, twenty-seven years old, pursued his servant into a neighbor's house but ran into an object and knocked himself out.

31. Ibid., pp. 28, 34, 75.

32. *Bedfordshire Wills, 1480–1519*, ed. Patricia Bell, Bedfordshire Historical Record Society 45 (1966), pp. 55–56. *English Wills, 1498–1526*, ed. A. F. Cirket, Bedfordshire Historical Record Society 87 (1956), pp. 17–18, 22, 70.

33. *Court Rolls of the Manor of Wakefield*, I, trans. W. P. Baildon, The Yorkshire Archaeological Society Record Series 29 (1901), pp. 164, 169.

Chapter 11. Childhood

1. Philippe Ariès, *Centuries of Childhood: A Social History of the Family*, trans. Robert Baldick (London, 1962), p. 368. Erik Erikson, *Childhood and Society* (New York, 1963), pp. 247–274, for a summary.

2. Mary Martin McLaughlin, "Survivors and Surrogates: Children and Parents from the Ninth to the Thirteenth Centuries," in *The History of Childhood*, ed. Lloyd deMause (New York, 1974), pp. 113–114. *Records of Medieval Oxford, Coroners' Inquests, The Walls of Oxford, etc.*, ed. H. E. Salter (Oxford, 1912), p. 27.

3. C. Wimberly, *Folklore in English and Scottish Ballads* (Chicago, 1928), pp. 371–376. James Francis Child, *English and Scottish Popular Ballads*, I, (Boston, 1883), nos. 5B, 5C.

4. Juha Pentikäinen, *The Nordic Dead-Child Tradition*, Folklore Fellows Communications, no. 201 (Helsinki, 1968), pp. 71–75. Nicole Belmont, "Levana: or How to Raise up Children," in *Family and Society: Selections from the Annales, Economies, Sociétés, Civilisation*, ed. Robert Forster and Orest Ranum, trans. Elborg Forster and Patricia M. Ranum (Baltimore, 1976), pp. 1–3. Thomas C. Rumble, *The Breton Lays in Middle English* (Detroit, 1965), pp. 49–50, 86–88.

5. Child, *Ballads*, I. 1A.

6. John Myrc, *Instructions for a Parish Priest*, ed. Edward Peacock, EETS, o.s. 209 (London, 1940), pp. 3–4, instructs the midwife to have clean water present at the birth, and if the child comes out by its head and shoulders and it appears it will not live, she is to baptize it. If the mother dies, the midwife is to take a knife and cut her open and extract the child. If her heart fails her, she can call upon a man for help. In folklore there was also considerable concern about the fate of children who "die without a name." Wimberly, *Folklore*, p. 409.

7. Charles H. E. White, "The Church and Parish of Chesham Bois, Bucks.," *Architectural and Archaeological Society for the County of Buckingham* 6 (1887), p. 195.

8. Louis Haas, "Baptism and Spiritual Kinship in the North of England, 1250–1450," M.A. Thesis (Ohio State University, 1982), pp. 69–80, describes the baptismal ceremony in detail. He has drawn on the manuals for priests and the proofs of age from the Inquisitions Post Mortem.

9. Ibid., pp. 76, 85.

10. Michael Bennett, "Spiritual Kinship and the Baptismal Name in Traditional European Society," in *Principalities, Powers and Estates: Studies in Medieval and Early Modern Government and Society*, ed. L. O. Frappell (Adelaide, 1979), p. 8, provides the information

on the proof of age from the Inquisitions Post Mortem, including the godparent who fought for his naming privileges. *English Wills, 1498–1526,* ed. A. F. Cirket, Bedfordshire Historical Record Society 37 (1956), p. 24. See also *Bedfordshire Wills, 1480–1519,* trans. Patricia Bell, Bedfordshire Historical Record Society 45 (1966), p. 60. The proof of English citizenship was used in York in the late fifteenth century when some tradesmen were accused of being Scots and refused the right to practice their trade. They proved their English origins by bringing evidence of their godparents from their baptismal records. Some of these are published in *A Volume of English Miscellanies,* Surtees Society 85 (1890), pp. 35–52.

11. Zvi Razi, *Life, Marriage and Death in the Medieval Parish: Economy, Society and Demography in Halesowen, 1270–1400* (Cambridge, 1980), p. 15.

12. Bennett, "Spiritual Kinship," p. 8.

13. Lawrence Stone, *Family, Sex, and Marriage in England, 1500–1800* (New York, 1977), p. 70, has concluded that parents gave two siblings the same name in the expectation that only one would survive.

14. J. C. Russell, "Demographic Limitations of the Spalding Serf Lists," *Economic History Review* 2, 15 (1962), pp. 138–144. F. S. Colman, *A History of the Parish of Barwick-in-Elmet, in the County of York,* Thoresby Society 12 (1908), p. 300.

15. A. C. Chibnall, *Sherington: Fiefs and Fields of a Buckinghamshire Village* (Cambridge, 1965), p. 95. *Chertsey Abbey Court Rolls, Abstract,* trans. Elsie Toms, Surrey Record Society 21 (1937), p. xxxix.

16. Thomas Wright, *A History of Domestic Manners and Sentiments in England in the Middle Ages* (London, 1862), pp. 48–51. McLaughlin, "Survivors and Surrogates," pp. 113–114.

17. Just. 2/77 m. 4.

18. Just. 2/111 m. 17; 2/112 m. 38; 2/113 ms. 27, 31; 2/255 m. 5. Beatrice, daughter of John Gous, fell in a ditch in her father's close when both her parents were in the fields: Just. 2/67 m. 9. Edith, wife of John le Taylor, put her infant daughter in a cradle by the fire at prime and went to hear Mass. A chicken in the house started a fire in the cradle by dropping embers on the child's hair: Just. 2/200 m. 6.

19. Beatrice White, "Poet and Peasant," in *The Reign of Richard II,* ed. F. R. H. DuBoulay and C. M. Barron (London, 1971), p. 70.

20. Just. 2/70 ms. 10d, 11; 2/67 m. 33.

21. Just. 2/18 ms. 42d, 45; 2/104 m. 18d; 2/200, m. 2; 2/199. *Bedfordshire Coroners' Rolls,* trans. R. F. Hunnisett, Bedfordshire Historical Record Society 41 (1961), pp. 25, 45.

22. Ibid., p. 93. Just. 2/18 m. 12d., 2/66 m. 2d., 2/67 m. 8d., 2/104 m. 13d.

23. Just. 2/105 m. 1d., 2/204 m. 1d., 2/104 m. 7. Richard Helmholtz, "Infanticide in the Province of Canterbury during the Fifteenth Century," *History of Childhood Quarterly* 2 (1974–75), pp. 282–390, for a discussion of the admonitions on childrearing that appear in penitential literature.

24. Wright, *Domestic Manners,* p. 51.

25. Just. 2/105 m. 6.

26. Frances M. M. Comper, *Spiritual Songs from English MSS. of Fourteenth to Sixteenth Centuries* (Cambridge, 1936), p. 27.

27. McLaughlin, "Survivors and Surrogates", pp. 115–116.

28. Just. 2/18 m. 57d., 2/85 m. 5, *Bedfordshire Coroners' Rolls,* p. 9.

29. Robert D. Stevick, ed., *One Hundred Middle English Lyrics* (Indianapolis, Ind., 1964), pp. 66–67.

30. Ibid., pp. 62–63.

31. Beth Lomax Hawes, "Folksong and Function: Some Thoughts on the American Lullaby," *Journal of American Folklore* 87 (1974), pp. 140–147, points out that mothers may sing any type of song to their infants, not just lullabies. The typical American lullaby not only speaks of a nice environment for the child, but one that is isolated from the parents and from the child's usual environment.

32. David Hunt, *Parents and Children in History: The Psychology of Family Life in Early Modern France* (New York, 1970), pp. 135–136, has applied Erik Erikson's model of child development to a historical content. In my initial work on the subject, "Childrearing among the Lower Classes," I too used this approach. The more broadly based biological approach seems more appropriate to me now.

33. Just. 2/18 m. 48d.; 2/74 m. 9; 2/201 m. 1; 2/106 m. 1d.; 2/109 m. 8; 2/77 m. 3d.; 2/113 ms. 32, 33, 37, 46; 2/194 ms. 2, 8d. *Bedfordshire Coroners' Rolls*, p. 35.

34. Just. 2/104 ms. 2, 12; 2/104 m. 2.

35. Albert P. Iskrant and Paul V. Joliet, *Accident and Homicide* (Cambridge, Mass., 1968), pp. 19, 22, 138.

36. *Bedfordshire Coroners' Rolls*, pp. 6, 11–12.

37. Carl Haffter, "The Changeling: History and Psychodynamics of Attitudes to Handicapped Children in European Folklore," *Journal of the History of the Behavioral Sciences* 4 (1968), pp. 55–61. Wimberly, *Folklore*, pp. 285, 325.

38. Hunt, *Parents and Children*, pp. 159–179. *Robert [Mannyng] of Brunne's Handlyng Synne*, ed. F. J. Furnivall, EETS, o.s. 119 (London, 1901), p. 244.

39. Mary Seger, *A Medieval Anthology, Being Lyrics and Other Short Poems Chiefly Religious* (London, 1915), p. 131.

40. F. J. Furnivall, *Manners and Meals in Olden Time*, EETS, o.s. 32 (London, 1868), pp. 33, 46. *Robert [Mannyng] of Brunne's Handlyng Synne*, pp. 45–46.

41. Just. 2/67 m. 40d. *Calendar Coroners' Rolls of the City of London*, ed. Reginald Sharpe (London, 1913), p. 83.

42. Just. 2/107 m. 5.

43. Just. 2/107 m. 7, 2/77 m. 3.

44. Ariès, *Centuries of Childhood*, p. 365. Stone, *Family, Marriage and Sex*, p. 6. *Bedfordshire Coroners' Rolls*, pp. 11, 27–28, 51–52, 93, 100–102, 103. Just. 2/106; 2/109 ms. 1, 7; 2/255 m. 6.

45. Barbara A. Hanawalt, *Crime and Conflict in English Communities, 1300–1348* (Cambridge, Mass., 1979), p. 161.

46. Just. 2/66 m. 6d, 2/102 m. 10d., 2/200 m. 7.

47. *Bedfordshire Coroners' Rolls*, p. 29.

48. *Records of Medieval Oxford, Coroners' Inquests, the Walls of Oxford, Etc.*, ed. H. E. Salter *(London, 1912), p. 7.*

49. *Bedfordshire Coroners' Rolls*, pp. 27–28, 33–34.

50. *Court Rolls of the Manor of Wakefield*, I, trans. W. P. Baildon, The Yorkshire Archaeological Society Record Series 29 (1901), p. 111. *Court Rolls of the Manor of Wakefield*, trans. Sue Sheridan Walker, The Yorkshire Archaeological Society Record Society, 2nd ser. 2 (forthcoming), p. 109. *Court Roll of Chalgrave Manor, 1278–1313*, ed. Marian K. Dale, Bedfordshire Historical Record Society 28 (1950), pp. 38–39. *Bedfordshire Wills*, pp. 43–47.

51. Adamson, *Treasury*, pp. 119, 152–153.

52. Segar, *Medieval Anthology*, pp. 109–110, cites a poem that praises women because they wrap the naked-born baby in weeds and foster and feed it and give it their love. Adamson, *Treasury*, p. 118, for another example.

53. *Robert [Mannyng] of Brunne's Handlyng Synne*, pp. 38–39, 40–43. *English Wills*, pp. 20, 23, 41, 44, 48, 56.

54. McLaughlin, "Survivors and Surrogates," pp. 117–120.

55. Ronald Knox, trans., *The Miracles of King Henry VI* (Cambridge, 1923).

56. William Holden Hutton, *The Lives and Legends of English Saints* (New York, 1903), pp. 324–327. E. Cobham Brewer, *A Dictionary of Miracles: Imitative, Realistic, and Dogmatic* (Philadelphia, 1884), pp. 171–175.

Chapter 12. Growing Up and Getting Married

1. Andreas Capellanus, *The Art of Courtly Love*, trans. John Jay Parry (New York, 1972), p. 24. Philippe Ariès, *Centuries of Childhood: A Social History of the Family*, trans. Robert Baldick (London, 1962), Ch. 6 and pp. 128–129. Edward Shorter, *The Making of the Modern Family* (New York, 1975), pp. 120–121.

2. Frederick J. Furnivall, ed., *Hymns to the Virgin and Christ, the Parliament of Devils, and Other Religious Poems*, EETS, o.s. 24 (London, 1868), p. 61.

3. Sue Sheridan Walker, "Proof of Age of Feudal Heirs in Medieval England," *Mediaeval Studies* 35 (1973), pp. 306–323. Zvi Razi, *Life, Marriage and Death in the Medieval Parish: Economy, Society and Demography in Halesowen, 1270–1400* (Cambridge, 1980), p. 43. *Court Roll of Chalgrave Manor*, ed. Marian K. Dale, Bedfordshire Historical Record Society, 28 (1950), p. 46. *The Court Rolls of the Manor of Wakefield*, trans. Sue Sheridan Walker, The Yorkshire Archaeological Society Record Series, 2nd ser. 2 (forthcoming), p. 33. Cicely Howell, "Peasant Inheritance Customs in the Midlands," in *Family and Inheritance*, ed. J. Goody, J. Thirsk, E. P. Thompson (Cambridge, 1976), pp. 145–146, found that in wills in Leicestershire the age of inheritance was variously described as sixteen, eighteen, twenty-one, or when they married. Edward Britton, *The Community of the Vill: A Study in the History of the Family and Village Life in Fourteenth-century England* (Toronto, 1977), pp. 46–47.

4. Just. 2/106 m. 2, 2/112 m. 1, 2/255 m. 6, 2/17 m. 6.

5. Antonia Gransden, "Childhood and Youth in Medieval England," *Nottingham Medieval Studies* 16 (1972), pp. 3–4.

6. Britton, *Community of the Vill*, pp. 38–43.

7. Just. 2/82, m. 4. *English Wills 1498–1526*, ed. A. F. Cirket, Bedfordshire Historical Record Society 37 (1956), pp. 62, 68. *Court Rolls of the Manor of Wakefield*, I, trans. W. P. Baildon, The Yorkshire Archaeological Society Record Series 36 (1906), p. 148.

8. *Court Rolls of the Manor of Wakefield*, IV, trans. John Lister, The Yorkshire Archaeological Society Record Series 78 (1970), p. 145. Walker, *Wakefield*, p. 153.

9. Just. 2/48 m. 13, 3/23 m. 1.

10. Francis James Child, *The English and Scottish Popular Ballads*, I, (Boston, 1883), nos. 13, 10A, and B, 11. *Chalgrave*, p. 49. Just. 2/108 m. 1.

11. Thomas C. Rumble, ed., *The Breton Lays in Middle English* (Detroit, 1965), pp. 13, 63–64, 90–91, 105–106. Child, *Ballads*, I, nos. 14, 17.

12. Margot Adamson, *A Treasury of Middle English Verse Selected and Rendered into Modern English* (London, 1930), p. 6.

13. Rossell Hope Robbins, *Secular Lyrics of the Fourteenth and Fifteenth Centuries* (Oxford, 1952), pp. 16–19. The poem titles give a good idea of content: "Careless Love," "A Forsaken Maiden's Lament," "The Wily Clerk."

14. R. T. Davies, *Medieval English Lyrics, A Critical Anthology* (Evanston, Ill., 1964), pp. 67–68, 260.

15. Robbins, *Secular Lyrics*, pp. 32–33: "A Young Girl's Ideal."

16. Fussell, "Countrywomen in Old England," p. 117.

17. Just. 2/104 m. 23. See also Just. 2/104 m. 42 and 2/200 m. 1.

18. *Church-Wardens' Accounts of Coscombe, Pilton, Latton, Tintinhull, Morebath, and St. Michael's Bath*, ed. Edmund Hobhouse, Somerset Record Society 4 (1890), p. 1.

19. *Robert [Mannyng] of Brunne's Handlyng Synne*, ed. F. J. Furnivall, EETS, o.s. 119 (London, 1901), p. 36. George Homans, *English Villagers of the Thirteenth Century* (Cambridge, Mass., 1941), pp. 366–367.

20. *Bedfordshire Coroners' Rolls*, trans. R. F. Hunnisett, Bedfordshire Historical Record Society 41 (1961), pp. 50–51.

21. Just. 2/116 ms. 6, 22.

22. *Robert [Mannyng] of Brunne's Handlyng Synne*, pp. 244, 257.

23. Britton, *Community of the Vill*, p. 51. *Wakefield*, IV, pp. 53–54. The way the entries appear in that one session is completely different from the random appearances in the other volumes including Walker's edition. Because of the unique nature of that session, Searle's table in "Merchet in Medieval England," p. 28, is somewhat misleading, although this does not change the conclusions she draws. Razi, *Halesowen*, pp. 64–66, 138–139. Razi states that the legerwite cases are always births out of wedlock, but his argument is not convincing and one can only take the legerwites as fornication unless the record also states that the woman bore a child out of wedlock. His argument that the legerwiters were actually pregnancies rests on a few cases in which the woman was described as both deflowered and pregnant. One cannot assume from these few cases that all are cases of the birth of a child out of wedlock.

24. Britton, *Community of the Vill*, p. 51. Razi, *Halesowen*, p. 66.

25. Michael Sheehan, "The Formation and Stability of Marriage in Fourteenth-Century England: Evidence of an Ely Register," *Mediaeval Studies* 33 (1971), pp. 241–243.

26. P. E. H. Hair, "Bridal Pregnancy in Rural England in Earlier Centuries," *Population Studies* 20 (1966–67), pp. 233–243, and "Bridal Pregnancy in Earlier Rural England, Further Examined," *Population Studies* 24 (1970), pp. 59–70. He found that a large proportion of the brides were three or more months pregnant, thus suggesting the betrothal resulted from conceptions. Peter Laslett, *Family Life and Illicit Love in Earlier Generations* (Cambridge, 1977), see Chapter 3, "Long-term Trends in Bastardy in England." Keith Wrightson and David Levine, *Poverty and Piety in an English Village: Terling, 1525–1700* (New York, 1979), pp. 126–128.

27. Just. 2/18 m. 2.

28. Child, *Ballads*, I., nos. 5, 25, 9A.

29. Judith Bennett, "Medieval Peasant Marriage: An Examination of Marriage Licence Fines in the *Liber Gersumarum*," in *Pathways to Medieval Peasants* ed. J. A. Raftis (Toronto, 1981), p. 200. The percentage marrying outside the village could be higher because the category of licenses to marry freemen probably also contained outsiders. But the addition of this group of forty-nine marriages might split along the same proportions. Sheehan, "Formation and Stability of Marriage," p. 251. Helmholz's estimates on marriage outside the village were included in an earlier chapter.

30. Adamson, *Treasury*, p. 147.

31. Sheehan, "Formation and Stability of Marriage," pp. 228–237. Richard Helmholz, *Marriage Litigation in Medieval England* (Cambridge, 1974), pp. 25–73, on marriage contracts.

32. Ibid., p. 248.

33. Eleanor Searle, "Seigneurial Control over Women's Marriages: The Antecedents and Function of Merchet in England," *Past and Present* 82 (1979), pp. 32–37. Razi, *Halesowen*, pp. 51–56. The same type of marriage strategy was used in urban centers as well: Colin Platt, *The English Medieval Town* (London, 1976), pp. 105–107. *Bedfordshire Wills, 1480–1519*, trans. Patricia Bell, Bedfordshire Historical Record Society 45 (1966), no. 172, shows that relations with a son-in-law could be very amicable. In this case the man called his son-in-law "his son John Huckell" and left him everything. The father-in-law did not live with them but in another village.

34. R. H. Hilton, *The English Peasantry in the Later Middle Ages* (Oxford, 1975), p. 59. Searle, "Seigneurial Control," p. 30, 37. A. E. Levett, *Studies In Manorial History*, ed. H. M. Cam, M. Coate, L. S. Sutherland (Oxford, 1938), p. 245. *Wakefield*, I, p. 183. *Calendar of the Court Rolls of the Manor of Wakefield*, V, ed. J. P. Walker, The Yorkshire Archaeological Society Record Series 109 (1945), p. 6.

35. Sheehan, "Formation and Stability of Marriage," p. 262. Helmholz, *Marriage Litigation*, pp. 90–94.

36. Razi, *Halesowen*, p. 66. K. H. Connell, "Peasant Marriage in Ireland: Its Structure and Development since the Famine," *Economic History Review*, 2nd. ser. 14 (1962), pp. 502–523.

37. Bennett, "Medieval Peasant Marriages," pp. 200–215.

38. Jean Schammell, "Freedom and Marriage in Medieval England," *Economic History Review* 2nd ser. 27 (1974), pp. 523–537, and "Wife-Rents and Merchet," *Economic History Review* 2nd ser., 29 (1976), pp. 487–490 has argued that merchet was a tax on people. Eleanor Searle, "Freedom and Marriage in Medieval England: An Alternative Hypothesis," *Economic History Review* 2nd ser., 29 (1976), pp. 482–486; "Seigneurial Control," pp. 3–43; and "A Rejoinder," *Past and Present* 99 (1983), pp. 149–160 argued to the contrary that it was a way for the lord to tax land and goods transferred at marriage. Paul A. Brand and Paul R. Hyams, "Debate: Seigneurial Control of Women's Marriage," *Past and Present* 99 (1983), pp. 123–133 concluded that it was a marriage levy on wealthy peasants. Rosamond Faith, "Debate: Seigneurial Control of Women's Marriage," *Past and Present* 99 (1983), pp. 133–148. For examples of relief and marriage fine connected, see *Chalgrave Manor*, p. 58. Levett, *Manorial History*, pp. 236–238, observed for St. Albans that the fees for merchet were rather low and not a hindrance to free choice in marriage. Hilton, *English Peasantry*, p. 58, observed much higher merchet fees in the west midlands.

40. Levett, *Manorial History*, pp. 237–244. Brand and Hyams, "Debate," p. 132. Faith, "Debate," p. 145. Hilton, *English Peasantry*, p. 108.

41. Sheehan, "Formation and Stability of Marriage," p. 263.

42. Kenneth Stevenson, *Nuptial Blessing: A Study of Christian Marriage Rites* (New York, 1983), pp. 76–80.

43. Ibid., pp. 237, 244–245. Helmholz, *Marriage Litigation*, p. 30, feels that it is fair to assume that most of the couples who had a private ceremony at home intended to have the church ceremony as well.

44. W. O. Hassall, *How They Lived: An Anthology of Original Accounts Written before 1485* (New York, 1962), p. 99.

45. Homans, *English Villagers*, p. 173. Faith, "Debate," pp. 137–138.

46. E. A. Wrigley and R. S. Schofield, *Population History of England, 1541–1871: A Reconstruction* (Cambridge, Mass., 1981), pp. 300, 519. Hair, "Bridal Pregnancy," p. 67.

Chapter 13. The Partnership Marriage

1. Geoffrey Chaucer, *Canterbury Tales*, trans. Neville Coghill (Harmondsworth, 1951), pp. 276–298.

2. Richard L. Greene, *The Early English Carols*, 2nd ed. (Oxford, 1977), nos. 407, 408, 409. In Rossell Hope Robbins, *Secular Lyrics of the Fourteenth and Fifteenth Centuries* (Oxford, 1952), pp. 38–40, the "Hen-pecked Husband" complains that if he asks for bread his wife takes a staff and breaks his head. In another poem the man complains that he cannot give orders because his wife abuses him. But one proverb preserved in a poem advises a woman how to win a husband's love: "Hold thy tonge stille/And have al thy wylle": Robert Stevick, *One Hundred Middle English Lyrics* (Indianapolis, In., 1964). p. 11.

3. John Myrc, *Instructions for Parish Priests*, ed. Edward Peacock, EETS, o.s. 209 (London, 1940), pp. 34, 42.

4. Frederick J. Furnivall, *Manners and Meals in Olden Times*, EETS, o.s. 32 (London, 1868), pp. 36–58.

5. Paul Hair, comp., *Before the Bawdy Court: Selections from Church Court and Other Records Relating to the Correction of Moral Offences in England, Scotland, and New England, 1300–1800* (New York, 1982). G. R. Quaife, *Wanton Wenches and Wayward Wives: Peasants and Illicit Sex in Early Seventeenth-Century England* (New Brunswick, 1979).

6. Barbara A. Hanawalt, *Crime and Conflict in English Communities, 1300–1348* (Cambridge, Mass., 1979), pp. 159–161. See particularly the histogram on p. 161 for comparison of the percentage of family members involved in jail delivery and manorial court cases. Compared with the modern figures on homicide among family members in England and the United States, the percentage of murders between spouses is very low. Richard Smith, "Kin and Neighbors in a Thirteenth Century Suffolk Community," *Journal of Family History* 4 (1979), has disputed the relatively low number of family members appearing in manorial court records, but he lumped pledging, a cooperative action, with debt, trespass, and assault. His figures are not useful for demonstrating intrafamiliar conflict.

7. *Court Rolls of the Manor of Wakefield*, trans. Sue Sheridan Walker, The Yorkshire Archaeological Society Record Series, 2nd ser. 2 (forthcoming), p. 113. *Court Rolls of the Manor of Wakefield*, V, J. W. Walker, ed., The Yorkshire Archaeological Society Record Series 109 (1945), p. 130. Just. 2/107 m. 7. Just. 2/195 m. 13.

8. *Robert [Mannyng] of Brunne's Handlyng Synne*, ed. F. J. Furnivall, EETS, o.s. 119 (London, 1901), pp. 63–68. He tells the story of the adulteress whose body was split in two; a dragon lived between the two halves in her tomb. He quotes a proverb on jealousy saying that when a man is jealous, there is a cuckold in the house, meaning that his jealousy will drive a woman to adultery. *Court Rolls of the Manor of Wakefield*, III, trans. John Lister, Yorkshire Archaeological Society Record Series 77 (1917), pp. 45, 108, 109. *Court Rolls of the Manor of Wakefield*, IV, trans. John Lister, The Yorkshire Archaeological Society Record Series 57 (1917), 33.

9. Just. 3/24/1 m. 2, 3/78 m. 2. *Chertsey Abbey Court Rolls, Abstract*, trans. Elsie Toms, Surrey Record Society 21 (1937), p. xiv, records a case in which a wife and her lover killed her husband and fled from the area. Many years later a son of the woman appeared and tried to claim his father's holding. But the murdered man's brother claimed that the boy was not the son of his brother.

10. *Bedfordshire Coroners' Rolls*, trans. R. F. Hunnisett, Bedfordshire Historical Record Society 41 (1961), p. 13.

11. Richard Helmholz, *Marriage Litigation in Medieval England* (Cambridge, 1974), pp. 74–111.

12. Sheehan, "The Formation and Stability of Marriage in Fourteenth-Century England: Evidence of an Ely Register," *Mediaeval Studies* 32 (1971), p. 252.

13. Helmholz, *Marriage Litigation*, pp. 88–89.

14. *Robert [Mannyng] of Brunne's Handlyng Synne*, pp. 237–238.

15. Sheehan, "Formation and Stability of Marriage," pp. 254–255.

16. Helmholz, *Marriage Litigation*, pp. 100–111.

17. A. C. Chibnall, *Sherington: Fiefs and Fields of a Buckinghamshire Village* (Cambridge, 1965), p. 118.

18. *The Book of Margery Kempe*, ed. Stanford B. Meech and Hope Emily Allen, EETS, o.s. 21 (London, 1940), pp. 6, 11–15, 21, 23–24.

19. Thomas C. Rumble, *The Breton Lays in Middle English* (Detroit, 1965), pp. 113, 118. Francis James Child, *The English and Scottish Popular Ballads*, I (Boston, 1883), no. 6A. Charles Wimberly, *Folklore in English and Scottish Ballads* (Chicago, 1928), pp. 205, 211. *Book of Margery Kempe*, pp. 221–227.

20. Helmholz, *Marriage Litigation*, pp. 102–105.

21. *Court Roll of Chalgrave Manor*, ed. Marian K. Dale, Bedfordshire Historical Record Society 28 (1950), p. 44.

22. *Wakefield*, I, p. 84. Just. 2/112 m. 22. *Robert [Mannyng] of Brunne's Handlyng Synne*, p. 69.

23. Margot R. Adamson, ed., *A Treasury of Middle English Verse Selected and Rendered into Modern English* (London 1950), p. 53. Other examples in Frances Comper, ed., *Spiritual Songs from English MSS. of the Fourteenth to Sixteenth Centuries* (Cambridge, 1936), pp. 4, 5, 12, 17.

24. Adamson, *Treasury*, p. 40. See also Comper, *Spiritual Songs*, pp. 18, 39. In the latter the poet puts into the mouth of Jesus the verse "Shall I, Moder, maiden and wife, My dear spouse, shall I so?"

25. Thomas Wright, ed., *Songs and Carols* (London, 1836), song XVI.

26. Rumble, *Breton Lays*, p. 85.

27. Beryl Rowland, *Medieval Woman's Guide to Health: The First English Gynecological Handbook* (Kent, Ohio, 1981), pp. 22–23.

28. Child, *Ballads*, I, no. 15. In France the *couvade*, or "man-childbirth," was practiced. Men had to imitate the labor pains of women: Madeleine Jeay, "Sexuality and Family in Fifteenth-Century France: Are Literary Sources a Mask or a Mirror?" *Journal of Family History* 4 (1979), p. 342.

29. Jeay, "Sexuality and Family," p. 41. Child, *Ballads*, I, no. 20, and II, no. 64. Wimberly, *Folklore in English and Scottish Ballads*, p. 124. He identifies it with an old Swedish custom and mentions the birth tree. The custom is more widespread and has been identified with birth being an act of "falling." See Nicole Belmont, "Levana: or How to Raise up Children," in *Family and Society*, ed. Robert Forster and Orest Ranum, trans. Elborg Forster and Patricia M. Ranum (Baltimore, 1976), pp. 11–12. For birthing positions, see George Engelmann, *Labor Among Primitive Peoples* (St. Louis, 1883); Harold Speert, *Iconographia Gyniatrica* (Philadelphia, 1973); and Palmer Fundley, *The Story of Childbirth* (New York, 1934).

30. Rowland, *Medieval Woman's Guide to Health*, see Introduction and Chapter Ten in the text. The advice deals in a practical way with difficult birthing positions, sickness in the woman, and sickness in the fetus.

31. Just. 2/105 m. 8. Wimberly, *Folklore in English and Scottish Ballads*, pp. 359, 409.

32. Jeay, "Sexuality and Family," pp. 331–342. Anthony Goodman, "The Piety of John Brunham's Daughter, of Lynn," in *Medieval Women: Dedicated and Presented to Professor Rosalind M. T. Hill*, ed. Derek Baker (Oxford, 1978), pp. 352–353. In general, the medieval French folklore is very different from the English, emphasizing virginity before marriage, marriage at the onset of puberty, and endogamy: E. A. Wrigley and R. S. Schofield, *The Population History of England, 1541–1871: A Reconstruction* (Cambridge, Mass., 1981), p. 254. In Colyton from 1560 to 1629 the average number of children by age of mother was 2.18 for women 20–24, 1.88 for women 25–29, 1.84 for women 30–34, 1.53 for women 35–39, 0.83 for women 40–44, and 0.09 for women 45–49. E. A. Wrigley, "Family Limitation in Pre-Industrial Europe," *Economic History Review*, 2nd ser. 19 (1966), p. 90.

33. Just. 2/18 m. 46, 2/104 m. 10, 2/195 m. 3d., 2/75 m. 1, 2/76 m. 1, 2/69 m. 7, 2/70 m. 7. The men of the village also enjoyed a good fight. Sometimes these appear as accidental deaths because a knife slipped out of a sheath or a punch was fatal: Just. 2/67, ms. 40, 45. But the number of fights that were fully described in the self-defense homicides indicate that the villagers stood around and watched the fight, and reported it in full to the coroner when one party died. Raphael Samuel, "'Quarry Roughs': Life and Labour in Headington Quarry, 1860–1920," in *Village Life and Labour*, ed. Raphael Samuel (London, 1975), pp. 148–151, found that people spoke with nostalgia about the fights of the "good old days."

34. Frances Baldwin, *Sumptuary Legislation and Personal Regulation in England* (Baltimore, 1926), pp. 83, 87. These provisions were directed specifically against laborers.

35. *Court Rolls of the Manor of Carshalton from the Reign of Edward III to that of Henry VII*, trans. D. L. Powell, Surrey Record Society 2 (1916), pp. 59–61. Thomas Wright, *A History of Domestic Manners and Sentiments in England During the Middle Ages* (London, 1862), pp. 226–255. Edward Britton, *The Community of the Vill: A Study in the History of the Family and Village Life in Fourteenth-Century England* (Toronto, 1977), pp. 42–43.

36. Barbara A. Hanawalt, "Keepers of the Lights, Late Medieval English Parish Gilds," *Journal of Medieval and Renaissance Studies* 14 (1984), pp. 21–37. Lawrence Stone, *The Family, Sex, and Marriage in England, 1500–1800* (New York, 1977), p. 102. Edward Shorter, *Making of the Modern Family* (New York, 1975), pp. 56–60.

37. Just. 2/66 m. 6d., 2/102 m. 10d., 2/200 m. 7.

38. Rumble, *Breton Lays*, pp. 176–177.

Chapter 14. Widowhood

1. Richard L. Greene, *The Early English Carols*, 2nd ed. (Oxford, 1977), no. 347.

2. *Court Rolls of the Manor of Wakefield*, ed. Sue Sheridan Walker, The Yorkshire Archaeological Society Record Series, 2nd ed. 2 (forthcoming), p. 26. *Chertsey Abbey Court Rolls, Abstract*, trans. Elsie Toms, Surrey Record Society 21 (1937), pp. xvii, 21.

3. *Bedfordshire Wills, 1408–1519*, trans. Patricia Bell, Bedfordshire Historical Record Society 45 (1966), nos. 164, 157. *English Wills, 1498–1526*, ed. A. F. Cirket, Bedfordshire Historical Record Society 37 (1956), pp. 10–11, 20, 27, 32, 49, 50, 51.

4. Zvi Razi, *Life, Marriage and Death in the Medieval Parish: Economy, Society and Demography in Halesowen, 1270–1400* (Cambridge, 1980), p. 40.

5. *English Wills*, pp. 20, 23, 41, 44, 48, 73.

6. *Court Roll of Chalgrave Manor*, ed. Marian K. Dale, Bedfordshire Historical Record Society 28 (1950), pp. 17, 54, 66; see p. 16 for another example. On taking land together, see pp. 63–64 and Walker, *Wakefield*, pp. 5, 40–41, 214, 288.

7. Walker, *Wakefield*, p. 308. *Court Rolls of the Manor of Wakefield*, I, trans. W. P. Baildon, The Yorkshire Archaeological Society Record Series 36 (1906), p. 182. Margaret Spufford, *Contrasting Communities: English Villagers in the Sixteenth and Seventeenth Centuries* (Cambridge, 1974), pp. 162–163. David Roden, "Fragmentation of Farms and Fields, in the Chiltern Hills, Thirteenth Century and Later" *Mediaeval Studies* 31 (1969), p. 229. *Court Rolls of the Manor of Wakefield*, IV, trans. John Lister, The Yorkshire Archaeological Record Society Series 78 (1950), p. 10.

8. R. H. Hilton, *The English Peasantry in the Later Middle Ages* (Oxford, 1975), p. 100. *Wakefield*, IV, pp. 19, 131. *The Court Rolls of the Manor of Wakefield*, V, trans. J. P. Walker, The Yorkshire Archaeological Society Record Series 109 (1945), p. 7. Walker, *Wakefield*, p. 25.

9. Eleanor Searle, "Seigneurial Control of Women's Marriages: The Antecedents and Function of Merchet in England," *Past and Present* 82 (1979), p. 40. Spufford, *Contrasting Communities*, pp. 116–117, 163. J. Z. Titow, "Some Differences between Manors and the Effects on the Condition of the Peasant in the Thirteenth Century," *Agricultural History Review* 10 (1962), pp. 7–13.

10. J. R. Ravensdale, "Deaths and Entries: The Reliability of the Figures of Mortality in the Black Death in Miss F. M. Page's *Estates of Crowland Abbey*, and Some Implications for Land Holding," in *Land, Kinship, and Life-Cycle*, ed. Richard Smith (forthcoming) and Judith Bennett, "Medieval Peasant Marriage: An Examination of Marriage Licence Fines in the *Liber Gersumarum*," in *Pathways to Medieval Peasants*, ed. J. A. Raftis (Toronto, 1981), p. 205, found that on Ramsey Abbey, from 1398 to 1458, only 47 of the 426 merchet payments recorded were from widows. Razi, *Halesowen*, pp. 63, 138, found 63 percent of widows remarrying shortly after the husband's death in the preplague period. Following the Black Death only 10 percent remarried.

11. Robert S. Gottfried, *Epidemic Disease in Fifteenth-Century England: The Medical Response and the Demographic Consequences* (New Brunswick, N.J., 1978), p. 180, found that 10 percent of the testators mentioned a second spouse. But wills could well have considerable underreporting. P. E. H. Hair, "Bridal Preganancy in Earlier Rural England, Further Examined," *Population Studies* 24 (1970), p. 64. R. S. Schofield and E. A. Wrigley, "Remarriage Intervals and the Effect of Marriage Order on Fertility," in *Marriage and Remarriage in Populations of the Past*, J. Dupâquier, E. Helin, P. Laslett, M. Livi-Bacci, S. Sogner, eds. (London, 1981), pp. 212, 214. In the eighteenth century 48 percent of the men remarried within one year and 37 percent of the women remarried. For men the interval was 12.6 months and for women, 19.4 months. Michael M. Sheehan, "The Influence of Canon Law on the Property Rights of Married Women in England," *Mediaeval Studies* 25 (1963), p. 121.

12. *Bedfordshire Wills*, no. 183, and *English Wills*, pp. 13–14.

13. *Bedfordshire Wills*, no. 62, and p. 55.

14. *Chalgrave*, p. 29. *Wakefield*, I, p. 232.

15. *Chalgrave*, p. 56. Walker, *Wakefield*, pp. 102, 104, 150, 253, 270, 285. *Wakefield*, I, pp. 140, 219, 223, 232, 243.

16. Just. 2/67 m. 15.

17. Hilton, *English Peasantry*, p. 108. *Bedfordshire Coroners' Rolls*, trans. R. F. Hunnisett, The Bedfordshire Historical Record Society 41 (1961), p. 42. Just. 2/104 m. 10d.

Chapter 15. Old Age and Death

1. One version is in *Robert [Mannyng] of Brunne's Handlyng Synne*, quoted in George

Homans, *English Villagers of the Thirteenth Century* (Cambridge, Mass., 1941), pp. 154–156. Homans took this as an indication that the son dwelling with the father was the norm.

2. Jack Goody, "Aging in Non Industrial Societies," in *Handbook of Aging and the Social Sciences* (New York, 1976), Robert H. Binstock and Ethel Shanas, eds., pp. 117–129. More detailed discussion may be found in Jack Goody, *Death, Property, and the Ancestors: A Study of the Mortuary Customs of the Lodagaa of West Africa* (Stanford, 1961), pp. 273–283. John C. Caldwell, *Theory of Fertility Decline* (New York, 1982), has proposed a theory that wealth (or benefits) always flow from the young to the old and as a consequence, in a family-based economy, the old benefit from having large families to take care of them. But, as he himself recognizes (pp. 217–222), the development of the West differed from that of current Third World economies. Furthermore, his model, being a demographic one, focuses on adults in their prime rather than the aged.

3. *Robert [Mannyng] of Brunne's Handlyng Synne*, ed. F. J. Furnivall, EETS, o.s. 19 (London, 1901), pp. 43, 202–206.

4. B. H. Putnam, *The Enforcement of the Statutes of Labourers during the First Decade after the Black Death* (New York, 1908), pp. 249–250. Gransden, "Childhood and Youth," pp. 12–14. She discusses the tensions between youth and old age that appear in chronicles. Creighton Gilbert, "When Did a Man in the Renaissance Grow Old?" *Studies in the Renaissance* 14 (1967), pp. 7–32, found that men described themselves as old at fifty or before.

5. E. A. Wrigley and R. S. Schofield, *The Population History of England, 1541–1871: A Reconstruction* (Cambridge, Mass., 1981), pp. 250–252, found that at age 30 for 1550–1599 expectation of life was 29.2 for males and 30.2 for females. The expectation of life at birth for the same period was 42.5. Their back projection for earlier in the century was 36.8. Don Brothwell, "Palaeodemography and Earlier British Populations," *World Archaeology* 4 (1972), p. 84. Robert Gottfried, *Epidemic Disease in Fifteenth-Century England: The Medical Response and the Demographic Consequences* (New Brunswick, N.J., 1978), p. 160, found that 22 percent of the testators could be estimated to be over 50, but this is too high for the overall population since only those with wealth to bestow left wills.

6. Peter Laslett, *Family Life and Illicit Love in Earlier Generations* (Cambridge, 1977), pp. 181–189.

7. David Herlihy and Christiane Klapisch-Zuber, *Les Toscans et leurs familles: Une étude du catasto Florentine de 1427* (Paris, 1978), pp. 374–378.

8. Barbara A. Hanawalt, *Crime and Conflict in English Communities, 1300–1348* (Cambridge, Mass., 1979), pp. 159–161.

9. Margaret Spufford, *Contrasting Communities: English Villagers in the Sixteenth and Seventeenth Centuries* (Cambridge, 1974), p. 112.

10. Elaine Clark, "Some Aspects of Social Security in Medieval England," *Journal of Family History* 7 (1982), pp. 307–320.

11. *Chertsey Abbey Court Rolls, Abstract*, ed. Elsie Toms, Surrey Record Society 21 (1937), p. xxix. See also *Court Roll of Chalgrave Manor*, ed. Marian K. Dale, Bedfordshire Historical Record Society 28 (1950), p. 18.

12. Clark, "Some Aspects of Social Security," p. 310.

13. Eleanor Searle, "Seigneurial Control of Women's Marriages: The Antecedents and Function of Merchet in England," *Past and Present* 82 (1979), p. 32. In another case the father held on to one-half the land for life, with that portion reverting to the son-in-law and daughter at his death.

14. *Chertsey Abbey*, p. xxix.

15. Clark, "Some Aspects of Social Security," p. 311.

16. Ibid., p. 312.

17. R. K. Field, "Worcestershire Peasant Buildings, Household Goods and Farming Equipment in the Later Middle Ages," *Medieval Archaeology* 9 (1965), pp. 126, 121. *Court Rolls of the Manor of Wakefield*, I, trans. W. P. Baildon, The Yorkshire Archaeological Society Record Series 29 (1901), pp. 86, 203.

18. Clark, "Some Aspects of the Social Security," pp. 313–314.

19. Ibid.

20. Ibid., pp. 314–315. In general in East Anglia a third to a half of the landholdings went outside the family on the head of household's death, so that this pattern was consistent with the norm.

21. Thomas Held, "Rural Retirement Arrangements in Seventeenth- to Nineteenth-Century Austria: A Cross-Community Analysis," *Journal of Family History* 7 (1982), pp. 228–252. Laslett, *Family Life*, pp. 208–213.

22. Clark, "Some Aspects of Social Security," p. 316.

23. Ibid.

24. Cicely Howell, "Peasant Inheritance Customs in the Midlands, 1280–1700," in *Family and Inheritance*, ed. J. Goody, J. Thirsk, and E. P. Thompson (Cambridge, 1976), pp. 137–139.

25. *Wakefield*, I, 235–236. J. A. Raftis, *Tenure and Mobility: Studies in the Social History of the Medieval English Village* (Toronto, 1964), pp. 42–46.

26. Clark, "Some Aspects of Social Security," p. 315.

27. *Bedfordshire Wills, 1480–1519*, trans. Patricia Bell, Bedfordshire Historical Record Society 48 (1966), no. 157. *English Wills, 1498–1516*, ed. A. F. Cirket, Bedfordshire Historical Record Society 37 (1956), pp. 46, 49, 63.

28. *English Wills*, p. 46.

29. *Bedfordshire Wills*, no. 55.

30. *English Wills*, 14.

31. Laslett, *Family Life*, pp. 208–213.

32. *English Wills*, pp. 17–18, 22, 24. K. L. Wood-Legh, *Perpetual Chantries in Britain* (Cambridge, 1965), pp. 212–233. On page 232 she has an interesting breakdown of the age of parish priests in various counties: Of a total of 672 priests 12 percent were under 39; 30 percent, 40–49; 30 percent, 30–59; 21 percent, 60–69; and 7 percent over 70. Chantry priests definitely belonged to a graying profession. Peter Heath, *The English Parish Clergy on the Eve of the Reformation* (London, 1969), pp. 183–186, has a discussion of various retirement arrangements for parish priests including keepers.

33. H. F. Westlake, *The Parish Gilds of Medieval England* (London, 1919), has an appendix with all of the extant returns of 1389 summarized. This has been used for information on provisions of parish gilds.

34. Just. 2/82 m. 3.

35. Just. 2/104 m. 7d.

36. *Bedfordshire Coroners' Rolls*, trans. R. F. Hunnisett, Bedfordshire Historical Record Society 41 (1961), p. 4.

37. Just. 2/200 m. 2. *Bedfordshire Coroners' Rolls*, p. 73.

38. Just. 2/17 m. 1d., 2/104 m. 32, 2/104 m. 10 an old woman (over sixty) was staying at the home of someone else and was crushed under a great cheese that fell on her; in 2/92 m. 4 a man (over sixty) was riding on a horse with two panniers on the side by the river when the horse tripped and he fell in.

39. Just. 2/18 m. 42.

40. *The Book of Margery Kempe*, ed. Sanford B. Meech and Hope Emily Allen, EETS o.s. (London, 1940), pp. 179–181.

41. Lowery Charles Wimberly, *Death and Burial Lore in the English and Scottish Popular Ballads*, University of Nebraska Studies in Language, Literature, and Criticism 8 (Lincon, 1927), pp. 215, 219, 224, 294, 307, 308.

42. Mary G. Segar, ed., *A Mediaeval Anthology Being Lyrics and Other Short Poems Chiefly Religious* (London, 1915), p. 132.

43. Thomas Wright and James O. Halliwell, eds., *Reliquiae Antiquae*, II, (London, 1841), pp. 210–212.

44. Ibid., I, p. 58.

45. *Bedfordshire Wills*, p. 50.

46. Ibid. For the Tichemarch network, see pp. 59–60, 68–69, 75. *English Wills*, p. 66.

47. Ibid., p. 28.

48. Ibid., p. 29.

49. J. A. Raftis, "Changes in an English Village after the Black Death," *Mediaeval Studies* 29 (1967), p. 167. *Bedfordshire Coroners' Rolls*, pp. 73, 49.

50. A. E. Levett, *Studies in Manorial History*, ed. H. M. Cam, M. Coate, and L. S. Sutherland (Oxford, 1938), pp. 221–222. *Calendar of Coroners' Rolls of the City of London*, ed. Reginald R. Sharpe (London, 1913), p. 5.

51. Richard Leighton Greene, *The Early English Carols*, 2nd ed. (Oxford, 1977), no. 374.

52. Wrigley and Schofield, *Population History of England*, p. 249.

53. R. T. Davies, ed., *Medieval English Lyrics, A Critical Anthology* (Evanston, Ill., 1964), pp. 73–74.

54. J. G. Hurst, "A Review of Archaeological Research to 1968," in *Deserted Medieval Villages*, ed. Maurice Beresford and J. G. Hurst (London, 1971), p. 135.

55. *Bedfordshire Coroners' Rolls*, p. 3.

56. Thomas Wright, *St. Patrick's Purgatory: An Essay on the Legends of Purgatory, Hell, and Paradise Current During the Middle Ages* (London, 1844), p. 31. Greene *English Carols*, pp. 216–232, for songs on preoccupation with death.

57. *Bedfordshire Wills*, p. 18.

Chapter 16. Surrogate Parents and Children

1. Peter Laslett, *Family Life and Illicit Love in Earlier Generations* (Cambridge, 1972), p. 162.

2. Louis Haas, "Baptism and Spiritual Kinship in the North of England, 1250–1450," M. A. Thesis, Ohio State University (1982), pp. 20–25.

3. *Robert [Mannyng] of Brunne's Handlyng Synne*, ed. F. J. Furnivall, EETS, o.s. 119 (1901), pp. 303–305.

4. Haas, "Baptism and Spiritual Kinship," pp. 78–79, 83–84, 86. Jack Goody, *The Development of Family and Marriage in Europe* (Cambridge, 1983), pp. 73–75, says that godparents were supposed to take in orphans.

5. *Bedfordshire Wills, 1480–1519*, trans. Patricia Bell, Bedfordshire Historical Record Society 45 (1966), p. 60.

6. Michael Bennett, "Spiritual Kinship and Baptismal Names in Traditional European Society," in *Principalities, Power, and Estates*, ed. L. O. Frappe (Adelaide, 1979), pp. 4–8.

7. *A Volume of English Miscellanies*, Surtees Society 85 (1890), pp. 35–52.

8. Zvi Razi, *Life, Marriage, and Death in the Medieval Parish: Economy, Society, and*

Demography in Halesowen, 1270–1400 (Cambridge, 1980), p. 105.

9. *English Wills, 1498–1526*, ed. A. F. Cirket, Bedfordshire Historical Record Society 37 (1956), p. 73. *Testamenta Eboracensia: A Selection of Wills from the Registry at York*, III, Surtees Society 45 (1865), p. 203.

10. *English Wills*, p. 20, 26. *Bedfordshire Wills*, pp. 89–90.

11. *English Wills*, pp. 27–28, 36, 29–30, 42.

12. *English Wills*, p. 82.

13. Just. 2/18 m. 57d., 2/204 m. 1d. *Bedfordshire Coroners' Rolls*, trans. R. F. Hunnisett, Bedfordshire Historical Record Society 41 (1961), p. 105.

14. In folklore evil stepmothers (mothers rather than fathers are prevalent) play a variety of nasty tricks on their stepchildren. One turns her stepson and stepdaughter into a "Laily worm and a mackrel of the sea"; others turn them into animals or very ugly women. Francis J. Child, *The English and Scottish Popular Ballads*, I, (Boston, 1883), nos. 31. 36. Charles Wimberley, *Folklore in English and Scottish Popular Ballads* (Chicago, 1928), pp. 51, 57, 62, 96, 207–213. In a poignant Danish ballad the mother's ghost returns and finds her children all crying and the baby not nursed. She feeds them and combs their hair and then threatens her former husband with another visitation if he does not look after their children. Ibid., pp. 266–267. Ronald C. Finucane, *Miracles and Pilgrims: Popular Beliefs in Medieval England* (Totowa, N.J., 1977), p. 110. *Court Rolls of the Manor of Wakefield*, V, trans. J. P. Walker, The Yorkshire Archaeological Society Record Series 109 (1945), p. 5, for example of stepdaughter suing stepfather.

15. W. G. Hoskins, "Murder and Sudden Death in Medieval Wigston," *Transactions of the Leicestershire Archaeological Society* 21 (1940–41), pp. 179–183.

16. *Bedfordshire Coroners' Rolls*, p. 73.

17. *Calendar of Nottinghamshire Coroners' Inquests, 1485–1558*, ed. R. F. Hunnisett, Thoroton Society Record Series 25 (1969), p. 93.

18. *English Wills*, p. 15, 32, 34.

19. A. E. Levett, *Studies in Manorial History*, ed. H. M. Cam, M. Coate, L. S. Sutherland (Oxford, 1958), pp. 242–243. *Chertsey Abbey Court Rolls, Abstract*, trans. Elsie Toms, Surrey Record Society 21 (1937), pp. xv, xx, xxviii. The widow was the most common guardian, but if the child were an orphan the court made guardian arrangements. The child and guardian came to the court and the guardian paid an entrance fine. Free peasants owed wardship to the lord: *Court Roll of Chalgrave Manor, 1278–1313*, ed. Marian K. Dale, Bedfordshire Historical Record Society 28 (1950), p. 63.

20. *Court Roll of the Manor of Wakefield*, IV, trans. John Lister, The Yorkshire Archaeological Society Record Series 78 (1930), pp. 126, 127, 130.

21. Just. 2/18 ms. 45, 5; 2/104 m. 27.

22. Thomas C. Rumble, *The Breton Lays in Middle English* (Detroit, 1965), pp. 49–50, 86–88, 128.

23. Mary Martin McLaughlin, "Survivors and Surrogates: Children and Parents from the Ninth to the Thirteenth Centuries," in *The History of Childhood*, ed. Lloyd deManse (New York, 1974), p. 122. Francis Gasquet, *English Monastic Life* (London, 1904), pp. 176–178.

24. Rotha M. Clay, *The Medieval Hospitals of England* (London, 1909), pp. 22–28.

25. Just. 2/18 m. 60, 2/104 m. 30.

26. *Bedfordshire Coroners' Rolls*, pp. 39–40.

27. Jack Goody, "Adoption in Cross-Cultural Perspective," *Comparative Studies in Society and History* 11 (1969), p. 57. McLaughlin, "Survivors and Surrogates," p. 122, found that in Europe in general, adoption was rare in the Middle Ages.

28. Eleanor Searle, "Seigneurial Control of Women's Marriages: The Anticedents and Function of Merchet in England," *Past and Present* 82 (1979), pp. 36–37.

29. Clay, *Medieval Hospitals*, p. 12. This is still an excellent description of medieval hospitals.

30. Jay Rowe, "The Medieval Hospitals of Bury St. Edmunds," *Medical History* 2 (1958), pp. 253–263.

31. Clay, *Medieval Hospitals*, pp. 212–225.

32. Peter Heath, *The English Parish Clergy on the Eve of the Reformation* (London, 1969), p. 141. Olwen Hufton, *The Poor of Eighteenth-Century France, 1750–1789* (Oxford, 1974), p. 151, shows village charity in practice. The priest broke up loaves of bread for poor women and children at mass. They then went and begged for milk among the peasants.

33. Just. 2/67 m. 50. *Bedfordshire Coroners' Rolls*, p. 47.

34. *English Wills*, p. 40.

35. *Bedfordshire Coroners' Rolls*, pp. 66–67, 74, 82, 83, 87, 89, 99, 239.

36. Ibid., pp. 64, 113–114.

37. *English Wills*, p. 16; see also pp. 19, 24, 30.

38. Just. 2/67 m. 40.

39. Geoffrey Chaucer, *The Canterbury Tales*, trans. Neville Coghill (Harmondsworth, 1951), p. 23.

40. Thomas Wright, *A History of Domestic Manners and Sentiments in England during the Middle Ages* (London, 1862); pp. 238–244. *Robert [Mannyng] of Brunne's Handlyng Synne*, p. 168, commended dogs for their faithfulness and attachment to their masters.

41. *Chalgrave*, p. 32.

42. R. H. Hilton and P A. Rahtz, "Upton, Gloucestershire, 1959–1964," *Transactions of the Bristol and Gloucestershire Archaeological Society* 85 (1966), pp. 140–142.

Chapter 17. Neighbors and Brotherhoods

1. Lawrence Stone, *The Family, Sex, and Marriage in England, 1500–1800* (New York, 1977), p. 93.

2. Richard M. Smith, "Kin and Neighbors in a Thirteenth Century Suffolk Community," *Journal of Family History* 4 (1979), pp. 224–225. Barbara A. Hanawalt, "The Peasant Family and Crime in Fourteenth-Century England," *Journal of British Studies* 8 (1974), pp. 1–18.

3. Edward Britton, *The Community of the Vill: A Study in the History of the Family and Village Life in Fourteenth-Century England* (Toronto, 1977).

4. *Court Rolls of the Manor of Carshalton*, trans. D. L. Powell, Surrey Record Society 2 (1916), pp. 38. 61.

5. Michael Bennett, "Spiritual Kinship and Baptismal Name in Traditional European Society," in *Principalities, Powers and Estates: Studies in Medieval and Early Modern Government and Society*, ed. L. O. Frappell (Adelaide, 1979), pp. 3–4. John Bossy, "Blood and Baptism: Kinship, Community and Christianity in Western Europe from the Fourteenth to the Seventeenth Centuries," in *Sanctity and Secularity: The Church and the World*, ed. Derek Baker (Oxford, 1973), pp. 129–144, has argued that feuds could be ended by the parents of a child asking an enemy to become coparents. While this is certainly possible, he has failed to produce evidence that it occurred in England. Mediterranean community activities cannot be transferred north just as their family organization, living arrangements, and marriage customs cannot be.

6. *Chertsey Abbey Court Rolls, Abstract,* trans. Elsie Toms, Surrey Record Society 21 (1937), p. xxix.

7. The difficulties of assessing the importance of pledging and other types of village aid relationships is that the studies are not strictly comparable since they used different means to form the categories of status in the village and were exploring somewhat different questions. The conclusions that can be drawn from the comparisons are of the most general order. Smith, "Kin and Neighbors," pp. 229–249, has done the most systematic work on village networks. Britton, *Community of the Vill,* pp. 103–108, has suggested the idea of dominance by village elite, and Martin Pimsler, "Solidarity in the Medieval Village? The Evidence of Personal Pledging at Elton, Huntingdonshire," *Journal of British Studies* 17 (1977), p. 11, seems to be in agreement. Edwin DeWindt, *Land and People in Holywell-cum-Needingworth* (Toronto, 1972), pp. 243–250, places somewhat more emphasis on village cooperation.

8. Ibid., pp. 265–274. Britton, *Community of the Vill,* pp. 105–114.

9. Just. 2/17 m. 1d., 2/17 m. 4d, 2/18 m. 1d.

10. In Just. 2/75 m. 1 a man was sitting at a bull baiting when the animal broke its ropes and ran over him; another case in Just. 2/76 m. 1. In Just. 2/18 m. 46 John Waryn was watching an archery contest on the church green on a Sunday in 1356 when he was hit by a stray arrow. Archery was the sport that Edward III encouraged in order to provide trained archers for his wars. Football was a favorite sport, but could be dangerous: Just. 2/69 m. 7, 2/70 m. 7. The official attitude toward ball games was that they should be banned. *Carshalton,* pp. 59, 62, 61, 65, fined peasants for playing handball. Statutes forbade ball games along with dice, stone throwing, and so on. Frances F. Baldwin, *Sumptuary Legislation and Personal Regulation in England* (Baltimore, 1926), pp. 83, 87. Just. 2/67 ms. 40, 45; 2/104; 2/195 m. 3d.

11. Lawrence Blair, *English Church Ales* (Ann Arbor, Mich., 1940).

12. *English Wills, 1498–1526,* ed. A. F. Cirket, Bedfordshire Historical Record Society 37 (1956), pp. 31. 41.

13. *Church-Wardens' Accounts of Coscombe, Pilton, Latton, Tintinhull, Morebath, and St. Michael's Bath,* ed. Edmund Hobhouse, Somerset Record Society, IV (1890), p. 1.

14. *Bedfordshire Wills, 1480–1519,* trans. Patricia Bell, Bedfordshire Historical Record Society 45 (1966), pp. 43–44, 59–60, 68–69, 92–93. For the Basse-Gere-Hafurne network, see pp. 67–68, 70, 80, 91–92.

15. F. W. Warren, "A Pre-Reformation Gild," *Proceedings of the Suffolk Institute of Archaeology* 11 (1903), p. 135.

16. Jacques Chiffoleau, *La compatabilité de L'Au-delà: les hommes, la mort et la religion dans la région d'Avignon à la fin du moyen âge (vers 1320–1480)* (Rome, 1980), pp. 167–285. For gild charters, see Toulmin Smith and Lucy Toulmin Smith, eds., *English Gilds: The Original Ordinances of More Than 100 English Gilds,* EETS, o.s. 40 (London, 1870), and the appendix to H. F. Westlake, *The Parish Gilds of Medieval England* (London, 1919). The Lincoln funeral provision: Westlake, pp. 167–168.

17. Westlake, *Parish Gilds,* p. 166.

18. Warren, "Pre-Reformation Gild," p. 185. *Churchwarden's Accounts of Croscombe,* pp. xxi–xxii. Dorothy Owen, *Church and Society in Medieval Lincolnshire* (Lincoln, 1971), p. 131.

19. Walter Rye, "The Guilds of Lynn Regis," *The Norfolk Antiquarian Miscellany* 1 (1877), pp. 158–159.

20. Smith and Smith, *English Gilds,* pp. xxxix–xxxx. Westlake, *Parish Gilds,* p. 35.

21. Ibid., p. 171.

22. *Cambridge Gild Records*, ed. Mary Batson, Cambridge Antiquarian Society Publications 39 (1903), p. xvi.

23. Westlake, *Parish Gilds*, pp. 61–62. Land and houses were also rented by gilds. Smith and Smith, *English Gilds*, p. xxxv.

24. Westlake, *Parish Gilds*, pp. 40–41. Cornelius Walford, *Gilds: Their Origin, Constitution, Objects, and Later History* (London, 1897), pp. 7, 20.

25. Westlake, *Parish Gilds*, p. 9 and appendix. Smith and Smith, *English Gilds*, p. xxxvi. Sometimes the limitation was three years' aid.

26. *Records of the Gild of St. George in Norwich, 1389–1547*, ed. Mary Grace, Norfolk Record Society 9 (1937), p. 24.

27. J. A. Raftis, "Changes in an English Village after the Black Death," *Mediaeval Studies* 29 (1967), pp. 158–177.

28. Zvi Razi, "Family, Land and the Village Community in Later Medieval England," *Past and Present* 93 (1981), p. 31.

29. DeWindt, *Holywell-cum-Needingworth*, pp. 263–275. Razi, "Family, Land and the Village Community," pp. 29–36, in his zeal to show that his evidence refutes Raftis and DeWindt, has tried to argue that the increased disparity of wealth and power in the villages did not destroy the community of Halesowen. He argues that the wealthy tended to employ their poorer neighbors. His argument ignores the obvious implications of this power relationship for discord in the community rather than as a continuation of the old balance in community relations. He also argues that the higher-status villagers were less involved in violence, but, as he fails to present any figures, one cannot accept this assertion.

30. Robert B. Goheen, "Social Ideas and Social Structure: Rural Gloucestershire, 1450–1500," *Histoire Sociale-Social History* 1 (1979), pp. 262–280, has developed an interesting argument about the transformation from community justice to royal justice in the fifteenth century. See also R. H. Hilton, *The English Peasantry in the Later Middle Ages* (Oxford, 1975) on the decline of serfdom and the manor court.

Appendix. Coroners' Rolls

1. R. F. Hunnisett, *The Medieval Coroner* (Cambridge, 1961), has a complete discussion of the coroners' duties and the rolls.

2. For Bedfordshire I used the published records: *Bedfordshire Coroners's Inquests*, trans. R. F. Hunnisett, Bedfordshire Historical Record Society 41 (1961).

Bibliography

Manuscripts

Great Britain. Coroners rolls (Just. 2).

Printed Documents

Bedfordshire Coroners' Rolls, trans. R. F. Hunnisett. Bedfordshire Historical Record Society 41 (1961).
Bedfordshire Wills, 1480–1519, trans. Patricia Bell. Bedfordshire Historical Record Society 45 (1966).
Bedfordshire Wills Proved in the Prerogative Court of Canterbury, 1383–1548, ed. Margaret McGregor. Bedfordshire Historical Record Society 58 (1979).
Before the Bawdy Court: Selections from Church Court and Other Records Relative to the Correction of Moral Offenses in England, Scotland, and New England, 1300–1800, comp. Paul Hair. New York, 1972.
Bishop Hatfield's Survey: A Record of the Possession of the See of Durham, ed. William Greenwell. Surtees Society 32 (1857).
Calendar of Coroners' Rolls of the City of London, ed. Reginald R. Sharpe, London, 1913.
Calendar of Nottinghamshire Coroners' Inquests, 1485–1558, ed. R. F. Hunnisett, Thoroton Society Record Series 25 (1969).
Cambridge Gild Records, 1298–1389, ed. Mary Bateson. Cambridge Antiquarian Society Publications, Octavo Ser. 39 (1903).
Carte Nativorum: A Peterborough Cartularly of the Fourteenth Century, ed. M. M. Postan and C. N. L. Brooke. Northamptonshire Record Society 20 (1960).
Chertsey Abbey Court Rolls, Abstract, trans. Elsie Toms. Surrey Record Society 21, Part I (1937), Part II (1954).
Church-Wardens' Accounts of Croscombe, Pilton, Latton, Tintinhull, Morebath, and St. Michael's Bath, ed. Edmund Hobhouse. Somerset Record Society 4 (1890).

The Court Baron, ed. Frederic W. Maitland and William P. Baildon. The Seldon Society 4. London, 1891.

Court Roll of Chalgrave Manor, 1278–1313, ed. Marian K. Dale. Bedfordshire Historical Record Society 28 (for 1948, published 1950).

Court Rolls of the Manor of Carshalton from the Reign of Edward III to That of Henry VII, trans. D. L. Powell. Surrey Record Society 2 (1916).

Court Rolls of the Manor of Ingoldmells in the County of Lincoln, ed. and trans. W. O. Massingberd. London, 1902.

Court Rolls of the Manor of Wakefield, 1274–1297, I, ed. and trans. W. P. Baildon. The Yorkshire Archaeological Society Record Series 29 (1901).

Court Rolls of the Manor of Wakefield, 1297–1309, II, ed. and trans. W. P. Baildon. The Yorkshire Archaeological Society Record Series 36 (1906).

Court Rolls of the Manor of Wakefield, 1313–1316, 1286, III, ed. and trans. John Lister. The Yorkshire Archaeological Society Record Series 57 (1917).

Court Rolls of the Manor of Wakefield, 1315–1317, IV, ed. and trans. John Lister. The Yorkshire Archaeological Society Record Series 78 (1930).

Court Rolls of the Manor of Wakefield, 1322–1331, V, ed. and trans, J. P. Walker. The Yorkshire Archaeological Society Record Series 109 (1945).

The Court Rolls of the Manor of Wakefield from October 1331 to September 1333, trans. Sue Sheridan Walker. The Yorkshire Archaeological Society Record Series, 2nd ser., 2 (forthcoming).

Documents Relating to the Manor and Soke of Newark-on-Trent, ed. M. W. Barley. Thoroton Society Record Series 16 (1956).

English Gilds: The Original Ordinances of More than 100 English Gilds, ed. Toulmin Smith and Lucy Toulmin Smith. Early English Text Society, o.s. 40 (1870).

English Wills, 1498–1526, ed. A. F. Cirket. Bedfordshire Historical Record Society 37 (1956).

"An Extent of Upton, 1431," pp. 26–38, ed. and trans. Violet W. Walker. In *A Second Miscellany of Nottinghamshire Records*. Thoroton Society Record Series 14 (1951).

Lathe Court Rolls and Views of Frankpledge in the Rape of Hastings, A.D. 1387 to 1474, ed. Elinor J. Courthope and Beryle E. R. Formoy. Sussex Record Society 37 (1931).

Records of the Gild of St. George in Norwich, 1389–1547, ed. Mary Grace. Norfolk Records Society 9 (1937).

The Records of the Guild of Holy Trinity, St. Mary, St. John the Baptist, and St. Katerine of Coventry, ed. Geoffrey Templeman. Dugdale Society 19. Oxford, 1944.

Records of Medieval Oxford, Coroners' Inquests, the Walls of Oxford, etc., ed. H. E. Salter. London, 1912.

Select Cases from the Coroners' Rolls, A.D. 1265–1413, ed. Charles Gross. Selden Society 9. London, 1896.

Select Pleas of the Forest, ed. G. J. Turner. Selden Society 13. London (1901).

A Small Household of the XVth Century: An Account Book of Munden's Chantry, Bridport, ed. K. L. Wood-Legh. Manchester, 1956.

Testamenta Eboracensia: A Selection of Wills from the Registry at York, III. Surtees Society 45 (1865).

"Three Records of the Alien Priory of Grove and the Manor of Leighton Buzzard," pp. 15–46, ed. Robert Richmond. In *Publications of the Bedfordshire Historical Record Society* 8 (1924).

A Volume of English Miscellanies. Surtees Society 85 (1890).

Wheatley Records, 956–1956, ed. W. O. Hassall. Oxfordshire Record Society 27 (1956).

Chronicles and Literary Sources

Adamson, Margot R., ed. *A Treasury of Middle English Verse Selected and Rendered into Modern English*. London, 1930.

Capellanus, Andreas. *The Art of Courtly Love*, trans. John Jay Parry. New York, 1972.

Chaucer, Geoffrey. *The Canterbury Tales*, trans. Neville Coghill. Harmondsworth, 1951.

Child, Francis James. *The English and Scottish Popular Ballads*, 5 vols. Boston, 1883–1894.

Comper, Frances M. M. *Spiritual Songs from English MSS. of the Fourteenth to Sixteenth Centuries*. Cambridge, 1936.

Davies, R. T. *Medieval English Lyrics, A Critical Anthology*. Evanston, Ill. 1964.

Furnivall, Frederick James. *Hymns to the Virgin and Christ, the Parliament of Devils, and Other Religious Poems*. Early English Text Society, o.s. 24. London, 1868.

——. *Manners and Meals in Olden Time*. Early English Text Society, o.s. 32. London, 1868.

Greene, Richard Leighton. *The Early English Carols*, 2nd ed. Oxford, 1977.

Harrison's Description of England in Shakespere's Youth, Being the Second and Third Books, Frederick J. Furnivall. New Shakespere Society, ser. 6, no 1 (1877), no. 8 (1881).

The Italian Relation of England: A Relation of the Island of England, ed. C. A. Sneyd. Camden Society 37 (1847).

Kempe, Margery. *The Book of Margery Kempe*, ed. Sanford B. Meech and Hope Emily Allen. Early English Text Society, o.s. 212. London, 1940.

Knox, Ronald and Leslie, Shane, eds. *The Miracles of King Henry VI*. Cambridge, 1923.

Langland, William. *Piers Plowman*, ed. W. W. Skeat. Oxford, 1886.

Myrc, John. *Instructions for Parish Priests*, ed. Edward Peacock. Early English Text Society, o.s. 209. London, 1940.

Pierce the Plowman's Crede, ed. W. W. Skeat. Early English Text Society, o.s. 30. London, 1906.

Robbins, Rossell Hope. *Secular Lyrics of the Fourteenth and Fifteenth Centuries*. Oxford, 1952.

Robert [Mannyng] of Brunne's Handlyng Synne, ed. Frederick J. Furnivall. Early English Text Society, o.s. 119. London, 1901.

Rumble, Thomas C., ed. *The Breton Lays in Middle English*. Detroit, 1965.

Segar, Mary G., ed. *A Mediaeval Anthology, Being Lyrics and Other Short Poems Chiefly Religious*. London, 1915.

Stevick, Robert D. ed. *One Hundred Middle English Lyrics*. Indianapolis, 1964.

Trokelowe, Johannes de. *Annales (Chronica Monasterii S. Albani)*, ed. H. T. Riley. Rolls Series 28. London, 1863.

Wright, Thomas, ed. *Songs and Carols*. London, 1836, and Halliwell, James Orchard, eds. *Reliquiae Antiquae: Scraps and Ancient Manuscripts Illustrating Chiefly Early English Literature and the English Language*, 2 vols. London, 1841.

Books and Articles

Alcock, N. W. "The Medieval Cottages of Bishops Clyst, Devon." *Medieval Archaeology* 9 (1965): 146–153.

Amundsen, Darrel, and Dreis, Carol Jean. "The Age of Menarche in Medieval England." *Human Biology* 45 (1973); 363–368.

Arensberg, Conrad. *The Irish Countryman*. Garden City, N.Y., 1968.

Ariès, Philippe. *Centuries of Childhood: A Social History of the Family*. trans. Robert Baldick. London, 1962.

Ault, Warren O. "By-Laws of Gleaning and the Problems of Harvest." *Economic History Review*, 2nd ser. 14 (1961): 210–217.

——. *Open-Field Farming in Medieval England*. London, 1972.

——. *Open-Field Husbandry and the Village Community: A Study of Agrarian By-Laws in Medieval England*. Transactions of the American Philosophical Society, new ser. 55. Philadelphia, 1965.

Ashley, William. *Bread of Our Forefathers*. Oxford, 1928.

Baker, A. R. H. "Open Fields and Partible Inheritance on a Kent Manor." *Economic History Review*, 2nd ser. 17 (1964): 1–23.

Baldwin, Frances Elizabeth. *Sumptuary Legislation and Personal Regulation in England*. Johns Hopkins University Studies in Historical and Political Science 44. Baltimore, 1926.

Barley, M. W. *The English Farmhouse and Cottage*. London, 1961.

——. "Farmhouses and Cottages, 1550–1725." *Economic History Review*, 2nd ser. 7 (1954–1955): 291–306.

Barnes, J. A. "Genetrix : Genitor :: Nature : Culture?" In *The Character of Kinship*, pp. 61–73, ed. Jack Goody. Cambridge, 1973.

Bean, J. M. W. "Plague, Population and Economic Decline in the Later Middle Ages." *Economic History Review*, 2nd ser. 15 (1963): 423–437.

Becker, Gary. "A Theory of Marriage: Part I." *Journal of Political Economy* 81 (1973): 813–146.

——. "A Theory of Marriage: Part II." *Journal of Political Economy* 82 (1974): S11–S26.

Belmont, Nicole. "Levana: or How to Raise Up Children." In *Family and Society: Selections from the Annales, Economies, Sociétés, Civilisations*, pp. 1–15, ed. Robert Forster and Orest Ranum, trans. Elborg Forster and Patricia M. Ranum. Baltimore, 1976.

Bennett, H. S. *Life on the English Manor*. Cambridge, 1937.

Bennett, Judith. "Medieval Peasant Marriage: An Examination of Marriage Licence Fines in the *Liber Gersumarum*." In *Pathways to Medieval Peasants*, pp. 193–246, ed. J. A. Raftis. Toronto, 1981.

——. "The Tie that Binds: Peasant Marriages and Peasant Families in Late Medieval England." *Journal of Interdisciplinary History* 15 (1984), pp. 111–129.

——. "Village Ale Wives." In *Women and Work in Preindustrial Europe*, ed. Barbara A. Hanawalt. Bloomington, Ind., forthcoming in 1986.

Bennett, Michael. "Spiritual Kinship and the Baptismal Name in Traditional European Society." In *Principalities, Powers and Estates: Studies in Medieval and Early Modern Government and Society*, pp. 1–12, ed. L. O. Frappell. Adelaide, 1979.

Beresford, Guy. *The Medieval Clay-Land Village: Excavations at Goltho and Barton Blount*. The Society for Medieval Archaeology, Monograph Series 6. London, 1975.

——. "Three Deserted Medieval Settlements on Dartmoor: A Report on the Late E. Marie Minter's Excavations." *Medieval Archaeology* 23 (1979): 98–158.

Beresford, Maurice. *The Lost Villages of the Middle Ages*. London, 1954.

Beresford, Maurice, and Hurst, John G., eds. *Deserted Medieval Villages*. London, 1971.

Berkner, Lutz K. "Recent Research on the History of the Family in Western Europe." *Journal of Marriage and the Family* 35 (1973): 395–405.

——. "Rural Family Organization in Europe: A Problem in Comparative History." *Peasant Studies Newsletter* 1 (1972): 145–156.

Berkner, Lutz K., and Mendels, Franklin F. "Inheritance Systems, Family Structure, and Demographic Patterns in Western Europe (1700–1900)." In *Historical Studies of Changing Fertility*, pp. 209–223, ed. Charles Tilly. Princeton, 1978.

Beveridge, William. "Wages in the Winchester Manors." *Economic History Review* 7 (1936): 22–43.

———. "Westminster Wages in the Manorial Era." *Economic History Review* 2nd ser., 8 (1955): 18–35.

Bigmore, Peter. "Villages and Towns." In *The English Medieval Landscape*, pp. 154–192, ed. Leonard Cantor. Philadelphia, 1982.

Biller, P. P. A. "Birth Control in the West in the Thirteenth and Early Fourteenth Centuries." *Past and Present* (1982): 3–26.

Blair, Lawrence A. *English Church Ales*. Ann Arbor, Mich., 1940.

Bloch, Maurice. "The Long Term and the Short Term: The Economic and Political Significance of the Morality of Kinship." In *The Character of Kinship*, pp. 75–87, ed. Jack Goody. Cambridge, 1973.

Blythe, Ronald. *Akenfield: Portrait of an English Village*. New York, 1969.

Bolton, J. L. *The Medieval English Economy, 1150–1500*. London, 1980.

Boserup, Ester. *Women's Role in Economic Development*. London, 1970.

Bossy, John. "Blood and Baptism: Kinship, Community and Christianity in Western Europe from the Fourteenth to the Seventeenth Centuries." In *Sanctity and Society: The Church and the World*, pp. 129–144, ed. Derek Baker. Oxford, 1973.

Brand, Paul A., and Hyams, Paul R. "Debate: Seigneurial Control of Women's Marriage." *Past and Present* 99 (1983): 123–133.

Braudel, Fernand. *Capitalism and Material Life, 1400–1800*, trans. Miriam Kochan. London, 1973.

Brewer, E. Cobham. *A Dictionary of Miracles: Imitative, Realistic, and Dogmatic*. Philadelphia, 1884.

Bridbury, A. R. "Before the Black Death." *Economic History Review* 2nd ser. 30 (1977): 393–410.

———. *Economic Growth: England in the Later Middle Ages*. London, 1962.

———. *England and the Salt Trade in the Late Middle Ages*. Oxford, 1955.

Britnell, R. H. "Agricultural Technology and the Margin of Cultivation in the Fourteenth Century." *Economic History Review* 2nd ser. 30 (1977): 53–66.

———. "Production for the Market on a Small Fourteenth-Century Estate." *Economic History Review* 2nd ser. 19 (1966): 380–387.

Britton, Edward. *The Community of the Vill: A Study in the History of the Family and Village Life in Fourteenth-Century England*. Toronto, 1977.

Brothwell, Don. "Palaeodemography and Earlier British Populations," *World Archaeology* 4 (1972): 75–87.

Bullough, D. A. "Early Medieval Social Groupings: The Terminology of Kinship." *Past and Present* 45 (1969): 3–18.

Caldwell, John C. *Theory of Fertility Decline*. New York, 1982.

Cam, H. M. *Liberties and Communities in Medieval England: Collected Studies in Local Administration and Topography*. Cambridge, 1944.

Charles, F. W. B. *Medieval Cruck Building and Its Derivatives*. London, 1967.

Charles-Edwards, T. M. "Kinship, Status and the Origins of the Hide." *Past and Present* 56 (1972): 3–33.

Chayanov, A. V. *The Theory of Peasant Economy*, ed. D. Thorner, B. Kerblay, and R. E. F. Smith. Homewood, Ill. 1966.

Chibnall, A. C. *Sherington: Fiefs and Fields of a Buckinghamshire Village*. Cambridge, 1965.

Chiffoleau, Jacques. *La compatibilité de l'au-delà: les hommes, la mort et la religion dans la région d'Avignon à la fin du moyen âge (vers 1320–1480)*. Rome, 1980.

Clark, Elaine. "Debt Litigation in a Late Medieval English Vill." In *Pathways to Medieval Peasants*, pp. 247–279, ed. J. Ambrose Raftis. Toronto, 1981.

———. "Some Aspects of Social Security in Medieval England." *Journal of Family History* 7 (1982): 307–320.

Clay, Rotha M. *The Medieval Hospitals of England*. London, 1909.

Colman, F. S. *A History of the Parish of Barwick-in-Elmet, in the County of York*. Thoresby Society, vol. 17. Leeds, 1908.

Colvin, H. M. "Farmhouses and Cottages." In *Medieval England*, vol. 1, pp. 77–97, ed. A. Lane Poole. London, 1958.

Connell, K. H. "Peasant Marriage in Ireland: Its Structure and Development since the Famine." *Economic History Review* 2nd ser. 14 (1962): 502–523.

Davenport, Frances G. "The Decay of Villeinage in East Anglia." In *Essays in Economic History*, vol. 2, pp. 112–124, ed. E. M. Carus-Wilson. London, 1962.

DeWindt, Anne. "A Peasant Land Market and Its Participants: King's Ripton, 1280–1400." *Midland History* 4 (1978): 142–158.

———. "Peasant Power Structures in Fourteenth-Century King's Ripton." *Mediaeval Studies* 38 (1976): 236–267.

DeWindt, Edwin B. *Land and People in Holywell-Cum-Needingworth*. Toronto, 1972.

Dodgshon, Robert A. "The Landholding Foundations of the Open-Field System." *Past and Present* 67 (1975); 3–29.

Dodwell, Barabara. "Holdings and Inheritance in Medieval East Anglia." *Economic History Review* 2nd ser. 20 (1967): 53–66.

Du Boulay, F. R. H. *An Age of Ambition*. London, 1970.

———. *The Lordship of Canterbury: An Essay on Medieval Society*. New York, 1966.

———. "Who Were Farming the English Demesnes at the End of the Middle Ages?" *Economic History Review* 2nd ser. 17 (1965): 443–455.

Duby, Georges. *Medieval Marriage: Two Models from Twelfth-Century France*, trans. Elborg Forster. Baltimore, 1978.

Dyer, Christopher. *Lords and Peasants in a Changing Society: The Estates of the Bishopric of Worcester, 680–1540*. Cambridge, 1980.

———. "A Small Landowner in the Fifteenth Century." *Midland History* 1 (1972): 1–14.

Elder, Glen. *Children of the Great Depression*. Chicago, 1974.

———. "Family History and the Life Course." *Journal of Family History* 2 (1977): 279–304.

Engelmann, George. *Labor Among Primitive Peoples*. St. Louis, 1883.

English, Barbara. *A Study in Feudal Society: The Lords of Holderness, 1086–1260*. Oxford, 1979.

Erikson, Erik. *Childhood and Society*. New York, 1963.

Faith, Rosamond J. "Debate: Seigneurial Control of Women's Marriage." *Past and Present* 99 (1983): 133–148.

———. "Peasant Families and Inheritance Customs in Medieval England." *Agricultural History Review* 14 (1966): 77–95.

Farmer, D. L. "Some Livestock Price Movements in Thirteenth-Century England." *Economic History Review* 2nd ser. 22 (1969): 1–16.

Field, R. K. "Worcestershire Peasant Buildings, Household Goods and Farming Equipment in the Later Middle Ages." *Medieval Archaeology* 9 (1965): 105–145.

Finucane, Ronald C. *Miracles and Pilgrims: Popular Beliefs in Medieval England*. Totowa, N.J., 1977.

Firth, Catherine B. "Village Gilds of Norfolk in the 15th Century." *Norfolk Archaeology* 18 (1914): 161–203.

Flandrin, Jean-Louis. *Families in Former Times: Kinship, Household, and Sexuality*, trans. Richard Southern. Cambridge, 1979.

Flinn, Michael W. *The European Demographic System, 1500–1820*. Baltimore, 1981.

Fundley, Palmer. *The Story of Childbirth*. New York, 1934.

Fussell, G. E. "Countrywomen in Old England." *Agricultural History* 50 (1976): 175–178.

Gilbert, Creighton. "When Did a Man in the Renaissance Grow Old?" *Studies in the Renaissance* 14 (1967): 7–32.

Given, James B. *Society and Homicide in Thirteenth-Century England*. Palo Alto, Calif., 1977.

Goode, William. *World Revolution and Family Patterns*. New York, 1963.

Goodman, Anthony. "The Piety of John Brunham's Daughter, of Lynn." In *Medieval Women: Dedicated and Presented to Professor Rosalind M. T. Hill*, pp. 347–358, ed. Derek Baker. Oxford, 1978.

Goody, Jack. "Adoption in Cross-Cultural Perspective." *Comparative Studies in Society and History* 11 (1969): 55–78.

——. "Aging in Non Industrial Societies." In *Handbook of Aging and the Social Sciences*, pp. 117–129, ed. Robert H. Binstock and Ethel Shanas. New York, 1976.

——. *Death, Property, and the Ancestors: A Study of the Mortuary Customs of the Lodagaa of West Africa*. Stanford, Calif., 1961.

——. *The Development of the Family and Marriage in Europe*, Cambridge, 1983.

——. *Production and Reproduction: A Comparative Study of the Domestic Domain*. Cambridge, 1976.

——. "The 'Family' and the 'Household.'" *Domestic Groups*, An Additon-Wessley Module in Anthropology 28 (1972): 1–32.

——. "Inheritance, Property and Women: Some Comparative Considerations." In *Family and Inheritance: Rural Society in Western Europe*, pp. 10–36, ed. Jack Goody, Joan Thirsk, and E. P. Thompson. Cambridge, 1976.

Goheen, Robert B. "Social Ideas and Social Structure: Rural Gloucestershire, 1450–1500." *Histoire Sociale—Social History* 1 (1979): 262–280.

Gottfried, Robert S. *Epidemic Disease in Fifteenth-Century England: The Medical Response and the Demographic Consequences*. New Brunswick, N.J., 1978.

Gransden, Antonia. "Childhood and Youth in Medieval England." *Nottingham Medieval Studies* 16 (1972): 3–19.

Gray, Howard L. *English Field Systems*. Harvard Historical Studies 22. Cambridge, Mass., 1915.

Greenwood, Davydd J. *Community-level Research, Local-Regional-Governmental Interactions and Development Planning: A Strategy for Baseline Studies*, Rural Development Occasional Paper no. 9, Center for International Studies at Cornell University. Ithaca, 1980.

Haas, Louis. "Baptism and Spiritual Kinship in the North of England, 1250–1450." M.A. thesis, Ohio State University, 1982.

Habakkuk, H. J. "Family Structure and Economic Change in Nineteenth-Century Europe." *Journal of Economic History* 15 (1955): 1–12.

Haffter, Carl. "The Changeling: History and Psychodynamics of Attitudes to Handicapped Children in European Folklore." *Journal of the History of the Behavorial Sciences* 4 (1968): 55–61.

Hair, P. E. H. "Bridal Pregnancy in Rural England in Earlier Centuries." *Population Studies* 20 (1966–67): 233–243.

——. "Bridal Pregnancy in Earlier Rural England, Further Examined." *Population Studies* 24 (1970): 59–70.

Hajnal, J. "European Marriage Patterns in Perspective." In *Population in History: Essays in Historical Demography*, pp. 101–143, ed. D. V. Glass and D. E. C. Eversley. Chicago, 1965.

Hallam, H. E. "Population Density in Medieval Fenland." *Economic History Review* 2nd ser. 14 (1961): 71–81.

——. "Some Thirteenth-Century Censuses." *Economic History Review* 2nd ser. 10 (1958): 340–361.

Hammel, E. A., and Laslett, Peter. "Comparing Household Structure over Time and Between Cultures." *Comparative Studies in Society and History* 16 (1974): 73–109.

Hanawalt, Barbara A. "Childrearing Among the Lower Classes of Late Medieval England." *Journal of Interdisciplinary History* 8 (1977): 1–22.

——. "Community Conflict and Social Control: Crime in the Ramsey Abbey Villages." *Mediaeval Studies* 39 (1977): 402–423.

——. "Conception Through Infancy in Medieval English Historical and Folklore Sources." *Folklore Forum* 13 (1980): 127–157.

——. *Crime and Conflict in English Communities, 1300–1348*. Cambridge, Mass., 1979.

——. Introduction to *Women and Work in Preindustrial Europe*. Bloomington, Ind. Forthcoming in 1986.

——. "Keepers of the Lights: Late Medieval English Parish Gilds." *Journal of Medieval and Renaissance Studies* 14 (1984): 21–37.

——. "The Peasant Family and Crime in Fourteenth-Century England," *Journal of British Studies* 8 (1974): 1–18.

Hareven, Tamara K. "The Family as Process: The Historical Study of the Family Cycle." *Journal of Social History* 7 (1973–74): 322–329.

——. ed. *Transitions: The Family and the Life Course in Historical Perspective*. New York, 1978.

Hareven, Tamara K., and Vinovskis, Maris A., eds. *Family and Population in Nineteenth-Century America*. Princeton, 1978.

Harvey, Barbara. *Westminster Abbey and Its Estates in the Middle Ages*. Oxford, 1977.

Hassall, W. O. *How They Lived: An Anthology of Original Accounts Written before 1485*. New York, 1962.

Hatcher, John. *Plague, Population, and the English Economy, 1348–1530*. London, 1977.

——. *Rural Economy and Society in the Duchy of Cornwall, 1300–1500*. Cambridge, 1970.

Hawes, Beth Lomax. "Folksong and Function: Some Thoughts on the American Lullaby." *Journal of American Folklore* 87 (1974): 140–148.

Heath, Peter. *The English Parish Clergy on the Eve of the Reformation*. London, 1969.

Heers, Jacques. *Le clan familial au moyen âge: Étude sur les structures politiques et sociales des milieux urbains*. Paris, 1974.

Held, Thomas. "Rural Retirement Arrangements in Seventeenth- to Nineteenth-Century Austria: A Cross-Community Analysis." *Journal of Family History* 7 (1982): 227–252.

Helmholz, Richard H. "Bastardy Litigation in Medieval England." *American Journal of Legal History* 13 (1969): 360–383.

——. "Infanticide in the Province of Canterbury during the Fifteenth Century." *History of Childhood Quarterly* 2 (1974–75): 282–390.

——. *Marriage Litigation in Medieval England*. Cambridge, 1974.

Herlihy, David. "Land, Family, and Women in Continental Europe, 710–1200." In *Women in Medieval Society*, pp. 13–46, ed. Susan Mosher Stuard. Philadelphia, 1976.

——. "Population, Plague, and Social Change in Rural Pistoia, 1201–1430." *Economic History Review* 2nd ser. 18 (1965): 225–244.

Herlihy, David, and Klapisch-Zuber, Christiane. *Les Toscans et leurs familles: Une étude du catasto florentin de 1427*. Paris, 1978.

Hilton, R. H. *The English Peasantry in the Later Middle Ages: The Ford Lectures for 1973 and Related Studies*. Oxford, 1975.

——. *A Medieval Society: The West Midlands at the End of the Thirteenth Century*. London, 1966.

Hilton, R. H., and Rahtz, P. A. "Upton, Gloucestershire, 1959–1964." *Transactions of the Bristol and Gloucestershire Archaeological Society* 85 (1966): 70–146.

Hollingsworth, T. H. "A Demographic Study of the British Ducal Families." *Population Studies* 11 (1957–58): 4–26.

——. *Historical Demography*. Ithaca, N.Y., 1969.

Homans, George C. *English Villagers of the Thirteenth Century*. Cambridge, Mass., 1941.

——. "The Frisians in East Anglia." *Economic History Review* 2nd ser. 10 (1957): 189–206.

——. "The Rural Sociology of Medieval England." *Past and Present* 4 (1953): 32–43.

Hoskins, W. G. *Leicestershire: An Illustrated Essay on the History of the Landscape*. London, 1957.

——. *Local History in England*. London, 1959.

——. *The Midland Peasant: The Economic and Social History of a Leicestershire Village*. London: 1957.

——. "Murder and Sudden Death in Medieval Wigston." *Transactions of the Leicestershire Archaeological Society* 21 (1940–1941): 176–186.

——. "The Rebuilding of Rural England, 1570–1640." *Past and Present* 4 (1953): 44–59.

Howell, Cicely. "Peasant Inheritance Customs in the Midlands, 1280–1700." In *Family and Inheritance: Rural Society in Western Europe*, pp. 112–155, ed. J. Goody, J. Thirsk, and E. P. Thompson. Cambridge, 1976.

Hufton, Olwen. *The Poor of Eighteenth-Century France, 1750–1789*. Oxford, 1974.

——. "Towards an Understanding of the Poor in Eighteenth-Century France." In *French Government and Society, 1500–1800*, pp. 143–165, ed. J. Bosher. London, 1954.

——. "Women and the Family Economy in Eighteenth-Century France." *French Historical Studies* 9 (1975): 1–22.

——. "Women in Revolution, 1789–1796." *Past and Present* 53 (1971): 90–108.

Hughes, Diane Owen. "Urban Growth and Family Structure in Medieval Genoa." *Past and Present* 66 (1975): 3–28.

Hunnisett, R. *The Medieval Coroner*. Cambridge, 1961.

Hunt, David. *Parents and Children in History: The Psychology of Family Life in Early Modern France*. New York, 1970.

Hurst, J. G. "The Changing Medieval Village in England." In *Pathways to Medieval Peasants*, pp. 27–64, ed. J. Ambrose Raftis. Toronto, 1981.

——. "A Review of Archaeological Research to 1968." In *Deserted Medieval Villages*, pp. 74–144, ed. Maurice Beresford and J. G. Hurst. London, 1971.

Hutton, William Holden. *The Lives and Legends of the English Saints*. New York, 1903.

Hyams, Paul. *King, Lords, and Peasants in Medieval England*. Oxford, 1980.

Iskrant, Albert P., and Joliet, Paul V. *Accidents and Homicide*. Cambridge, Mass., 1968.

Jeay, Madeleine. "Sexuality and Family in Fifteenth-Century France: Are Literary Sources a Mask or a Mirror?" *Journal of Family History* 4 (1979): 328–345.

Jones, Andrew. "Harvest Customs and Labourers' Perquisites in Southern England, 1150–1350." *Agricultural History Review* 25 (1977): 14–22, 98–107.

——. "Land and People at Leighton Buzzard in the Late Fifteenth Century." *Economic History Review* 2nd ser. 25 (1972): 18–27.

Kellum, Barbara A. "Infanticide in England in the Later Middle Ages." *History of Childhood Quarterly* 1 (1973–74): 367–388.

Kennedy, Marjorie J. O. "Resourceful Villeins: The Cellarer Family of Wawne in Holderness." *Yorkshire Archaeological Journal* 48 (1976): 107–117.

King, Edmund. *Peterborough Abbey, 1086–1310: A Study in the Land Market.* Cambridge, 1973.

Kitteringham, Jennie. "Country Work Girls in Nineteenth-Century England." In *Village Life and Labor*, pp. 73–138, ed. Raphael Samuel. London, 1975.

Klapisch. Christiane. "Household and Family in Tuscany in 1427." In *Household and Family in Past Time*, pp. 267–281, ed. Peter Laslett. Cambridge, 1972.

Kosminsky, E. A. *Studies in the Agrarian History of England in the Thirteenth Century.* Oxford, 1965.

Krause, J. "The Medieval Household: Large or Small?" *Economic History Review* 2nd ser. 9 (1957): 420–432.

Kussmaul, Ann. *Servants in Husbandry in Early Modern England.* Cambridge, 1981.

Lancaster, Lorraine. "Kinship in Anglo-Saxon Society." *British Journal of Sociology* 9 (1958): 230–250, 359–377.

Laslett, Peter. *Family Life and Illicit Love in Earlier Generations: Essays in Historical Sociology.* Cambridge, 1977.

——. "Mean Household Size in England since the Sixteenth Century." In *Household and Family in Past Time*, pp. 125–158, ed. Peter Laslett. Cambridge, 1972.

——. *The World We have Lost.* New York, 1965.

Lee, Ronald. "Models of Preindustrial Population Dynamics with Application to England." In *Historical Studies in Changing Fertility*, pp. 155–207, ed. Charles Tilly. Princeton, 1978.

LeRoy Ladurie, Emmanuel. *Montaillou: The Promised Land of Error*, trans. Barbara Bray. New York, 1978.

Levett, A. E. *Studies in Manorial History*, ed. H. M. Cam, M. Coate, and L. S. Sutherland. Oxford, 1938.

Levine, David. *Family Formation in an Age of Nascent Capitalism.* New York, 1977.

Macfarlane, Alan. *The Origins of English Individualism.* New York, 1979.

McLaughlin, Mary Martin. "Survivors and Surrogates: Children and Parents from the Ninth to the Thirteenth Centuries." In *The History of Childhood*, pp. 101–181, ed. Lloyd deMause. New York, 1974.

Maddicott, J. R. *The English Peasantry and the Demands of the Crown, 1294–1341.* Past and Present Supplements, 1. Oxford, 1975.

Mendels, Franklin. "Industry and Marriages in Flanders before the Industrial Revolution." In *Population and Economics*, Proceedings of Section V of the Fourth Congress of the International Economic History Association, pp. 81–93, ed. P. Deprez. Winnipeg, 1970.

Mercer, Eric. *English Vernacular Houses: A Study of Traditional Farmhouses and Cottages.* London, 1975.

Miller, E., and Hatcher, J. *Medieval England: Rural Society and Economic Change, 1086–1348.* London, 1978.

Mitterauer, Michael, and Sieder, Reinhard. *The European Family: Patriarchy to Partnership from the Middle Ages to the Present*, trans. Karla Oosterveen and Manfred Horzinger. Chicago, 1982.

Moorhouse, S. "A Late Medieval Domestic Rubbish Deposit from Broughton, Lincolnshire." *Lincolnshire History and Archaeology* 9 (1974): 3–16.

Morgan, David H. "The Place of Harvesters in Nineteenth-Century Village Life." In *Village Life and Labour*, pp. 26–72, ed. Raphael Samuel. London, 1975.

Nimkoff, M. F., and Middleton, Russell. "Types of Family and Types of Economy." *American Journal of Sociology* 66 (1960): 215–225.

Noonan, John T., Jr. *Conception: A History of Its Treatment by the Catholic Theologians and Canonists*. Cambridge, Mass., 1965.

Orwin, Charles, and Orwin, Christabel. *The Open Fields*. Oxford, 1938.

Owen, Dorothy. *Church and Society in Medieval Lincolnshire*. Lincolnshire Local History Society, vol. 5. Lincoln, 1971.

Pentikäinen, Juha. *The Nordic Dead-Child Tradition*. Folklore Fellows Communications, no. 201. Helsinki, 1968.

Phelps Brown, E. H., and Hopkins, Sheila V. "Seven Centuries of the Price of Consumables, Compared with Builders' Wage-Rates." In *Essays in Economic History*, vol. 2, pp. 179–196, ed. E. M. Carus-Wilson. London, 1962.

Phillpots, Bertha S. *Kindred and Clan in the Middle Ages and After: A Study in the Sociology of the Teutonic Races*. Cambridge, 1913.

Phythian-Adams, Charles. *Continuity, Fields and Fission: The Making of a Midland Parish*. Department of English Local History, Occasional Papers, 3rd ser., 4. Leicester, 1978.

Pimsler, Martin. "Solidarity in the Medieval Village? The Evidence of Personal Pledging at Elton, Huntingdonshire." *Journal of British Studies* 17 (1977): 1–11.

Platt, Colin. *The English Medieval Town*. London, 1976.

——. *Medieval England: A Social History and Archaeology from the Conquest to 1600 A.D.* New York, 1978.

Pollock, F., and Maitland, F. W. *History of English Law before Edward I*, new ed., 2 vols. Cambridge, 1968.

Poni, Carlo. "Family and 'Podere' in Emilia Romagna." *The Journal of Italian History* 1 (1978): 201–234.

Popkin, Samuel. *The Rational Peasant*. Berkeley, 1979.

Postan, M. M. "The Charters of the Villeins." In *Carte Nativorum: A Peterborough Cartulary of the Fourteenth Century*, Ch. 2, ed. C. N. L. Brooke and M. M. Postan. Northamptonshire Record Society 20 (1960).

——. "Some Economic Evidence of Declining Population in the Later Middle Ages." *Economic History Review* 2nd ser. 2 (1950): 221–246.

——. "Village Livestock in the Thirteenth Century." *Economic History Review* 2nd ser. 15 (1952): 219–249.

Postan, M. M., and J. Z. Titow. "Heriots and the Prices on Winchester Manors." *Economic History Review* 2nd ser. 11 (1959): 392–411.

Powell, Edgar. *The Rising in East Anglia in 1381*. Cambridge, 1896.

Putnam, B. H. *The Enforcement of the Statutes of Laborers during the First Decade after the Black Death, 1349–1359*. New York, 1908.

Quaife, G. R. *Wanton Wenches and Wayward Wives: Peasants and Illicit Sex in Early Seventeenth-Century England*. New Brunswick, 1979.

Raftis, J. Ambrose. "Changes in an English Village after the Black Death." *Mediaeval Studies* 29 (1967): 158–177.

——. "The Concentration of Responsibility in Five Villages." *Mediaeval Studies* 28 (1966): 92–118.

——. "Social Structure in Five East Midlands Villages: A Study of Possibilities in the Use of Court Roll Data." *Economic History Review* 2nd ser. 18 (1965): 83–100.

——. *Tenure and Mobility: Studies in the Social History of the Medieval English Village.* Toronto, 1964.

——. "Town and Country Migration." In *Studies of Peasant Mobility in a Region of Late Thirteenth and Early Fourteenth Century*, ed. Edward Britton and J. Ambrose Raftis. In manuscript.

——. *Warboys: Two Hundred Years in the Life of an English Medieval Village.* Toronto, 1974.

Raistrick, A. "A Fourteenth-Century Regional Survey." *Sociological Review* 21 (1929): 241–249.

Ravensdale, J. R. "Deaths and Entries: The Reliability of the Figures of Mortality in the Black Death in Miss F. M. Page's *Estates of Crowland Abbey*, and Some Implications for Landholding." In *Land, Kinship and Life-Cycle*, ed. Richard Smith. Forthcoming.

——. *Liable to Floods: Village Lands Cope on the Edge of the Fens. A.D. 450–1850.* Cambridge, 1974.

Razi, Zvi. "Family, Land and the Village Community in Later Medieval England." *Past and Present* 93 (1981): 4–36.

——. *Life, Marriage, and Death in the Medieval Parish: Economy, Society, and Demography in Halesowen, 1270–1400.* Cambridge, 1980.

Ritchie (née Kenyon), Nora. "Labor Conditions in Essex in the Reign of Richard II." In *Essays in Economic History*, II, pp. 91–111, ed. E. M. Carus-Wilson. London, 1962.

Roberts, Brian K. *Rural Settlement in Britain.* Folkestone, Kent, 1977.

Roden, David. "Fragmentation of Farms and Fields in the Chiltern Hills, Thirteenth Century and Later." *Mediaeval Studies* 31 (1969): 225–238.

Rogers, James E. Thorold. *Six Centuries of Work and Wages: The History of English Labour.* London, 1884.

Rossiaud, Jacques. "Prostitution, Youth, and Society in the Towns of Southeastern France in the Fifteenth Century." In *Deviants and the Abandoned in French Society: Selections from the Annales, Economies, Sociétés, Civilisations*, vol. 4, pp. 1–46, ed. Robert Forster and Orest Ranum, trans. Elborg Forster and Patricia M. Ranum. Baltimore, 1978.

Rowe, Jay. "The Medieval Hospitals of Bury St. Edmunds." *Medical History* 2 (1958): 253–263.

Rowland, Beryl. *Medieval Woman's Guide to Health, the First English Gynecological Handbook.* Kent, Ohio, 1981.

Rowley, Trevor. "Medieval Field Systems." In *The English Medieval Landscape*, pp. 25–55, ed. Leonard Cantor. Philadelphia, 1982.

Russell, Josiah Cox. *British Medieval Population.* Albuquerque, 1948.

——. "Demographic Limitations of the Spalding Serf Lists." *Economic History Review* 2nd ser. 15 (1962): 138–144.

Rye, Walter. "The Guilds of Lynn Regis." *The Norfolk Antiquarian Miscellany* 1 (1877): 153–183.

Sabean, David. "Aspects of Kinship Behaviour and Property in Rural Western Europe before 1800." In *Family and Inheritance: Rural Society in Western Europe, 1200–1800*, pp. 96–111, ed. J. Goody, J. Thirsk, E. P. Thompson. Cambridge, 1976.

Salzman, L. F. *English Industries of the Middle Ages.* New York, 1913.

Samuel, Raphael. "'Quarry Roughs': Life and Labour in Headington Quarry, 1860–1920." In *Village Life and Labour*, pp. 139–263, ed. Raphael Samuel. London, 1965.

Santos, Fredricka Pickford. "The Economics of Marital Status." In *Sex, Discrimination, and the Division of Labor*, pp. 244–268, ed. Cynthia Lloyd. New York, 1975.

Schammell, Jean. "Freedom and Marriage in Medieval England." *Economic History Review* 2nd ser. 27 (1974): 523–537.

———. "Wife-Rents and Merchet." *Economic History Review* 2nd ser. 29 (1976): 487–490.

Schofield, R. S., and Wrigley, E. A. "Remarriage Intervals and the Effect of Marriage Order on Fertility." In *Marriage and Remarriage in Populations of the Past*, pp. 211–227, ed. J. Dupaquier, E. Helin, P. Laslett, M. Livi-Bacci, and S. Sogner. London, 1981.

Scott, James C. *The Moral Economy of the Peasant*. New Haven, 1976.

Scott, Joan W., and Tilly, Louise A. "Women's Work and the Family in Nineteenth-Century Europe." *Comparative Studies in Society and History* 17 (1975): 36–64.

Searle, Eleanor. "Freedom and Marriage in Medieval England: An Alternative Hypothesis." *Economic History Review* 2nd ser. 29 (1976): 482–486.

———. "Seigneurial Control of Women's Marriages: The Antecedents and Function of Merchet in England." *Past and Present* 82 (1979): 3–43.

———. "A Rejoinder." *Past and Present* 99 (1983): 149–160.

Shanin, Teodor, ed. *Peasants and Peasant Societies: Selected Readings*. Harmondsworth, 1971.

Sheehan, Michael M. "The Formation and Stability of Marriage in Fourteenth-Century England: Evidence of an Ely Register." *Mediaeval Studies* 33 (1971): 228–263.

———. "The Influence of Canon Law on the Property Rights of Married Women in England." *Mediaeval Studies* 25 (1963): 109–124.

Shorter, Edward. *The Making of the Modern Family*. New York, 1975.

Smith, Richard M. "Kin and Neighbors in a Thirteenth-Century Suffolk Community." *Journal of Family History* 4 (1979): 89–115.

———. "Hypothèses sur la nuptialité en Angleterre au XIIe–XIVe siècles." *Annales, Economies, Sociétés, Civilisations* 38 (1983): 107–136.

Speert, Harold. *Iconographia Gyniatrica*. Philadelphia, 1973.

Spufford, Margaret. *Contrasting Communities: English Villagers in the Sixteenth and Seventeenth Centuries*. Cambridge, 1974.

———. "Peasant Inheritance Customs and Land Distribution in Cambridgeshire from the Sixteenth to the Eighteenth Centuries." In *Family and Inheritance: Rural Society in Western Europe, 1200–1800*, pp. 156–176, ed. J. Goody, J. Thirsk, and E. P. Thompson. Cambridge, 1976.

Stenton, Doris Mary. *English Society in the Early Middle Ages, 1066–1307*, 4th ed. Harmondsworth, 1971.

Stevenson, Kenneth. *Nuptial Blessing: A Study of Christian Marriage Rites*. New York, 1983.

Stone, Lawrence. *The Family, Sex and Marriage in England, 1500–1800*. New York, 1977.

Thirsk, Joan. "The Family." *Past and Present* 27 (1964): 116–122.

Thrupp, Sylvia. *The Merchant Class of Medieval London*. Chicago, 1948.

———. "The Problem of Replacement Rates in Late Medieval English Population." *Economic History Review* 2nd ser. 18 (1965): 101–119.

Tickner, F. W. *Women in English Economic History*. London, 1923.

Tilly, Louise, and Cohen, Miriam. "Does the Family Have a History? A Review of Theory and Practice in Family History." *Social Science History* 6 (1982): 131–180.

Tilly, Louise and Scott, Joan W. *Women, Work, and Family*. New York. 1978.

Titow, J. Z. *English Rural Society, 1200–1350*. New York, 1969.

———. "Some Evidence of the Thirteenth-Century Population Increase." *Economic History Review* 2nd ser. 14 (1961): 218–224.

———. "Some Differences between Manors and the Effects on the Condition of the Peasant in the Thirteenth Century." *Agricultural History Review* 10 (1962): 1–13.

Trumbach, Randolph. *The Rise of the Egalitarian Family: Aristocratic Kinship and Domestic Relations in Eighteenth-Century England.* New York, 1978.

Vinogradoff, Paul. *English Society in the Eleventh Century: Essays in English Mediaeval History.* Oxford, 1908.

Wachter, Kenneth, with Hammel, Eugene, A., and Laslett, Peter. *Statistical Studies of Historical Social Structure.* New York, 1978.

Walford, Cornelius. *Gilds: Their Origin, Constitution, Objects, and Later History.* London, 1879.

Walker, Sue Sheridan. "Proof of Age of Feudal Heirs in Medieval England." *Mediaeval Studies* 35 (1973): 306–323.

Warren, F. W. "A Pre-Reformation Gild." *Proceedings of the Suffolk Institute of Archaeology* 11 (1903): 134–147.

Weissman, Hope Phyllis. "Why Chaucer's Wife Is from Bath." *The Chaucer Review* 15 (1980-81): 12–35.

Wells, C. "A Leper Cemetery at South Acre, Norfolk." *Medieval Archaeology* 11 (1967): 242–248.

Westlake, H. F. *The Parish Gilds of Medieval England.* London, 1919.

White, Beatrice. "Poet and Peasant." In *The Reign of Richard II*, pp. 58–74, ed. F. R. H. DuBoulay and C. M. Barron. London, 1971.

White, Charles H. E. "The Church and Parish of Chesham Bois, Bucks." *Architectural and Archaeological Society for the County of Buckingham* 6 (1887): 179–211.

Wimberly, Charles. *Death and Burial Lore in the English and Scottish Popular Ballads.* University of Nebraska Studies in Language and Criticism, no. 8. Lincoln, 1927.

———. *Folklore in English and Scottish Ballads.* Chicago, 1928.

Wolf, Eric R. *Peasants.* Englewood Cliffs, N.J., 1966.

Wood-Legh, K. L. *Perpetual Chantries in Britain.* Cambridge, 1965.

Wright, Thomas. *A History of Domestic Manners and Sentiments in England during the Middle Ages.* London, 1862.

———. *St. Patrick's Purgatory: An Essay on the Legends of Purgatory, Hell, and Paradise Current during the Middle Ages.* London, 1844.

Wrightson, Keith, and Levine, David. *Poverty and Piety in an English Village: Terling, 1525–1700.* New York, 1979.

Wrigley, E. A. "Family Limitation in Pre-Industrial Europe." *Economic History Review* 2nd ser. 19 (1966): 82–109.

———. "Fertility Strategy for the Individual and the Group." In *Historical Studies of Changing Fertility*, pp. 135–154, ed. Charles Tilly. Princeton, 1978.

Wrigley, E. A., and Schofield, R. S. *The Population History of England, 1541–1871: A Reconstruction.* Cambridge, Mass., 1981.

Index

Abortion. *See* Family, limitation

Accidental death, 11, 13, 27, 62, 87, 125–30, 145–46, 156, 160, 164, 177, 180–84, 218, 236–40, 269–74

age at time of accident, 128, 158–60

time of day, 128–30, 145, 146, 176

Adamson, Margot R., 280 *n*, 305–7 *n*, 310 *n*

Adolescence, 95–100, 142, 156, 159–68, 188–204, 220, 237

Adoption, 73, 83, 233, 252

Adultery, 209–12, 258, 263

Aerial photographs, 24

Age of majority, 76, 98, 143, 189, 221, 265

Agricultural implements, 44, 46, 47, 51, 114, 124, 126, 151

Alcock, N. W., 279 *n*

Algor, William son of Stephen, and family, 122

Allen, Hope Emily, 293 *n*, 310 *n*, 314 *n*

Almar, Richard, 190

Almshouses. *See* Hospitals

Alvirthorp, Gerbot de, 76

Alyne, Alice, 249

Amundsen, Darrel, 293 *n*

Andrew family, 86

Andrewe, Agnes, 259

Anglo-Saxon, 13, 56, 79, 80, 83, 173, 175, 245

Annotson, William, 183

Anthropology, 7, 79

Apprenticeship, 157, 161, 253

Archaeology, 19, 21, 25, 42–43, 46, 52–53, 93

Archery. *See* Play

Ariès, Philippe, 9, 83, 160, 171, 183, 186, 188, 245, 257–58, 266 *n*, 303 *n*, 305–6 *n*

Arson, 23

Ashley, William, 282 *n*

Asplon, Robert, 249

Assarts, 112

Assholff, Thomas, 108

Assize of Bread and Ale, 132

Atkyn, Batholomew, 76, 77

Attemore, William, 195

Atwell, Agnes daughter of Daniel, 194

Ault, Warren O., 277 *n*, 280 *n*, 282 *n*, 296 *n*, 301 *n*

Avon Valley, 164

Baildon, W. P., 278 *n*, 280–81 *n*, 285 *n*, 288 *n*, 296 *n*, 299–300 *n*, 303–5 *n*, 312 *n*, 314 *n*

Baker, A. R. H., 285 *n*

Baker, John, 250

Bakhampton, Richard, 137

Baking, 132, 146, 158

Baldwin, Francis Elizabeth, 283 *n*, 311 *n*

Ball, John, 144

Ball, John of Pynchbeck, 132

Ball, Robert, 194

"Ballad of the Tyrannical Husband," 141

Ballads, 98–99, 100, 172, 191–92, 196–97, 216

Ballard, John, 237

Ballard, Richard son of Thomas, 71

Baly, William son of Nicholas, 158

Banbury, Adam, 28

335

Baptism, 80, 103, 111, 172–74, 196, 246

Barbo, Thomas, 211

Barbor, William, 259

Bardolfeston, 24

Bardwell, 262, 263

Barley, M. W., 277 *n*, 290 *n*

Barn, 23, 42, 44

Barnes, J. A., 294 *n*

Baronn, John, 60

Barton Blount, 41

Basse family, 262

Bastardy, 72–73, 76, 82, 100, 103, 156, 176, 194–97, 212, 251–52

Bate, Maud daughter of Ellis, 178

Bate, Thomas and Walter, 135

Bathing, 61

Batson, Mary, 319 *n*

Baumburg, John son of Henry of, 92

Bauserman, Robert le, 209

Bear, 13, 23, 39

Beauchamp, Juliana de, 12, 162

Beaumonds, 230

Becahe, Henry de, 260

Becker, Gary, 301 *n*

Bedel, Walter le, 209

Bedford, 59, 165

Bedfordshire, 13, 24, 27, 42–43, 71, 77, 87, 93, 142, 194, 225, 239–40, 249, 256, 261, 269

Beggar, 236–37, 255–56. *See also* Vagabond

Belamy, Amice daughter of Robert, 12, 162

Bell, Patricia, 286 *n*, 288 *n*, 300 *n*, 303 *n*, 308 *n*, 311 *n*, 314 *n*

Bell ringing, 134

Belling, John of, 28

Belmont, Nicole, 303 *n*, 310 *n*

Bennett, H. S., 11, 14, 275 *n*, 297 *n*

Bennett, Judith, 288 *n*, 293 *n*, 296–97 *n*, 300 *n*, 307 *n*, 308 *n*, 312 *n*

Bennett, Michael, 303 *n*, 315 *n*, 317 *n*

Bentley, Agnes, 121, 199

Berdholf, Alice, 236

Beresford, Guy, 278–80 *n*

Beresford, Maurice, 277 *n*, 290 *n*

Berkner, Lutz, 290 *n*

Berkshire, 193, 199

Bernard, Peter, 72

Bernard, William and Isabel, 63

Best, John, 251

Beveridge, William, 298 *n*, 301 *n*

Biblesworth, Walter, 175, 177

Bigamy, 198, 210

Bigge, Maude daughter of William, 177

Bigmore, Peter, 277 *n*

Bigod, Juliana, 195

Biller, P. P. A., 294 *n*

Birth control. *See* Family, limitation

Births, 100–101, 192, 216–17, 245, 249, 252–53

Bishops Clyst, 36

Bishopstone, 58

Blac, Isabel daughter of William le, 253

Black Death. *See* Plague

Blair, Lawrence, 318 *n*

Blakewode, Clare de, 224

Bloyou family, 134

Blythe, Ronald, 276 *n*

Boating, 132, 162, 194

Bodekesham, Isabella wife of John son of Margery of, 237

Bodleian Library, 129, 131, 148–50, 176

Bolton, J. L., 276 *n*

Bonchevaler, Sibyle, 12

Bone, Beatrice, 254

Bony, Katherine, 27

Bookham, 69

Boonwork, 58

Borewelle, John, 198

Boserup, Ester, 300 *n*

Bossy, John, 317 *n*

Bothes, Johanna widow of William of the, 223

Bothes, Simon de, 136

Boundaries, 23

 beating of the bounds, 21, 261

Bovate, 22

Bowes, Matilda, 259

Bracton, Henry de, 68, 100

Brakest family, 138

Brand, Paul A., 308 *n*

Braudel, Fernand, 57, 283 *n*

Breton Lays, 172, 192, 213, 251

Brewer, Cobham, 306 *n*

Brewing, 40, 51, 116, 132, 134, 140, 145–46, 158, 162, 264

Brid, Thomas, 231

Bridbury, A. R., 283–84 *n*

Bridport, 57

Brien, William son of John Alymar of Salford, 39

Bristowe, John de, 239

Britnell, R. H., 301 *n*

Britton, Edward, 275 *n*, 286 *n*, 296–97 *n*, 300 *n*, 306–7 *n*, 311 *n*, 317 *n*, 318 *n*

Bromham, 27, 59

Bromhurst, 34

Brondroke, John del, 36

Bronn, John, 249

Brooke, C. N. L., 286 *n*
Brotherhood. *See* Gilds
Brothwell, Don, 294 *n*, 313 *n*
Broughton, 148, 190, 194–96, 218
Brown, Robert son of John, 178
Brun, 25
Buckland, 164
Bullok, John son of John, 178
Bune, Richard, of London, 111
Burglary, 23, 30, 39, 44, 117, 137
Burgoyne, John de, 249
Burial, 236, 240, 250, 262–63
Buxale, Thomas, 218
Bylaws, 22–23, 25, 51–54, 58, 63, 237, 261
Byre, 33, 38, 42, 44

Caldwell, John, 289 *n*, 313 *n*
Caldwell Priory, 130
Cam, 27
Cambridgeshire, 13, 28, 42–43, 87, 116, 132, 158, 264, 269
Candles, 51, 152
Canon law, 79–81, 89, 98, 172–74, 192, 195–204, 209–14, 246
Canterbury, 199, 210
Cantor, Leonard, 276–77 *n*
Capellanus, Andreas, 188, 306 *n*
Caretaker, 231, 235
Carpenter, Emma former wife of William le, 209
Carshalton, 132, 136, 218
Carter, Reginald, 166
Carter, William son of Nicholas, 132
Carting, 126, 127, 131–32
Carus-Wilson, E. M., 283 *n*
Castle, 25, 41, 44
Catelyne, John, 233
Cattle. *See* Livestock
Cellarer family, 85, 121
Chalgrave, 37, 47, 71, 151, 189, 191, 214, 259
Changeling, 181
Charity, 55, 225, 235–37, 242, 251–55, 264–65
Charles, F. W. B., 279 *n*
Chaucer's *Canterbury Tales*, 14, 45, 50, 52, 98, 121, 131, 205, 226, 255, 281–82 *n*, 309 *n*, 317 *n*
Chawston, 12
Chayanov, A. V., 7, 107, 294 *n*
Chellington, Geoffrey son of William of, 194
Chertsey Abbey, 71, 72, 229

Cheshire, 20
Chevage, 138
Chibnall, A. C., 288 *n*, 304 *n*, 310 *n*
Chiffoleau, Jacques, 318 *n*
Child, Francis James, 293 *n*, 294 *n*, 303 *n*, 306–7 *n*, 310 *n*, 316 *n*
Childbirth. *See* Births
Childe, Richard, 208
Children, 23, 26–27, 29, 39, 40, 42–43, 51, 53, 56, 61, 76, 87, 94, 101, 146, 148, 151, 156–68, 171–87, 220, 222–23, 249–53, 217–18, 245–52
  handicapped, 101, 103
Chilterne, William, 210
Chimney, 40
Chirston, Henry, 190
Christmas, 28, 58, 235
Church, 25, 34, 54, 68, 176, 192, 203, 236, 240, 241, 260, 261
  law. *See* Canon law
  yards, 28, 102, 240
Churching of women, 217
Chyld, Joan, Henry, Walter, 82
Cirket, A. F., 281 *n*, 285 *n*, 295 *n*, 300 *n*, 306 *n*, 314 *n*, 316 *n*, 318 *n*
Cistern, 41
Clarice, John, 39
Clark, Elaine, 229, 231–32, 288 *n*, 293 *n*, 296–97 *n*, 299 *n*, 301 *n*, 313 *n*, 314 *n*
Clay, Rotha M., 283 *n*, 316–17 *n*
Clay, Thomas, 223
Close. *See* Croft
Cloth, 116, 117, 175
  making, 133, 146, 161
Clothing, 49, 62, 89, 144, 146, 231, 263
Clyne, Simon son of Hugh of, 252
Cob, 34
Cobbler, Hue the, 86
Cohen, Miriam, 275 *n*
Coke, Alice, 254
Colburne, Agnes, 165
Colley, Eve widow of William de, 223
Colman, F. S., 304 *n*
Colmworth, 12
Colville, Emma, 166
Colvin, H. M., 279 *n*
Colwell, 212
Colyn, Edward, 77
Colyn, John, 167
Common law, 72, 75, 142–43
Comper, Frances M. M., 304 *n*, 310 *n*
Concubine, 209, 211
Connell, K. H., 308 *n*
Construction, 128, 133, 145, 159
Cornwall, 20, 73, 133–34, 136

Coroners, 11, 269–70
  inquests, 12–13, 38–39, 41, 61, 90, 93,
    109, 140, 142, 145, 149, 151, 156,
    158, 163–64, 171, 175–76, 182, 184,
    186, 193–94, 196–97, 208–9, 228,
    236–37, 249–52, 254–55, 260
Cotiller, Robert, 39
Cotswolds, 165
Cottage industry, 115, 142
Cottars. *See* Villagers, tertiary
Craftsmen, 42, 114, 124, 131, 139, 163,
    190, 247
Craucester, Richard, 247
Credit, 134–35, 151, 165, 258
Croft, 23–25, 33, 40–44, 56, 145, 159,
    180, 196
Croscombe, 27, 193
Crow, 44
Crowland Abbey, 224
Cruck, 35, 39
Cumberland, 20
Customary law, 71–72, 142–43
Cyne, Thomas, 135

Dale, Marian K., 279 *n*, 285 *n*, 288 *n*,
    297 *n*, 306 *n*, 310–11 *n*, 313 *n*, 316 *n*
Dancing, 26, 193
Davenport, Frances F., 295 *n*, 299 *n*
Davies, R. T., 280 *n*, 303 *n*
Davy, Henry, 143
Dawson, Bartran, 247
Death, 239–42
Debt, 119, 122
Demesne, 22, 138
Deodand, 13, 269
Derbyshire, 264
Derlynge, John, 143
Devonshire, 20, 34, 36, 39
DeWindt, Anne, 286–87 *n*, 297 *n*
DeWindt, Edwin, 275 *n*, 286 *n*, 288 *n*,
    295 *n*, 299 *n*, 318–19 *n*
Diet, 48, 52–60, 108–9, 117, 122, 140,
    148, 151–52, 158–61, 231, 263
Dinna Clerks, 39
Ditch, 24, 27, 43, 145, 209
Divorce, 14, 81, 200, 209–14. *See also*
    Marriage, incompatibility in
Dodghson, Robert A., 287 *n*
Dodwell, Barbara, 284 *n*
Doghty, John, 209
Dogs, 53, 256
Dolle, Robert son of Robert, 27
Doomesday Book, 45, 92
Door, 38–39
Dorset, 24

Dower, 71, 121–22, 142–43, 203, 221–22,
    228
Dowry, 68, 70, 78, 89, 112, 142–44, 201,
    203, 222
Dreis, Carol Jean, 293 *n*
Drinking, 26, 44, 55–57, 59–60, 128, 181,
    189–91, 236–37, 240
Drowning, 27, 125, 145, 158, 177, 190,
    241
DuBoulay, R. H., 284 *n*
Duby, Georges, 276 *n*
Duloe, Henry son of Thomas of, 241
Dung heap, 41, 42
Dyer, Christopher, 286 *n*, 296 *n*, 298–99 *n*

East Anglia, 13, 22, 33, 43, 70, 91, 137–
    38, 229
Eaton, 12
Ecclesiastical law. *See* Canon law
Edmond, Isabel, 226
Edworth, 28
Edwyne, John, 209
Eggs, 27, 54, 56–57, 154
Elder, Glen, 295 *n*
Ely, 200, 202, 210–11
Enclosure, 21
  acts of, 20
Engelmann, George, 310 *n*
Engleys, William le, 116
English, Barbara, 290 *n*
Erikson, Erik, 305 *n*
Essex, 20, 84, 122, 134
Exposure. *See* Accidental death

Fairs, 132
Faith, Rosamond J., 285–86 *n*, 308 *n*
Familia, 4, 156
Family. *See also* Household size; House-
    hold structure
  extended, 67, 78, 80, 83, 86, 88–90,
    261
  genealogy, 81
  labor, 107, 112–13
  land, 67–68, 77–78, 107, 112, 233
  limitation, 90, 95–96, 100–103, 215–16
  nuclear or conjugal, 5, 67, 79–80, 83,
    86, 88, 90–91, 245, 257
  reconstitution of, 96
  stem, 92, 103, 235
  surrogate, 8, 84, 242, 245–67
Famine, 3, 6
Felony, 23, 63, 137, 152, 164, 214
Fenkyll, Bartran, 247
Fenlands, 21, 27, 70, 112
Fertility, 90, 95, 215

Field, R. K., 278–79 *n*, 281 *n*, 314 *n*
Fields, 19, 21, 53, 140, 145, 150, 176
  open, 20–23, 70
  systems (woodland and champion), 20,
    70
Fights, 26
Fine, Joan, 254
Finucane, Ronald C., 316 *n*
First finder, 12, 87, 184, 197, 238
Firth, Catherine B., 283 *n*
Fish, 53, 57, 132
Fisher family, 28, 194
Flandrin, Jean-Louis, 290 *n*, 292 *n*
Flinn, Michael, 292 *n*, 294 *n*
Floor, 37, 39
Fohester, Edith, 127
Foleweye, William and his wife Albreda,
    43
Ford, John de and his wife Alice, 72
Fordham, Johanna daughter of Alice, 196
Forester, Joan wife of Hugh, 154
Forncett, 138, 139
Fostering, 93, 156–57, 253
Foundlings. *See* Orphans
France, 11, 47
Frankpledge, 43
Freemen, 75, 139, 140, 201
Friends. *See* Neighbors
Fruit and berries, 23, 43, 56
Frythe, Thomas atte, 46
Fuel, 23, 49–50, 125, 128, 158–61
Fundley, Palmer, 310 *n*
Funeral. *See* Burial
Furnivall, Frederick J., 283 *n*, 293 *n*,
    300 *n*, 301 *n*, 305 *n*, 306 *n*, 309 *n*,
    313 *n*, 315 *n*
Fussell, G. E., 302 *n*, 307 *n*

Gallerer, John son of John, 127
Games. *See* Play
Gardens, 21, 23–25, 43, 53, 56, 158, 161
Gardyner, Cecilia wife of Richard le, 152
Gasquet, Francis, 316 *n*
Gere family, 262
Germany, 11, 74
Gilbert, Creighton, 313 *n*
Gilds, 8, 56, 59–60, 118, 218, 235–36,
    239, 241–42, 258, 262–67
Given, James B., 284 *n*
Glass, 39
Gleaning, 54, 117–18, 147, 151–52, 236–
    37
Glebe, 22
Glotho, 42
Gloucestershire, 52, 163

Gobat, Stephen, 195
Godparents, 56, 173–76, 239, 246–48,
    252, 257–59, 265, 267
Goheens, Robert B., 319 *n*
Goldington, John of, 140
Goldington, Ralph of, 12
Goldisborowe, William, 247
Goode, William, 289 *n*
Goodman, Anthony, 311 *n*
Goody, Jack, 10, 227, 236–37, 252, 275 *n*,
    284 *n*, 287 *n*, 291 *n*, 295 *n*, 313 *n*
Gossip, 44, 258–59
Gothe, William, 163
Gotter, Felicia daughter of John, 251
Gottfried, Robert S., 291 *n*, 312–13 *n*
Gower, John, 55, 62, 282 *n*
Grace, Mary, 319 *n*
Grain, 21, 24, 54–56, 88, 117, 143–44,
    237
Gransden, Antonia, 306 *n*, 313 *n*
Graveyard. *See* Church, yards
Gray, 262
Gray, Howard L., 277 *n*
Greene, Richard Leighton, 293 *n*, 301 *n*,
    303 *n*, 309 *n*, 311 *n*, 315 *n*
Greens, village, 24, 25, 27, 158
Greenwood, Davydd, 295 *n*
Grene, Alice daughter of William of the,
    163
Grimsby, 41
Gross, Charles, 276 *n*
Grosseteste, Robert, 212
Guardians, 222, 246, 248–51, 259
Gylemyn, Agatha, 152

Haas, Louis, 303 *n*, 315 *n*
Habakkuk, H. J., 291 *n*
Hache, Thomas atte, 69
Haffter, Carl, 305 *n*
Hafune family, 262
Hair, P. E. H., 307 *n*, 309 *n*, 312 *n*
Hajnal, John, 95, 99, 292 *n*
Halesowen, 82, 94, 96–97, 175, 189, 194,
    222, 248
Hallam, H. E., 285 *n*, 290–91 *n*, 293 *n*,
    295 *n*
Halliwell, James Orchard, 282 *n*, 297 *n*,
    299 *n*, 315 *n*
Hamlets, 20–21
Hammel, Eugene A., 288 *n*, 290 *n*
Hammell, 91
Hampton Lucy, 121
Hanawalt, Barbara A., 277 *n*, 281 *n*,
    284 *n*, 293 *n*, 294 *n*, 296 *n*, 300–
    301 *n*, 305 *n*, 309 *n*, 311–12 *n*, 317 *n*

Handenby, Robert and wife Margaret, 211

Haraven, Tamara K., 295 *n*

Hardy, Hawisa wife of Alan, 28

Harlewlyne, Emma, 116

Harrison, 48–49, 59

Harrison, Robert, 262

Harvest, 126, 130, 165, 176

Hassall, W. O., 279 *n*, 308 *n*

Hatcher, John, 276 *n*, 283 *n*, 286 *n*, 293 *n*, 299 *n*

Hawes, Beth Lomax, 305 *n*

Hay, 23, 42–43, 126, 151, 194

Hearth, 39, 40, 175

Heath, Peter, 283 *n*, 314 *n*, 317 *n*

Hedges, 21

Heers, Jacques, 276 *n*

Held, Thomas, 314 *n*

Helmholz, Richard, 210, 285 *n*, 287 *n*, 293 *n*, 307 *n*, 308 *n*, 311 *n*

Hemmingford Abbots, 23

Hepworth, Alice daughter of Simon de, 209

Heriot, 110, 114, 240

Herlihy, David, 276 *n*, 288 *n*, 290 *n*, 291–92 *n*, 313 *n*

Herney, John, 225

Hertfordshire, 20

High Easter, Alwin of, and family, 198–99

Hillyng family, 138

Hilton, R. H., 5, 9, 110, 165, 275–76 *n*, 280–82 *n*, 285 *n*, 290 *n*, 298 *n*, 301–2 *n*, 308 *n*, 312 *n*, 317 *n*, 319 *n*

Himgeleys, Margery, 214

Hinton-on-the-Green, 25

Hobhouse, Edmund, 278 *n*, 307 *n*, 319 *n*

Hode, Thomas son of John le, 194

Holderness, 93

Holidays, 261

Hollingsworth, T. H., 292 *n*

Holywell-cum-Needingworth, 136, 260

Homans, George, 11, 14, 68, 70, 276 *n*, 278 *n*, 282–85 *n*, 290 *n*, 292 *n*, 295 *n*, 297 *n*, 307 *n*, 308 *n*, 313 *n*

Homicide, 11, 13, 26, 102, 155, 166, 183, 184, 191, 194, 208–9, 213, 227, 229, 239, 250, 257, 264

Hood, Robin, 54, 193

Hopkins, Shiela V., 283 *n*

Horn, Isabella and Paganus, 116

Hoskins, W. G., 21, 277 *n*, 285 *n*, 316 *n*

Hospitals, 58, 111, 132, 235, 251–53

Houghton Regis, 174, 254

Houlot family, 138

Houseful, 91, 93, 167

Household goods, 44, 46–49, 60, 77, 88, 112, 143, 180, 261–62

Household size, 90–104, 107

Household structure, 90–103

  complex, 67

  conjugal or simple, 67, 91–94, 103

  extended, 91, 94, 103

  joint, 93, 103

  multiple, 91, 94

  solitaries, 91, 93, 220

Houses, 19, 21, 23–25, 28–29, 31–43, 92, 94, 137, 145, 177, 180, 234, 239

  bays in, 31–37

  cottage, 32, 35–36, 42, 166, 230, 232, 238

  dower cottage, 92, 222

  long house, 33, 36, 42

  second stories in, 39

Housework, 146–47, 161–62

Howell, Cicely, 285–87 *n*, 290 *n*, 292 *n*, 306 *n*, 314 *n*

Hudde, Margaret, 247

Hufton, Olwen, 151, 218, 295 *n*, 299 *n*, 301 *n*, 317 *n*

Hughes, Diane Owen, 276 *n*

Humber, 27, 132, 158

Hundred Years' War, 112

Hunestere, Christiane le, 28

Hunnisett, R. F., 277 *n*, 279 *n*, 282 *n*, 289 *n*, 294 *n*, 296 *n*, 298 *n*, 300 *n*, 302 *n*, 305 *n*, 307 *n*, 309 *n*, 312 *n*, 314 *n*, 316 *n*, 319 *n*

Hunt, David, 305 *n*

Hunting and gathering, 116–17, 148, 158–61. *See also* Poaching

Huntingdonshire, 209, 260, 266

Hurst, J. G., 32, 277 *n*, 278–83 *n*, 290 *n*, 315 *n*

Husbandman, 31, 124–40, 161, 177, 190

  seasonality of work, 124–28, 140

Hutton, William Holden, 306 *n*

Hyams, Paul R., 284 *n*, 308 *n*

Illegitimacy. *See* Bastardy

Incest, 191–92

Infanticide, 95, 101–3, 156

Ingelforn, Isabell, 259

Inheritance, 67–78, 83, 107–8, 154, 191, 208, 221, 223, 250–52, 256

  daughters, 71, 121, 142–43, 198–203, 230

  friends, 261–62

  gavelkind, 69

  impartible, 69

partible, 11, 69–70, 91–92, 103
primogeniture, 69
ultimogeniture or Borough English,
    69–70
Inn, 39
Inter vivos settlements, 68, 73, 75, 77
Iskrant, Albert P., 305 *n*
Italy, 11

Jail delivery, 47, 102
Jeay, Madeleine, 310 *n*
Joliet, Paul V., 305 *n*
Jones, Andrew, 286 *n*, 198 *n*
Jordan, Thomas, 23
Juries, 12, 23, 81, 98, 102, 118–19, 140,
    167, 183, 189–90, 196, 208, 233

Kellum, Barbara A., 294 *n*
Kemp, Margery, 99, 212–13, 217–18,
    238, 293 *n*, 310 *n*, 314 *n*
Kempsford, 163
Kennedy, Marjorie J. O., 280 *n*, 288 *n*,
    297 *n*
Kent, 20, 22–33, 69–70, 91
Kenward, John, 209
Kenygall, Thomas, 262
Kettlewell, 114, 163
Kibworth Harcourt, 73–75, 94
Kiln, 42–44
King, E. J., 286 *n*
King, Thomas, 196
King's Ripton, 75
Kinship, 67, 73, 79–89, 91, 229, 259
    affins, 73, 80, 87
    bilateral, 79
    lineage, 8, 80–82
    obligations to, 83–84, 86–89
    prohibition to marriage, 80–81, 89
    terminology, 79–80
Kitteringham, Jennie, 282 *n*
Klapisch-Zuber, Christiane, 276 *n*, 290–
    91 *n*, 292 *n*, 313 *n*
Knox, Ronald, 306 *n*
Krause, J., 290 *n*
Kroyl family, 86
Kussmaul, Ann, 302 *n*
Kynde, Samina, 259

Ladder, 42, 127
Lamkyn, Elizabeth, 167
Lancaster, Loraine, 287–88 *n*
Lancastershire, 20, 62
Land, Agnes of the, 223
Land market, 7, 74, 120, 135, 151

Langland's *Piers Plowman*, 14, 50, 54, 56,
    124, 281–83 *n*
Langnoe, Simon of, 130
Langsfeld, wife of Thomas de, 209
Languedoc, 93
Larceny, 23. *See also* Burglary; Theft
Laslett, Peter, 91, 245, 288 *n*, 290–92 *n*,
    294 *n*, 307 *n*, 313 *n*, 314–15 *n*
Latrine, 41
Laundry, 61, 162
Legerwite, 110, 194–95
Leicestershire, 36, 73–74
Leighton Buzzard, 75
Le Play, Frederick, 95
LeRoy Ladurie, Emmanuel, 258–59,
    278 *n*
Levett, A. E., 284 *n*, 297 *n*, 300 *n*, 302 *n*,
    308 *n*, 315 *n*, 316 *n*
Levine, David, 288–89 *n*, 292 *n*, 307 *n*
Life course. *See* Life cycle
Life cycle, 73, 76, 107, 113, 135, 142, 157,
    167, 189, 220
Life expectancy, 229
Lincoln, St. Hugh of, 187
Lincolnshire, 13, 27–28, 70, 84, 96, 132,
    269
Lineage. *See* Kinship
Lister, John, 298 *n*, 302 *n*, 306 *n*, 308 *n*,
    312 *n*, 316 *n*
Livestock, 21, 24, 29, 42, 51–53, 77, 89,
    107, 112, 114, 117, 120, 124, 134–37,
    143–45, 147, 152, 158–59, 161, 177,
    261, 264
Locks, 39
Lodey, John son of Hugh de, 240
Lodgers, 116
London, 190
London, Maude of, 116
Lorkyn, Robert, 30
Love, 188, 200, 203
Love, John, 121, 199
Loverd, Richard and Emma, 230
Ludlow, 264
Luffe, John, 250
Lullabies, 179
Lutterell Psalter, 125, 127–28, 207
Luwyne, Gilbert, 69
Lyght, John, 250
Lynn, 99, 212

Macfarlane, Alan, 5, 9, 73, 162, 275–76 *n*,
    286 *n*, 302 *n*
McGregor, Margaret, 299 *n*
McLaughlin, Mary Martin, 303–4 *n*,
    306 *n*, 316 *n*

Maddicott, J. R., 295 *n*
Maitland, Frederic W., 282 *n*, 300 *n*
"Man in the Moon," 45, 49–50
Manning, John, 185
Mannyng, Robert, *Handlyng Synne*, 59, 98,
    182, 185, 193–94, 209, 211, 214, 228,
    246, 283 *n*, 293 *n*, 306–7 *n*, 309 *n*,
    310 *n*, 312–13 *n*, 315 *n*
Manor, 22, 25, 41, 71, 121, 130, 137–39,
    150, 162, 167, 174
    courts, 39, 46–47, 53, 70, 75, 77, 84–
      85, 87, 90, 92, 95, 109, 117, 122, 132,
      136–37, 141–42, 144, 154–56, 158–
      59, 163–64, 183, 197, 207, 218, 221,
      223–25, 228–29, 250–51, 254, 256,
      258–59, 261, 267
    officials, 118, 121, 136, 162, 189, 199,
      230–34, 237, 239
Manorialism, 5, 7, 110
Market, 24, 110, 116, 121, 132, 140
Marriage, 96, 99, 120–21, 130, 142–44,
    151, 165, 167, 189, 191, 196–204,
    228, 230, 232, 251, 265
    age of, 11, 74, 90, 95–100
    bars to, 198–203. *See also* Kinship
    ceremony, 203–4
    consensual theory of, 197–203. *See also*
      Trothplight
    endogamy and exogamy, 81, 200–201
    incompatibility in, 205–14, 228, 258. *See*
      also Divorce
    partnership, 154–55, 186, 205–19
    remarriage, 143, 154–55, 221, 224–25,
      249–50
    vows, 203
Martyn, Elena, 233
Maulden, Roger son of Agnes of, 252
Meadow, 21–23
Meaux Abbey, 85
Meech, Sanford B., 293 *n*, 310 *n*, 314 *n*
Mendels, Franklin, 290 *n*, 295 *n*
Mercer, Eric, 279 *n*
Merchet, 110, 138, 197–203, 208
Mere, Alice widow of John of the, 223
Messuage, 23
Metfield, 138
Middlesex, 20
Middleton, Russell, 288 *n*, 290 *n*
Midlands, 13, 20, 25, 33, 43, 51, 71
Midwives, 102, 172–73, 216, 264
Mildenhall, 164
Miller, Cecily wife of John the, 189
Miller, Edward, 283 *n*
Miller, Philip le, 214
Mining, 133–34, 151

Mirror, 62
Misadventure. *See* Accidental death
Misogyny, 153–54, 205
Missenden Abby, 173
Mitterauer, Michael, 275 *n*, 278 *n*, 288 *n*
Model for household economy, 7, 8, 107–
    23, 245
    assests of household, 109, 112–15
    ceremonial expenses, 108, 111–12, 137,
      242
    demands on the household economy,
      108–12
    division of labor in household, 108,
      113, 116, 144–55, 157–67, 215
    supplemental economic activities, 115–
      20, 134, 136, 158, 160–61
Model, simulation, 92
Montaillou, 258, 259
Moody, Thomas, 46
Moorhouse, S., 279 *n*
Mora, Moll de, 233, 256
Mordant, Amice, 254
Mordema, Robert, 218
Morgan, David H., 297 *n*
Mortality, 95, 96
Mortuary beast, 111, 114, 240
Mull, Agnes atte, 46
Mulleward, Agnes, 259
Multon, 158
Muth, Roger son of Walter le, 160
Myrc, John, 206, 303 *n*, 309 *n*

Neighbors, 23, 63, 75, 88–89, 116, 136–
    37, 140, 165, 181, 214, 225, 252,
    257–67
Nene, Amicia, 210
Newark-on-Trent, 121
Newham Priory, 162
Nimkoff, M. R., 288 *n*, 290 *n*
Noonan, John T. Jr., 294 *n*
Norfolk, 13, 21, 23–24, 38, 87, 132, 269
Norman Conquest, 81
North Sea, 20
Northamptonshire, 13, 36, 42, 133, 230,
    269
Northolt, 25
Norton, 162
Norwich, 139, 265
    St. William, 186
Nursing, 178, 179

Old age, 227–40, 253
Ombersley, 93
Orphans, 93, 167, 179, 245, 250–53, 255

Orwell, 71
Orwell, George, 6
Orwin, Charles, 277 *n*
Orwin, Christabel, 277 *n*
Outbuildings, 21, 42
Outshoot, 35, 39
Oven, 40, 42
Overton, 266
Owen, Dorothy, 278, 318 *n*
Oxgang. *See* Bovate

Parish registers, 95, 196
Parker, Robert and Thomas le, 191
Partition, 40
Passelewe, William, 27
Paston, Margaret, 10
Pasture, 22, 23
Paterfamilias, 10, 11, 219
Payne, John, 223
Paysele, Beatrice, 179, 249
Peasant, defined, 5
Peasant Revolt, 81, 110, 112
Pengelly, John de, 134
Penifader family, 86
Penlyn family, 103
Pensioner, 231
Pentikäinen, Juha, 294 *n*, 302 *n*
Pertefeu, Stephan, 195
Perus, John, Parnel his wife, and John his
    son, 75
Pets, 255, 256
Peyndell, Simon, 262
Phelps Brown, E. H., 283 *n*
Phillpots, Bertha, 287 *n*
Pigs (hogs), 23, 38, 42, 53, 180
    pigherd, 30, 40
Pimsler, Martin, 288 *n*, 318 *n*
Pistoia, 94
Pits, 27, 40, 41, 133
Plague, 3, 21, 24, 48, 74, 79, 81, 89, 94,
    96, 100, 103, 108, 115, 121, 130, 134,
    137–39, 151, 165, 231–32, 266
Planting, 126
Platt, Colin, 277 *n*, 308 *n*
Play, 25–26, 29, 140, 157–59, 171, 180,
    183–87, 189–90, 193, 217–18, 260–
    61
Pledging, 84, 201, 259–60, 267
Plow. *See* Agricultural implements
Poaching, 53, 117, 132–33, 137, 140. *See
    also* Hunting and gathering
Pofot, Lucy, widow of Thomas of Hough-
    ton, 226
Poket, Henry, 199
Polehanger, Warren, 166

Polet, Bertran, 166
Pole-vault, 27
Pollock, F., 300 *n*
Pond, 27
Poni, Carlo, 291 *n*, 296 *n*, 300 *n*
Poor Law, 266
Popkin, Samuel, 295 *n*
Porter, Anicia, 178
Postan, M. M., 74, 276 *n*, 282 *n*, 286 *n*,
    295 *n*
Poultry, 38, 42, 53
Powell, D. L., 298 *n*, 311 *n*, 317 *n*
Powell, Edgar, 292 *n*, 296 *n*
Prat, Thomas Jr., 26
Pregnancy, 146, 212
Prestisman, Simon le and his wife Agnes,
    28
Principalia, 45–46, 51, 60
Prostitution, 61, 142, 209, 211, 226
Prothos, John Major and John Minor, 191
Proudfoot, William, 28
Punting, 27, 132
Purgatory, 111, 241, 242
Putnam, Bertha Haven, 301 *n*, 313 *n*
Putton, Emma daughter of Edward, 39

Quaife, G. R., 309 *n*
Quarry, 41, 133
Quege, Thomas, 50

Raftis, J. Ambrose, 6, 275 *n*, 276 *n*, 277 *n*,
    278 *n*, 284–85 *n*, 288 *n*, 296 *n*, 299 *n*,
    314–15 *n*, 319 *n*
Rahtz, P. W., 281–82 *n*, 317 *n*
Raistrick, A., 296 *n*, 302 *n*
Ramsey Abbey, 23, 58, 97, 119, 191, 197,
    201–2
Rape, 23, 98, 196, 214
Rat, 44
Ravensdale, J. R., 224, 282 *n*, 293 *n*,
    296 *n*, 312 *n*
Rayward, Thomas son of John, 30
Razi, Zvi, 275 *n*, 284–88 *n*, 291–93 *n*,
    304 *n*, 306 *n*, 308 *n*, 311 *n*, 315 *n*,
    319 *n*
Receiving, 23
Reciprocity, 114, 118–19, 165
Rectory, 38, 132, 252
Red, Richard, 254
Red, William the, 140
Redgrave, 84, 94, 119, 260
Reeve. *See* Manor, officials
Rent, 108, 110, 112

Retirement, 74, 97, 166
   contracts, 39, 75, 97, 103, 229–34, 237,
      242, 251, 253, 259
Richmond, Robert, 302 *n*
Rickinghall, 94
Ring, 203
Risler, John, 288 *n*
Risseleye, John del, 209
Risseworth, Richard de, 72
Ritchie, Nora (nee Kenyon), 299 *n*
River, 27
Roads, 24, 25, 26, 29, 53, 181
Robbery, 23, 117
Robbins, Rossell Hope, 283 *n*, 293 *n*,
   296 *n*, 300–301 *n*, 306–7 *n*, 309 *n*
Roberts, Brian K., 277 *n*
Roden, David, 285 *n*, 312 *n*
Rogers, James E. Thorold, 280 *n*, 282 *n*,
   298 *n*, 302 *n*
Room, 40
Rose, Adam, 214
Rossiaud, Jacques, 283 *n*
Rowe, Jay, 317 *n*
Rowland, Beryl, 310 *n*
Rowley, Trevor, 276 *n*
Rumble, Thomas C., 306 *n*, 310–11 *n*,
   316 *n*
Russel family, 78
Russell, J. C., 142, 291–92 *n*, 299 *n*, 304 *n*
Rye, Walter, 318 *n*

Sabean, David, 284 *n*
Salisbury, 208
Salter, H. E., 303 *n*, 305 *n*
Saly, John and Christina, 256
Saly, John and Walter, 191
Salzman, L. R., 298–99 *n*
Samuel, Raphael, 282, 311 *n*
Santos, Fredricka Pickford, 301 *n*
Sarreman, Beatrice le, 165
Scaly family, 122
Schammell, Jean, 308 *n*
Schofield, Roger, 293 *n*, 299–200 *n*, 309 *n*,
   311–13 *n*, 315 *n*
Scoles, John de, 208
Scott, James C., 295 *n*
Scott, Joan, 153, 296 *n*, 299 *n*, 301 *n*
Searle, Eleanor, 297 *n*, 308 *n*, 312–13 *n*,
   317 *n*
See, Johanna del, 165
Seger, Mary, 305 *n*, 315 *n*
Senenok family, 177
Senility, 238
Serfdom, 7, 47, 90, 93, 137–39, 174,
   201–2, 267

Serle, Henry, 76
Servants, 51, 56, 84, 115, 130, 142, 144,
   146, 156–68, 194, 239, 247, 254–55
Seustere, Joan, 211
Sex, 14, 98, 188–97, 208–14, 217, 246
Shanin, Teodor, 275 *n*, 295 *n*
Sharp, Reginald, 315 *n*
Sharp, Thomas, 217
Shayle, Joan wife of William, 26
Sheehan, Michael, 307 *n*, 308 *n*, 310 *n*,
   312 *n*
Sherington, 212
Sherlok, Matilda, 225
Shirford, Thomas de, 212
Shorter, Edward, 8, 89, 188, 218–19, 245,
   257–58, 266, 276 *n*, 306 *n*, 311 *n*
Shortnekke, Isabel daughter and servant
   of John, 164
Sibbeson, Juliana daughter of John, 195
Sieder, Reinhard, 275 *n*, 277 *n*, 288 *n*
Skeat, W. W., 295 *n*
Skipton, 114, 163
Smith. *See* Craftsmen
Smith, Agnes, 199
Smith, Lucy Toulmin, 318–19 *n*
Smith, Richard, 288 *n*, 291–92 *n*, 296 *n*,
   309 *n*, 317 *n*, 318 *n*
Smith, Toulmin, 318–19 *n*
Smyth, Thomas, 234
Sneuth, Ralph, 248
Sneyd, C. A., 301 *n*
Solar, 39, 237
Somerset, 28, 261
"Song of the Husbandman," 113
Sourhale, Alice, 199
Spalding, 41
Speert, Harold, 310 *n*
Spinning, 116, 141, 144, 149–50
Spufford, Margaret, 284–85 *n*, 312–13 *n*
Squire, Joan, 210
Stable, 42
Staplehoe, 12
Statute of Labourers, 85, 139, 229
Stenton, Doris M., 283 *n*
Stepparents, 249–50
Stevenson, Kenneth, 308 *n*
Stistede, Margaret, 198
Stoke, Thomas, 39
Stokeley, George, 250
Stone, 36–37
Stone, Lawrence, 9, 89, 218–19, 245,
   257–58, 276 *n*, 280 *n*, 304–5 *n*, 311 *n*,
   317 *n*
Stotford, 24
Stourbridge Fair, 211

Stowe, 164
Strangers (outsiders), 23
Straw, 37, 42, 128, 237
Streets. *See* Roads
Subsistence crisis, 3, 71, 74, 102, 103, 108, 115, 120, 130, 144, 152, 232
Suffolk, 20, 84, 94, 95, 138, 164, 166, 260
Suger, William, 177
Suicide, 11, 13
Sulung, 22
Sumptuary legislation, 62, 217
Surety. *See* Pledging
Surnames
  geographic, 82
  lack of identity with, 83, 252
  matronymic, 82, 175
  occupational, 82, 113
  patronymic, 80, 82
Surrey, 20, 69
Sussex, 58
Sutton, Adam de, 250
Swerd, Henry, 103
Swon, Nicholas le, 249
Syger, John, 27

Tailor, John, 34
Tailur family, 250
Tanning, 133
Tavern, 28–30, 60, 132, 260
Taylor, John, 262
Taxes, 3, 5, 90, 92–93, 95–96, 109–10, 112, 114, 142, 156, 163, 166
Tebworth, John son of Jordan of, 189
Teddy, Thomas, 260
Tempsford, Reynold son of Thomas, 185
Terling, 84
Thames, 172
Thatch, 35, 150, 159
Theft, 117, 118, 136. *See* Burglary; Larceny
Thingowe, 164
Thrale, John, 167
Threscher, John, 194
Throdholm, Thomas of, 137
Thrupp, Sylvia, 100, 276 *n,* 294 *n*
Tichemarch family, 239, 247, 262
Tickner, F. W., 301 *n*
Tilly, Louise, 153, 275 *n,* 296 *n,* 299 *n,* 301 *n*
Timpon, Alice, 63
Tin, 73
Tithe, 5, 111–12
Titow, J. Z., 276 *n,* 285 *n,* 293–95 *n,* 312 *n*
Toft, 23, 31, 36, 41, 43
Tolle, John, 199

Tompkyns family, 249
Toms, Elsie, 279 *n,* 284 *n,* 288 *n,* 313 *n,* 316 *n,* 318 *n*
Tothale, John de of Chobham, 72
Totti, William, 73
Toutere, John le, 165
Towns, 21, 116, 142
Trespass, 117–18, 136, 267
Tripes, Matilda, 213
Trivaler family, 185
Troklowe, Johannes de, 294 *n*
Trothplight, 72, 199–202. *See also* Marriage
Trub, Adam, 165
Trubb, Robert, 50
Trumpington, 252
Truss, 35
Tudor, 21
Turner, J. G., 282 *n,* 298 *n*
Tuscany, 93, 229
Tyringham, Arnold of, 130, 165

Upton, 52, 256
Upwood, 239

Vagabond, 47, 62, 97, 159, 190, 236. *See also* Beggar
Village
  deserted, 21, 24
  officers. *See* Manor officials
  plans, 19–30
Villagers
  primary, 6, 49, 58, 84, 94–95, 97, 107–8, 111–12, 114–16, 118–20, 122–23, 130, 134, 136, 148, 165, 195, 199, 266
  secondary (middling), 6, 84–85, 95, 97, 107–8, 111, 114–16, 118–20, 122–23, 165, 195, 199
  tertiary (cottars), 6, 7, 24, 32, 46, 51, 55, 58, 84, 93–95, 97, 107–8, 111, 114–20, 122–23, 134, 136, 149, 165–66, 195, 199, 230, 232, 266
Villein, 6, 45, 68, 75, 81, 85, 140. *See also* Serfdom
Vinogradoff, Paul, 284 *n*
Vinovskis, Maris A., 295 *n*
Virgate, 22
Virgaters, 24, 33, 46, 120
  half-virgaters, 24, 33, 46, 47, 120, 198
Vyncent, Katherine, 235

Wachter, Kenneth W., 288 *n,* 290 *n*
Waeng, Robert, 181

Wage labor, 73, 76, 84, 108, 114–15, 130–31, 137, 141, 144, 149, 163–66
Wagon, 44
Wake, 111, 196. *See also* Burial
Wakefield, 28, 35, 40, 47, 72, 117, 133–34, 136–37, 163, 189, 193, 195, 214, 232
Wales, Thomas, 248
Walker, J. P., 308–9 *n*, 312 *n*, 316 *n*
Walker, Sue Sheridan, 278 *n*, 281 *n*, 283 *n*, 285 *n*, 287 *n*, 289 *n*, 298 *n*, 300 *n*, 302 *n*, 306 *n*, 309 *n*, 310 *n*, 312 *n*
Wall, John atte, 46
Walle, William, 174
Walls, 24
Waralynton, Thomas, 213
Wardship. *See* Guardians
Warren, F. W., 318 *n*
Waste, 22
Water
bodies of, 125, 180, 181
drinking, 21
Wattle and daub, 34, 40
Wawne, 25
Wayhe, John, 158
Weisman, Hope Phyllis, 283 *n*
Wells, 21, 26–27, 40–41, 62, 237
Wells, C., 283 *n*
Wellester, Alice, mother of Agnes, daughter of Nicholas, 27
Wellyng, Simon, 130
West Acton, 236
Westlake, H. R., 314 *n*, 218–19 *n*
Westminster, 85, 130
Wether, William, 137
Wet-nurse, 249
Wharram Percy, 24–25, 33, 36, 41, 43, 50, 52, 56, 240
White, Beatrice, 295 *n*, 304 *n*
White, Charles H. E., 303 *n*
Whytyng, John, 230
Widowers, 135, 154, 225
Widows, 69, 71, 74–75, 87, 93, 97, 121–22, 135, 142–43, 154–55, 190–91, 201–2, 209, 217, 220–26, 228, 230–31, 233–39, 247–50, 254, 256, 262, 265

Wills, 14, 49, 51, 68, 70–71, 75–78, 85, 87–89, 90, 95, 109, 111, 142–43, 154–55, 174, 222, 225, 230, 234–35, 238–41, 247, 249, 252, 254–56, 261–62, 265
Wiltshire, 13, 42, 87, 127, 270
Wimberly, C., 303 *n*, 310 *n*, 315 *n*, 316 *n*
Winchester, 130, 224
Windows, 38
Wisbech, Isabel daughter of Joan of, 203
Wistowe, 233
Wodemous, William, 233
Wolf, Eric, 7, 107–10, 275 *n*, 293–95 *n*
Women, 26, 29, 43, 50, 53, 56, 60–61, 113, 116, 117, 132, 134, 137, 141–55
Wood, 34–35, 38
Wood-Legh, K. L., 283 *n*, 314 *n*
Woods, 21–22, 38, 50
Worcestershire, 34–36, 39, 121
Wrestling. *See* Play
Wright, Thomas, 281–83 *n*, 293 *n*, 297 *n*, 299 *n*, 304 *n*, 310 *n*, 315 *n*, 317 *n*
Wrighte, Alexander, 203
Wrightson, Keith, 288–89 *n*, 292 *n*, 307 *n*
Wrigley, E. A., 289 *n*, 292–93 *n*, 299 *n*, 300 *n*, 308 *n*, 311 *n*, 312–13 *n*, 315 *n*
Writtle, 84, 118, 122, 134
Wrynbe, Cecilia de, 178
Wrythe, Agnes daughter of William, 26
Wuale, Osbert le, son of William Christemasse, 59
Wycliff, John, 81
Wygod, Richard, 34
Wyle, John atte, 229
Wyndover, John, 239
Wysman, John son and servant of John, 164
Wyt, Reynold le, 252
Wyte, William le, 158

Yardland. *See* Virgate
Yeoman, 62, 119, 140, 166, 266, 267
Yngeleys, William, 256
York, 14, 49, 174, 210–11, 247
Yorkshire, 24, 25, 133, 152, 154
Young, Richard, 199